NEW JERSEY

DURING THE REVOLUTION

*as
Related in the
News Items of the Day*

Richard B. Marrin

HERITAGE BOOKS
2009

HERITAGE BOOKS
AN IMPRINT OF HERITAGE BOOKS, INC.

Books, CDs, and more—Worldwide

For our listing of thousands of titles see our website at
www.HeritageBooks.com

Published 2009 by
HERITAGE BOOKS, INC.
Publishing Division
100 Railroad Ave. #104
Westminster, Maryland 21157

Copyright © 2009 Richard B. Marrin

All rights reserved. No part of this book may be reproduced or transmitted in any form or by any means, electronic or mechanical, including photocopying, recording or by any information storage and retrieval system without written permission from the author, except for the inclusion of brief quotations in a review.

International Standard Book Numbers
Paperbound: 978-0-7884-3587-4
Clothbound: 978-0-7884-8148-2

INTRODUCTION

CHAPTER 1: an Overview of Life in New Jersey in the 1770's	1
CHAPTER 2: The Approaching Revolution	17
CHAPTER 3: 1775: The War Begins	51
CHAPTER 4: War: 1776	63
CHAPTER 5: Propaganda War	99
CHAPTER 6: The War: 1777	127
CHAPTER 7: Life in the War Zone	147
CHAPTER 8: The War: 1778	175
CHAPTER 9: The Soldiers of the Revolution	195
CHAPTER 10: The War: 1779	229
CHAPTER 11: *Banditti*	251
CHAPTER 12: The War Years: 1780	263
CHAPTER 13: The War at Sea	295
CHAPTER 14: The War: 1781	307
CHAPTER 15: The War's End: 1782 and 1783	329
ENDNOTES	347
INDICES	375

INTRODUCTION

The richer and more diverse a nation's history becomes, the longer grows the list of the heroic exploits, pivotal battles and major personalities responsible for its success. There is a sad corollary to that axiom. As the nation's proud history expands, less will be the attention paid to any individual scene within the tapestry of yesterday. The United States is not exempt from the operation of these principles. There are scores of fascinating eras among the more than fifty decades since the European colonization of America --- exciting periods of history that have become virtually forgotten by our citizenry. Some of those periods should have a greater value to us than others. Their neglect is, therefore, all the more troubling.

One such era of American history, both valuable and forgotten, is that of our Revolutionary War. Begun with an exchange of gunfire in Massachusetts on April 19, 1775, literally *the shot heard round the world*, it lasted eight years, and, when it was over, a new world order had emerged. The period 1771 through 1783 saw the Revolution's fermentation, eruption and resolution. In those years can be viewed -- almost in slow motion -- the issues at play that shaped the conflict, the Authority of the Monarchy and Parliament, the adoration given by the upstart colonist to the philosophical concept of *liberty* and his yen for independence --*to be left alone by government*-- in the land he had husbanded. It is a sometimes revealing, sometimes stirring tale. Its retelling perhaps can give perspective to Americans of every age and origin.

Happily, the events of the Revolutionary War period can be observed, almost as one would view a documentary film -- slowly, with images fashioned from words, rather than by the camera. With New Jersey as its focus -- after all, it was called the *cock pit of the Revolution*, situated, as it was, between the key cities of New York and Philadelphia -- news accounts of the period, a sometimes forgotten resource, reveal the sentiments of the participants to the conflict as it was being waged, not how it sometimes is recast by legends or in history books. Indeed, if studied hard and long enough, newspapers can become mirrors in which we can see America in her youth.

CHAPTER 1

An Overview of Life in New Jersey in the 1770's

The New Jersey of the 21st Century is the most densely populated state in the nation, with more people per square mile than even crowded India or Japan. Many view portions of the state as grimy and deteriorating. Certain sections have been highly industrialized since the Civil War with factories, refineries and warehouses.

However, most of the state has not been so altered as to be unrecognizable to some colonist magically transported back in time. There is still much farmland in the central and southern portions of the state, mountains and woodlands to the north and west, pine barrens to the southeast and, of course, more than a hundred miles of seacoast, little changed.

By its second century of settlement, the Provinces of East and West New Jersey were no longer the dangerous frontiers they had once been. Indians, pirates and savage beasts were things of the past. The American colonies were enjoying a period of tremendous prosperity and growth. The Treaty of Paris in 1759 had ended the recurring wars with Spain and France and the latter's ceding Canada to the British removed the threat of invasion. Thousands of western Europeans, mostly from the British Isles, were immigrating to America's shores, even as the descendants of the earlier inhabitants were restlessly moving westward, penetrating the habitat of only the Indian.

New Jersey was an agricultural economy at the eve of the Revolution -- a sea of farms with waves of wheat and corn. Good land was available at reasonable prices, the climate favorable. An average farm was a hundred acres in size and was worked by a single family.[1] The brute force of harnessed oxen helped clear the land. The soil was readied by hand and mule, often with barely effective wooden plows. Harvesting was by means, such as scythes, unchanged since Biblical times. Hired hands were scarce. The abundance of available land allowed every man to have his own farm. As a result, neighbors had to help neighbors in barn raisings, cattle drives, harvests and the like. These became social events with the men working during the day, while the women prepared vast amounts of food for dinner. Afterward, there would be dancing, wooing and gossip. It is hard to imagine that New Jersey was once like a Kansas or Nebraska.

Winter wheat was a big crop in both the eastern and western divisions of the Province of New Jersey[2] as were barley, oats, rye, buckwheat, flax, vegetables and fruits of many varieties, including apple, plum, peaches and cherries. Livestock on the typical farm consisted of hogs, horses, "horned" cattle, sheep and poultry. In the southern counties, like Cape May and Cumberland, with their extensive meadows of salt hay, cattle raising was a principal industry. Herds of these animals would be driven by men, called "cowboys," to Philadelphia and New York for sale in their markets. Hogs were slaughtered, packed in barrels of brine and shipped to the islands of the Caribbean. The produce of the orchards was distilled into ciders and brandies, for personal consumption as well as export. They made linen from flax, boots and shoes from leather and homespun wool. In short, most of what was produced on the Jersey farm of the 1770's was consumed there by the farm families.

Sometimes, farms expanded beyond agriculture. A few had blacksmith operations, saw mills and grist mills associated with them. Gradually they provided enough employment to non family members as to become the hub of a village. An advertisement for the sale of a piece of land bordering Sandy Hook Bay in Middletown, Monmouth County gives us an idea of the various crops, including those of the sea and forest, that an enterprising and industrious farmer could expect to reap:

TO BE SOLD, a Farm, lying in Middletown, in the County of Monmouth and Province of East New Jersey, pleasantly situated on the Bay, that leads from Sandy Hook to Amboy and New York, being a neck enclosed with one and forty panel of fence. It contains by estimation between three and four hundred acres of upland and as much salt meadow and sedge and will produce four score or a hundred tons of hay per year. The land is natural to grain, viz., wheat, rye, Indian corn &c. It is also natural to grass, a considerable part of it will mow two and sometimes thirty tons has been mowed in a year, chiefly of the best sort of hay; there is thirty

or forty acres of low land to clear that will make good meadow; it has plenty of wood and timber for fencing and well watered. There is on it a convenient dwelling house, kitchen, barn and sundry out houses. Also a sawmill lately built, and when timber fails, it is very convenient for a grist mill, either for the country or bolting; there is on it between two and three hundred bearing apple trees; also a good assortment of peach trees and sundry other sorts of fruits. It has a great advantage of manure, such as seaweed, sand &c, which, being experienced, admits of no doubt. It is convenient for fishing, oystering and clamming. Any person inclining to purchase the same may apply to the subscriber on the Premises and be further informed.
John Stevenson
The New York Journal, April 11, 1771

New Jersey has a seacoast 127 miles long. That has not changed. However, in colonial days, Jersey's ports, lying between two great rivers, the Hudson and Delaware, that serviced New York and Philadelphia, were more popular than today. In the 1770's, Perth Amboy, the Capital of the Eastern Province of New Jersey, was a principal port for international and inter colonial trade alike. So was Egg Harbor and towns like Salem and Burlington along the Delaware River. Sandy Hook Bay, blessed by such a convenient and reliable spring of fresh water that it became known as the "Watering Place," attracted hundreds of transatlantic vessels, needing to refill their casks before a long voyage. The Provinces of New Jersey were, without a doubt, important cogs in the American works.

We can see evidences of colonial trade routes and cargos from newspaper notices that informed the public as to arriving and departing ships and their ports of origin and destination. Sloops named *Good Intent, Hope, Prosperous, Endeavor, Abigail, Robinhood, Charming Molly, Sea Flower, Little John* and *Black Jake* sailed to and from Jersey ports with brigantines, bearing the names of *Industry, Jupiter, Dove, Friendship, Polly, Charming Peggy, Unity* and schooners christened *Sally, Swan, Chance, Two Friends, Three Brothers* and *Dolphin*. Some of the vessels were engaged in the coastal trade, plying among New York, Amboy, Philadelphia, Newport, Piscataway in New Hampshire, Boston, Virginia, Charleston and Georgia. Others went to ports in Europe: Hamburg, Lisbon, London, Liverpool, Glasgow, Dublin, Bristol, and Newry in

Ireland. Still others sailed to the islands of the Caribbean and other exotic sounding ports: the Bay of Honduras, Surinam, Curacao, Bermuda, Antigua, Jamaica, Barbados, St. Eustatia, St. Christopher's, Nevis, St. Martins, St. Kitts, Santo Domingo, Martinico, Exuma, and Madeira and the Azores. The cargos rarely were as exotic, being mostly the staples imported by the colonists or the raw materials exported by them: salt, sugar, lumbers of all varieties, barrels of hog lard, pork, and beef, wheat, tobacco, Indian corn, pitch, tar and other marine and military stores, fish, indigo and, of course, rum. Some fineries from London were imported too: knives, forks, scissors, pewter quart and pint mugs, tea pots, basins, dishes, plates, penknives, ivory combs, metal buttons, snuff boxes, buckles, women's and mens' silk stockings, silk caps and handkerchiefs, Irish camblets, linens, looking glasses, tea boards and Madeira wine. Britain did not encourage manufacturing in its colonies. They were to be the markets of the English manufacturers.

But what of the people of the Provinces of New Jersey? Who were they and from where did they come? New Jersey had 130,000 inhabitants in 1774, out of the colonies total population of over three million.[3] The press reported the American demographics of the time:

An estimate of the number of souls in the following provinces, made in Congress, September, 1774

New Hampshire.	150,000
Massachusetts.	400,000
Rhode Island.	59,678
Connecticut.	192,000
New York.	250,000
New Jersey	130,000
Pennsylvania.	350,000
(including the lower counties [Delaware])	
Maryland	320,000
Virginia	650,000
North Carolina	300,000
South Carolina	225,000
Total	3,026,678

The New York Journal, November 24, 1774

Very few of the New Jersey inhabitants were Native American by as late as 1770. When the first Europeans had arrived, the Atlantic coastline from the southern portion of Long Island down to the Virginia Capes and inland for hundreds of miles had been the domain of a tribe of Indians who had named themselves the Lenni Lenape, meaning in their tongue, "the real people." They were a peaceful nation and relations between the Indians and the white settlers had generally been good. As their number waned, the Lenni Lenape were given a reservation, called Brotherton, in the Western Province of New Jersey, but soon sold it and moved to upstate New York, beginning an odyssey that eventually took them to Oklahoma where their descendants, called the Delaware, can still be found.

Some of the Jersey inhabitants of the 1770's were descendants of the first colonists a century earlier, religious dissenters including the Quakers, Baptists, Huguenots and political refugees from the Civil War in England. Many more were immigrants themselves or the sons and daughters of recent immigrants. Perhaps, fifty per cent of the population was of English descent and another 15% from elsewhere in the British Isles -- Scotland, Ireland or Wales. Another 15% were Dutch. They inhabited mostly Bergen and Sussex counties, having migrated west from the New York Hudson Valley into the fertile valleys of the Hackensack, Passaic and the Raritan. Ten per cent more of the colonial was German, French, Swedish or other European stock. Slightly less than 10% was African, almost all of whom were slaves.

Seventy-five per cent of these immigrants, south of New England, had arrived in America as indentured servants, a term of bondage to their master/owner that, unlike the slave, was measured in years, rather than in perpetuity. By mid 18th century, more and more of these new immigrants were coming from Northern Ireland. These were the Scotch-Irish, who were called Irish, only because Ulster in Northern Ireland had been the last place from which they had come.[4] Transported to Northern Ireland to relieve England's population explosion and act as a buffer against the Celtic native Irish, large numbers began leaving Ulster in the 1730's for the colonies. Thousands and thousands settled in western New Jersey, Pennsylvania and Appalachia and, as the frontier moved westward, the most adventuresome moved with it. Presbyterian in religious belief and, politically, staunchly in favor of the common man, they were to play an important part in the upcoming Revolution, both in the spirit of and the skill of battle.[5]

> *Four ships, the Captains of which were Montgomery, Pharis, M'Cutchen and Chevers, full of passengers, [have] lately sailed from [Newry, Ireland], for Philadelphia, where two of them have arrived. Another ship of 300 tons, Capt. Cunningham, for Philadelphia and the Brig Eliot, Capt. Waring, for South Carolina, both full of passengers, were expected to sail from Newry about the 25th of May. From the same place also, other vessels are going with settlers. We hear also that great numbers of vessels from Dublin, Londonderry, Belfast, Learn, Cork, and other ports have lately sailed or are soon expected to sail, full of passengers, for different parts of North America. These emigrations, it is thought, have already drained the northern parts of Ireland of near a third part of its most useful and industrious inhabitants. Nearly all of them being Protestants, those left behind begin to be greatly alarmed.*
>
> *Most of these people being well skilled in the linen manufactory, if proper encouragement is given to them, will be an important acquisition to the British colonies. The Pennsylvania Chronicle, July 19, 1773*

Almost ten per cent of the population, both in New Jersey as well as generally throughout the colonies, was African -- some 300,000 poor wretches. Slaves had come to the British colonies even before the Pilgrims had. A Dutch pirate reportedly brought the first nineteen African "indentured servants"[6] to James Town in 1619. It had obtained them after capturing a Spanish vessel, bound with its human cargo to Santo Domingo. By 1770, many slaves continued to come directly from Africa; others came from the plantations of the West Indies. A large population of Afro Americans had also developed within the colonies.

Advertisements for the sale of slaves were common in the newspapers of the 1770s:

> *Two Negro men, both under thirty, healthy and strong, one of them a valuable and complete farmer in all its branches, to which he*

has been bred since a child and is very stout. The other a genteel footman and waiter, who understands the care of horses well, the management of a carriage, drives either on the box or as a postilion and, in every respect, suitable for a genteel family or single gentleman and is fond of farming. Both have had the smallpox. Enquire of Mr. Coxe at Trenton or of Doctor Redman at Philadelphia. The Pennsylvania Journal, February 28, 1776

TO BE SOLD

Sundry Negroes, consisting of two men and two women, two boys and two girls. The oldest of the men is a miller, a carter and a farmer and is about 50 years old. The other is a stout likely fellow, a farmer, and about 35 years old; he is father to three of the children viz. one girl nine years old, one six years and a boy ten months old by the oldest wench who is a good cook and dairy woman. The youngest wench, about twenty seven years old, is an excellent house servant and, besides washing and ironing, can spin wool and flax, knit &c., understands the management of a dairy and making butter and cheese; she is the mother of the other boy, about eleven years old and as fine a boy of his age as any in America. The man and wife and three children must not be parted, nor the mother and son, as they have lived long in one family together; it would be most agreeable if they could be fixed near each other. They are sold for no fault, the owner only intending to change his plan of life. Whoever the above may suit will please to inquire of Mr. Henry Worly, Inn Keeper at the North Branch of Raritan, Somerset County, East New Jersey. The Pennsylvania Packet, March 18, 1778

In addition to the willing and unwilling immigrants to America, the native born populations of America, white and black, began to multiply rapidly. America was a healthy place to live, with many births and few deaths. The population had doubled every 25 years, "a rapidity of population not to be paralleled in the annals of Europe. It has never been equaled since the patriarchal ages."[7] The press reported feats of fertility such as the woman from Morris County, New Jersey, who had borne 18 sons and two daughters in 17 years of marriage. It also offered as "a specimen to the longevity of its inhabitant" items such as that reported by the Elizabeth correspondent that the last three deaths in that place were to "Mrs.

Crane. aged 74; Mr. Price, 97; and Mrs. Garthwait, 73"[8] or the obituary of Elizabeth Thatcher of Kingwood in West Jersey, who died at the age of 87, having had 17 children, 118 grandchildren, 133 great grandchildren and one great, great grandchild.[9]

The fecundity and longevity of the population, suggested by items like these, appear to be borne out by contemporaneous population statistics. In fact, we are fortunate to have a thumbnail statistical sketch of the people and their lives back then. The Royal Governor of the Provinces of East New Jersey and West New Jersey, William Franklin, had requested all the townships of New Jersey to report certain statistics about themselves to the Legislature. Apparently, only the township of Windsor complied. Happily, however, the material it provided was detailed and gives us an idea of the population makeup of Windsor and presumably other colonial towns, in New Jersey and elsewhere, during the period just before the Revolution.

Windsor, near Princeton, was described as a small town, fourteen miles long and five miles wide, some 29,000 acres in size. Formed in 1733, when it had about forty farms, it had grown to three hundred farms by the time of the report, fewer than forty years later.

Windsor had a population of 1,908 souls, broken down to "white persons" and "Negroes" with each classification further broken down by sex and age.[10] There were 1,823 whites in the town, with an imbalance of 69 more females than males. Curiously, almost exactly half of the white population was under the age of 16 and, in that instance, there were only two more females than males. However, that ratio changed dramatically for the age group 16 to 50, where there were 78 more females than males, the jump, one suspects being that military service, accidents and adventuring to the west reduced the ranks of the men, more than did death in childbirth kill the women. Yet, obviously - at least in Windsor at the time - women died sooner than men because, in the population of the ages 50 to 80, the women lost their significant advantage and there were actually 14 fewer women than men in this age group. For those in the over 80 age group (there were nine of them), however, women regained their superiority and there were twice as many women as men in this group.

Oddly, the percentages were markedly different in the Negro population, which totaled 95 individuals, and suggest something else, perhaps the cruel possibility that young black lads were sold off while they were young for training elsewhere, or that maidens were sold to distant places later on when they reached child bearing age, or a combination of the two. Under the age of 16, there were 31 females and only 18 males; however, over the age of 16, the numbers flipped flopped to 33 males and only 13 females. One slave woman was 108 years old.

The town assessor produced other statistics that shed some light on life in 1771 in the farming town of Windsor. During the year, there were four marriages, 29 births (15 male, 14 female) and 9 burials. Of the deceased, 4 were under the age of 16, 3 from 16 to 50 and 2 over the age of 50.

The township of Windsor still exists. It has been treated better by time, however, than have some of New Jersey's other first towns. Their fates were to become cities and centers of commerce. For example, the following advertisement by Jacob Cooper for the sale of land along the Delaware River boldly predicts that the spot would be ideal for the formation of a town:

A certain tract of land in Glouster county, West New Jersey, directly opposite Market and Chestnut streets in Philadelphia; contains 100 acres, 70 whereof is woodland; bounded northerly by a street 100 Feet wide; southerly and easterly by the lands of Daniel and William Cooper, and westerly by the River Delaware on the front of which its breadth is about 900 feet; which tract from its situation, is capable of great improvement as it is a suitable place for erecting another Ferry and in all probability may, in a few years, be disposed of in lots to great advantage in erecting a Town, as it will suit the many persons who reside there and carry on different occupations, as in Philadelphia. Any person inclining to purchase or exchange is desired to apply to the subscriber, in Philadelphia. The Pennsylvania Gazette, March 11, 1771

This spot, in the area known as Coopers Ferry, was to become the nucleus of the City of Camden. Similarly, the following advertisement describes an idyllic plantation for sale, located in the heart of New Jersey's largest city, Newark:

That pleasant situated house and lot of ground at Newark on Passaic River, belonging to John Low, Esq. now occupied by Mr. Anthony Rutgers and opposite Captain Kennedy's. The house is built of stone, 56 feet front, and 36 feet deep, two and a half stories high; the walls as substantial as can be made; two rooms on the lower floor; one large stone cellar; one stone cellar for provisions and liquors; one stone cellar for a dairy, all on the lowest floor; the second floor enters with one step from the garden and has four rooms on it; in each room, a fireplace, a large entry, in the upper half story are three bedrooms, a large garret and an upper loft; a large stone kitchen at one end of the house, with lodging for servants, a poultry yard and house &c., a large garden very level, that joins the poultry yard and contains a great variety of grafted fruit trees of the best kind. The lot contains about twenty two and a half acres, about twelve acres of which is an orchard of many grafted apple trees and is remarkable for making the best of cider, 200 barrels having been made in a plentiful year; also a piece of mowing ground which is very good. There is also another stone house on the same lot of ground, about ten rods from the large stone house. It has four rooms on a floor and four fireplaces, a good garden with several fruit trees, a dock or wharf before the large house; a mill brook runs near the house through a marsh, where a dock may be made at small expense, so that three or four boats may load at a time; staves and timbers of all sorts come from the back parts of the country and down the river, which makes it very convenient for a merchant or storekeeper; also a store house, 42 feet long and 28 feet wide, two stories high; a boat may load or unload aside the store; a barn that can stable eight horses; a chair or coach house; a fine spring of water; a well near the kitchen; and another well that is fed by a spring a small distance from the house; plenty of fish and fowl in their season; oysters and fish are frequently brought to the door for sale and boats go from said dock to New York almost every day and return the next; it is only 9 miles from Powles Hook Ferry. The whole will be sold together or separate, as may best suit the purchasers. The New York Gazette, August 3, 1772

Although rural, the inhabitants of the Eastern and Western Provinces of New Jersey had become as literate and well informed a population as the vast majority of their English cousins. Situated between Philadelphia and New York City, New Jersey's land owners, many of whose families had lived there for more than a century already, had become something of an American gentry.

Their schools concentrated on the liberal arts, which included Latin, Greek, English, philosophy, rhetoric as well as mathematics and the sciences. Often fostered by the Protestant churches of America, the purpose of an institution of learning was to produce public spirited leaders, hopefully ministers of the Gospel, and it was geared to teach gentlemen to think, rather than to accumulate facts or to earn a living, as seems to be the thrust of much of higher learning today. The effect that these teachers and their students had upon the coming American Revolution and the birth of the United States is incalculable. The faculty and students, almost to a man, supported, often led, the War for Independence.

After the young man -- women were not educated in the same manner -- received some initial tutoring at home or studied on a local level[11], he went off to a boarding Grammar School, which was a program of college preparation:

The Mattisonia Grammar School in Lower Freehold is still continued under the patronage of the Rev. Messrs. William Tennent[12], Charles M'Knight[13] and William Ayres and Doctor Nathaniel Scudder[14], who purpose constantly to provide such school with an able teacher and visit it as often as may be necessary.

The Gentleman who now presides in the School and gives singular satisfaction, is Mr. Moses Allen, late of Nassau Hall[15].
He teaches the Latin and Greek Languages with accuracy and is particularly attentive to the reading and pronunciation of the English tongue.

The situation of the School is such that the pupils are as little exposed to temptation or any thing that may corrupt their morals, as in any part of America.

N.B. Board, including washing, fire wood and candles is at present no higher than seven shillings and six pence proclamation money per week. The New York Journal, January 30, 1772

The Province of New Jersey had two institutions of higher learning. The more recent one was named Queens College then, but today is known as Rutgers University. Founded just as the 1770's began, the newspapers of the day witnessed and recorded her birth, formation and first graduating class[16] Her first leader was Frederick Frelinghousen, who was himself to become a Patriot and leader in the post Revolution New Jersey[17]. He was replaced by Rev. J. R. Hardenbergh, a clergyman in the Dutch Reformed Church. Hardenberg was a patriot and a delegate to the New Jersey Provincial Congress. After the War, he became president of Rutgers.

The older university in New Jersey was known as Kings College or, more affectionately, Old Nassau. Today, we know it as Princeton. Its curriculum, and that of the few other colleges in the colonies, was far different from the course of study at the university level today. There being so few institutions of higher learning, only the more intelligent of the more affluent received the benefits of a liberal arts education, an education that made them leaders of the next generation. Witness the following spirited competition for cash awards among Princeton undergraduates in connection with the anniversary of the founding of its sibling Princeton Grammar School. Also note the identity of some of the students participating. They would be the leaders in the approaching Revolution and extremely influential in the shaping of America in the years ahead:

Yesterday was held in the Public Library of the College in this Place, before about twenty gentlemen of liberal education, a Competition for Premiums, in the following branches of study:

1. Reading the English language with propriety and answering the questions on the Orthography.[18] On a decision by ballot, the first premium was adjudged to Aaron Burr[19] of the junior class; the second to William Linn[20] of the junior class; the third to Belcher Peartree Smith of the Sophomore class

2. Extempore -- exercises in the Latin language. The judges thought it proper that the premium should be divided equally between Brockholst Livingston[21] and David Witherspoon[22], both of the freshman class

3. Reading the Latin and Greek languages with propriety. The first premium was given to John Witherspoon of the sophomore class; the second to Aaron Burr of the junior; the third to Henry Lee[23] of the sophomore class.

4. Written translation of English into Latin. The Judges, on reading the several pieces, decided in favor of Henry Lee of the sophomore class.

5. Public Speaking. As the competitors were numerous and the Judges were highly pleased with each of the performances, it was very difficult to decide the pre-eminence. On a division, the majority of the votes adjudged the first premium to William Bradford [24] of the junior class; the second to William Linn of the junior class; the third to Hugh Hodge of the freshman class. The Pennsylvania Journal, October 3, 1771

At graduation of the College the next day, the faculty and audience were treated to a number of orations and debates by the graduates, again a tradition lost to today. The subjects debated suggest an education similarly long vanished:

The exercises were conducted in the following order:
1. Mr. Brackenridge[25] delivered a Salutatory Latin Oration "De Societate Hominium[26]"

2. The following Proposition "Mendacium est semper illicitum[27]" was defended by Mr. Williamson, who was opposed in the syllogistic form by Messrs. McKnight[28] and Taylor.

3. Mr. Black supported this thesis "Moral qualities are confessedly more excellent than natural; yet, the latter are much more envied in the possessor by the generality of mankind. A sure sign of the corrupt bias of human nature?" Mr. Cheeseman opposed him and was answered by Mr. Taylor.

4. Mr. Campell[29] pronounced an English Oration on "the advantages of an active life"; and the business of the forenoon was ended with an Anthem by the Students.

5. At three o'clock, the Audience again convened and, after singing by the Students, Mr. Spring[30] delivered an English Oration on: "The idea of a Patriot King".

6. An English forensic Debate on this question,"Does ancient Poetry excel the modern?" Mr. Freneau[31], the respondent, being necessarily absent, his arguments in favor of the ancients were read to the Assembly. Mr. Williamson answered him and supported the moderns and Mr. McKnight replied.

7. A Poem on "The rising glory of America" was spoken by Mr. Brackenridge and received with great applause by the Audience.

8. Mr. Ross delivered an English Oration on "The Power of Eloquence".

9. The Students sung an Anthem, after which, the following young Gentlemen were admitted to the first Degree in the Arts viz. Gunning Bedford[32], John Black[33], Hugh Brackinridge, Donald Campbell, Edmund Cheeseman, Philip Freneau, Charles M'Knight, James Madison[34], Joseph Ross, Samuel Spring, James Taylor and Jacob Williamson. *The Pennsylvania Journal, October 3, 1771*

While only a few received higher education at Princeton or Rutgers, a large portion of the citizenry was nevertheless literate and their literary tastes were wide ranging, including religious and tomes on morality, works on science and mathematics, almanacs and, of course, newspapers.

The citizen of New Jersey in the years immediately prior to the Revolution, like his counterparts in other provinces, had a social side too. Life was not all hard work and virtue. He was attracted to performing charitable works, attending music recitals, visiting health spas, sightseeing and other forms of entertainment. Some of it was proper enough, inspired by London fads:

Mr. Hoar begs leave to acquaint the ladies and gentlemen of this neighborhood that on Monday evening the 22nd instant, at Mr. Whitehead's Long Room, in this Town [Princeton], he will have a concert, of vocal and instrumental music, and hopes for their patronage as he has not only engaged the best performers here but is to have from New York the assistance of two gentlemen and a young lady.

The vocal music will consist of a select and well chosen number of songs, cantatas and duets, among which will be the following:

The Highland Queen

The British Fair

Say little foolish fluttering thing

May Day, a Cantata

Were I a Shepherd's Maid

The Gaudy Tulip

    Cleone, a Cantata

    The Lass with one Eye

    Sweet Willy O

    The Sheep in her Clusters

    The English Padlock

    Favorite Hunting Song

The Concert will be divided into three parts, with four songs in each part and the whole to conclude with a Ball, which shall be conducted on the same plan, as at Bath, Tunbridge, Scarborough and all the polite assemblies in London or any other part of Great Britain.
Price of Tickets, one dollar each. Tea and coffee included.
The New York Journal, August 11, 1774

Other entertainment was more American home spun:

The subscriber has lately built a new and very commodious house for tavern keeping about 200 yards away from his late dwelling, at the foot of the bridge, and on the King's Highway to Newark, and intends, God willing, to leave all business as shop keeping and farming and to apply himself solely to tavern keeping and to keep as good a house as the country can afford, viz. eating, drinking and lodging, with the best accommodations for horses. All gentlemen and ladies who will favor him with their company, may depend upon the best and gentlest treatment. Should it appear too great a distance from his house to the falls any gentleman or lady who chose to go there shall be supplied with horses, gratis.
By the public's most humble servant
Abraham Godwin, commonly called Gordon
N.B. A convenient room for dancing and a fiddler will always be ready for the service of ladies and gentlemen who may require it. Also a guide to attend any strangers, who shall show them all the natural curiosities at the falls. The New York Gazette, September 5, 1774

There was even the beginning of some of the attractions for which the Jersey Shore has become so well known:

Lately erected, and as soon as the Season will permit, will be opened, a New and Convenient Bath, in which is a room, properly constructed to undress and dress in, with a Stair Case leading into the Bathing Room, where Persons of either Sex may bathe in Salt Water, in the greatest Privacy, and for those who choose to swim off in deeper Water, a Door is so placed in the Bath that they can conveniently go out and return. The Building is near the End of a Wharf, opposite to the Bay, at the Mouth of the Raritan River. This Bath will be more beneficial as, at about two Miles Distance, is a Mineral Water, similar to the German Spa, which has proved of the greatest efficacy in many Disorders; its proper distance, procuring moderate Exercise after Bathing, has proved in many instances very assistant to the Medicinal Quality of the Waters, which, with great success, have been directed after bathing in Sea Water. The Qualities of this Spa have been well examined by several Physicians of ability and frequently recommended by them, particularly by the present Doctor Johnson, as well as his Father. The *New York Gazette,* March 9, 1772

CHAPTER 2

The Approaching Revolution

The American Revolution, of course, did not start spontaneously at Lexington and Concord in 1775. The essence of this enormous event that changed the world -- and continues to change it over two centuries later -- had been building in the minds of many for some years.

In America, the roles of the governor and the governed were not quite the same as they had been in England, a faraway land across a wide, dangerous ocean that took months to cross. In America, there was no King, no Parliament, no ancient system of nobility with its lords, dukes and earls. In America, the local ruler needed to seek a workable understanding with a citizenry that did not hesitate to challenge things when necessary.

To the rest of Europe, the British had always been considered a troublesome, difficult people, given to mobs and rioting when too long oppressed by another force. Some attribute this spirit to the genetic amalgamation of the various warring peoples that combined to form the English nation. Others believe it due to its island environment and its concomitant isolation. Still others claim that the Englishman's perceived willingness to challenge authority as a member of a mob really was not rebellion at all but a warning, a harmless growl of an otherwise obedient dog. What is certain is that these characteristics and customs of demonstrating public displeasure with government were passed along to America and evolved there even more.

The mobs of common men protesting a practice of government --rioting, as the forces of government term it -- had had several manifestations in New Jersey before the ultimate mob transformed itself into a new nation. The action of the mob was how the common man voiced a deeply felt concern. Paradoxically, the "riots" were usually orderly, sometimes even polite, described by some historians as more a "ritual" than an actual insurrection. They did little damage, except to an effigy or two that would be symbolically burned, but it released the pressure that had caused it and usually brought some accommodation from government.

Sometimes, it could get a little rougher. For example, in the 1740's, there was great uncertainty in New Jersey as to the legal title to certain lands of the Province. Settlers had carved farms from the wilderness, believing that they owned the land, a belief the law courts overturned, in favor of affluent owners, much to the displeasure of many:

> *We have just received the following account of a very extraordinary riot at Newark on Thursday last viz. The day before one Nehemiah Baldwin with two others were apprehended there by order of the Governor in Council for being concerned in a former riot and committed to jail; In the morning one of them offered to give bail and the sheriff for that purpose took him out in order to carry him to the judge; but on their way thither, a great number of persons appeared armed with cudgels, coming down from the back settlements, who immediately rescued the prisoner in a very violent manner, contrary to his own desire; upon this the Sheriff retreated to the jail, where he raised 30 men of the militia, with their officers, in order to guard it; but by two o'clock in the afternoon the mob being increased to about 300 strong, marched with the utmost intrepidity to the prison, declaring if they were fired on, they would kill every man; and after breaking through the guard, wounding and being wounded, they got to the jail which they broke open, setting at liberty all the prisoners they could find, as well as debtors and others, and then marched off in triumph, using many threatening expressions against all those who has assisted the authority. Several of the guard as well as of the mob were much wounded and bruised and 'tis thought one of the latter is past recovery. What may be the consequence of this affair is not easy to guess.* The New York Weekly Post Boy, January 20, 1746

Not unexpectedly, the official reaction to the riot was outrage. However, the authorities did little more than to try to arrest some of the participants who could be identified. The mob returned and freed the prisoners, conduct that both frightened and angered the Royal Governor of the Province:

The Governor of New Jersey's Speech to the General Assembly

Gentlemen of the Assembly:

His Majesty's Attorney General will lay before you an account of a great riot, or rather Insurrection, at Newark. This was a natural consequence of one that was some time before that; and, although I did what, by advice of his Majesty's Council they judged at that time sufficient to put a check to an evil that had been too great a probability of growing bigger and to prevent its doing so, yet (as appears) it was without the effect intended. So open and avowed an attempt in defiance of the government and in contempt of the laws, if not high treason, make so nigh approaches to it, as seems but too likely to end in rebellion, and throwing off His Majesty's authority, if timely measures be not taken to check the Intemperance of too licentious multitude; I therefore recommend this matter to your most serious consideration...

Lewis Morris
The New York Weekly Post Boy, March 31, 1746

The riots did spark exchanges of opinion as to their legitimacy and, underlying that, what the rights of the common man were to change his lot in life, an issue to be answered years later in the American Revolution. The range of views on how far the common man could go is illustrated by the following trio of early Letters to the Editor regarding the right to rebel against existing authority. The first argued natural law justified revolution, a sentiment later to be found in our Declaration of Independence.

As several of your late Papers have been almost filled with Matter relating to the Proprietors and their disputed lands in New Jersey, I desire you'd give the following short Piece a Place in your Paper, for although it was not written designedly, yet it may fully serve as an answer thereto and which, tho' it not be Law, yet 'tis Equity and Reason, and therefore ought to be Law, as 'tis Better than any Law without reason, viz.

No Man is naturally entitled to a greater Proportion of the Earth, than another; but tho' it was made for the equal Use of all, it may nonetheless be appropriated by every Individual. This done by the Improvement of any Part of it lying vacant, which is thereupon distinguished from the great Common of Nature and made the property of that Man, who bestowed his Labor on it, from whom it cannot afterwards be taken, without breaking through the Rule of Natural Justice, for thereby he would actually be deprived of the Fruits of his Industry.

Yet, if Mankind, who was designed by the Almighty to be Tenants in Common of the Habitable Globe, should agree to divide it among themselves into certain Shares or Parts, the Contract will be by binding by the Laws of Nature and ought therefore to be inviolably observed. Such a Division has been attempted by the Treaties made between the several Princes and States of Europe, with Regard to the vast Desert of America. But each Prince stipulated, or ought to be understood to have stipulated, for the general Benefit of the People under his Government and not for his particular Profit. The Kings of England have always held the Lands of America, ceded to them by Treaties, in Trust for their Subjects, which Lands, having lain uncultivated from the Beginnings of the World, were therefore as free and as common for all to settle upon, as the Waters of the Rivers are to all to drink of. Yet to prevent the Confusion that would follow on every Man's being his own Carver, Governor's were from time to time appointed by the Crown to parcel out to the Subjects as much Land as each could occupy. But the Mischief of it was that the best Parts and most commodiously situated have been granted to a few Particulars, in such exorbitant Quantities that the rest of the Subjects have been obliged to buy it for their use, at an extravagant Price, a Hardship that seems as great, as if they had been put under the necessity of Buying the Waters of the Rivers. The New York Weekly Post Boy, June 9, 1746

The second letter advanced the Divine direction to obey the authority of Caesar that had been given the common man in the New Testament.

I think it necessary at present to speak a few words on several verses of Paul to the Romans. St. Paul's Words are so very plain and conspicuous that they need but little Explanation. I shall a little open the first Verse and the rest I hope will be clearly understood.

1st. Verse "Let every Soul be subject to the higher Powers, for there is no power but of God. The powers that be are ordained by God." This Text divides itself into three parts.

1st. That it's every Christian's Duty to be subject to the Higher Powers, that is, to the present temporal Authority or the Laws of our country that are now in force.

2dly, "For there is no Power but of God." That is, all temporal Government that is established in any Country is of God, tho' its done and acted by Men, yet it's by God's Permission and Appointment.

3dly, "The powers that be or the present powers are Ordained of God." By this we may plainly see that we are not to Dispute how the supreme Magistrate came by his power or whether he has a Lawful Right or not; but whoever has got the Government in their Hands, it immediately becomes our Duty to be subject in all things that are not contrary to our Duty to God and, there, we may say we ought to obey God rather than Man.

2d Verse "Whosoever therefor resists the Power resists the Ordinance of God and they that resist shall receive to themselves Damnation."

By this it is evidently clear that whosoever resists any Officer, even the lowest Officer, that comes lawfully in the King's or supreme Magistrate's Name and Authority, resists the Ordinance of God and they that resist shall receive to themselves Damnation. . . . .

Now, beloved Brethren, seeing the resisting of the powers that we live under is so great a sin, what shall we think of those who live under the best and mildest Government in the World, who have always been protected in their Lawful Rights and Privileges, according to the known good laws of the Land and Nation to which they belong? And only because they can't have a litigious Case tried just according to their own Humor and their own will, be it right or wrong, . . . will rise up in rebellion against the powers that be by raising of Mobs, become guilty of Riots, beating the Officers of the present Government when they are upon their lawful Duty, breaking open Jails, setting fellows at liberty, gathering in great numbers with Clubs, beating down all that oppose them, turning poor people out of their possessions and standing in Defiance of all Laws and Government, trusting to their great Numbers to protect them in all their Villainy. . .

I accuse no particulars; if there be any that find the Coat does fit them, they are welcome to wear it. The New York Evening Post, August 3, 1747

The third letter, which urged a reasonable approach, predicted, quite correctly, as proved in Boston some years later, that riots would lead to the invasion of America by British soldiers, which would in turn lead to even greater regulation

On reading the New York Evening Post, No. 141, I find a Discourse on St. Paul to the Romans, showing the Danger and sin of resisting the Powers that be or the present Government. Tho' he mentions no Time or Place, yet he certainly points at the present New Jersey Rioters, who have run on to a great height and still going from bad to worse (as if they had no remorse) which is to be feared will bring Destruction on themselves, both to Soul and Body, and it will be a singular Providence, if the innocent do not at last suffer in same Measure with the Guilty.

It is an old Maxim "The strictest laws is the greatest Oppression." And it may happen so sometimes in some intricate Cases and there are so many tricks and advantages to be taken in the Law, whereby an innocent Person may suffer and I do not doubt but some of these poor people has suffered very much. If I am rightly informed there are some very industrious, hard laboring People in both the Eastern and Western Divisions of New Jersey that have bought their land and paid for it, once or twice, and some three times, and now they expect to lose it at last.

There are Grievances and Oppressions or Misfortunes, call them how you please, that is too hard for Nature to bear. But all that are guilty in these Riots are not in this case for most of them have no title to land at all and the rest but Blind ones. Doubtless, the Indians have a just Right and may justly Keep others off that they will not buy. But had not the King got a good right also by virtue of Discovery to dispose of to whom he pleases of his own subjects, born in his Dominions. So that none has a right to hold by Indian Title, till they buy of the King also or from those whom the King sold to. And whoever will pretend to hold lands alone, without any regard to the King's Patents, ought to be looked upon as enemies to his Majesty.

Tho' I am neither Proprietor or Lawyer, nor any way by interest concerned, yet I shall venture to give a little advice in this case. It is an old and true saying "Take away the Cause and the effect will cease"... Let some reasonable and easy proposals be made to those that are the real Sufferers with a prudent mixture of Lenity and Justice and let everything be carried fairly; and then, it is hopeful, with a little wise Management, these warm Resentments will cool and be forgotten. And those that are the Advisors and Ringleaders in the Club, they would do well to consider speedily of some method to keep their own Necks out of the Collar. I am not going to Justify them in the least for their wicked Rebellious behavior, for except they repent and forebear such doings, I do not see how they can expect any Favor or Protection, but to be treated as common Enemies and Rebels to the present Government.

Now Gentlemen, you that are so warm in the Club Affair, I shall only ask you one civil Question, how would you like it to have three or four thousand Soldiers sent over as a standing Army to be Quartered upon you?   The New York Evening Post, September 7, 1747

Among the many reasons for the evolution of the mob in America was the Crown's benign neglect of the colonies during those earlier decades, when the British Lion was preoccupied with fighting the French and Spanish. This parental neglect allowed an already independent colonist to grow more so. Never again would he be easily prodded by those who thought themselves still his master.

The opportunity for the colonist to demonstrate his irritation at being told what to do and for Britain, in turn, to respond as it always responded when it confronted mobs, presented itself in 1763. England had changed her policies regarding her colonist children. The Treaty of Paris, four years earlier, had provided the thriving colonies with more growing room and safety, eliminating enemy France from the North American continent. But, it had come at decades of great financial cost to Britain. King George III and Parliament thought it only proper that the now flourishing colonies should help pay the costs of these years of war, plus assume a greater share of the annual costs of its own administration. This policy, reflected in a handful of "Acts" of Parliament, would, within a dozen years, divide irreconcilably the American colonies from their mother land. The Proclamation Act of 1763 shut off the colonists from settling in the fertile lands west of the Allegheny Mountains. The Sugar Act in 1764 imposed taxes designed to raise general revenues for England, without any direct colonial benefit. It started the shout of "no taxation without representation," which would turn into a battle cry. The Quartering Act of 1765 required colonists to provide housing and provisions to the very British troops who had been sent to stand guard over them. It was the Stamp Act in 1765, however, that forever created in the minds of some colonists the "us" against "them" view of the English. The Stamp Act sought to impose taxes on all types of printed documents, including newspapers. The revenues it raised were to pay for Britain's costs of administering her colonial empire. The common man detested the tax. It spawned a mob with a name, the Sons of Liberty, and, while still kin to the English mob, it showed signs of actual rebellion, a shadow of things to come. The newspapers of the time tell the story:

On Saturday last, the 28th Instant, the Sons of Liberty of Woodbridge and the Parts adjacent had a Meeting here, and not sufficiently assured that Mr. Coxe of Philadelphia, who was appointed Distributor of Stamps for New Jersey, had resigned that Office, they deputized and instructed two of their Number to wait on Mr. Coxe, with a Letter, praying a satisfactory Account of his Resignation. Instructions were forthwith made out and delivered to the deputies, together with a Letter to Mr. Coxe which were as follows, viz.

Instructions given by the Sons of Liberty to their deputies to Mr. Coxe, who is appointed distributor of stamps, for the Province of New-Jersey.

First. We command and strictly enjoin it upon you, upon pain of our high displeasure, that you do immediately, with the greatest expedition possible, repair to the house of Mr. Coxe, our stamp distributor, in Philadelphia, and into his hands deliver our letter, praying his resignation, according to the tenor of said letter which, if he complies with, you are to bear the same to us and, in the name of every Son of Liberty in the Province of New-Jersey, to return him your thanks therefor.

Second. Upon Mr. Coxe's refusal, we command you to return immediately and make report to us of the same.

Third. We command and strictly enjoin it upon you, that whether said Mr. Coxe resign his commission &c or not, you do treat him with that complaisance and decorum, becoming a gentleman of Honor. The New York Gazette, January 9, 1766

Coxe resigned his commission forthwith

"I do hereby resign into the hands of the right honourable the lords commissioners of his majesty's treasury, the office of distributor of stamps for the province of New-Jersey. Witness my hand and seal, this third day of September, in the Year of Our Lord 1765.
   William Coxe (seal)
Sealed and delivered in the presence of William Humphreys and Tench Tilgman". The New York Gazette, January 9, 1766

That the opposition to the Stamp Act was universal can be seen in the following warning to the populace of New Jersey:

A large Gallows was erected in Elizabeth-Town last Week with a Rope already fixed thereto, and the inhabitants there vow and declare that the first Person that either distributes or takes out a Stamped Paper shall be hung thereon without Judge or Jury. The New York Gazette, February 27, 1766

Among the items to be taxed by the Stamp Act were legal documents. This caused a problem. Were the Courts to be shut down? The English legal system -- the common law -- was much prized then, as now, by Americans. It was a protector of the citizen against arbitrary power. The colonists did not want to be without it. On the other hand, they did not want to pay the tax and thereby appear to subject itself to Parliament's authority. And, even to a mob, intimidating a tax collector was less revolutionary than threatening a judge and the law. The dilemma was solved in a simple fashion. Everyone, including the court, its clerks and lawyers, ignored the tax and business went forward as usual, without stamps:

We hear from New-Jersey that the gentlemen of the law in that Province met last Thursday at New-Brunswick, to consider the propriety of resuming their practice, which they have discontinued since the 1st of November, where they were waited upon by a deputation of the Sons of Liberty, who expressed their uneasiness about the suspension of law proceedings, and it was decided by a majority of the lawyers then convened "that they would resume their practice the 1st Day of April next, whatever accounts may be received from England or sooner, if earlier intelligence arrives of the determination of Parliament respecting the Stamp Act", which being communicated to the deputies, who then attended, they appeared to be satisfied therewith. And at the same time, deputies from the Sons of Liberty of the County of Hunterdon, waited on Mr. White, prothonotary of that County, with a request that he open his office to transact business as usual, who received them politely and they received assurances that the office should be opened the first day of April.

We likewise hear from the same quarter that a certain person being dunned for a debt, he gave his creditor to understand that as there was no law, he would not pay him, whereupon the creditor seized him by the shoulders and called out "here is a man that wants stamps!" He was in a little time surrounded by a number of people who would make a sacrifice of him, who dared to take the advantage of the distressing situation of his Country, had he not immediately paid the money and made an acknowledgment of his fault. The Pennsylvania Journal, February 20, 1766

Remarkably, opposition to the Stamp Act unified the colonies and networks formed among towns, counties and even the provinces. Each tried to voice and publish its reasoning for challenging the Stamp Act, expressions in which, centuries later, Americans can recognize the essential tenets of their own form of self government:

To the Printer
Please to insert the following Resolves, in your next Paper.
At a meeting of the Sons of Liberty, of Woodbridge in New-Jersey, they have come unto the following resolves.
I. Resolv'd, that we yield hearty and unfeigned obedience to His Majesty King George the Third

II. Resolv'd, that we maintain and abide by all and singular the constitutional laws of our Mother Country; but no other laws or impositions whatsoever

III. Resolv'd, that a Committee of five Persons be immediately chosen to act in conjunction with the several committees of our neighboring township in the counties of Middlesex, in order that the respective committees of the several Townships may form a Committee out of their own body, to act in conjunction with the several committees of the neighboring counties of the Province of New Jersey, that we may be in actual readiness on any emergency.

IV. Resolv'd, that our Committee are hereby authorized to transact all affairs relating to the Stamp Act, any three of which acting, shall be decisive.

V. Resolv'd, that we commit these resolves to the press, without any design to dictate to our neighboring Towns or Counties, but only to communicate our sentiments for them to improve upon and shall be ever ready to hear all other proposals that they shall think more conducive to the public end aimed at, namely, the Union of the Provinces throughout the Continent.

P.S. We have taken the above measures in consequence of a letter from a Committee of the Sons of Liberty of the City of New-York, recommending such a step as a necessary precaution against the Stamp Act. The New York Gazette, March 6, 1766

Much to the colonists' pleasure -- and undoubtedly fostering a sense of power that would encourage them in years to follow -- the news arrived in Philadelphia, in a round about way but typical of the times, that Parliament had relented and repealed the Stamp Act:

On Sunday night an express arrived here, dispatched by the Sons of Liberty of Baltimore in Maryland to the Sons of Liberty here, with the following glorious news.

Baltimore, April 3, 1766, 8 o'clock at night.

About a quarter of an hour ago, Mr. Ploughman came here from lower Marlborough and brings a letter from Mr. George Maxwell, of Benedict, on Patuxent River, to Mr. Charles Graham of Marlborough, advising him of the arrival of Capt. Brook from London and his receiving by him a letter from Messrs R. and J. Day, merchants in London, dated the 8th of February, in which they say,

"We congratulate you on the repeal of the Stamp Act, which, Thanks to God, is just now resolved here by a very great majority in parliament. On which I sincerely congratulate you and all lovers of Liberty."

This account, it is thought, there is great reason to believe, as all the gentlemen mentioned in it are persons of the highest credit. And what seems to strengthen the above intelligence is that a gentleman of this place, ten days ago, met another from Virginia, in the Jersies, who told him that he had left York Town on the 27th of March, that the day before a vessel arrived there from London, in 43 days passage, which brought letters to the tenth of February, one of which to Col. Ayres and which the gentleman saw, wherein the writer tells him the Stamp Act was REPEALED, whereof he gave him joy. The Pennsylvania Journal, April 10, 1766

Needless to say, the colonists celebrated the great news:

On Saturday last, on account of the Glorious News of the Repeal of the Stamp-Act, an elegant entertainment was prepared in the City of Burlington, at which his Excellency the Governor and the principal inhabitants of the place were present, when the following Toasts were drank viz. The King, The Queen, and Royal Family, the Parliament of Great Britain, the present worthy Ministry, The Governor and Province, the glorious Mr. Pitt, Lord Cambden, Lord Dartmouth, General Howard, Colonel Barre, Doctor Franklin, Trecothic and Hanbury, Friends to America on this and the other side of the Atlantic. May the Stamp Act be buried in Oblivion. Increase to the manufacturers of Britain and prosperity to the agriculture of America.

The city was handsomely illuminated; bonfires were lighted and other demonstrations of joy were shown and every thing was conducted with the greatest order and decorum. The Pennsylvania Gazette, May 29, 1766

A crisis had been averted. The American merchants thanked the London merchants for their assistance and the colonies each thanked the King:

To Barlow Trecothick, Esq. and the Committee of Merchants, London, trading to North America

This acknowledges receipt of your much esteemed favours the 28th of February and the 18th of March, which severally afforded us the highest pleasures, the former as presaging and the latter confirming the repeal of the unhappy stamp act.

As that act, had it been enforced, must have necessarily deprived his Majesty's subjects in North America of their most invaluable privileges, at the same time that it imposed burdens grievous, and, as we apprehend, unconstitutional, thence the account of its being repealed could not fail of diffusing universal joy throughout the continent.

The various difficulties and the relentless opposition which the friends of liberty had to encounter in bringing about this happy event, fill our minds with a high sense of their eminent, inflexible virtues.

In regard to the riots or tumults that have appeared at times in some particular places among the colonies, they were sallies of less considerate men. History furnishes proof that even the best regulated states have not been at all times able to restrain such, far less could it be expected in our infant country. Hence, we are inclined to think that these would not have preponderated so much in England, had they not been greatly exaggerated and, probably, misrepresented there by mercenary or otherwise ill-affected persons, for, we hope, the conduct of the more thinking men among us stood unexceptionable.

We conceived the imposition to be unconstitutional and the distress on our trade to be highly impolitic. We saw the co-operation of these measures, if persisted in, must inevitably issue in the ruin of the colonies and that England would sensibly feel the direful effects.

The then Administration seemed regardless of every remonstrance from that quarter whence we were left to pour out our complaints to private friends on your side and urge their aid, in warding off the impending evil. Had not a repeal of the stamp act (accompanied with the prospect of the extension of trade) taken place, commerce must have ceased here, agriculture, manufacture and economy become the sole object of the attention and pursuit of these colonies.

We flatter ourselves that the discussion of that important point before the parliament had thrown in such a light upon the minds of the people of Great Britain that men in power will see, and be persuaded, that fettering the trade of America and over burthening its inhabitants, is, in fact, cropping the flowers and distressing the bees of their own hive; that, on the other hand, keeping up an attention to the prosperity of the colonies and the extension of the commerce, as it is the most natural, must prove the most efficacious means of promoting the best interest of Great Britain.

We cannot take our leave without expressing our most affectionate loyalty to his present Majesty, our gratitude to his ministers, to the majority of parliament, to Mr. Pitt, that eminent friend of Liberty, and you, gentlemen, the Committee of North-American Merchants, for your unwearied endeavors on this most important occasion. And we trust that the behavior of the colonies will always fully justify what you were so kind as to assert in their behalf.

(signed by fourteen principal merchants)
The Pennsylvania Gazette, October 23, 1766

However, the repeal of the Stamp Act, far from being the resolution of the conflict, was only the beginning. The Ministry and King George III could not end it with a victory by the mob and with it, the loss of authority by proper Government. They quickly enacted the Townshend Acts of 1767, a new set of revenue producing taxes for the colonies. This time, when the citizens of Boston protested, Britain barked back by sending 4,000 British troops to Boston. The friction between these soldiers and the Boston towns people was great and a number of "incidents" erupted, the most infamous being the Boston Massacre of 1770, when five colonists were killed when the British soldiers fired into the mob.

Feeling their strength, the colonists escalated their protests to Parliament and the British Ministry over the change of policies of governing the colonies. Their spokesmen were no longer only the common citizen and the Sons of Liberty, but also the Provincial Legislators, elected by the common man. Suffering Massachusetts took the lead. The following reports show how the Massachusetts Assembly encouraged sister colony New Jersey to send a message from it directly to the King of England himself, bypassing his Ministers:

> We have the Pleasure to inform our readers, that the House of Representatives in the present session of the General Assembly, have received very agreeable letters from divers House of Representatives, etc. of other Colonies, in Answer to the circular letter of the late House of the 11th of February. Whatever the opinion of some on the other side of the water may be, of this letter, who have had representations of it being the rash and hasty production of a spirit of faction, it seems that one respectable body after another in America, having judged it worthy of their attention. "The little dirty expiring faction", as the well known true Patriot and his few adherents have affected to call it [in Parliament], will, without peradventure, appear to his and their astonishment and grief, to be the sober and enlightened sentiments of by far the greater part of the most respectable inhabitants, not of Massachusetts-Bay only, but the whole American continent!

> Sir,
> As soon as the House of Representatives of this Colony met, which was on the 12th of April, I laid your letter of the 11th of February before them.
> Sensible that the law you complain of is a subject in which every Colony is interested, the House of Representatives readily perceived the necessity of an immediate application to the King, and that it should correspond with those of the other Colonies; but as they have not had an opportunity of knowing the sentiments of any other Colony, but that of Massachusetts-Bay, they have endeavored to conform themselves to the mode adopted by you.
> They have therefore given instructions to their Agent, and enjoined his attention to the subject of their Opinion.
> "The freedom with which the House of Representatives of the Massachusetts-Bay have communicated their sentiments on a matter of such great concern to all the Colonies, hath been received by this House, with that Candor, the spirit and design of your letter merit. And at the same time, that they acknowledge themselves obliged to you for communicating your sentiments to them, they have directed me to assure you, that they are desirous to keep up a correspondence

with you, and to unite with the Colonies, if necessary, in further supplications to his Majesty, to relieve his distressed, American subjects."

In the name and by the order of the House of Representatives, I am, Sir, your most Obedient humble servant.
Cortland Skinner[35]
The Pennsylvania Gazette, May 15, 1768

The underlying issue was, in the American mind, a straight forward one. The Magna Carta of 1215 had been regarded as a pact between the King and, at first, his Vassal Lords, and, then by the 1770's with all Englishmen, the Houses of Parliament having replaced the feudal lords. One term in that agreement was that the King would not take an Englishman's property without either his direct or indirect (through the Parliament) consent. Money, of course, was a form of property. If a colonist had to pay money, in the form of a tax, then he was in fact having his property taken away by the Crown without his consent. He did not have a chance to approve or disapprove because the American colonists had no representatives in the English Parliament that voted the taxes. In an effort to help the King understand the views of his subjects in the Provinces of East and West New Jersey, the New Jersey Assembly sent him a letter. After displaying proper deference to the Monarch, the letter eloquently presented the colonists' position and determination. As it would turn out, it would all be to no avail:

Most Gracious Sovereign

We Your Majesty's loyal subjects, the Representatives of Your colony of New-Jersey, confiding in Your Majesty's paternal affection for Your people, humbly implore permission to approach the throne and to present our supplications in Behalf of ourselves and our constituents, Your Majesty's faithful and afflicted subjects.

Before that happy period, in which the empire of the British dominion was, by the favor of divine Providence, for the felicity of those Dominions, and of Europe in general, established in your illustrious House, our ancestors, with the consent of the Crown, removed from their Native land, then abounding in all Blessings, but perfect Security of Liberty, and that merciful Spirit of Administration, which render your Royal Family so justly dear to your remotest subjects, and ventured with their hapless Relatives, through a vast Ocean, and trusted themselves with their tender Companions to the inhospitable and unknown wilderness of this new World, the Horrors of which no consideration could render tolerable, but the prospect of enjoying complete Freedom, which Britons never thought could be purchased at too great a Price.

The Subjects thus emigrating, brought with them, as inherent in their Persons, all the Rights and Liberties of natural-born subjects within the Parent State: In consequence of these, a Government was formed, under which they have been constantly exercised and enjoyed by the Inhabitants, and repeatedly and solemnly recognized and confirmed by your Royal Predecessors, and the Legislature of Great Britain.

One of these Rights and Liberties, vested in the People of this Colony, is the Privilege of being exempt from any Taxation, but such as are imposed upon them by themselves, or by their Representatives; and this they esteem so valuable, that they are fully persuaded, no other can exist without it.

Your Majesty's signal Distinction is, that you reign over Freemen, and your peculiar Glory, that you reign in such a Manner, is that your Subjects, the Disposers of their own Property, are ready and willing whenever your Service calls upon them, with their Lives and Fortunes, to assist your Cause. Your People of this Colony, who share in the Blessings flowing from your Wisdom and Knowledge, most gratefully sensible of their Obligations to so excellent a Prince, humbly hope that they have never been deficient in duly acknowledging them. Whenever it has been necessary that Supplies should be levied within this Colony, Requisitions by your Majesty, or by your Royal Predecessor, conformable to the Rights and Liberties of the People, have been made, and by them loyally and liberally complied with.

We beseech your Majesty to do them the Justice to believe that they can never fail on any future Occasion to demonstrate their Devotion to your Majesty; nor can they resign, without unutterable Shame and Grief, the Honor and Satisfaction of voluntarily and cheerfully expressing in the strongest Manner their Circumstances will permit, their unfeigned Affection for your Majesty's Person, their distinguished Duty to your Government, and their inflexible Resolution to maintain your authority, and defend your Dominions.

Penetrated with these Sentiments, this your People, with the utmost Concern and Anxiety, observe, that Duties have lately been imposed on them by Parliament, for the sole and express Purposes of raising a Revenue. This is a Taxation upon them, from which they conceive they ought to be protected, by the acknowledged Principles of the Constitution, that Freemen cannot be legally taxed but by themselves, or by their Representatives; and that they are not represented in Parliament, they not only cannot allow, but are convinced, that from their local Circumstances they never can be.

Very far is it from our Intention, to deny our Subordination to that August Body, or our Dependence on the Kingdom of Great-Britain; in these Connections, and in the Settlement of our Liberties, under the auspicious Influence of your Royal house, we know our Happiness consists; and, therefore, to confine these Connections, and to strengthen this Settlement, is at once our Interest, Duty, and Delight. Nor do we apprehend that it lies within our Power, by any Means more effectually to promote these great Purposes, than by zealously striving to preserve in perfect Vigor, those sacred Rights and Liberties, under the inspiring Sanction of which, inconceivable Difficulties and Dangers opposing, this Colony has been rescued from the rudest State of Nature, converted into a populous, flourishing, and valuable Territory and has contributed to a very considerable Degree, to the Welfare of Great-Britain.

Most Gracious Sovereign, the incessant exertion of your truly Royal Cares, to Procure your People a Prosperity equal to your Love of them, encourages us with all Humility to pray, that your Majesty's Clemency will be graciously pleased to take into Consideration our unhappy Circumstances and to afford us such relief, as your Majesty's Wisdom shall judge to be most proper." The Pennsylvania Gazette, July 21, 1768

Courts of Admiralty did not have juries, a cherished right of English common law. Instead, the judge alone determined the facts, the law and the punishment and then he was paid from what he recovered. Obviously, this was a tremendous temptation to the unscrupulous. When the jurisdiction of these courts was expanded to include enforcement of the shipping, revenue and other laws, they became objects of great oppression in the eyes of the colonists and resistance to them grew as the following extract from a letter indicates:

> *I've been seeing my Relations in Virginia whom I have not visited these 14 years past, and in taverns and friends houses where I lodged on my way through the Jerseys, Pennsylvania and Maryland, I found the people of all sorts greatly alarmed by the late revenue acts; the dissolving of our provincial Parliaments or Assemblies; the new Courts of Admiralty erected on our coasts; being denied of juries in many cases to be tried; the British Government's rejecting the Petitions lately sent them from the colonies, and their now proposing to send for Otis, Cushing &c. to carry them home as Traitors and try them for their lives. These things have blown up the minds of the people into a high flame for industry all over the countries, so that several townships, as I came along, were resolving speedily to meet and to enter into strict agreements against buying any more English goods, especially their woolen, silk and calico fineries, but each family vigorously to set about manufacturing their own clothing and every other necessary article. I happened also into company where some farmers and a physician were set about agreeing with an eminent silk weaver, late from Dublin, about erecting a silk manufactory, as mulberries grow freely in the woods. At another gentleman's house where I was, his lady was spinning fast and had five clever girls spinning alongside her ever since they heard the Boston Parliament was dissolved. It's expected that they soon will have a great deal of cloth to sell. When riding along the road last week, I saw sometimes Country girls pointed out and hissed at for wearing scarlet and calicoes; "beh!" says a bachelor, "there ride two saucy dames, none of them a match for me; she will never make a coat for me, when it seems her mamma never learned her to spin a coat nor mantle for her dear sweet self." This put the girls to blush and so rode off. The Pennsylvania Journal, April 20, 1769*

The Ministers of Great Britain were mocked in the press for their laws against the colonies:

> *On the Virginia Assembly offering up their prayers for wisdom for Lord B----t.*

The Assembly in devoutest strain
Ask for my Lord the gift of Brain
Wisdom alone will hardly do
Next beg a little patience too
The Pennsylvania Chronicle, June 5, 1769

In 1770, at about the same time as the Boston Massacre was taking place in Massachusetts, there was more civil disobedience in New Jersey. Now, the rioting seemed to come easier. The riots ensued after years and years of litigation had gone against those claiming to have purchased good title from the Indians in favor of those who claimed title from the Crown. Despite threats to burn down Newark, mobs of self viewed defranchised citizens and arrests of the mob's leaders, violence was minimal and damage limited. The leaders, who stood trial were convicted by a jury of freeholders and fined. In Monmouth county, the problem was blamed on the lawyers, who had represented the winning side, and the mob shut down the court:

From Freehold in Monmouth County in New Jersey, we learn that the inhabitants of that County are so irritated at the lawyers there, that on Tuesday the 23rd of January, being the Time appointed for the holding Courts of Pleas and General Sessions of the Peace there, a great number of them assembled there in a tumultuous and riotous Manner and absolutely refused to permit one lawyer to come; the Magistrates were so intimidated that no Courts were opened or held there that time. The Pennsylvania Journal, February 12, 1770

Despite the growing anger and resentment of the Americans, Britain was not giving up its colonial policies. Far from it. Parliament and its Prime Minister were alarmed and angered by the actions of the colonists and would not be intimidated again by what they considered to be just another manifestation of the old English mob. An event that gave tinder to the growing flame of conflict was the renowned Gaspee Affair. The *HMS Gaspee* was a royal revenue -- and anti- smuggler -- cutter, which had been seized and burned by a mob, after it had run aground in Narragansett Bay, off Rhode Island. Perhaps, more accurately, as pointed out in the following, it was

Britain's handling of the matter which revealed to the colonists their second class status. It was evident that American colonists simply did not enjoy the same civil rights as did Englishmen in Britain. Rumors regarding the Crown's methods of investigation and its proposed plan of prosecuting the accused both frightened and angered those in other colonies, who compared it to the oppressive conduct they had suffered at the hands of the British:

> *We hear that a Commission is to make inquiry into the affair of burning his Majesty's Schooner Gaspee. If the burning [of] the Gaspee Schooner was a matter of serious importance, much more so are the methods pursued by the British administration in consequence of it. This affair was transacted within the body of a county, in a free English government; one would think therefore it should be the subject of the inquiry of the grand jury of inquest of that county. Instead of which, we are told that five gentlemen, four of whom are of superior rank in other colonies, the other, indeed, a judge of the Admiralty, are appointed by commission to make the enquiry. By a gentleman lately from Rhode Island, we are informed, that three of these commissioners are empowered to act, at whose call the army and navy are to attend; that any persons accused, against whom the commissioners shall judge there is sufficient evidence to convict, are to be apprehended and, together with the evidences, sent to England for trial. . . It is said that he [the British admiral in Newport, from whose fleet the Gaspee came,] has recommended that those who, it is supposed, can give evidence of this matter, and refuse to do it, be put on board the men of war and there kept, until they do. The indignity offered to all the Colonies, and particularly Rhode Island, says a gentleman of a neighboring town to a friend of his in this city [Philadelphia], is not to be equaled. To have a set of crown officers, commissioned by the Ministry and supported by ships and troops, to enquire into offenses against the crown, instead of the ordinary and constitutional method of a grand jury, carries an implication that the people of that colony are so deeply tinctured with rebellious principles as they are not to be trusted by the crown.*
>
> *The inhabitants of Philadelphia can feel for their brethren of Rhode Island, having themselves tasted of the cup of ministerial vengeance, when, to aid and protect the commissioners of the*

customs, in carrying in execution a revenue act of the British parliament, [British] troops were stationed in the capitol and the city turned into a garrison! And though these troops, after slaughtering some of our innocent inhabitants, were obliged to retire from the town, they are yet posted in the principal fortress and key of the Province. What shall hinder the like scene of blood, rapine and slaughter in the Capitol of Rhode Island, if the commission of enquiry there, should so readily call for the military aid as the commissioners of the customs did here? Such treatment of the Colonies calls for most serious attention; and, however profane it may be called by Draper [the editor of the pro British Boston News Letter], we have reason with firm affiance in HIM who hateth oppression and tyranny, devoutly to acclaim "How Long! O Lord! How Long!" The Pennsylvania Journal, December 30, 1772

The Pennsylvania Chronicle was in complete accord. After outlining the same tales of intimidation by the British in its own account on the Gaspee case, it concluded:

In this situation of affairs, every friend of our violated constitution cannot be but greatly alarmed. The idea of seizing a number of persons, under the points of bayonets, and transporting them nearly three thousand miles for trial, where, guilty or innocent, they must unavoidably fall victim alike to revenge or prejudice, is shocking to humanity, repugnant to every dictate of reason, liberty and justice and in which Americans and freemen ought never to acquiesce.
The following law was made and passed by the General Assembly of the Colony, on their sessions in Newport on the 1st of March, 1663 and not since repealed, viz.: "Be it enacted that no freeman shall be taken, imprisoned or deprived of his freehold or Liberty or free Custom, or be outlawed or exiled or otherwise destroyed, nor shall be passed upon, judged or condemned but by the lawful judgment of his Peers or by the Law of this Colony." The Pennsylvania Chronicle, January 2, 1773

Further fanning the flame among the citizens of Pennsylvania, *The Pennsylvania Journal* published portions of a letter from Lord Dartmouth at White Hall in London to the Governor of Rhode Island, confirming the rumors that Britain had already concluded that this was a matter of treason, not piracy, that troops would be at the Commission's disposal to quell crowds and that the Commission was to send everyone to London for trial. Lord Dartmouth's letter, reported in the press, advised the Governor and the Commission:

> *The particulars of that atrocious proceeding [the burning of the Gaspee] have by the King's Command been examined and considered with the greatest attention . . . in the obvious view of the whole transaction and taking all the circumstances together, the offense is in the opinion of the servants of the crown, who have been consulted upon that question, of a much deeper dye [than merely piracy] and is considered in no other light than as an act of high treason, viz. levying war against the King. . .*
>
> *The King trusts that all persons in the colony will pay a due respect to his royal commission and that the business of it will be carried on without molestation. At the same time, the nature of this offence and the great number of persons who appear to have been concerned in it make every precaution necessary. His Majesty has therefore, for the further support in the execution of this duty thought fit to direct me to signify his pleasure to Lieutenant General Gage that he do hold himself in readiness to send troops to Rhode Island, whenever he shall be called upon by the commissioners for that purpose in order to aid and assist the civil magistrate in the suppression of any riot or disturbances and in the preservation of the public peace. . . It is his Majesty's intention, in consequence of the advice of his privy council, that the persons concerned in the burning of the Gaspee schooner and in the other violences that attended that daring insult, should be brought to England to be tried . . . taking care that you do give notice to the persons accused in order that they may procure such witnesses on their behalf as they shall judge necessary, which witnesses, together with all such as may be proper to support the charges against them, will be received and sent hither with the prisoners. The Pennsylvania Journal, January 20, 1773*

In 1773, the colonies were advised of Parliament's enactment of the Tea Act, which gave a group in London a monopoly on the shipment of all tea to the Americas. The Massachusetts patriots responded with the famous Boston Tea Party, where colonists, thinly disguised as Mohawk Indians, dumped several hundred chests of tea from several British cargo ships into the harbor. Britain countered by closing Boston Harbor and taking over the civilian government of the city, pursuant to a series of parliamentary enactments, known on this side of the Atlantic, as the Intolerable Acts.

Many colonists, outside Massachusetts, also resolved to have nothing to do with the tea tax. Some protest was symbolic:

Philadelphia, February 16. We hear from Princeton, in New Jersey, that the Officers and Students of the College have unanimously agreed to drink no more TEA. The Pennsylvania Journal, February 9, 1774

Most of it, however, was deadly serious and was intended to prevent entry of any tea into America. Boston had not been the only town that threatened a "Tea Party". It was happening throughout the colonies[36]. In New York, for example, peaceful means of persuasion were first employed, with not so veiled economic and physical threats clearly visible, lurking in the background, if needed. Witness how the mob, growing more powerful and organized by the minute, reasoned with the pilots not to assist an expected tea ship into that port:

To the Stated Pilots of the Port of New York and to all others whom it may concern,
Gentlemen:
We need not inform you that the ship is hourly expected with the tea from England, which, if landed here, will entail slavery on this colony and ruin its commerce. No class of men are more interested in the last but you; nor none have it more in their power to prevent the introduction of which the tyrannical Ministry intend as the badge of our slavery. You are, therefore, called upon to give the first obstruction. The ship cannot enter this port unless you direct her. Acquit yourselves in this as become free men and friends of commerce. Much depends upon your conduct in this interesting crisis, no less than whether you or your posterity shall be free men or slaves -- whether you shall have property or be beggars. You have had many proofs of the disapprobation of your fellow citizens to the

importation of any article, subject to a duty by the British Parliament, for the purpose of raising a revenue in America. You have therefore nothing to fear from doing your duty to your country. The merchants and all the inhabitants, friends of liberty, are concerned in your giving the obstruction and will support you. We cannot therefore doubt that these are sufficient motives to induce you to demonstrate to all the world, that you will not have the least agency in the destruction of your country. But, if contrary to our just expectations, any of you should be so lost to all sense of obligation to your country as not to follow the directions hereinafter mentioned, the vengeance of a free people, struggling for their liberties, await and will surely be executed upon you. Should you be told that the Wardens will remove any of you who refuse to pilot a ship into this port or prosecute your bonds, they dare not do either, for they are within the reach of the same vengeance and therefore will not hazard their own safety.

Whenever you board a vessel, enquire carelessly of the sailors, where she is from, and if she is from London, whether she has any tea on board, for the Captain of the tea ship may conceal it from you. If the sailors were not on board at the loading of her, and cannot inform you, enquire of the Captain. If he is unwilling to tell you, rest assured there is tea there. In this case, or if you are informed that there is tea on board, bring her to anchor in Sandy Hook Bay and no farther, where she may be supplied with provisions or other articles she might want for her return. Upon her anchoring, quit her immediately and make the best of your way to this city and inform the citizens of her arrival. You should be provided with a red flag to hoist as a signal to the other Pilots, whenever you discover her to be the tea ship, in order that they may keep clear of her after you quit her.

Let every pilot possess himself with a copy of this for his government.

Legion
The Pennsylvania Journal, November 24, 1773

The next tea ship bound for New York encountered the same such scrutiny:

On Friday last, about four o'clock in the afternoon, the ship London, Capt. Chambers, came up into the harbor. As soon as she arrived at Sandy Hook, two of the Committee (who went down to watch the Tea ship) went on board her & informed Chambers of the intelligence [they] had received respecting the Tea on board his ship, which he positively denied and produced for them his file of cockets on which there was no cocket for Tea. When the ship came to the wharf, the Committee and some of his owners went on board and interrogated him on the subject, but he still persisted in denying it, 'till Capt. S., (a member of the Committee and who is likewise a proprietor of the ship) told him it was in vain to deny it and that he had better acknowledge it, if he knew anything of the matter, as he may be assured, that every suspicious package may be opened. Upon which he took the cocket out of his pocket and presented it to Capt. S, who immediately withdrew, with the rest of the Committee and the owners of the ship to Queen's Head Tavern, where, upon opening the cocket, they discovered to their astonishment that Chambers was the proprietor of the Tea. . . . As soon as it was known, the people began to assemble and, by evening, a large body was collected, a number of whom went on board the ship, broke open the boxes and emptied every ounce of it into the river. About eight o'clock, a number of men, disguised, came alongside the ship for the same purpose, not suspecting that the business had already been effected. Chambers somehow managed to escape in the bustle[37]. " The Pennsylvania Journal, April 27, 1774

In Philadelphia, the tea tax and the other revenue raising measures, inflicted by Parliament on the colonies, were equally detested by the common people, the ultimate mob. They viewed the tax as a symbol of the greater struggle between the English speaking peoples on opposite sides of the Atlantic on issues such as taxation and representation:

Philadelphia, Monday, December 27, 1773. A Public Meeting of the inhabitants was held at the State House on the 18th of October, at which great numbers attended and the sense of the city was expressed in the following resolves:
1. That the disposal of their property is the inherent right of freemen; that there can be no property in that which another can, of

right, take from us without our consent; that the claim of Parliament to tax America is, in other words, a claim of right to levy contributions on us at pleasure

2. That the duty imposed by Parliament upon tea landed in America, is a tax on the Americans or levying contributions on them without their consent

3. That the express purpose for which the tax is levied on the Americans, namely for the support of government, administration of justice and defense of his Majesty's dominions in America, has a direct tendency to render Assemblies useless and to introduce arbitrary government and slavery.

4. That a virtuous and steady opposition to this ministerial plan of governing America is absolutely necessary to preserve even the shadow of liberty and is a duty which every freeman in America owes to his country, to himself and to his posterity.

5. That the resolution lately entered into by the East India Company to send out their Tea to America, subject to the payment of duties on its being landed there, is an open attempt to enforce this ministerial plan and a violent attack upon the liberties of America.

6. That it is the duty of every American to oppose this attempt.

7. That whosoever shall, directly or indirectly, countenance this attempt, or in any way aid or abet in unloading, receiving or vending the tea sent or to be sent out by the East India Tea Company, while it remains subject to the payment of a duty here, is an enemy to his country.

8. That a Committee be immediately chosen to wait on those gentlemen who, it is reported, are appointed by the East India Company to receive and sell said tea and request them, from a regard to their own character, and the peace and good order of the city and the province, immediately to resign their appointment.

It is not easy to describe the anxiety and suspense of the City in this interval. Sundry reports of her arrival were received which proved premature. But, on Saturday evening last, an express came up from Chester to inform the Town that the Tea Ship, commanded by Capt. Ayres, with her detestable Cargo, was arrived there, having followed another ship up the river so far. The Committee then appointed three of their members to go to Chester and two others to Glouster Point, in order to have the earliest opportunity of meeting Capt. Ayres and representing to him the sense of the Public, respecting his voyage and cargo . . . This [the meeting] the Captain complied with and was handed through a lane made by the People to the Gentlemen appointed to confer with him. They represented to him the general sentiments, together with the dangers and difficulties that would attend his refusal to comply with the wishes of the inhabitants. . . [and they] desired him to proceed with them to Town where he would be more fully informed of the temper and resolution of the People. He was accordingly accompanied to Town by a number of Persons where he was soon convinced of the truth and propriety of the representations, which had been made to him and agreed, upon the desire of the Inhabitants being publicly expressed, he would conduct himself accordingly. Some small rudeness being offered to the Captain afterwards in the street by some small boys, several gentlemen interposed and suppressed it before he received the least injury. Upon an hour's notice this morning, a public meeting was called, and the State House not being sufficient to hold the numbers assembled, they adjourned into the Square. This meeting is allowed by all to be the most respectable, both in the numbers and ranks of those that attended it that has been known in this City. After a short introduction, the following resolutions were not only agreed to, but the public approbation testified in the warmest manner.

RESOLVED,

1. that the Tea on board the Ship Polly, Capt. Ayres, shall not be landed.

2. That Capt. Ayres shall neither enter nor report his vessel at the Custom House.

3. That Capt. Ayres shall carry back the Tea immediately.

4. That Capt. Ayres shall immediately send a pilot on board his vessel with orders to take charge of her and to proceed to Reedy Island next high water.

5. That the Captain shall be allowed to stay in Town till tomorrow to provide necessaries for his voyage.

6. That he shall then be obliged to leave the Town and proceed to his vessel and make the best of his way out of our river and bay.

7. That a Committee of four Gentlemen be appointed to see the Resolves are carried into execution.

The whole business was conducted with decorum and order worthy the importance of the cause. Capt. Ayres, being present at this meeting, solemnly and publicly engaged that he would literally comply with the sense of the City, as expressed in the above resolutions.

A proper supply of necessaries and fresh provisions being then procured, in about two hours the Tea Ship weighted anchor from Glouster Point, where she lay in sight of the Town, and has proceeded, with her whole cargo, on her return to the East India Company. The Pennsylvania Gazette, December 29, 1773

The colonists' resistance to Parliaments' efforts to force them to accede to the hated revenue acts intensified, especially as they viewed Boston's being punished for its earlier insubordination. The colonists increased communication among the different provinces, encouraging each other to prepare for the period ahead. The mob still professed loyalty and affection to the Crown. Its language was polite and diplomatic. Its initial threat was economic, a colonial boycott against goods manufactured in England:

At a Meeting of the Freeholders and inhabitants of the county of Essex, in the Province of New Jersey, at Newark, in the said county, on Saturday, the 11th of June, 1774.

This meeting taking into serious consideration some late alarming measures, adopted by the British Parliament, for depriving his Majesty's American subjects of their undoubted and constitutional rights and privileges, and particularly, the act of blockading the port of Boston which appears to them pregnant with the most dangerous consequences to all his Majesty's dominions in North America, do unanimously resolve and agree:

1. That, under the enjoyment of our constitutional privileges and immunities, we will ever cheerfully render all due obedience to the Crown of Great Britain, as well as full faith and allegiance to his most gracious Majesty King George the Third and do esteem a firm dependence on the mother country essential to our political security and happiness;

2. That the late act of Parliament relative to Boston, which so absolutely destroys every idea of safety and confidence, appears to us big with the most dangerous and alarming consequences, especially as subversive of that very dependence which we would earnestly hope to continue, as our best safeguard and protection, and we conceive every well wisher to Great Britain and her Colonies is now called upon to exert his utmost abilities, in promoting every loyal and prudent measure towards obtaining a repeal of the said act of Parliament and all others subversive of the undoubted rights and liberties of his Majesty's American subjects;

3. That it is our unanimous opinion that it would conduce to the restoration of the liberties of America, should the colonies enter into a joint agreement not to purchase or use any articles of British manufactory and especially any commodities imported from the East Indies, under such restrictions as may be agreed upon by a general congress of the said colonies to be hereinafter appointed;

4. That this county [Essex] will most readily and cheerfully join their brethren of the other counties of this province, in promoting such a congress of deputies, to be sent from each of the colonies to form a general plan of union, so that the measures to be pursued for the important ends in view may be uniform and firm, to which plan, when concluded upon, we do agree faithfully to adhere. And now, we declare ourselves ready to send a committee to meet with those from the other colonies at such time and place as may be by them agreed upon, in order to elect proper persons to represent this province in the said general congress;

5. That the freeholders and inhabitants of the other counties of this province be requested to speedily convene themselves to consider the present distressing state of our public affairs and to correspond and to consult with such other committees as also with those of any other province and, particularly, to meet with the said county committees in order to nominate and appoint deputies to represent this province on the general congress;

6. We do hereby unanimously request the following gentlemen to accept of that trust and, accordingly, do appoint them our committee for the purposes aforesaid, viz. Stephen Crane, Henry Gariste, Joseph Riggs, William Livingston, William P. Smith, John De Hart, John Chetwood, Isaac Ogden and Elias Boudinot, Esquires.
The Pennsylvania Gazette, June 29, 1774

Committees formed throughout the provinces, in towns and counties. In constant communication with one another, all the provinces enthusiastically prepared for what lay ahead:

Boston, June 20. The present aspect of public affairs is highly favorable to the liberties of America. The whole continent seems inspired by one soul and that soul a vigorous and determined one.

Virginia is all in motion and Maryland has made amazing progress for the short space since they have taken this fresh alarm from the Boston port bill. . . Besides the doings of Annapolis and Baltimore, those of Chester are deserving our warmest acknowledgments. Subscription papers have been set on foot in that county and considerable sums already subscribed for the relief of our poor in that devoted town. Philadelphia is following in the generous example, as well as the Jersies, New York and Connecticut. New Jersey is very forward and are on the point of choosing their deputies for the Congress by a very regular method viz. of meetings in towns and neighborhoods, sending deputies from those meetings to county meetings and others from those to a provincial one. Rivington's New York Gazetteer, June 30, 1774

As the towns within each county and the counties within each province began to unify, the various provinces did likewise. The First Continental Congress was called for Philadelphia and, for six weeks, beginning in September 1774, delegates from each province, except Georgia, met there in Carpenter Hall to determine what the provinces should do as a group. A plan for reconciliation was rejected in favor of forcing a confrontation over colonial rights. Congress sent a resolution embodying their grievances and in putting the blame on the change in colonial policy that began in 1763. It then backed it up with a trade embargo with Britain. The stage was set for war

RESOLUTION

The good people of the several colonies of New Hampshire, Massachusetts Bay, Rhode Island and Providence Plantations, Connecticut, New York, New Jersey, Pennsylvania, New Castle, Kent and Sussex on Delaware, Maryland, Virginia, North Carolina and

South Carolina, justly alarmed at these arbitrary proceedings of Parliament and administration, have severally elected, constituted and appointed deputies to meet and sit in General Congress in the City of Philadelphia in order to obtain such establishment, as their religion, laws and liberties may not be subverted. Whereupon, the deputies so appointed being now assembled, in a full and free representation of these colonies, taking into their consideration the best means of attaining the ends aforesaid, do, in the first place, as Englishmen in like cases have usually done, for asserting and vindicating their rights and liberties declare:

We, his majesty's most loyal subjects, the delegates of the several colonies, deputed to represent them in a continental Congress, held in the city of Philadelphia on the 5th Day of September, 1774, avowing our allegiance to his Majesty, our affection and regard for our fellow subjects in Great Britain and elsewhere, affected with the deepest anxiety and most alarming apprehensions at those grievances and distresses, with which his Majesty's American subjects are oppressed, and having taken under our most serious deliberations, the state of the whole continent, find that the present unhappy situation of our affairs is occasioned by a ruinous system of colonial administration adopted by the British ministry about the year 1763, evidently calculated for enslaving these colonies and with them the British Empire. Dunlop's Pennsylvania Packet, October 31, 1774

However, while messages and petitions crossed the Atlantic, Britain had escalated hostilities. The King had not the slightest intention of relenting. Nor, aside for some merchants and liberals like Lord Pitt, no one suggested that the Colonial insubordination be handled any differently. The colonies had flourished at the expense of those in England. Now, it was time for the Provinces to pay their share of the costs of their administration and defense. To the man in the street in London, had he been asked, it would also been logical and fair. The King was firm with his resolve to discipline his unruly colonists and his ministers agreed. The Earl of Sandwich, Ruler of the King's Navy, described the patriots to his peers in the House of Lords. "They are raw, undisciplined cowardly men. I wish instead of forty or fifty thousand of these brave fellows, they would produce in the field at 200,000. The more, the better and easier will be the conquest. If they do not run away, they will starve to death by our measures." To teach the Boston rebels in specific a lesson for throwing the Tea Party, the city was attacked by British troops and occupied as enemy territory. The year 1774 ended in tension as the following news item from around the colonies illustrates:

Philadelphia. Yesterday afternoon arrived here an express from the Committee at Elizabeth Town, with the following letter from Col. Israel Putnam of Pomfret, in Connecticut, to one of his captains, handed them by expresses sent by the different Committees through Connecticut, &c.

Sept. 3, 1774
Capt. Cleveland,
Mr. Keys has this moment brought us the news that the Men of War and troops began to fire on the people last night at sunset at Boston, when a post was immediately sent off to inform the country. He informs that the Artillery played all night [and] that the people were universally rallying from Boston as far as here and desire all the assistance possible. The first was occasioned by the country being robbed of their Powder from Boston as far as Farmingham, and, when found out, the persons that went to take them were immediately fired on. Six of our number were killed the first shot and a number wounded. Beg you will collect all the forces you can and be on the march immediately, for the relief of Boston and the people that way.
Israel Putnam
The Pennsylvania Journal, September 7, 1774

Philadelphia. Notwithstanding the eight Regiments, now at Boston, the General has thought proper to remove the Royal Irish from the [New York] City to Amboy and, it is supposed, from thence to Boston, as well as two regiments from Quebec and it is said that troops in New York and New Jersey are to move that way in a short time, after which, if Gen. Gage thinks his army is strong enough, he will rob the Americans of their lives or liberties. The Pennsylvania Journal, September 14, 1774

Added to all of this, the town [Boston] is surrounded by Ships of War and, it is said, the Fleet of Newfoundland is to winter in this harbor. Formidable fortifications have been erected and are erecting at the only Avenue of the town; chains and chevaux de frise already provided to stop up the entrance at pleasure. Four Regiments are encamped on the Common, with a large train of artillery and matrosses; one Regiment on Fort Hill, one on the new fortifications on the Neck and another Regiment at Castle William; three Companies just arrived on the Rose Man of war from Newfoundland; transports dispatched some time past to New York for two Regiments from thence and the Jersies and to Quebec for two Regiments from that quarter; military stores and implements of all kinds are collecting in this town, which has now the appearance of a garrison . The Pennsylvania Journal, October 26, 1774

CHAPTER 3

1775: The War Begins

The pleas to King George to reconsider Britain's colonial policies, made by both individual provinces, like New Jersey, and by the Continental Congress on behalf of all, were ignored. The King was convinced of the equity of the Crown's position that the Colonies begin repaying it for the vast sums spent protecting them and to henceforth become self supporting - but not self ruling. More importantly, King George and his ministers had concluded that force was necessary, reconciliation not either feasible or desirable. The King had told Lord North: "I am not sorry that the line of conduct now seems chalked out. I know I am doing my duty and have no reason to retreat. I wish nothing but good. Therefore, anyone who does not agree with me is a traitor and a scoundrel."

In March of 1775, Parliament formally declared Massachusetts to be in rebellion. British General Thomas Gage increased his already tight grip on the city and its surrounding countryside. Throughout the colonies, men and women of like mind with those under siege in Boston, began to arm themselves, form militias, and to consider a war with their motherland as a likely possibility.

On the night of April 18, 1775, Gage's troops marched to Lexington and Concord, two villages outside the city of Boston. The Americans had been on the alert for this. When the British direction was ascertained, Paul Revere made his famous ride through the countryside to Lexington to warn that the British were coming. Next morning, Wednesday April 19, 1775, some of those whom Revere had called to arms encountered the British. A stray gun shot -- forever "the shot heard round the world" -- pierced the silence, its source no one knows. In response, the British troops opened fired and eight Americans lay dead, the first heroes of the American War for Independence. Later that same day, the scene was reenacted at Concord, but the ending was different. The colonists, ready and angry, fired upon the British from all sides, killing and capturing 273 of the red coated enemy.

Express riders from the Committee of Safety from the Boston area furiously rode in relay to Worcester, then through the Connecticut towns of Norwich, New London, Lyme, Saybrook, Guildford, Branford, New Haven and Fairfield, spreading the word of the hostilities. The news reached New York, at four o'clock on Sunday afternoon, the 23rd, four days after the gunfire. Those further to the south would not learn of it until weeks later. A state of war existed, but between whom? Without a doubt, on one side was Great Britain in all her power and majesty. On the eve of the Revolution, Britain was the greatest empire since Rome. She was intent on disciplining obstinate and too independent colonists, grown wild from having been ignored by their parent during her long struggles with France and Spain. But who was on the other side? Were there few or many of them? Would they come to give the Boston mob's assistance or would they break up and run for cover when they saw the British troops approach their own town and invade it as they had with Boston? Time was to show that there were indeed many of the same mentality as those of Boston and, over the next seven years of war, they would also prove themselves as resolute as had their New England cousins.

At first, the other provinces, including a number of New Jersey counties and towns, provided food and other support to those besieged in Boston:

Boston, October 24. Capt. Brown arrived at Salem, with a generous donation from our worthy sympathizing brethren of the county of Monmouth, New Jersey, consisting of twelve hundred bushels of rye and fifty barrels of rye flower. The New York Gazette, October 31, 1774

Philadelphia, November 16, 1774. We are informed that a few days ago Jesse Hand, Esq., of Cape May, came to this city with a genteel amount of money, generously subscribed by the people of that place, to be laid out for the use of the suffering poor of Boston. The Pennsylvania Gazette, November 16, 1774

We hear that Mr. Joseph Ellis of Glouster County, lately paid into the hands of Thomas Cushing Esq. five hundred and thirty four dollars, subscribed by the people of that County, for the relief of the poor of Boston. The Pennsylvania Gazette, November 23, 1774

The farmers in and about Allen Town and Freehold, having opened a subscription for the relief of Boston, in a very short time collected as much grain as loaded a sloop, which sailed from Elizabeth Town Point last week for Salem. The Pennsylvania Journal, September 14, 1774

Last Saturday, the Committee of Trenton, in Hunterdon County, New Jersey, paid into the hands of Samuel Adams Esq., seventy pounds as a donation from that county for the use of the poor of Boston. The above Committee, last fall, also paid one hundred pounds into the hands of Mr. Jeffries for the above use. The Pennsylvania Journal, June 7, 1775

Support for the effort -- and a realization that it would be a long struggle, not the usual mob's climax of a few rocks thrown and then dispersal -- came in other ways. Everyone was to help, the fair maidens included:

At a meeting of the inhabitants of the county of Glouster, held at the court house, on the twelfth day of December, 1774 it was resolved unanimously that it will be proper, and appears at this meeting absolutely necessary, that our farmers should as much as possible, apply their ground to raising fax and hemp and that our young women, instead of trifling their time away, do prudently employ it in learning the use of the spinning wheel. The time calls for diligence and no hand ought to be idle that is capable of contributing, in the least degree, to the support of the public cause. The Pennsylvania Gazette, December 21, 1774

America had always considered herself especially blessed by the Divine and the patriots acknowledged their dependence upon God.

In the Provincial Congress of New Jersey

RESOLVED, that this Congress do earnestly recommend to the inhabitants of every religious denomination throughout this province that Thursday, the 29th of June inst., be observed by them as a day of fasting, humiliation and prayer in order to deprecate the displeasure of Almighty God in this season of public calamity and humbly to implore his divine blessing on such measures as may be used for supporting our invaluable rights and privileges and restoring concord and harmony between Great Britain and her American Colonies.
    H. Fisher, President
    The Pennsylvania Journal, June 7, 1775

More than prayer, food and clothing would be needed, if a loosely connected group of provinces, each of which barely governed itself, were to go to war with the greatest power on earth. Leadership and a cause for which men would die were both necessary. So were men and money. The colonists went about this Revolution, in an orderly, serious manner. They elected a Congress of their finest citizens to lead them on a national level:

Last week in Philadelphia ended the Grand Continental Congress of Delegates from all the British American colonies from New Hampshire to South Carolina, inclusively, they having, in a manner highly honorable to themselves and their constituents and serviceable to their country, finished the important business on which they were appointed and met to deliberate and determine for a great and increasing Nation.
The world has hardly seen any Assembly that had matters of greater consequence, that were chosen in a more honorable manner, were better qualified for the high trust reposed in them, executed it in a more faithful, judicious manner, or were more free and unanimous in their conclusions than this. *The New York Journal, November 3, 1774*

Leadership was also required at the town, county and state levels. The Continental Congress in Philadelphia directed the representatives from its member states to organize their citizens locally. To each citizen fell the individual duty to follow the patriot standard, as the following exhortations to the citizens of Essex and

Glouster counties respectively indicate. They were to elect Committees of Observation", the purpose of which was to make certain there were no British loyalists --potential traitors -- among the townspeople :

The zeal you [citizens of Essex] have heretofore manifested in support of the constitutional liberties of our country will unquestionably prompt you to carry into execution, with firmness and unanimity, the wise and prudent resolutions lately entered into by the delegates of this continent in General Congress. In the eleventh article of the Association formed in behalf of themselves and their constituents, it was agreed "that a Committee be chosen in every county, city and town by those who are qualified to vote for representatives in the legislature, whose business it should be to observe the conduct of all persons, touching the Association." We, your Committee of Correspondence, cannot in the least doubt your ready and willing compliance with this article, for, as the salutary effects to rise from this association must, under God, depend upon the fidelity of individuals in carrying it precisely into execution, so, should any inhabitant of this colony be found so lost to a sense of public virtue as to violate the same in any instance, such person, pursuant to said article, may by your committee be held up to public notice as unfriendly to the liberties of his country and all dealings with him or her be thenceforward broken off.. The New York Gazette, December 5, 1774

And as carrying the said association properly and faithfully into execution is the only peaceable way we [the inhabitants of Glouster county] can hope to obtain relief from the arbitrary and detestable measures of the British Parliament, so truly alarming to the colonies, and as carrying it into execution will so very much depend upon the vigilance, prudence and firmness of the said committee, when appointed, and as the said committee ought to be very large, consisting of trusted members from every part of the country, it is hoped that the inhabitants, qualified as aforesaid, will generally attend and assist in electing the same. The New York Gazette, December 5, 1774

Congresses, Committees of Observation and alert loyal citizens were only the first steps. Soldiers were necessary, warriors for the conflict which all thought was inevitable. In June, 1775, the Provincial Congress of the Colony of New Jersey, sitting in Trenton, resolved that because of "the cruel and arbitrary measures of the British Parliament and Ministry to enslave the American Colonies", it was now necessary "to arm and discipline the inhabitants, in defense of their rights and freedoms" and that each county within the Province was to respond to this war effort with both men and money:

Persons in whom they [the inhabitants of each County] can confide are to be chosen to command in the militia. It is recommended and advised that one or more companies, consisting of 80 men (aged from 16 to 50) each, be formed in each Township or Corporation; That each of these companies meet and choose from among themselves, 1 Captain, 2 Lieutenants and 1 Ensign, which officers of each Company shall choose their Sergeants, Corporals and drummers; That each Captain provide a muster role, which everyone at enlisting is to subscribe, and, according as the proper officers shall direct, to meet for improvement in military discipline, the whole Companies at least once a month and at a general muster or review of the whole regiment, as a often as the field officers shall appoint. Each person enlisted to be equipped as soon as possible with arms, ammunition &c.

That in the present state of public affairs, as the usual resources of government appear to be insufficient, a fund extraordinary be provided for the use of the Province of 10,000 pounds Proclamation money, to be immediately raised, at which the proportions of the several counties are to be as follows:

> Bergen......................664.8.0
> Essex.......................742.18.0
> Middlesex..................872.6.8
> Somerset...................904.2.0
> Monmouth................1,069.2.8
> Morris........................723.6.0
> Sussex.......................593.5.4
> Hunterdon.................1,363.16.8
> Burlington.................1,071.13.4

>   *Glouster 763.2.8*
>   *Salem. 679.12.0*
>   *Cumberland 385. 6.8*
>   *Cape May 166.18.0*
>   *10,000.0.0*
> *For raising this money, persons are to be appointed by the Committees in each town. The New York Journal, June 29, 1775*

While there was clearly broad support in the country side for this challenge, it was not universal by any means. Indeed, there were a number of diverse views, both in American and back in England, regarding Colonial resistance to British authority. Some advocated it and openly, although orderly, challenged the King and his officers. For example, in the following item, the Grand Jury, sitting in Newark, in Essex County, responded to some remarks made by the English appointed Chief Judge:

> *May it please Your Honor, [with respect to] your Honor's charge from the bench we think ourselves obliged to express our gratitude to your Honor's friendly admonition and at the same time to inform you how far we have the misfortune to differ from you in sentiment, both as to the origin and tendency of the present uneasiness, so generally diffused through the colony. If we rightly understand a particular part of your Honor's charge, you were pleased to tell us, that while we were employed in guarding against "imaginary tyranny, three thousand miles distant" we ought not to expose ourselves to a "real tyranny at our own doors". We are utterly at a loss for the idea thereby intended to be communicated. But respecting the tyranny at a distance of three thousand miles, which your Honor is pleased to represent as imaginary, we have the unhappiness to differ from you in opinion. The effect, Sir, of that tyranny is too severely felt to have it felt altogether visionary. We cannot think, Sir, that taxes imposed upon us by our fellow subjects in a legislature in which we are not represented is imaginary, but that it is a real and actual tyranny. We cannot think, Sir, that depriving us of the inestimable right of a trial by jury, seizing our persons and carrying us to trial in Great Britain, is a tyranny merely imaginary. Nor can we think with your Honor that destroying characters and changing the forms of our government is a tyranny altogether ideal. In a word, Sir, we cannot convince ourselves that*

the fleet now blocking up the Port of Boston, consisting of ships built of real English oak and solid iron and armed with cannon and ponderous metal, with actual powder and ball; nor the army lodged in the town of Boston and the fortifications thrown around it (substantial and formidable realities) are all creatures of the imagination. These, Sir, are but a few of the grievances under which America now groans. To procure redress of these grievances we have the happiness to represent to your Honor that in the prosecution of measures for preserving American Liberties and obtaining the removal of oppressions, the people have acted in all their popular assemblies (which is the right of Englishmen to convene whenever they please) with the spirit, temper and prudence becoming freemen and loyal subjects. The New York Journal, November 17, 1774

In local communities and between neighboring towns, there was disagreement over which side of the growing issue should the citizenry take:

Whereas, in a meeting in the town of Ridgefield, held on the 30th of January last, the question was put, whether the town would adopt and conform to the resolves contained in the association of the Continental Congress or not, which question was resolved in the negative, we, the subscribers, inhabitants of the society of Ridgbury, within the town of Ridgefield, do hereby declare that we were not on the negative side of the above question and are very sorry that the town did not adopt the said Association, as we think it of the utmost importance to the cause of American freedom that it should be faithfully observed, and do accordingly purpose to observe it ourselves, as far as we can under our present circumstances and stand ready to concur with the town, if a majority could be obtained for that purpose, in appointing a Committee of Observation. The New York Journal, February 9, 1775

Elizabeth Town, February 13, 1775. Whereas the inhabitants of Staten Island[38] have manifested an unfriendly disposition towards the Liberties of America and, among other things, have neglected to join the General Association proposed by the Continental Congress, and entered into by most of the townships in America, the Committee for Observation for this town [Elizabeth], taking the same into consideration, are of the opinion that the inhabitants of their district ought, and by the aforesaid Association are bound, to break off all trade, commerce and dealings and [that] intercourse whatsoever be suspended accordingly, which suspension is hereby notified and recommended to the inhabitants of their district, to be by them, universally observed and adopted.. The New York Journal, February 16, 1775

Some were opposed to the colonial disobedience on intellectual grounds, logically deduced and based on the reality that an island nation, like Britain, needed subservient colonies in order to survive. These were not taxes at all, but custom duties, which the King had a right to impose and from which the Colonists had always benefitted.

Friends and Countrymen:
In a late address to you, I have endeavored to distinguish between Taxes and Duties, that the former ought to be imposed upon our own estates, by our representatives, that the latter cannot properly be laid by any authority, but that of Great Britain.
That we are a part of the great British Empire, and without losing every idea of a colony, we cannot claim an exemption from duties and restraints on trade. I now beg leave to add that this country was settled for the purpose of trade and an absolute submission to the laws of the mother country, in paying customs and duties, was one of the terms our forefathers settled under.
The British Legislature have always made the trade of the colonies their object and ever kept in view the first intention in settling them. Under these laws, our forefathers settled and improved their plantations; under them, they and we ourselves have happily lived and enjoyed all the liberty that men could or can wish and may yet do it, if we will refuse to hearken to the sedition --nay, treason -- that is daily buzzed into our ears, by men who do not design our happiness, but only study their own emolument. They tell us we are cramped in our trade and that, if we permit this duty, another will follow and another, until we are ruined and deprived of all liberty.
It is true that duties will be laid for revenue or prohibitions, but these will never be calculated to destroy trade, but to encourage beneficial, and to destroy destructive, commerce, by which the smuggler will be restrained and the fair trader enjoy the fruits of his

industry and honesty. But what right do we have to enter into a quarrel about it? Let us remember our duty to the parent state, the terms on which our forefathers settled, lived and prospered, under which we ourselves have grown rich and lived happily. Let us request the parent state to leave the taxation of our estates to our own representatives, while we act within the sphere of our duty and pursue not measures destructive of her commerce and bid defiance to her laws. I have hope (I wish I could say more) that the intended Congress, if it should calmly enter into the dispute with the mother country, has it in its power to preserve our liberties and to restore harmony between the colonies and the mother state, but, should they listen to and be governed by the folly of the times and think that these colonies were not planted and not protected for the extension of commerce, but for a new empire, then will our once happy country become a scene of blood and destruction. We can have no recourse but to arms and, alas, how shall we face the force of our mother country in the day of trial, when roused by our repeated insults and enraged by our avowed declarations against her authority, her fleets and armies seize our cities, stop our trade and, we, by conquest, are reduced to a state, our mother country will even grieve to see.
    Z.
Rivington's New York Gazetteer, September 8, 1774

In London, there were many who sympathized with the colonists as they had, more than a decade earlier, with regard to the Stamp Act. They debated the point:

House of Commons, April 5. At five o'clock, the order of the day . . . to restrain the trade and commerce of the colonies of New Jersey, Pennsylvania, Maryland, Virginia and South Carolina . . . produced a debate that continued within a few minutes of eight o'clock, when, the question being put, the House divided upon the Yeas 192, Noes 46.

Mr. Hartley opposed the bill as beyond measure cruel and oppressive. . . Lord North replied that the bill [may] exist or not exist at the options of the Americans, for, if they have a mind to seek the friendship and protection of Great Britain, they would comply with the conditions of the bill, which were a free importation and exportation to and from the Mother Country as usual.

> Mr. Alderman Sawbridge spoke very strongly against the bill, observing, as it originated manifest injustice, so it inflicted a punishment to the last degree cruel and oppressive. He added he hoped America would never tamely acquiesce to be dragooned and compelled to submit to terms as unjust as the power, which dictated them, was obnoxious to the natural rights of mankind in general and distinctive of those they were entitled to as freeman and British subjects.
>
> Mr. Alderman Bull adopted the ideas of his worthy friend and dwelt very pathetically on the certain ruin the present measures must inevitably be productive of, by their operation, on our trade and manufactures. Though the right were on our side, he said, it would be folly to enforce it. But, when it was evident to every impartial man that our claims were founded on principles diametrically opposed to those of the Constitution and to the established municipal rights and privileges of our colonies, it was at once uniting folly and wickedness in the extreme. Dunlap's Penn's Packet, June 5, 1775

Some, especially the Society of Friends, known as Quakers, who were pacifists and lived in large numbers in the Jerseys and neighboring Pennsylvania, tried to remain neutral:

> The Quakers of Pennsylvania much alarmed at the present distracted proceedings of the Colonies, in the opposition making to the authority to the Parliament of Great Britain, foresee the most fatal consequences, both to themselves and to the parent country, have thought it necessary to address their Brethren in the adjacent Provinces and publish an Epistle, declaring their disapprobation of the measures prosecuting for obtaining redress and earnestly requesting all of their communion to avoid joining in such measures as are totally inconsistent with their religious principles. Rivington' New York Gazetteer, January 26, 1775
>
> Philadelphia. We are informed that the people called Quakers, at a meeting in this city a few days since, have agreed to recommend it to their brethren in their meetings in this province and in New Jersey to promote subscriptions to raise money for the relief of the necessitous of all religious denominations, who are reduced to losses and distress in this time of public calamity, to be distributed

among them by a Committee of their brethren in New England and a Committee appointed for the same purpose here. The Pennsylvania Gazette, July 12, 1775

But meanwhile, the war continued. Some sixteen hundred Americans occupied a piece of higher ground across the Charles River from Boston, known as Breed's Hill, often called Bunker Hill. On June 17, 1775, the British, led by General William Howe, attacked the hill three times with some 2,400 British troops. Short of gun powder, the American soldiers were admonished not to fire until "you see the whites of their eyes". By the time the American ammunition was exhausted, eleven hundred British soldiers were killed or wounded.[39]

The Continental Congress had just appointed 43 year old George Washington as Commander in Chief of the Continental Army, which was still in the process being formed. Washington immediately left for Boston to fortify the country side outside the British occupied city.

CHAPTER 4

War: 1776

1776 is a magical date in United States history, the year in which the thirteen colonies declared their collective independence from Great Britain. Theirs was the first of a hundred of revolutions that have since circled the globe, overthrowing tyranny and elevating the rights and dignity of mankind.

The war had begun the prior April in Boston. However, aside from the battles there and a failed invasion of Canada,[40] much of the remainder of that year had been spent by both sides in mobilizing for the war effort. These were no longer the actions of the typical mob, if that, in fact, was what it had been at the beginning. Now it was more profound, the origin of the American nation. Having vented its anger in Boston, the mob did not disperse, returning to things as usual. Instead, it took control of the provincial governments, focused its collective attention on beginning a government to replace the one that had been overthrown and then preparing to fight a war. The newspapers reported on all of these events and preserved for us today the thoughts, fears and hopes of those turbulent times.

Among the first measures that the Rebels needed to take was to declare the prior Royal government as invalid, declare their predecessors in power to have been the equivalent of outlaws and then legitimize their own authority as originating from the people. "Out with the old":

In Provincial Congress, New Jersey, Burlington, June 14, 1776

Resolved that, in the opinion of this congress, the proclamation of William Franklin Esq, late Governor of New Jersey, bearing the date the 30th of May last, in the name of the King of Great Britain, appointing a meeting of the General Assembly, to be held on the 20th day of this instant June, ought not to be obeyed.

Resolved that, in the opinion of this Congress, the said William Franklin Esq, by such his proclamation, has acted in direct contempt and violation of the Resolve of the Continental Congress of the fifteenth of May last.

Resolved, that in the opinion of this Congress, all payments of money, on account of salary or otherwise, to the said William Franklin Esq, as Governor, ought from henceforth to cease and that the Treasurer or Treasurers of this Province should account for the monies in their hands to this Congress or to the future Legislatures of this colony.
By Order of Congress
Samuel Tucker, President
The Pennsylvania Evening Post, June 18, 1776

Then it was "in with the new". Pending the People's selecting their leaders directly in an election, temporary, emergency powers were established. They boiled down to this: if one were opposed to the insurrection, he should gather his family and portable property and leave New Jersey; those who remained in New Jersey, or even passed through her lands, were presumed to be patriots and expected to be totally loyal to the insurrection, under penalty of being declared a traitor and executed. Interestingly, however urgent the need and drastic the sanction, the common law right to a trial by jury was to be preserved. This might have begun as a mob, but it knew the restraints of what later would be termed "due process":

In the Convention of the State of New Jersey, Trenton July 18, 1776

Whereas it is necessary in these times of danger that crimes should receive their due punishment, and the safety of the people more requires, that all persons who have been found to be so wicked as to devise the destruction of good government, or to aid or assist the avowed enemies of the State, be punished with death. Therefore, be it established and ordained by the authority of the same, that all persons abiding within this State of New Jersey, and deriving protection from the laws thereof, do owe allegiance to the government of this State, as of late established on the authority of the people, and are to be deemed as members of this State, and that all persons, passing through, visiting, or making a temporary stay in this State, being entitled to the protection of its laws during passage, visitation or temporary stay, during the same time, owe allegiance to this Government.

And be it further resolved and ordained, that all and every person or persons, members of or owing allegiance to, this government, as before described, who, from and after the date hereof, shall levy war against this State within the same, or be adherent to the King of Great Britain or others, the enemies of this State, within the same, or to the enemies of the United States of North America, giving to him or them aid or comfort, shall be adjudged guilty of High Treason and suffer the pains and penalties thereof, in like manner as by the ancient laws of this state he or they should have suffered in cases of high treason.

And be it further resolved and ordained, that all and every person or persons, who, from and after the date hereof, shall be found guilty of reviling the government of this state, as by this Convention established, or other seditious speeches or practices, shall be punished in like manner as by the former laws of this state such person or persons might or ought to have been punished for such seditious speeches and practices against the Government then in being.

Provided always, that no person or persons shall suffer death or other pain or penalty for any of the offences aforesaid, until he or they had first been found guilty of the same offence or offences whereof he or they shall be charged or accused in a due course of law and by the verdict of a jury.

Resolved that, in order to prevent a failure of justice, all judges, justices of the peace, sheriffs, coroners, and other inferior officers of the late Government within this colony, proceed in the execution of their several duties under the authority of the People, until the intended legislature and the several officers of the new government be settled and perfected, having respect to the present constitution of New Jersey, as by the Congress of late ordained and the others of the Continental and Provincial Congresses and that all actions, suits and processes be continued, altering only the style and form thereof, according to the terms by the said constitution prescribed in the further prosecution thereof.   William Paterson, Secretary The Pennsylvania Journal, July 10, 1776

There was no neutral ground recognized in the common defense, save, in some respects, for the non violent Quakers. They were excused from the militia because of their religious beliefs. However, all inhabitants, including Quakers, were expected to contribute in some manner:

In the Convention of the State of New Jersey, Brunswick, August 3, 1776

Whereas, by the arrival of the enemy in the neighborhood of this State, the burden is becoming much greater to the Militia thereof, numbers being obliged to leave their families and march to the defense of their country [it has become] highly just and equitable proportionally to increase the sums formerly directed to be paid by those who refuse to bear arms for the protection of the State and also to inflict greater punishment on those who, although associated [with the militia]. . . yet neglect to attend on days appointed for musterings and who are unwilling, at this great time of danger, to step forth with their countrymen, to oppose the enemies of freedom. It is therefore

RESOLVED and ordained that all able bodied persons, between the ages of sixteen and fifty years, who, on any account, refuse to bear arms, do pay, as an equivalent for their actual service, the sum of twenty shilling proclamation money monthly and every month during the present alarming time. And that all persons who neglect to attend on days of muster, do pay double the sums directed [by Congress]; all such sums shall be recovered without regard to religious denomination. . .

William Paterson, Secretary
The Pennsylvania Packet, August 13, 1776

Along with establishing the authority of the new political entity, the State of New Jersey, and the inhabitants' duty to obey it in this time of crisis, the new government also had to issue a wide set of regulations, deemed necessary for the defense of the people of the state, such as:

The Public are desired to take Notice that no Person whatever, either Male or Female, above the Age of 14, will be permitted to pass any of the Ferries in the State of New Jersey, without a proper pass from the Place they leave. The New York Gazette, August 5, 1776

It was also necessary that offenders of the rules and spirit of the new order be punished, either by the State or, as likely, by the community, as a lesson to deter others. The offenses were many and the punishments varied:

In the Convention of the State of New Jersey, Brunswick, August 2, 1776
RESOLVED that the several County Committees within this State do cause inventories and appraisements to be made to the estates, real as well as personal, of all such persons within their respective bounds, as have, absconded, from their homes and joined themselves to the enemies of this State, causing all perishable articles to be sold and the monies arising therefrom and all the other goods and estates of such persons, that they keep in safe and secure custody, until the further order of this Convention or the determination of other proper judicature; provided, that the said Committees be empowered to leave any part of the said estate in the hands of the relations or friends of such absconding persons, taking such security as they may think proper for the return thereof, or, of the value. The Pennsylvania Packet, August 13, 1776

Hanover, Committee Chambers, February 5, 1776. Ananias Halsey, being brought before the committee on complaint and upon hearing the evidences, we judge that he is guilty of vilifying and disregarding the measures pursued for the redress of our grievances and has defamed the office of the continental service, for which we judge him to be an enemy of his country and desire all persons to break off all trading with him, agreeable to the rules of Congress and that this be printed in the public prints. The New York Gazette, March 4, 1776

In the Provincial Congress of New York
The Memorial of Robert and John Murray, on the subject of the breach of the Association of the late Continental Congress[41] whereby they pray to be restored to their former commercial powers and it appearing that they, the said Robert and John Murray, have

published a printed hand bill, expressing their contrition for their offense and their resolution for the future strictly to adhere to the said Association, RESOLVED therefore that the said Robert and John Murray shall be and hereby are restored to their commercial purposes and declared to be entitled to the forgiveness of the public. The New York Gazette, June 12, 1775

The 6th December, Quibble Town, Middlesex county, Piscataqua Township, New Jersey:

Thomas Randolf, cooper, who had publicly proved himself an enemy to his country, by revealing and using his utmost endeavors to oppose the proceedings of the Continental and Provincial Convention and Committees, in defense of their rights and liberties, and he, being judged a person of not consequence for a severer punishment, was ordered to be stripped naked, well coated with tar and feathers and carried in a wagon publicly round the town, which punishment was accordingly inflicted; and, as he soon became duly sensible to his offense, for which he earnestly begged pardon, and promised us to atone, so far as he was able, by a contrary behavior in the future, he was released and suffered to return to his house in less than half an hour. The whole was conducted with that regularity and decorum that ought to be observed in all public punishments. The New York Journal, December 28, 1775

I, Ezekiel Beach, of the township of Mendham, in the county of Morris, have heretofore, by my words and conduct, been guilty of opposing the good people of the country in the measures, by them adopted, in preserving American Freedom, particularly saying "I had rather the Ministerial troops would conquer the Continental," and further declared that "the Parliament of Great Britain had a right to levy the oppressive taxes and acts upon America, particularly the act for changing the government of Massachusetts Bay" and further declared that "I would assist the Ministerial troops with provisions and other necessaries, provided that they would pay for same"; and, having thus on the most mature deliberations, considered of such my conduct, do most heartily disapprove of the same and do hereby promise that for the future, I will observe, as far as within me lie, the rules and regulations of the honorable Continental Congress and the Provincial Congress of New Jersey, and will use my best endeavors to promote and to carry into execution every measure adopted already or that may be hereafter adopted by said Congress for preserving the rights and liberties of this country, and I will most cheerfully sign the Association adopted by said Provincial Congress, when thereunto required, and do hereby desire that in the future the good people of this country would consider me as a friend to the same, which I hope to manifest by my conduct.

Ezekiel Beach
The New York Journal, December 28, 1775

Sometimes, the colonists' enthusiasm for the cause of liberty, combined with their ancestry as a mob, made them more resemble vigilantes than patriots. The press, loyal to Britain, did not hesitate to highlight this failing:

Newtown, Sussex County, New Jersey. Last Tuesday, about four hundred of the militia of this county, under the command of Colonel Ephraim Martin and Mark Thompson, assembled and proceeded in good order and regularity in quest of Tories, a considerable number of whom, (inhabitants of this county) had entered into a combination and agreement not to comply with any of the Congress measures; about forty, we hear, are taken, most of whom have recanted, signed the Association and professed themselves to be true sons of liberty, being fully convinced of their error; and that two or three that remain incorrigible are to be sent to the congress to be dealt with. The New York Journal, December 28, 1775

Two Gentlemen, one from Cumberland County and the other from Glouster County, arrived here since our last, and inform that on their journey hither, on Sunday night the 24th ultimo, they arrived at the Rev. Samuel Peters' house, in Hebron, Connecticut, and that, at about sunrise the next morning, they were surprised by about 300 men who came to the house on horseback, about ten of which came into the house and informed Mrs. Peters that they were a committee chosen by the body of men waiting without to enquire whether he (Mr. Peters) had not written to England in a manner unfriendly to the rights and privileges of the colony? Mr. Peters declared to them that he had not wrote in such a manner, whereupon they informed him that they expected he would show the copies of such letters that he had written [to England and to newspapers]. Mr. Peters, perceiving the vengeance that seemed to sit on the brows of the formidable multitude that surrounded the house, thought it prudent to show them all such papers as they requested and did do it . . . The said Committee declared themselves satisfied that Mr. Peters was innocent of all the crimes he was suspected of being guilty of and went to their brethren, the mob, that surrounded the house and reported that Mr. Peters was innocent; this was apparently satisfactory to most of them. To the honor of the Committee, it may justly be said that they treated Mr. Peters with as much civility as might any way be expected from men that forgot it was indecent, unjust and cruel to terrify a British subject to such a degree as to force him to lay open to public view his letters &c. as it is by force and terror to extort from a man all the secrets of his family. The Committee further insisted that Mr. Peters sign a declaration that he had not wrote, nor did he intend to write, to Great Britain relating to the controversy between her and the colonies, all which Peters complied with. The mob now seemed quite satisfied and a great majority of them mounted their horses to retire, thanking Mr. Peters for his civility. But about the number of twenty of the mob, headed by one Hatch and one White, tarried and insisted on Mr. Peter's asking forgiveness, acknowledging his faults etc. A considerable number of Mr. Peter's friends assembled, the appearance of whom struck such terror in Hatch, White and the other creatures that attended them that they soon followed their more sensible friends, without administering to Mr. Peters tar, feathers or other violence.

What is very remarkable, this large body of people call themselves the Sons of Liberty. O poor degenerate children! Such destroyers of liberty itself are a disgrace to their mother, if she is the goddess of Liberty. For does not Liberty allow every man to enjoy his own sentiments? Does not she allow him to enjoy his leisure hours in contemplation? Does she forbid him committing by ink to paper his thoughts? Does she justify others when they break the cabinet of her sins and peep into their secrets? Are these burglarians her dutiful sons or are they destroyers of her family, the disgrace of their mother? Surely they are cursed children, to whom is reserved the blackness of death for ever. The New York Gazette, September 5, 1776

Finally, completing its transition, the former Province of East and West New Jersey, now the State of New Jersey, elected, through its Assembly, a Governor, William Livingston. Governor Livingston was to prove to be a firm and wise leader throughout the war. In his inaugural speech, he set out squarely the situation in which he and his fellow patriots now found themselves, how they had gotten there and how they could get out of it:

It may afford some consolation to every man duly regardful of the convictions of his own mind, and the honor and reputation of his country, that America deferred this important step, till the decisive alternate of absolute submission or utter destruction, announced by a numerous fleet and army, had extinguished all hope of obtaining justice and the whole continent, save a few self interested individuals, were unanimous in the separation...

Thus, constrained to assert our own independence and dissolve all political connection with a nation insatiate with plunder and deaf to the voice of reason, of justice, of humanity, the late Representatives of the Colony of New Jersey in congress assembled, did, pursuant to the advice of the Honorable Continental Congress, the Supreme Council of the American Colonies, agree upon a form of Constitution, which, by tacit acquiescence and open approbation, hath since received the assent and concurrence of the good people of this state, to whose consideration it was for that purpose submitted.. The Pennsylvania Gazette, October 1, 1776

As the new government was still creating itself, preparations for war were ongoing. First, an army had to be raised:

Province of New Jersey in Congress, February 5, 1776.
Whereas by a Resolution of the Continental Congress, a third Battalion is recommended immediately to be raised in this Colony, for service and at the expense of the United Colonies, consisting of eight companies and each company of seventy eight privates and officers with one Captain, two Lieutenants, one Ensign, four Sergeants, and four Corporals, which recommendations this

Congress being desirous fully to comply with, do therefore resolve, that Officers of said Battalion be immediately recommended for Commissions and that the Captains and Subalterns be appointed and warrants issued for enlisting the aforesaid compliment of men,

Resolved, that agreeable to the recommendations of the Honorable Continental Congress, the recruiting officers enlist none but healthy, sound, and able bodied freemen, not under sixteen years of age. The form of the enlistment to be in the following words:

"I, ----, have this day enlisted myself as a soldier in the American Continental Army for one year, unless sooner discharged, and do bind myself to conform in all instances to such rules and regulations as are or shall be established for the government of said army."

Resolved, that no apprentice whatsoever be enlisted within this colony, without the consent of his master or mistress first obtained in writing and that every person under the age of twenty one years, enlisting himself as aforesaid, within twenty fours hours after their parents or guardians have notice of said enlistment, obtain his discharge, by refunding the money received from the recruiting officer and returning such necessaries as may have been supplied him by the officer or the value thereof in money.
That it be recommended to the officers of said battalion, to pay the strictest attention to the behavior of the troops in quarters or on their march that they give no reasonable cause of complaint.
The New York Gazette, February 19, 1776

A statewide militia was formed, under the command of Governor Livingston, totaling several thousand men and drawing at least one regiment[42] per county. In addition, New Jersey contributed three battalions to George Washington's Continental Army.

The cooperation and assistance of the ordinary citizen were also requested -- and expected. There were many ways for the non combatant to help the war effort, many which, at first blush, might seem odd to us today. For example, wool was necessary for the manufacture of clothing, a product heretofore supplied the colonists from the factories of Britain. America needed to maintain large flocks of sheep to produce that wool. Slaughtering a sheep for mutton was downright unpatriotic:

> *Committee Chamber, Newark, May 20, 1776. Resolved, that it be recommended to the inhabitants of this Township that they do not kill nor eat any Lamb or Sheep of any kind, from this Day to the first Day of August next, nor sell them to any person whom they shall have reason to suspect design to kill them within the said Time and, that, upon Proof being made to this Committee of any Person or Persons contravening the above Recommendations, the Delinquent or Delinquents shall be held up to the Public as Enemies to their Country and all Persons prohibited from having any Dealings or Correspondence with them. The New York Gazette, June 10, 1776*

Equally precious in a war economy was salt petre, a nitrate needed for the manufacture of gun powder:

> *A powder works in consequence of an agreement with the committee of safety, made at the session at Trenton, May 11th last, is in the new erection in the Town of Morris Town in the County of Morris and Province of New Jersey, by Jacob Ford, jun. All Persons in said Province, who now have, and may hereafter have, any good merchantable salt-peter to dispose of, are requested to carry it to Samuel Tucker, Esq. or to his father at Morris Town, of whom they will receive four shillings and two pence, proclamation money and a certificate of the quantity delivered by which certificate they will be entitled to receive one shilling per lb. And all merchants and traders in such Province of New Jersey, who have any sulphur on hand, are earnestly requested to carry it to the above named gentlemen, for which they will receive cash, at the rate of forty-six shillings, New York currency, per hundred weight. And, whereas the Province is in the greatest want of the article powder, at this time of most imminent danger, when the collecting strength of Great Britain and the mercenary aid of neighboring powers, threatens the rights and liberties of the thirteen United Colonies with ruin and destruction, it is hoped and humbly requested of the respective County and Town Committees, that they will assist said Ford, by encouraging the inhabitants (in their respective Districts) to immediately go into the manufacturing of salt peter.[43] The New York Gazette, June 10, 1776*

The war resumed in March of 1776 in Massachusetts as General Washington and his newly formed Continental Army bombarded the British with their own armaments. Ethan Allen had captured the artillery from the British at Fort Ticonderoga the prior year and then, under the watchful eye of artillery commander Colonel Knox, sledded it across mountainous New England during the winter to Boston. It was a bold move by Washington. The artillery was most effective on the British huddled in Boston. After two weeks of it, their entire force of 12,000 evacuated the city by sea, to Halifax.

A battle won rarely means that a war is over. Usually, it is prelude to a counter offensive, as proved the case in 1776. Retreating to Halifax, General Howe regrouped there and awaited expected reinforcements from Britain. When they arrived, he attacked and took New York City. For the rest of the war, New York would be an occupied city and New Jersey a no man's land, at times a battle field, at other times the source of fodder, food and booty for both plundering armies. New Jersey, lay between New York and Philadelphia, two of the epicenters of the war. It legitimately earned the title of "Cockpit of the Revolution." The war was constantly there, often on its soils, always on its border. New Jersey would enjoy no peace for the next seven years.

Even before General Howe and his troops arrived there from Halifax in July of 1776, the British had displayed an interest in New York. The Hudson River, beginning in Canada and emptying into New York harbor, cuts off the New England colonies from those to the south. If it could be controlled, the land route across the interiors of the colonies would be blocked and the colonies chopped into two pieces, each of which to be dealt with separately.

Of course, Washington had recognized the possibility that the British would attack New York City and had begun preparations for its defense. New Jersey was key to that effort. Her citizens were cautioned of the situation, apprized of what defense the Continental Army would try to provide and told what would be expected of them. They were reminded too of the noble struggle in which they were engaged and exhorted to bravery for the protection of liberty. It was here, as it had been in Lexington and Concord and other battle grounds throughout the new born nation, where the American spirit was cast:

Countrymen and Friends

This Province has been requested by the Continental Congress to send, without delay, from their Militia, three thousand three hundred men to New York in consequence of authentic information that the grand attack of our common enemy this summer, which will probably prove the decisive campaign, is to be upon that city and that their force might be expected there in a few days. Your representatives in this Congress, with all the dispatch in their power, and with the utmost unanimity, prepared an ordinance for raising the number called for, as equally from the different parts of the province, as possible. They have determined to raise the men by voluntary enlistment in the several counties, in full confidence that, in this way, they will be raised most speedily, as well as consist of persons with the greatest spirit and alacrity for the important service. Filled with the same zeal for the defense of their country, they appeal to you by this short address to entreat you to give a new proof to the public of your courage and intrepidity as men, of you unalterable attachment to the liberties of America and the sincerity of your unanimous resolutions from the beginning of this contest.

The danger is not only certain but immediate and imminent. It does not admit of even a moment's delay, for our unjust and implacable enemy is at hand. The place where the attack is expected is of the last importance, not only a city of great extent, the interest of whose numerous inhabitants must be exceedingly dear to us, but situated in the middle of the Colonies and where the success of the enemy would separate the provinces and disunite their efforts by land, which are, of necessity, liable to interruption from the enemy's fleet by sea. It is scarce worth while to add that this Province, by its vicinity, would then be exposed to the cruel depredations of the enemy, who happily heretofore, have been able to do us little or no mischief but by theft and rapine.

We cannot help putting you in mind how significantly Almighty God has prospered us hitherto and crowned our virtuous efforts with success. The expulsion of the enemy from Boston, where they first took possession and the oppressive measures was an event as disgraceful to them as it was advantageous to the public cause and honorable to that brave and resolute army by which it was accomplished.

We must not forget the activity and success of the inhabitants of the southern colonies. They run to arms in the thousands the moment they hear of an attack, both in Virginia and in North Carolina. God was pleased in both instances to reward their alacrity, for they obtained a complete victory over their enemy with so little loss of blood as it was not barely wonderful, but scarcely incredible.

Everyone is now obliged to confess what many saw long ago, that entire and unconditional submission is the point to which our enemies are determined to bring us, if in their power, so that nothing remains for us but either the abject slavery of tributary slaves or to maintain our rights and liberties by force of arms and hand down the fair inheritance to our posterity, by a brave and determined defense.

We desire and expect that, in such a situation of things, all particular difference of small moment, arising from whatever the cause, whether religious denominations, rivalship of different classes of men, scarcity of some articles of commerce, or any other, may be entirely laid aside. The present danger requires the most perfect union.

That you may be under no apprehension, either of inequality of the burden or that of our coasts will be left unguarded by the destination of this brigade, we have thought it best to inform you that the Continental Congress have amply provided for the defense of this Province . . . and that a flying camp of ten thousand men is now forming for the protection of the middle colonies, which we are credibly informed, is to have its chief station in this province.[44]

We add no more, but that we trust and hope, that, While every province is making the most spirited efforts, New Jersey, in its place and duty, will be second to none.

Signed in name and by appointment of Congress at Burlington

Samuel Tucker, President
The New York Gazette, June 17, 1776

By early in July, 1776, Howe's 10,000 soldiers established a beach head on Staten Island. During the summer, reinforcements arrived from Europe, including 9,000 Hessian mercenaries from the

German state of Hesse-Cassel. Soon, Howe had at least 32,000 troops at his disposal.

Staten Island, remained the British' stronghold in New York throughout the war, a safe haven where the British and their mercenaries could group and plan. The British troops did not have to conquer the island. The local citizenry, strongly royalist in their allegiance, had welcomed the English troops to their soil and, for the next seven years, contentedly lived alongside them.

Only narrow waterways, not more than a few hundred yards wide in places, separated loyalist Staten Island from towns, like Elizabeth and Perth Amboy, on the Jersey side, whose patriot citizens momentarily expected an invasion of their homeland by those whom the Staten Islanders were befriending. The ribbons of waterways were not very effective barriers against the bad blood that existed between the warring populations. As a result, a war within a war developed, a conflict between eastern New Jersey and Staten Island only. It was one where neighbors plotted against neighbors and engaged in night raids, kidnaping and atrocities. Sometimes it seems that vestiges of the animosity between the New Jersey shoreline and Staten Island communities still exist, although the source of the dislike long forgotten. Friction came early and then often between the two:

The fleet from Halifax, we informed our readers in our last, was arrived at Sandy Hook, to the amount of one hundred and thirteen sail.

Part of the Army is now encamped on Staten Island and, we have not the least reason to doubt, will endeavor to secure the north side thereof by entrenchments, while the shipping protects the other parts of it.

As soon as the troops were landed, they paraded the North shore and, on Wednesday morning, made their appearance near Elizabeth Town point, but the country being soon alarmed, they retreated, took up the floor of the drawbridge in the salt meadows and immediately threw up some works.

Their near approach to Elizabeth Town Point greatly alarmed the inhabitants of Essex county and, particularly, the people of Elizabeth Town and Newark, but they are now in a condition to receive them whenever they may think proper to approach.

> Two young men from Elizabeth Town crossed the river in a canoe last Thursday and fired upon the regulars but a number of them, rushing from the woods, they were obliged to retreat and cross the river again.
>
> Yesterday, nine of our riflemen [from Elizabeth] crossed the river in order to harass some Regulars who were throwing up a kind of breastwork on a bridge. Their sentries kept firing on our men for some time without doing any execution till one of the brave fellows went within a few yards of the enemy and desired them to surrender. At that instant, he received a ball through the head, which killed him on the spot. The Pennsylvania Gazette, July 31, 1776

> Our people at Elizabeth Town and the enemy on Staten Island, cannonaded each other yesterday afternoon without doing any damage except disturbing the congregation.The Pennsylvania Journal, August 28, 1776

The British also sought to sail up the Hudson River, but to do so meant that they had to run a gauntlet of shore batteries on both the New York and Jersey sides:

> Last Friday morning it was reported in town that Lord Howe was arrived at Sandy Hook, with a large fleet from England. Between one and two o'clock P.M. two ships hove in sight and joined the fleet at the Watering Place; about an hour after, ship, supposed to be the Phoenix of 44 guns, a frigate of 28 and three tenders, got underway at Staten Island and stood up for this city. The army soon took its alarm and, in a few minutes, everyone was at his station, well provided with all necessaries for a vigorous defense, but, as soon as the ships came near Bedlow's Island[45], they inclined to the Jersey shore to avoid our batteries that then began to play upon them from every quarter on both sides of the River, and, notwithstanding that they must have received considerable damage, they stood their course up Hudson's River, firing several broadsides as they went along, without either killing or wounding any of our people, who, on the occasion, behaved with uncommon bravery. A strong southerly wind, and the tide of flood facilitated the ships getting above the batteries near the town, but we hear that they were roughly handled about 12 miles up the river, from whence they have not yet attempted

to return, but, we hear, laid at Tarry Town about 50 miles up the river, on Saturday evening. *The Pennsylvania Journal, July 17, 1776*

The Ships of War in the North River are now at Haverstraw. It is evident that their designs are frustrated, not expecting we were so well prepared to receive them. Last Thursday, a man made his escape from aboard the Rose by swimming. He is well known here by officers and men from Boston, in the Train. He was taken last summer by the Rose, in going to the West Indies. He says . . . that the most damage they received was in passing the Battery at Powles Hook. The cook of the ship had a leg shot off; some others wounded; a 12 pounder lodged in their foremast; one came through her Quarter Galley into the Cabin and that her shrouds and rigging suffered much. The Phoenix's damages he could not tell, only that she had received a shot in her bowsprit. What he saw, he declared. As he was a prisoner, 'tis not likely they would not let him know their disasters. The New York Gazette, August 5, 1776

General Washington and his army were nearby and harassed the British as they probed New York's defenses. Washington, correctly anticipating New York City as the likely next target of the British, had moved his army from Boston to eastern New Jersey, Westchester, Manhattan and Long Island in April, 1776, when the British had departed Boston for Halifax. The American army had taken advantage of the several month interim, to amass more troops from neighboring regions to help defend against the British invasion. Never would the American forces, however, exceed two thirds of the size of the enemy:

New York, June 17th. Colonel Magaw's and Col. Shea's Battalions are this Day expected from Pennsylvania and a great number of Militia from the different Parts of New Jersey, Connecticut and this Province, so that in the course of this week, we may expect to have here an Army of at least 25,000 Men The New York Gazette, June 17, 1776

Since our last, a great number of troops from Maryland and the different counties of this Province, have passed through this city

[Phildelphia] on their way to the Jersies, where no doubt, if Howe gives them an opportunity, they will prove to the world, they deserve liberty. The New York Gazette, July 29, 1776

The Militia of this State [Pennsylvania] continues to pass through this city daily on their way to New Jersey. It is thought that Pennsylvania will send 20,000 men to the assistance of our neighbors. The New York Gazette, August 5, 1776

Our posts, which we found almost without any defense, are now pretty well secured. We have above five thousand troops at the different stations from Newark round Staten Island Sound to South Amboy, where our greatest strength lies. . . The strength of the enemy is very much uncertain. It was generally agreed that they had about 8,000 effective men when we first arrived, it is said two thousand Highlanders have joined them. They have sentinels all round our side of [Staten] Island[46] and the houses and barns all appear to be full. Their chief encampment is said to be on the sea or bay side next to their shipping, but we have great reason to believe they have a considerable encampment also behind a hill immediately opposite Amboy. I believe they are uninformed of our numbers and believe them to be greater than they are and are apprehensive of our going over. They have cannon planted along the shore, but concealed from our view. The Pennsylvania Journal, August 7, 1776

War means casualties -- bleeding, dying men, who need medical care. Arrangements were made for the carnage anticipated in the invasion and the inhabitants of Jersey were asked for their assistance:

The good people of this city [Philadelphia] and province and the province of New Jersey, are earnestly desired to send all the old sheets and other old linen which they could possibly spare to Dr. Shippen, jun., for the Jersey hospital. None will refuse complying with this request, when they consider that the lint and bandages made of this linen may be used in dressing and curing the wounds of their own fathers, husbands, brethren or sons.

The good people of New Jersey are desired to send their donations to Dr. Cowell in Trenton, Dr. Bainbridge in Princeton, Dr.

Cochran in New Brunswick, Mr. C. Petit in Amboy and the Rev. Mr. Caldwell[47] in Elizabeth Town. The Pennsylvania Journal, July 17, 1776

Imagine the dread in the mind of the New Jersey citizen that summer, while awaiting the appearance of the reinforcement fleet from Britain and the invasion that would inevitably follow. But, along with the fear, lay resolve. The American was ready to fight for liberty and independence. The fifteen months of hostilities between Lexington and the expected attack upon New York City and the writings of patriots such as Thomas Paine had steeled most Americans to the realization that the King was not worthy of allegiance. War that would end either in freedom or, in slavery, was now inevitable. It is appropriate that it was during this period of waiting for the invasion, that the Declaration of Independence was read to a crowd of patriots in Philadelphia. The People of America, including those of New Jersey, celebrated the news, while under the shadow of the English battle axe:

The Declaration of Independence was this day proclaimed here [Trenton], together with the new constitution of the colony of late established, and the resolve of the Provincial Congress for continuing the Administration of justice during the interim.

The members of the Provincial Congress, the gentlemen of the Committee, the officers and privates of the Militia under arms and a large concourse of the inhabitants attended on this great and solemn occasion. The declaration and other proceedings were received with loud acclamations.

The people are now convinced of what we ought long since to have known, that our enemies have left us no middle way between perfect freedom and abject slavery. In the field we hope, as well as in Council, the inhabitants of New Jersey will be found ever ready to support the Freedom and Independence of America. The Pennsylvania Packet, July 15, 1776

Last night Nassau Hall was grandly illuminated and Independency proclaimed under a triple volley of musketry and universal acclamation for the prosperity of the United States. The ceremony was conducted with the utmost decorum. The Pennsylvania Packet, July 15, 1776

On Wednesday the 7th instant, the Committee of Inspection for the County of Cumberland, in the State of New Jersey, the officers of the militia & a great number of other inhabitants, having met at Bridgetown, went in procession to the Courthouse, where The Declaration of Independence, The Constitution of New Jersey and the Trenton Ordinance were publicly read and unanimously approved of. These were followed with a spirited address by Dr. Elmer, Chairman of the Committee, after which the peace officers staves, on which were depicted the King's Coats of Arms, with other ensigns of Royalty, were burnt in the street. The whole was conducted with the greatest decency and regularity. The Pennsylvania Journal, August 28, 1776

The day of the invasion by the British appeared at hand, although the exact location of the assault was not yet known. A later published extract of a letter from an officer in the Second Battalion of Philadelphia, stationed on the Jersey coast at Amboy, and dated August 12, 9 o'clock A.M., records the British approach:

We have now in sight upwards of 60 sail of top sail vessels coming in to Sandy Hook; I suppose many more will appear, for every quarter of an hour, they make their appearance round the Highlands. I suppose this is their grand fleet. Our Battalion is ordered to New York. Saturday, Colonel Miles' two battalions and, this morning, Col. Atlee's battalion and a part of the Jersey militia, marched for New York; and, in a few days, most of the troops that are here will march for the same place, where they are in great want of men.
P.S. Half after ten o'clock, 90 sail in sight".
The Pennsylvania Journal, August 14, 1776

They landed in great numbers and camped in Tory Staten Island. Washington learned what was facing him:

This night we have reason to suspect the grand attack from our enemies, the reason why follows: The night before last a lad went over to Staten Island, supped there with a friend, and got safe back again undiscovered; soon after, he went to General Washington and, upon good authority, reported that the English army amounting to 15 to 20,000 had embarked and was in readiness for an engagement; that seven ships of the line and a number of other vessels of war were to surround the city and cover their landing; that the Hessians, being 15,000, were to remain on the island and attack Perth Amboy, Elizabeth Town point and Bergen, while the main body were doing its best here. The Pennsylvania Journal, August 28, 1776

Washington had split his forces into two camps, one in Manhattan, the other out on Long Island, a positioning he was later to regret. Those who were out on Long Island were literally out on a limb, easily cut off from retreat to the mainland. Consequently, the British attacked them first and the Americans suffered well over a thousand casualties:

New York, August 29. The great, the important day, big with the fate of America and liberty, seems to draw near! The British troops began to land on Long Island last Thursday, nearly their whole force, supposed to be more than 20,000 British and foreign troops. The marched through the small town of New Utrecht, in the way to Flatbush, another town about five miles from the city, near which they encamped; but were much harassed by our riflemen. Scouting parties were sent from our army into the adjoining woods, but were rather scanty in their numbers, considering the extent of ground they had to cover. The British forces, in three divisions, taking three different roads, and with the advantages of the night, almost surrounded the whole of our parties, who, although encircled with more than treble their number, bravely fought their way through the enemy, killing great numbers of them and brought off some prisoners. The New York first battalion behaved with great bravery. Lord Sterling's Brigade sustained the hottest of the enemy's fire;[48] it consisted of Col. Miles' two battalions, Col. Atlee's, Col. Smallwood's and Col. Hatch's regiments; they were all surrounded by the enemy and had to fight their way through the blaze of their fire. They fought and fell like Romans! The major part of Col. Atlee's, and Col. Piper's regiments are missing. Doctor Davis and his mate were both taken prisoners as they were dressing a wounded person in the wood. Col. Miles is missing (a truly amiable character) and supposed to be slain. Our killed, wounded and missing are imagined to be about 1000, but for our encouragement, the missing are hourly coming in. The Pennsylvania Journal, September 4, 1776

Through a combination of daring and bravery[49] and a British slow pursuit, Washington was able to evacuate at night the remnant of his Long Island troops to Manhattan to join the main army, thus preserving their chance to fight another day. Washington had learned a lesson. He was determined not to risk his army -- and with it the hope of the Revolution -- in a major engagement. He began to move away from the European battle plan where two armies would confront each other head to head. Instead, Washington adopted the advice of his General Nathaniel Greene to throw a quick punch and retreat: "We fight, get beat, rise and fight again." Indeed, over the ensuing several months, increasingly it would become General Washington's reluctant strategy to keep falling back to avoid a decisive battle with the British that would wipe out the dwindling American army.

But first, there would be the battle for New York City. Newspapers published extracts of letters from soldiers to families and friends or even journal entries from eyewitnesses to the shelling of Manhattan and its evacuation by the Americans during September of 1776:

Since our last. . . we have collected the following intelligence relative to the fleets and armies of our enemies. viz. that a battery was opened on a point of land on Long Island, opposite the east end of Blackwell's Island, which cannonaded our Fort at Hoorn's Hook for several days but to little purpose, we having no more than two men killed and four wounded.

Wednesday, the eleventh [of September], a number of the enemy took possession of Bahanna and Montrefour's islands, from whence it was imagined they intended to land at Harlem or Morrissania.

Thursday the 12th, two ships of War made their appearance at Hell Gate, having come through the Sound.

Friday the 13th, a signal gun was fired from the admiral's ship at three o'clock, P.M., when the Phoenix and Roebuck of forty four guns each, the Orpheus of thirty and another frigate, got under way and went up the East River, through a very hot fire from our batteries.

Saturday the 14th, in the evening, four other frigates and two transports run up the East River to join those that went up the day before.

Sunday the 15th, the Asia and two other ships of war proceeded up the North River but were roughly handled by our battery at Powles Hook.

And the next morning [Monday, the 16th], the Asia, by daylight, coming down much faster than she went up, three ships of war being nearly destroyed by four of our fire ships that run in among them and nothing prevented their total destruction but a gale of wind that sprung up that instant.

The same day, about eleven o'clock, the enemy effected the landing of a number of men near Mr. Stuyvesant's House in the Bowery, about two miles from the City, under cover of a most tremendous fire from eight or ten ships of war and in a few hours after took possession of the City of New York.

We hear that the English troops attacked part of our army near the Blue Ball, last Monday, about four o'clock in the afternoon, that the enemy was twice repulsed and beat back near two miles, leaving behind them many killed and taken prisoner, with three field pieces, luggage &c

Wednesday last [the 18th], the Asia went up the North River again. The same day there was a smart firing from Bergen point, at two tenders, a sloop and a schooner that lay neat Shutter's island at the mouth of Newark bay.

Yesterday morning [the 20th], a very heavy firing was heard on York Island, at Bergen town. We hear that there are no more than one thousand of the King's troops now in New York and those principally Englishmen. The Pennsylvania Evening Post, October 1, 1776

The patriot Sons of Liberty were determined to leave the British a burned out New York City. Fires were begun in brothels and taverns in lower Manhattan.[50] There had been a horrible drought all summer, the wooden buildings like tinder and no water for the fire equipment, even if the patriots had not disabled it already. Most the homes and businesses up to Chatham Square and all along the Hudson River were consumed. At the foot of Broadway, a large statute of King George was dragged down, cut up and put on wagons for

Connecticut to be melted into rebel bullets.[51] The British reacted swiftly, nabbing suspected American saboteurs, bayoneting or hanging them on the spot.

While General Washington and the main army were compelled to yield New York City to the British and to begin two months of fighting in Westchester, the Flying Camp, promised by Washington for the protection of New Jersey and commanded by General Mercer, together with the Jersey Militia, were patrolling the eastern corridor from Perth Amboy, all the way north to Bergen County. They had built a fort at Paulus Hook, today the Jersey City waterfront, which was across the bay from New York City.[52] A little further north, on the towering Palisades of the Hudson River, they had built Fort Lee, a companion shield to Fort Washington on the New York side of the Hudson. As soon as the British had captured New York City, the fort at Paulus Hook had to be abandoned. The British took it over and, for the first time in the war, occupied a piece of New Jersey. Entries from the journal of the Rev. Benjamin Boardman of Middle Haddam, Connecticut, Chaplain to the Continental troops, stationed at Paulus Hook, as published in the Pennsylvania Post, told the week's sad tale:

Paulus Hook, September 15, 1776. After Long Island was evacuated, it was judged impossible to hold the City of New York, and, for several days, the artillery and stores of every kind had been removed, and last night the sick were ordered to Newark, in the Jersies, but most of them could get no farther than this place and Hoebuck, and as there is but one house at each of these places, many were obliged to lie in the open air till this morning, whose distress, when I walked out at daybreak, gave me a livelier idea of the horror of war than anything I ever met with before.

About eight this morning, three large ships came to sail and made up towards the Hook. The garrison was ordered into our works. Soon after, they had taken their posts, the ships came up near the Jersey shore, to avoid our shot from the grand battery and, as they passed up the North River, kept up an incessant fire upon us. Their shot, a large part of which was grape, raked the whole Hook, but providentially one horse was all we lost by it.

It gave me great pleasure to see the spirit of the troops around me, who were evidently animated by the whistling of the enemy's shot, which often struck so near as to cover them with dust. About eleven o'clock, a furious cannonade was heard a little bit above New York and, before Night, numbers came over from the City and informed that it was evacuated by our troops and, about, sunset, we saw the tyrant's flag flying on Fort George.

September 16th. About two o'clock this morning an attempt was made to burn the ships that passed up the North River yesterday and anchored about three miles above us. One of them, the Renown of fifty guns, was grappled but broke her grappling and came down by us again.

September 17th. This day a large quantity of lead, musket ball and buckshot was discovered in a suspected house about a mile and a half above us and brought down to this place and properly secured for the United States.

September 18th. Nothing material happened here. Just at evening, intelligence was received that the brave Lieut. Col. Knowlton of our regiment was killed in the action that happened a little bit below Kingsbridge [between the northern tip of Manhattan and the Bronx] on Monday, as he was fighting with undaunted courage at the head of a body of rangers.

September 20th. The Renown returned back again to the fleet, and though she passed close in with New York shore, yet as there was very little wind, about forty shot from our battery were fired at her, many of which took effect. She lay all next day upon a careen to repair.

September 21. At two this morning we were waked by the guards, who informed us that New York was on fire. As the fire began on the south east end of the city, a little east of the grand battery, it was spread by a strong south wind, first on the East River, then northward, across the Broadway, opposite to the old English Church (if I mistake not the name) from thence it consumed all before it between Broadway and the North River, near to the college, laying about one third of the city in ashes (the opinion of those best acquainted with it).

September 22d. As no reinforcements could be sent us, we received orders this morning to remove our artillery, stores and baggage and hold ourselves in readiness to retreat and, before night, most of them were removed.

September 23. At one o'clock P.M., having removed every thing of value, we were ordered to retreat from the Hook. As soon as we began our march, four ships came up and anchored near the shore around the Hook, at the same time a great number of boats and floating batteries came down from just above New York. After taking a considerable time to see that there was nobody to hurt them, they began a most furious cannonade on our empty works, which continued until they wearied themselves.

Meanwhile, our little battalion retreated, with drums beating and colors flying, to Bergen, and, before night, the brave Britons ventured onshore and took possession of our evacuated works.

The post we now possess covers the Jersies. Here, we are reinforced by a number of regiments; more are daily coming in; the sick are recovering; the troops in high spirits and we have no fear but we shall be able to maintain our ground against all the banditti of [King] George. The Pennsylvania Evening Post, November 19, 1776

In October, the Americans had suffered a loss at White Plains. Washington crossed the Hudson to Hackensack, New Jersey, with 5,000 troops, anticipating that the British, having captured New York, might invade New Jersey and then attack the Capital of the rebellion, Philadelphia.

The enemy has not decamped, as was reported, but are still at Dobb's Ferry. Part of our army have come this side of the river. General Washington will cross today. Deserters confirm the suspicions of the enemy's design to pay us a visit in the Jerseys, but the attempt is so dangerous and so long delayed that I can scarcely believe it is seriously in agitation. Yesterday, Col. Magaw's men killed thirteen Hessians and an officer and stripped them. This little enterprise gives spirit to our men and insensibly reduces the number of the enemy. The Pennsylvania Journal, November 13, 1776

The committee of the county of Essex think it proper to inform the inhabitants of it that they have received intelligence, by a letter from his Excellency General Washington at White Plains, dated the 7th instant, that General Howe, with the army under his command, had retreated from that place with an intention, as he supposed, of sending a detachment of his troops into the Jerseys. The general

therefore advises all those who live near the water to be ready to move their stock, grain, carriages, and other effects back into the country. He adds that, if not done, the calamities we must suffer will be beyond all description and the advantages the enemy will receive immensely great. They have treated all here without discrimination, the distinction of Whig and Tory has been lost in one general scene of ravage and desolation. The article of forage is of great importance to them; not a blade, he says, should be left; what cannot with convenience be moved, must be consumed without the least hesitation. They have further intelligence, by a letter of this day from General Mercer, at Fort Lee, per express, that General Green had just received advice from General Washington that he was now fully convinced the enemy intended to cross the North River and make an incursion into this state, desiring we may be prepared in the best manner possible to defeat the design of their coming.
    By order of the Committee
    William Burney, Chairman
    The Pennsylvania Packet, November 19, 1776

To slow their invasion of New Jersey, if indeed that were the British plan, Washington sent Lord Stirling with eight regiments to Rahway and New Brunswick. On November 15, 1776, Fort Washington on the New York side of the Hudson fell, with the loss of 2,500 soldiers, a huge blow to the American cause. A few days later, Lord Cornwallis executed a daring surprise attack on Fort Lee, high on the Palisades of New Jersey. While the American garrison was able to flee and avoid capture, a large amount of badly needed munitions and supplies fell into the enemy's hands.

The enemy has been busy all day, in removing the stores at Fort Washington and have burnt several houses, for what reason we cannot conjecture. As this post was intended to keep the communication open, and has now become useless, it will probably be abandoned as soon as the stores can be removed. Whether the army will move higher up the river or westward into the country, I imagine is not yet agreed upon. The Pennsylvania Journal, November 27, 1776

You have no doubt heard all the particulars about our retreat from Fort Lee to Hackensack, from Hackensack to Acquaconack, and, from thence, to this place [Newark]. Nothing material has happened in the fighting way. We lost some of our large mortars, part of our cannon and stores at Fort Lee as well as at Hackensack. I believe the Generals intend to make a stand at this place. I hope these losses will rouse the virtue of America. If she does not exert herself now, she deserves not the independence she has declared. I still have hopes of success. I heard a great man say many months ago that America would not purchase her freedom at so cheap a rate as was imagined; nor is it proper she should. What costs us a little, we do not value enough. The Pennsylvania Journal, November 27, 1776

Unhappy with Hackensack or Newark as possible battle grounds, Washington moved his army to New Brunswick. Some viewed the withdrawal as a temporary strategic maneuver, not one of desperation. A letter from Headquarters, published in the press, justified the withdrawal from the parts of New Jersey adjacent to Bergen Neck[53].

Tomorrow, we evacuate Bergen, a measure, which will at first be condemned and, afterwards, approved of. For my own part, I am sorry that the enemy should possess another inch of American ground, but prudence requires a further sacrifice. The reasons of leaving this place, I take to be these. Bergen is a narrow neck of land, accessible on three sides by water and exposed to a variety of attacks in different places at one and the same time. A large body of the enemy might infallibly take possession of that place whenever they pleased, unless we keep a stronger force there than our numbers will allow. The spot itself is not an object of their arms. If they attacked, it would be to cut off those who defended it and to secure the grain and military stores. These have been removed and, when we have gone, a naked spot is all they will find. No other damage will follow except a depression of some people's spirits, who, unacquainted with places, circumstances and the secret reasons of such relinquishments, are apt to respond as if everything was lost. We go to Fort Constitution as soon as we have seen the troops marched off. We shall leave a guard of observation behind us. This may prevent the enemy's discovering our removal for a day or two. The Pennsylvania Journal, October 9, 1776

Realists might not be so easily calmed. Washington, in withdrawing to Newark and then New Brunswick, had made a call for help to the New Jersey militia that had been ignored. His competence to lead was beginning to be questioned by some. Moreover, many of the Flying Camp, whose enlistments were up, had gone home. Washington now barely had 4,000 troops under his command. The American candle, without doubt, was flickering, more in danger of expiring than it had ever been before. The last several months had been disastrous for morale. New York City had fallen and the Hudson River was in jeopardy. The strength of the army was at its weakest and its morale at its lowest. It was exhausted and, if the British kept up their pursuit of it, was likely to be crushed by year's end. What better indication of the plunging public sentiment than the response which the citizens of New Jersey gave an offer of clemency by the British General Lord Howe. Over three thousand "patriots" accepted it, including members of the legislature, judges and even a signer of the Declaration of Independence![54]

Fortunately, General Washington, other leaders and a core of true patriots would not succumb to despair, however bleak the future appeared. Governor Livingston attempted to rally the spirits and resolve of the New Jersey militia, as evidenced by his letter to the colonels of the New Jersey militia:

Sirs,

General Howe, after having been presented with the fairest opportunity to come to a general engagement with the brave troops of the United States, at White Plains, thought proper to decline a battle and suddenly retreated to New York. In his return thither, he [captured] Fort Washington, and by the mere dint of numbers, possessed himself of that garrison, with considerable slaughter on his side, reported to be equal the number of prisoners he took in the fortress. This being the only thing of consequence effected by the British Arms during a whole summer's campaign (the Americans having had the advantage in almost every skirmish) the enemy, despairing of conquest, seemed determined to plunder and, reduced to the greatest straights for want of forage and provisions, will, as there is reason to apprehend, endeavor to make an incursion into this state to supply those necessaries. To check their progress General Washington (whose fame is deservedly above applause) has transported a considerable body of Continental troops to the eastern parts of this state, who, with the assistance of our militia, will doubtless be able to give them such a reception as their rashness deserves.

As the war in which we are engaged is founded on the principles of self defense and self preservation and to save ourselves and posterity from the most ignominious slavery, . . . as the eyes of all Europe are fixed on the brave Americans, as a people resolved, at all hazards, to maintain that independence, which British injustice and British cruelty compelled us to adopt, [and]. . . as we ought not to be unwilling to do for our descendants what our ancestors have done for us. . . it is expected that the New Jersey Militia will not forfeit, by any unworthy conduct, the favorable sentiments entertained of their prowess. In full confidence of not being disappointed in those expectations, you are hereby directed to have the battalion under your command ready to march at the shortest notice. The Pennsylvania Evening Post, November 28, 1776

To reverse their losses since the summer and to prevent what appeared to be the beginning of a rout, the American patriot had to reach deeply within himself for the necessary courage to choose death over slavery:

I have just time enough to inform you that there is very good intelligence that the enemy intends to make a push for Philadelphia. . . We look to New Jersey and Pennsylvania for their Militia and, on their spirit, depends the preservation of America. If in this hour of adversity, they shrink from danger, they deserve to be slaves, indeed. If the freedom which success will assure us, if the misery that awaits our subjection, will not rouse them, why let them sleep on till they awake in bondage. The Pennsylvania Evening Post, November 28, 1776

On a national level as well, Thomas Paine, who had helped spark the Revolution by his essay Common Sense and who was now serving in the retreating army at Newark, wrote, by night, another essay, entitled Crisis. Published immediately, it gripped the Americans and renewed their spirits:

These are the times that try mens' souls. The summer soldier and the sunshine patriot will, in this crisis, shrink from the service of his country, but he, who stands it now, deserves the love and thanks of man and woman.

For reasons never fully known, the British pursued Washington's army at a snail's pace.[55] They approached New Brunswick where the Americans had camped on December 11 and Washington quickly moved his troops further south to Trenton, on the Delaware River. At Trenton, he issued an order taking up all the boats along that stretch of the River. The British dawdled another five days in their pursuit of the Americans and, when they finally appeared, Washington had already transported his troops across the river into Pennsylvania. Unable to follow him because they had no craft with which to cross the river, the British halted the chase until spring and, as was the custom among European armies, settled down for the winter. British headquarters were at New Brunswick on the Raritan River but, so as to control as much of New Jersey as possible, troops were wintered across the State from Hackensack to the Delaware. Many of the major towns of the state were occupied, including Trenton, Burlington, Bordentown and Princeton. The countryside provided forage for the foreign troops. The Americans resisted the attempts to the extent they could:

Philadelphia, December 24. We hear from good authority that on Sunday last, betwixt Slab Town[56], and Black Horse[57], in the Jersies, a party of our army under the command of Col. Griffin, had a skirmish with the Hessians and that the enemy were forced to retreat with precipitation, having some killed and leaving behind them many knapsacks and other necessaries, among which was a hat shot through the crown. But, the next morning, the enemy advanced with considerable reinforcement, supposed to be about 2000 men with seven or eight field pieces, our little army was obliged to retreat (which they performed with great regularity) to prevent their being outflanked by superior numbers and, in the evening, they had another skirmish at Mount Holly, in which the enemy, as an intelligent person informs, had several killed or wounded. Our army is at Moorestown and that of the enemy is at Mount Holly. The Pennsylvania Evening Post, December 19, 1776

General Washington, however, had not retired for the winter. Far from it. Aware of America's need for a change in her fortunes and having been reinforced from a number of quarters, he was willing to be bold. He and his staff decided to cross the ice filled Delaware River, and surprise one of the British winter camps. On the eve of battle, Thomas Paine's *Crisis* was read to the troops, leaving no doubt as to the importance of the mission or what was expected of them. The next day -- Christmas, 1776 -- Washington with 2,400 men, crossed the Delaware[58], attacking the 1,400 man Hessian garrison at Trenton. The plan worked better than could have been hoped. A hundred Hessians were killed, including their commanding officer Colonel Joann Rall; 900 were captured and 400 escaped to tell of the American victory. The Americans had four men wounded[59]:

It was determined, some three days ago, that our army should pass over to Jersey, in three different places and attack the enemy. About two thousand five hundred men and twenty brass fieldpieces, with his Excellency George Washington at its head, and Major Generals Sullivan and Greene, in command of two divisions passed over on the night of Christmas and, at about three a.m. were on their march, by two routes, towards Trenton. The night was sleety and the roads so slippery that it was daybreak, when we were two miles from Trenton. But, happily, the enemy was not apprised of our design. The enemy consisted of about fifteen hundred Hessians, under Col. Rall, formed and made some smart fire from the musketry and six field pieces, but our people pressed from every quarter and drove them from their cannon. They retreated toward a field behind a piece of wood up the creek from Trenton and formed in two bodies. As I came in full view of them, from the back of the wood, with his Excellency George Washington, an officer informed him that the enemy had grounded their arms and surrendered prisoners. . . .

I was immediately sent off with the prisoners to M'Conkey's ferry and have got about seven hundred and fifty safe in town. We lost but two of our men that I can hear of, a few wounded and one brave officer, Captain Washington, who assisted in securing their artillery, shot in both hands. Indeed, every officer and private behaved well and it was a fortunate day to our arms, which I more rejoice at having an active part in it. The success of this day will greatly animate our

friends and add fresh courage to our new army, which, when formed, will be sufficient to secure us from the depredations or insults of our enemy. We took three standards, six fine brass cannon and about one thousand stands of arms.
> *Published by Order of the Council on Safety*
> *Geo. Bickham, Secretary pro tem*

Although the calendar was about to slip from 1776 to 1777, General Washington did not want to end the 1776 campaign and lose the momentum he had created at Trenton. Briefly, he returned back across the Delaware to rest his men, who had spent the last 36 hours marching and fighting. The British, stung by the attack, were rethinking their strategy of thinly scattering their troops for the winter across the Jersey country side. They began to gather them at Princeton and New Brunswick. Meanwhile, American forces began to pester the British outposts. A little victory had gone a long way.

Washington and his staff had one more trick up their sleeve. On December 30, he re-crossed the Delaware with 5,000 soldiers, encamped at Trenton and waited for the British, stationed at Princeton, to come and get them. The British, some 8,000 troops led by Lord Cornwallis, took the bait. Harassed all the way from Princeton by American troops, the British did not reach the outskirts of Trenton until dusk on January 2, 1777 and, facing the artillery fire of the Americans, decided to postpone their attack until the morning.

At one o'clock in the morning of January 3, 1777, while their watch fires were kept burning to fool the enemy, all the Americans except a few props, stole away and, by dawn that day, were only two miles from Princeton. A series of attacks drove the British from Princeton. The British suffered a 100 dead and another 300 captured, as well as the embarrassment of having been fooled by a colonial. The Americans had forty casualties.[60] The story is related in a letter received from an officer of General Washington's and published in the newspaper:

We left Crosswicks on the first, instant, about ten o'clock in the morning, and arrived a little after sunset in Trenton, through the worst roads that were ever seen. About eleven o'clock, we were alarmed by the approach of the enemy. We only sent a brigade out to amuse them, while we took post on the lower side of the creek and back in the woods. There was a pretty fair cannonade, till dark, when both sides ceased firing. The men ordered to keep their posts and lie on their arms. A council of war was held and it was determined to file off to the right, through the woods and by bye roads, leaving the enemy on the left, and attack Princeton by daylight; about 500 men and two pieces of iron cannon were left to amuse the enemy. [At Princeton], about seven hundred British troops saw our army about a mile and a half distant. They returned to the town and made ready to receive us. General Mercer's Brigade did not fire until the enemy advanced within forty yards. The enemy received the brigade with charged bayonets. General Mercer was wounded (it is said by a ball filed but it is a fact that he was afterwards wounded in the belly by a bayonet). I fancy the enemy found it impossible to escape, as our troops all began to rally and join in the pursuit. They all dropped their packs and flew with the utmost precipitation and we pursued with great eagerness. The town surrendered and about sixty, including fourteen officers, surrendered. We have taken in the whole about three hundred, about thirty killed and fifty wounded. I have no doubt that others will be brought in. We lost about thirty killed and thirty wounded. We took three pieces of brass artillery. The enemy proceeded towards Brunswick, with the utmost expedition, the British arrived there about daylight and the Hessians at twelve yesterday. All was in the greatest confusion. We marched immediately to Morristown where we shall be ready to fall down on Elizabeth Town, Newark or Amboy. The Pennsylvania Evening Post, January 16, 1777

The maneuver had been not only a military success but another morale booster for the patriots:

I almost think the author of the Crisis [Thomas Paine] a prophet when he says the Tories will curse the day when Howe arrived upon the Delaware. I verily believe the observation is coming true. The two late actions at Trenton and Princeton have put a new face upon affairs . Within a fortnight past, we have taken and killed of Howe's army between two and three thousand men. Our loss is trifling. We are daily picking up their parties. Yesterday, we took seventy prisoner and thirty loads of baggage. The Pennsylvania Evening Post, January 14, 1777

After the victory at Princeton, Washington considered marching to New Brunswick to take on the British there. But his troops were tired and the morale of both the soldiers as well as the nation's had been restored at Trenton and Princeton. Instead, he decided to winter at Morristown, New Jersey, where he could rest his troops and regroup for the next campaign. It was time to close 1776, a year that had started well with the British fleeing Boston and some key American victories in the South and which also had ended well, with these victories of Trenton and Princeton. The months in between, however, had not been as successful. The Americans were defeated at the Battles of Long Island, Kingsbridge, White Plains and Fort Lee. New York City, bombarded and burned, was now in English hands.

CHAPTER 5

Propaganda War

There were no neutral newspapers in America during the Revolutionary War. A paper's political affiliations could be quickly gleaned from the subtleties of its expressions, such as its use of the term "rebels", rather than "patriots", or calling New Jersey a "state", not a "province". Most of the newspapers strongly supported the American Revolutionary cause, including *The New Jersey Gazette* and *The New Jersey Journal*. Both of these papers -- the first newspapers ever published in New Jersey -- were born during the Revolution, when the printing presses of New York City and Philadelphia were in British hands.

The most notorious Loyalist journal was *Rivington's New York Gazetteer*[61], later called *Rivington's New York Loyal Gazette,* and finally *The Royal Gazette*, all published at Hanover Square in New York City by the same man, James Rivington. He might have been the most hated man in America.

James Rivington had been born in London and bred into the bookseller business, his father, Charles, having had a stall in Paternoster Row in London since 1711.[62] In 1742, James and his brother John took over the business from their father and prospered. James put out Smollet's *History Of England*, which enjoyed ten thousand pounds of sales, a record at the time. Talented, well mannered and informed, James became affluent enough to be able to keep a carriage, a sign of rank in the London of the 1750's. He also liked to have a good time, especially with some of his new friends -- many with the titles of nobility -- whom he had met at the horse races of Newmarket and other places of amusement for the jet set of the day. After one especially bad day at Newmarket where he had a lost a small fortune, Rivington gave up. Dissipated, he was no longer able to keep up with wealthier friends who did not have business duties which required regular attention. He declared bankruptcy. Surprisingly, despite his spendthrift ways, he had still had more assets than debts, so he was able to pay off everyone and still have a little left to start anew, this time in a more responsible manner. He surrendered the family business to his brother John and sailed for America, as have many others, looking for a fresh start in life.

In 1760, James Rivington became a bookseller in Philadelphia. A year later, turning the business there over to a partner to run, he came to New York City where he opened a bookstore on the lower end of Wall Street, as well as a shop in Boston. On April 22, 1773, he published the first issue of *Rivington's New York Gazetteer or The Connecticut, New Jersey, Hudson's River and Quebec Weekly Advertiser*. It was printed weekly on Thursday. At first, it bore the motto on its masthead: "Printed at his ever open and uninfluenced press, fronting Hanover Square". A wood cut of a ship under sail completed his logo. Within two years, the Gazette had a circulation of 3,600 readers and regularly reached as far away as England, France and the West Indies. Because of both the number and the width of this circulation, it became one of the most read journals in the colonies.

These first two years of *The New York Gazette* coincided with the birthing of the Revolution. In the beginning, Rivington reported on events with moderation and impartiality. Soon, however, he became increasingly Tory, loyal to the Crown and disdainful of the mob. On his front page, the King's Arms replaced the image of the ship and the motto "ever open and uninfluenced" was dropped. He remarks in the press towards the rebels became more derogatory, his comments more cutting and taunting and his conduct toward the American cause more offensive:

New-Town, Sussex County. Yesterday a certain David Campell, a pedlar, was discovered in offering for sale a pamphlet, entitled "A Friendly Address to all reasonable Americans on the subject of our political contentions", a work highly injurious to the cause of American liberty, speciously recommending the base principles of passive obedience to tyranny, calculated to excite jealousies and divisions among the inhabitants of the different colonies and to terrify weak minded persons into submission to the late oppressive acts of Parliament. The man, as soon as questioned, protested his innocence and, the dangerous tendency of the pamphlet declared to him, he promised to sell no more of them (one only having been disposed of).

This day, the county committee called him before them, when he declared that these infamous pamphlets were delivered to him by James Rivington of New York, printer, who recommended them as excellent pamphlets and very saleable, and, upon his assuring the printer, he had already expended all his money, Rivington urged him to take a dozen copies upon trust, in confirmation of which he produced the original invoice, in the handwriting of Rivington himself. Previous to his appearance before the committee, the man, being convinced of his offence and desirous to satisfy the people, had voluntarily consented to their being burned by the hands of the common hangman and they were burnt accordingly, in the presence of a numerous concourse of people, from the different parts of this extensive county. The committee being informed of this, the pedlar, discovering great candor and the appearance of innocence, and having most heartedly promised to be more cautious in the future, he was dismissed.

Mr. James Rivington:
Sir, when I purchased a gross of the proceedings of the Congress and two dozen almanacs, for which I paid you 4 pounds, 17 shillings, you at that time solicited me to take along to sell, a dozen of what you called a friendly address. I knew no other than it being an address to the good people of this land to exert themselves for the preservation of their ancient liberties and privileges. But how was I surprised to find them the reverse and were sufficient to expose me to the prejudice of every gentleman in the county. Well! They have been publicly burned here. I aided and assisted in performing the same and have been had up and examined before the gentlemen and the committee of this county. Thus, Mr. Rivington's friendship has turned out to be the highest vexation and trouble to me. David Campell The New York Journal, December 8, 1774

Elizabeth Town, December 19. The committee of observation for the free borough and town of Elizabeth, taking into consideration that James Rivington, printer of one of the New York Gazettes, having published many pieces in his paper and divers pamphlets, inimical to the liberties of America, by which we have reason to suspect that he is a vile ministerial hireling, employed to disunite the colonies and calumniate all their measures entered into for the public good, in order therefore to discountenance the attempts of every person unfriendly to American liberty.

RESOLVED unanimously, by this Committee, that they will take no more of Rivington's Gazettes, nor send any advertisements to be inserted therein, or have any further dealings or commerce with him. And that we will recommend it to our constituents to observe the same conduct towards said Rivington or to any other printer who shall publish or print any pieces or pamphlets tending to break the happy union now subsisting throughout the American colonies. The New York Journal, December 22, 1774

Rivington's mocking style was indeed offensive to the Jersey rebels and he knew how to get that reader's goat. The following, somewhat less than objective, reporting by Rivington of an event in Elizabeth certainly was meant by Rivington, in part at least, to repay the citizens of that town for the burning his books a few months earlier:

Some particulars of a riot that happened at Elizabeth Town in east Jersey, on Wednesday, the 8th of February.

The scene opened in the face of day, between twelve and one o'clock, with seizing a poor Staten Islander, for no other reason than because some people of that loyal island were supposed to have been ready to assist in landing some goods from Captain Watson' Scotch ship, which lately left New York and is departed with his cargo for Jamaica, having arrived at New York after the first of February, the day limited by the Congress for the importation of goods. The man's boat was dragged ashore and his oysters distributed to the hungry vagabonds, who were visibly headed in the center of town by Jonathan Hampton, a Justice of the Peace, a Judge of the County Court, and Chairman of the Committee. Hampton was the man who attempted lately to obstruct the passage of his Majesty's Royal Regiment of Ireland over the ferries and prevented wagons from carrying their baggage; this same Hampton was the man who had raised a riot lately in Sussex County, attacked a pedlar and destroyed his property. At about four o'clock when the mob discharged the poor oysterman, they proceeded to abuse all the people in town who were known to be well affected to the Constitution[63]; they erected a gallows in order to more particularly insult them and fixed up a liberty pole in the middle of town. It must be observed that the worshipful Judge Hampton was, as usual, completely drunk when the riot commenced. For the honor of the police, it must be recorded that two of the Aldermen, Messrs. Blanchard and Dayton, exerted themselves greatly to suppress those violences but they were able only to check them. Two of the Delegates contributed to a collection that was made for their staunch friends, the mob. Mr. Alderman Blanchard ordered the gallows to be demolished after it had existed two hours and their deity, the liberty pole, after standing to Monday evening, was struck by an order of the Committee, without the consent of that exemplary and able guarantee of American freedom, the righteous and immaculate Judge Jonathan Hampton.

This was a glorious day to the sons of licentiousness and it was also a glorious day for the sons of loyalty for it has made in Elizabeth more proselytes to the side of order and government than all the other endeavors that have been exerted to abate the fever of the times. Rivington's New York Gazetteer, March 2, 1775

Among the many who developed a deep hatred of Rivington were the Sons of Liberty of New York and its radical leader, Isaac Sears. Rivington's press was attacked and, for a brief period, he was held prisoner by the patriot mob. Then, on November 27, 1775, -- the war already in process in Massachusetts but before the Declaration of Independence - a number of armed men from Connecticut broke into Rivington's printing house, destroyed his press, and carried a way a large quantity of his types to be melted and formed into rebel bullets. This was enough. In January, 1776, Rivington abandoned New York for England.

But, unfortunately, he was not gone for good. Back in England, he purchased a new press, was officially named the King's Printer in New York, and came back to the City, when the British forces, led by General Howe, captured it. Now under the protection of the British army and no longer frightened of the mob, Rivington re-opened his paper on October 4, 1777, changing its title to *Rivington's New York Loyal Gazette,* then simply to *The Royal Gazette.* It proudly proclaimed that it was published by "James Rivington, Printer to the King, his most Excellent Majesty". As their titles suggest, these journals were stridently pro British and, as he had earlier, Rivington became a tremendous irritant to the Americans and the subject of curses and threats alike.[64]

Rivington maintained his knack at making money and spending it as quickly. In addition to the newspaper, the bookstores and then a stationer's business, Rivington had a business relationship with his friend and fellow reveler, New York City merchant and trader, Robert Townsend. Townsend had a hidden ownership interest in Rivington's newspapers and often contributed anti-American editorials for him to publish. Together, they also owned the British Coffee House, a tavern frequented by English army officers, as well as a boarding house, catering to the same clientele.

At the time of the Revolution in America, newspapers had existed for less than a century. During that time, there had been no war between nations that shared a common language and, hence, that could communicate with the other's general populace on a large scale. Therefore, it would seem safe to assume that the war of words -- alternatively, the truth, exaggerations, scoldings, recriminations, lies -- in which Mr. Rivington and his American counterparts of the colonial press were about to engage was the beginning of mass propaganda, today a standard of all warfare.

An aim of propaganda and misinformation is to intimidate and undermine the confidence and resolve of enemy troops and civilians alike. At the same time, the press serves up optimistic and encouraging news accounts for its own citizens.

For example, in an effort to demoralize the Americans, Rivington published articles designed to question whether the ordinary American was in favor of the rebellion and to hold up to ridicule those who espoused the rebel cause, as, for example, the following letter supposedly to Deputies of Continental Congress from Essex:

Gentlemen: Your notice to the Freeholders of Essex, of the 28th of November, was conveyed to me by Holt's paper of Thursday last, and as your purpose in convening us was declared to be, in conformity to the wise and prudent resolves of Congress, of which I had before heard, I determined to read their resolves with the greatest attention and, therefore, sent Tom, with my best horse, who soon brought me the extracts of the proceedings of the Congress. I

eagerly sat down and read them, but, alas, how I was disappointed. Instead of wise and prudent, I found nothing but rude, insolent and absurd resolves, calculated to answer no end but to stir up strife and increase confusion among us and to unite every spirited Briton against us. Did I think them wise and prudent, or believed that you could think them so, I would have unquestionably supported them, but when the Congress, instead of healing differences, create confusion, when under the pretense of limiting the power of the King, Lords and Commons, they create a power unknown to our constitution what do they make of us? Do you and they apprehend us to be fools and that we are implicitly to be led as you direct? We know what it is to be governed by acts of parliament and never thought ill of them, until we were alarmed in other sentiments"
A Freeholder of Essex and a Real Lover of Liberty. Rivington's New York Gazetteer, January 5, 1775

In consequence of an anonymous advertisement fixed up at this place [Shrewsbury, New Jersey], giving notice to the freeholders and others to meet on Tuesday, the 17th instant, in order to form a Committee of Inspection etc., etc., between thirty and forty of the most respectable freeholders accordingly met, and after a few debates on the business of the day, which were carried on with great decency and moderation, it was generally agreed (there not being more than four or five dissentient vote) that an appointment of a committee was not only useless, but they were apprehensive that it would prove a means that peace and quiet, which had heretofore existed in the township, and which they were extremely desirous and would continue to use their utmost efforts to preserve, and [they agreed] to guard themselves against running upon that rock, on which, with much concern, they behold others, through an inattentive rashness, daily splitting. Rivington's New York Gazetteer, January 26, 1775

Mr. Printer: We hear from Woodbridge-Rahway, New Jersey, that on the 17th instant, notwithstanding the badness of the weather, the sons of Bacchus went several miles to procure an emblem of licentiousness, by them miscalled a Liberty pole, which was of the stupendous height of four score feet; they dragged it with much ado and no small fear to the place of its destination, the crossroads, a proper place of erecting a pillory, stocks or whipping post (which are all extremely necessary in that place). And, after having got it so far safe, according to the custom common in such achievements, repaired to the nearest tavern and, between seven and eight o'clock, their tumblers being empty and the landlord somewhat weary of their company, they repaired to the shrine to pay the final homage of the night to their ever adorable goddess, when, to their remorse, they found her cut in twain by means of a handsaw, agitated, as they suppose, by some fiend of a Tory. Rivington's New York Gazetteer, March 30, 1775

The following Anecdote we believe may be depended upon.
Whilst the Count D'Estaing's Squadron lay off Sandy Hook, a Marine Officer belonging to one of the ships, a Scotch Man by birth, went on Shore at Shrewsbury. The Inhabitants, finding that he spoke good English, crowded to converse with him and told him how happy they were made by the arrival of the French Fleet, as they did not doubt that their Independence would be delivered by their co-operation. Whereat the Scotch Soldier with a significant shake of the head answered them "he believed they were mistaken, that he looked upon their independence only as a dream for either France or England must have this Country."
The effect this Speech had may be better conceived than described. Rivington's New York Loyal Gazette, August 10, 1778

The American papers also engaged in disseminating propaganda. Some of it was of the positive, morale uplifting variety, designed to increase patriotism, fervor and confidence:

New York, July 29. An old Gentleman between 60 and 70, now does duty in the Militia near Newark, in New Jersey, is the Father of about 15 Children now alive, 9 of which are in the Continental Army, from Captains to Privates. The New York Gazette, July 29,1776[65]

New York, August 8. We hear from Elizabeth Town, that on a late alarm there, when an immediate attack of the Regulars was expected, and every man capable of bearing arms was summoned to defend it, there were three or four young men, brothers, going out from one house, an elderly lady, mother or grandmother to the young men, who, without displaying the least signs of timidity, had, with a resolute calmness, encouraged and assisted them to arm. When they were ready to go, and, just setting out, she addressed them thus: "My children, I have a few words to say to you. You are going out on a just cause to fight for the rights and liberties of your country. You have my blessings and prayers that God will protect you and assist you. But, if you fall, his will be done. Let me beg of you, my children, that if you fall, it be like men, and that your wounds may not be in your back parts. *The Pennsylvania Evening Post, August 10, 1776*

From New Jersey, we learn, that the 20th ult., a woman passing an evacuated house in Woodbridge, saw, through a window, a drunken Hessian soldier, who had straggled from his party; there being no men within less than a mile of the town, she went home, dressed herself in a man's apparel and, armed with an old firelock, returned to the house, entered it and took the Hessian prisoner whom she stripped of his arms and was leading off, when she fell in with the patrol guard of a New Jersey regiment to whom she delivered her prisoner. *The Pennsylvania Journal, April 2, 1777*

Mr. Collins,
I do not remember whether your Gazette has hitherto given us the production of any woman correspondent. Indeed, nothing but the most pressing call of my country could have induced me to appear in Print. But rather than suffer your sex to be caught by the bait of that arch foe to American Liberty, Lord North, I think that ours ought, to a woman, to draw their pens and enter our solemn protest against it. Nay, the fair ones in our neighborhood have already entered into a resolve for every mother to disown her son and refuse the caresses of her husband and for every maiden to reject the advances of her gallant, where such husband, son or gallant, shows the least symptoms of being imposed upon by this flimsy subterfuge, which, I call, the dying speech, and last groans of Great Britain, pronounced and grunted out by her great oracle, and little politician, who now appears ready to hang himself, for having brought the nation to the brink of that ruin from which he can not deliver her. You will be kind enough to correct my spelling, a part of my education in which I have been much neglected.

I am your sincere friend
BELINDA[66]
The New Jersey Gazette, May 6, 1778

The American newspapers, however, engaged in their share of belittling the British and Loyalists and their alleged military prowess. Ridicule was an excellent weapon:

A Poem on General Howe's late expedition to attack the army of the United States

> *Threat'ning to drive us from the hill,*
> *Sir William march'd t' attack our men;*
> *But finding that we all stood still,*
> *Sir William, he marched back again.*
> *The New Jersey Gazette, January 7, 1778*

This city has lately been entertained with a most astonishing instance of the activity, bravery, and military skill of the Royal Navy of Great Britain. The affair is somewhat peculiar and deserves your notice. Some time last week, two boys observed a keg of a singular construction, floating in the river opposite to the city; they got into a small boat, and, attempting to take up the keg, it burst with a great explosion and blew up the unfortunate boys. On Monday last, several more kegs of the same construction made their appearance. An alarm was immediately spread through the City. Various reports prevailed, filling the city and the royal troops with unspeakable consternation. Some reported that these kegs were filled with armed rebels, who were to issue forth in the dead of the night, as the Grecians did of old from their wooden horse at the siege of Troy, and take the city by surprise, asserting that they had seen the points of their bayonets through the bung holes of the kegs. Others said they were charged with the most inveterate combustibles, to be kindled by secret machinery and, setting the whole Delaware in flames, were to consume all the shipping in the harbor; while others asserted that they were constructed by art magic, would themselves ascend the wharfs in the night time and roll, all flaming, through the streets of the city, destroying everything. Be this as it may, certain it is that the shipping in the harbor and all the wharfs of the city were manned.

The battle begun and it was surprising to behold the incessant blaze that was kept up against the enemy, the kegs. Both officers and men exhibited the most unparalleled skill and bravery on the occasion, whilst the citizens stood gazing, as solemn witnesses of their prowess. From the Roebuck and other ships of war, whole broadsides were poured into the Delaware. In short, not a wandering chip, stick or drift log but felt the vigor of the British arms. The action began at about sunrise and would have been completed by noon, had not an old market woman coming down the river with provisions, unfortunately let a small keg of butter fall overboard, which (as it was then ebb) floated down to the scene of action. At the sight of this unexpected reinforcement of the enemy, the battle was renewed with fresh fury; the firing was incessant till the evening closed the affair. The kegs were either totally demolished or obliged to fly, as none of them has shown their heads since. It is said that his Excellency Lord Howe has dispatched a swift sailing packet with an account of this victory to the court of London. In a Word, Monday the 5th of January, 1778, must ever be distinguished in history for the memorable BATTLE OF THE KEGS. The New Jersey Gazette, January 21, 1778

By a gentleman from Newark we are informed that a certain James Nutman . . . when the British troops landed on the Jersey Shore, was so exceedingly pleased that he invited his friends and neighbors to keep thanksgiving, as he termed it, by spending the day and taking dinner with him, on the happy occasion, often saying with much seeming satisfaction, his dear brethren and protectors had come, frequently repeating the questions to his guests "Aren't you glad that they have come?" The next day they [the British troops] arrived in Newark and his dear friends and protectors stripped him of all his moveable property, even to his shoes and stockings; and the poor wretch of a Tory was under the necessity of begging from his neighbors something to cover his nakedness.
The Pennsylvania Evening Post, March 6, 1777

Both sides reported on how the enemy troops were small in number, ill, unhappy, starving or ready to desert. In the beginning of the war, it was the Rebel position that was reported to be deteriorating:

By the nearest calculation that can be formed, the Rebels, in the course of the last year, did not lose by sickness and battle less than 25,000 men --an immense draught in a country, where the price of labor is so great and the hands so few. Rivington's New York Loyal Gazette, January 13, 1777

The Rebels are inoculating great numbers for small pox at Hanover in New Jersey[67]. Rivington's New York Loyal Gazette, March 31, 1777

Mr. Washington remains as yet at Morris Town, with not above 4 or 500 men. The rest of his people are stationed at Quibbletown and other parts of the country most of the New Englanders have gone home, some to their farms, others to their merchandize. Their new levies[68] have succeeded very ill and men are not to be had upon any terms.

Since our last, a number of persons have left the Rebel Army in New Jersey, and came in with their arms &c. to our troops, in consequence of the General's late indulgent Proclamation and have joined the several Provincial Corps already appointed, which are now very nearly complete. Rivington's New York Loyal Gazette, March 31, 1777

By several persons come in from the Jersies, we are informed, that Mr. Washington's whole force in that colony does not exceed 4000 men, who are for the most part in a very ragged condition. Their provisions are likewise very bad and scarce. Most of their beef and pork is stinking for want of salt to cure it properly; and, for several days, they were at short allowance. By their preparations, they seem to intend shortly to repass the Delaware. Rivington's New York Loyal Gazette, April 7, 1777

Suddenly, the tide turned and it was the British whom the press reported to be in difficulty:

Deserters from the British Army are daily coming out of Philadelphia and it remains to be confidently asserted that the enemy are making every preparation to evacuate that city in a short time.

We have many corroborating accounts that the enemy in New York and Philadelphia having lately been impressing refugees and young men inhabitants of those places and putting them handcuffed on board their ships. The New Jersey Gazette, May 27, 1778

There never was an instance of so much desertion in a British army, as what now prevails in the Jersies; near five hundred have already come into Philadelphia since they left it, besides great numbers who go up the country. From accounts by them, we learn that they have been much impeded and harassed in their march and have lost numbers of their grenadiers and light infantry. The Pennsylvania Evening Post, June 25, 1778

Two persons came out of New York, the 5th instant, who inform us there was great uneasiness in that city among the Tories, on account of an exceedingly great mob in London, which after much difficulty over a number of days, was quelled. The mob arose partly on account of the hot press in England and partly because the manufacturers were out of employment and in want of bread. They were enraged at the administration as the cause of the American war, which was the source of all their distresses. They pulled down the houses of the Arch fiend Bute and his second North and insulted a number of the king's friends and tools. But these things are only the beginning of sorrow to Britain. The New Jersey Gazette, February 11, 1778

I doubt not that you have heard of the great fire in New York City. Yesterday came out from thence, two Hessian officers. They were of those taken at Trenton and had contracted an affection for the country. Therefore, shortly after they were exchanged, as they tell the story, they resigned their commissions, but not being able to obtain leave to come out, they at length effected their escape. They left the city just about 8 o'clock in the evening, the 6th inst. and passed King's Bridge at about one in the morning. One of them, a handsome young fellow whose brother is aide de camp to Gen. Clinton, tells me he saw the fire, that it began in a house filled with the King's stores, [that] 68 houses were consumed and a vast quantity of stores, amongst which 30,000 blankets or pairs of blankets, I think the latter, 10,000 suits of clothes, and a great deal of provisions, computed at a four weeks supply. Sometime afterwards, a vessel struck with lightning blew up. This Hessian says she had on board upwards of 200 tons of powder but other accounts say from 70 to 90 barrels; either was a great quantity for an explosion and did great damage to the town. They say the inhabitants are much distressed at their present situation and many want to take their chances in the country but cannot obtain permission. The New Jersey Gazette, August 12, 1778

We hear that Colonel William Allens's regiment of Pennsylvania Royalists is entirely broken up and what few men were deluded in so infamous a service as that of taking up arms against their native country, have been incorporated into other regiments. The New Jersey Gazette, February 11, 1778

Last week five Hessians deserters arrived here from Fort Washington.
A correspondent at Pitts-Town, who conversed with many of the principal officers of the Convention troops as they passed through that place on their way to Virginia informs us, that they appeared to be much cast down, and seemed very desirous that an exchange might take place to facilitate their return to Europe - many of whom declared, that, were they once there, they would never return to engage in so fruitless a business as that as attempting to conquer America. The Hessian officers, in particular, expressed great dissatisfaction -- complaining that many of them had been deceived, not expecting to have come further than England and that, in every respect, since their arrival in America, they conceived themselves to have been very basely treated. The New Jersey Gazette, January 13, 1779

Friday last, 200 American sailors and Masters of ships were exchanged at Elizabeth town. By several of those, who arrived here [Trenton] on Monday, we learn, that they have drafted every sixth man in New York and on Long Island from 16 to 20 years of age, and those who do not turn out are put into the Provost; that a number of

Hessians left in New York as a garrison, lately mutinied, many of whom having absolutely refused to go on duty; and that our prisoners on board the prison ships suffer beyond description, being turned down in great numbers below then decks, where they are obliged to languish in stench and dirt, by which cruel treatment, many have fallen sacrifice to diseases and the cruel hand of oppression. The New Jersey Gazette, June 16, 1779

Last Friday night, se'nnight[69], orders were issued by the commandant of the city, for all male inhabitants of a proper age, to assist in throwing up works on Governor's Island. The number of inhabitants it was imagined amounted to 4,000, half of whom were to go on fatigue one day and the other half the ensuing, Sundays not excepted. This our information were an eye witness to. The New Jersey Gazette, October 20, 1779

The fortunes of war changed a third time in 1779 and 1780 and it was the Americans who were reported as being bankrupt, ill supplied, starving and deserting in large numbers. Although exaggerated, there was discontent among many soldiers at their always late pay in virtually worthless script:

We hear that the General Assembly of New Jersey is now meeting and they are busy framing a law to impress every 8th Man in the Province to serve in the militia for the campaign of the year 1779. The New York Gazette, April 19, 1779

The clamor among the officers and men is so great in Elizabeth Town, owing to the little value of their pay, that a deputation lately went off to Head Quarters, demanding a gratuity of two hundred pounds per officer and forty dollars for each private, without which they determined not to serve, in consequence of which it was granted.
A dollar is usually paid a tonsor[70] to smooth the chin of a poor militia man. The Royal Gazette, May 22, 1779

The militia of Elizabeth town, which were reckoned to be 1,000 being last Monday ordered out to be drafted for service, the officers appeared, but not a single private soldier, the latter having declared that they would no longer leave their families to fight without pay, as the continental paper dollars are depreciated at Elizabeth town to a ridiculous estimate, a single silver Spanish dollar having there last week purchased thirty of the continental paper dollars. The Royal Gazette, June 12, 1779

Every fourth man has been ordered to be drafted from the Jersey militia to serve in the rebel army until the 26th of December; each devoted racoon to receive down forty soft or paper dollars, which rags now pass at the rate of near forty for one solid Spaniard dollar at the city of Philadelphia, the seat of the Rebel Rumps. The Royal Gazette, October 23. 1779

New York, July 17. In a small Township in New Jersey, called Pacquanock, about 8 miles from Morristown, containing about 300 houses, their Fines for not turning out on the late Alarm, amounted to 20,000 pounds. The inhabitants are chiefly Low Dutch. The New York Gazette, July 17, 1780

The obnoxious Rivington was anxious to publish these low points in patriot morale to all the world.

New York, August 26. The Debates in every Session of the Parliament affirming us, on this side of the Atlantic, continued proofs of their want of information concerning the real state of the Rebel Army, the Congress, their Finances &c, &c. The Printer,[James Rivington] with humble deference, presumes to address the following sketches found in truth, to the noble and honorable Members of both Houses in their approaching Session, as well as the Good People of England and Ireland at large.

Without money and without credit, the rebel interest is now supported by depredation and spoil. No man will now part with anything for paper money, old or new. The rebel commissaries have not credit for a farthing, in any part of the continent. In every place, they take what they want from the farmers, a horse, a cow, grain, hay, straw and leave a certificate to be paid at Doom's Day and, in spite of all this licentious, Washington's army between Pompton and Tapan are at three quarters of a pound allowance of flour and fresh meat.

At the late irruption of the Light Horse (about 60) to Bergen, on Sunday the 13th instant, they found the inhabitants going to church; some they insulted; others they robbed and condescended to such pitiful exploits as changing hats and clothes, taking the buckles from their shoes and, in one instance, stripping off a man's breeches and leaving an old pair of trousers to cover his nakedness.

The most horrible oppressions are at the same time used to force the militia to join them in their career of destruction. All their bands are made up of men and boys drafted from an unwilling militia, except the continentals who had earlier been beguiled to enlist in the continental army and whose times are not yet out or who, if they are, cannot get their dismissions.

The loyalists increase hourly. Scarce a day passes without fugitives to this place [New York], from the barbarities perpetrated by the usurpers in the upper parts of this, as well as from the neighboring provinces.

Resolutions are forming in the divers colonies to resist the freedoms taken with private property to support what the rebels call their army. In the southern part of Virginia, certain militia officers have laid down their commissions and several thousand have gone from North Carolina to join the King's troops on the advance into that province.

Yet, for all of this, Mr. Joseph Reed [President of the State of Pennsylvania] struts through Prince Town, boasting that his 500 recruits are 3,000, crying along the road our independency is established. So a drunken beggar calls himself a King, the sober spectators laugh at such a King and such a President, General or Counselor, or whatever else he is pleased to be settled, at the head of a mob, notoriously the minority of the province. The Royal Gazette, August 26, 1780

Indeed, in 1780 the odious, Rivington smugly advised the rebels that their cause was lost and urged them to seek their King's forgiveness:

To the Inhabitants of New Jersey.
To repeat former arguments against rebellion at this time would be useless. You have felt the effects of Congress in the ruin of your estates by their taxation as well as by the calamities of the war.

You have tried to start a new government and, instead of that liberty which you had fondly thought to attain, you have tyrants increase without number and your property taken from you without the least hope of satisfaction. You have been promised much by your French alliance, I appeal to yourselves for any benefit received by it. Every measure adopted has turned out to your distress. Is it not then the time to look back and restore that government, under which you flourished and grew rich and, I am truly sorry to tell you, wanton. You did not prize your happy state as you ought. Happy beyond any other people, you foolishly though to get more, by grasping at a phantom, you have lost substantial freedom. It is not yet too late. You see one GENERAL make his peace, and, in justifying his conduct, pointed out his duty. The conduct of others should show you that private interest, not public good, was and is the view of your leaders. Colonel Hamilton, in his letter to Sears, declares the Congress incompetent to govern and openly proposes ABSOLUTE GOVERNMENT. Be wise then. Take time by the forelock and, as I know you want a restoration of government, rather than a continuance of your agony and distress, rouse then, lest not a mistaken persistence in revolution (which is not fortitude but a false pride in being ashamed to acknowledge your errors) lead you to utter ruin. Return to the government of your merciful King, who, notwithstanding your unprovoked rebellion, is ready to receive you. One exertion makes you free. Try it. You will find the delusion vanish and will be amazed to see yourself once more happy and will only have to wonder and regret that you have been such dupes. One struggle will do it. Exert yourselves and you need not fear the event.
Z
The Royal Gazette, November 8, 1780

Without doubt, James Rivington knew how to infuriate the American rebels. He published an account as to how "Clarinda", a rebel maid had given a rose to British Lieutenant Colonel Cosmo Gordon to protect him from rebel sniper fire. "Clarinda", it was suggested, was Susan Livingston, daughter of Governor Livingston of New Jersey, a staunch foe of the British and the rose was intended to mean her virginity. Despite the purported protecting power of the flower Clarinda had given him, Gordon was nonetheless wounded.

The story brought an attack upon Rivington in the Jersey Journal of July 12, 1780 by the wronged lady:

Mr. Rivington, according to his usual practice, has asserted in his Gazette on the 29th ult., under the signature of one of my sex, the grossest falsehoods respecting what happened to Col. Gordon, near Governor Livingston's house, that ever entered into the hearts of man. Almost every syllable of that publication is a most villainous lie. There was not a single musket fired from behind the Governor's house nor field's, nor was it the Colonel that was wounded who had the rose in the morning, but a Colonel Wormb, an Hessian officer, who asked leave to pick one, as he was on his horse. This, Mr. Printer, you may depend upon as fact, and it is in the power of both Colonel Gordon and Col. Wormb to confirm my words.
I am your humble servant
CLARINDA

Rivington published Clarinda's charge, along with his own apology. He followed that with a fresh slur of Clarinda's chastity, this in the form of a gossipy letter received from "Rosalinda":

Mr. Rivington presents his most respectful compliments to Clarinda and assures her he is perfectly innocent of the charge respecting the Rose and all other imputations in the above address. He has not printed or published directly or indirectly, a single title upon the subject and he takes leave to add that no Lady will from his performances, ever meet with injury or disgust.

CARD to Mr. Rivington
Rosalinda presents her compliments to Mr. Rivington, regretting the name of one of her sex should be connected with terms [as used by Clarinda]. However his [Rivington's] zeal and loyalty may urge him to be poetical in his prose productions occasionally, the world at large must acquit him of having merited the unguarded attack of the Clarinda of Chatham.. Rosalinda is informed that the British officer [Gordon] refused the honor of the Rose by Clarinda, very grateful for the favor that he will not relinquish his right to it and for the first time (and, as he says, he hopes the last time in his life) he brags of the Lady's Favor. It is whispered that on return from

the excursion, notwithstanding that he wore the sweet present next to his left breast, the afternoon he received another, in the vicinity of Mr. Livingston's house, tho' also very honorable, was not so agreeable as that he had the pleasure to receive at 4 o'clock that morning!" The Royal Gazette, July 22, 1780

A form of propaganda was the reporting -- and often the misreporting and exaggeration -- of atrocities committed by the enemy army. All too often, however, as set out in a chapter within, there were in fact some ugly incidents of barbarism on both sides, an unattractive aspect of the Revolution rarely reviewed. How much truth is there and how much propaganda in the following accounts? First, English allegations of American atrocities:

New York, October 21. A body of the Rebels skulked over on Saturday sen'night from the New Jersey shore to Staten Island, and, after, cowardly setting fire to two or three farm houses, skulked back again to their former station. Probably, from their conduct, it might be judged that these were the same people, who, about the middle of last August, committed such an act of villainous barbarity, as cannot be recited without indignation. A very little boy, belonging to an officer of the army, was playing by himself upon the shore of Staten Island, when about seven or eight of the rifle men or Ragged Men, came down slyly and discharged their muskets upon him. Immediately upon the small creature's falling, they gave three cheers and retired. This was a most cruel, dastardly and infamous Murder upon a defenseless, innocent child. Rivington's New York Loyal Gazette, October 20, 1777

On Sunday morning last, a party of refugees went from New York, in boats, to Closter, a settlement abounding with many violent rebels and persecutors of loyal subjects and who are almost daily offering some fresh instance of barbarity. The party, on their approach to the settlement, being fired upon by the militia from the houses, were obliged to lay them in ashes, and after pursuing the runaways, killing five or six and wounding many and bringing in four prisoners, returned to this City, having one man slightly wounded from a random shot on re-embarking. On the party's first arrival at

Closter, they found a sign affixed on several houses, printed papers with the following:
"No Quarters shall be given to Refugees"

Some time since, Mr. Meyers, an Ensign in a company of refugees, was killed in a skirmish with a party of rebels near Closter, the inhabitants of that place after his death, stripped his corpse naked, hung him up by the neck, where he was exhibited as a public spectacle for many hours.

The inhabitants of Closter have been remarkable for their persecution of, and cruelty to all the friends of government and had fixed up in many of their houses advertisements, in which they expressed their determination of giving no quarter to refugees and requested all Continental soldiers and militia to refuse them quarters. The Royal Gazette, May 13, 1779

Likewise, the Americans told sensational tales of British atrocities to excite their readership to a hatred of the foe, as evidence by the following extract of a letter "from an officer of distinction in the American Camp":

Since I wrote to you this morning, I have had an opportunity of hearing a number of the particulars of the horrid depredations committed by that part of the British army, which was stationed at and near Pennytown, under the command of Lord Cornwallis. Besides the sixteen young women who fled into the woods in order to avoid their brutality, and were there seized and carried off, one man had the cruel mortification to have his wife and only daughter (a child of ten years of age) ravished; this he himself, almost choked with grief, uttered in lamentation to his friend, who told me of it and also informed me that another girl of thirteen years of age was taken from her father's house, carried to a barn about a mile and then ravished, and, afterwards, made use of by five more of these brutes. Wanton mischief was seen in every part of the country; everything portable, they plunder and carry off; neither age nor sex, Whig or Tory, is spared. Infants, children, old men and women are left in their shirts, without a blanket to cover them in this inclement season; furniture of every kind, destroyed or burnt; windows and doors, broken to pieces; in short, the house left uninhabitable, the people left without provisions. Another instance of their brutality happened near Woodbridge. One of the most respectable men in that part of the country was alarmed by the cries and shrieks of a most lovely daughter. He found an officer, a British officer, in the act of ravishing her. He instantly put him to death. Two other officers rushed in with fusees and fired two balls in to the father, who is now languishing under his wounds.

I am tired of this horrid scene. Almighty justice cannot suffer it to go unpunished. He will inspirit his people (who only claim the liberty to which he has entitled them) to do themselves justice, to rise universally in arms and drive these invading tyrants out of the country.

Published by Order of the Council on Safety
Geo. Bickham, Secretary pro tem
The Pennsylvania Evening Post, December 28, 1776

The enemy was very cruel in their retreat. They, seeing a poor countryman standing at his door, laid hold of him; he showed a protection signed by Gen. Howe's secretary. They damned him and his protection and immediately sent a ball through his body, which not proving instant death, they stabbed him with bayonets. After such an instance, it is not to be wondered at their beating the brains out of our wounded. The Pennsylvania Journal, March 5, 1777

In his rout [from Brunswick to Amboy], he, Sir William Howe, stole everything worth carrying off, burnt Somerset Court House, meeting house and a great number of other houses, wheat &c. and hung up three women (two of them by their feet at the head of the army) whom he imagined were spies. In short, his whole progress through this part of the country is marked with devastation and cruelty, more like the savages of the wilderness, than that of Britons, once famed for honor and humanity, the characteristics of brave men. The Pennsylvania Journal, June 25, 1777

Examination of Abraham Orsoe, late of Sing Sing,[71] in Westchester county, state of New York, taken before Brigadier Gen. M'Dougall, at Peet's-kill,[72]

June 15, 1777

> He declares that he left this place on the 11th of May last and, on the 13th, he was taken by a party of Capt. Pike's Company of the enemy's new levies, between Pumpton and Morristown, and by them carried to the guardhouse, where he was very ill treated for five days and obliged to enlist; that he received no pay, nor could he learn whether any of the new corps on Bergen had received any; that they were frequently told by their officers, when they asked for pay, that they must plunder for it; that no provisions were served to the levies but subsisted wholly by plunder from the inhabitants; that their officers always told them, when out on a party, to take care of themselves; that Tory women frequently came to the officers to inform them where they might take Whigs. The Pennsylvania Evening Post, July 1, 1777

The ultimate "insult" to the American cause was the charge made by Rivington that Congress, predominantly, if not exclusive, Protestant, was embracing Roman Catholic rituals, so as to curry French and Spanish assistance

> On Monday the 4th instant was celebrated at Philadelphia, the funeral of the Spanish Resident[73] who lately died at Morris Town. The following was the order of Procession

The Bier covered with Black Cloth
Monsieur Lucerne, the French Resident
The Congress
The General Officers
The Citizens

> When the procession arrived at the Roman Catholic chapel, the priest presented the holy water to Monsieur Lucerne, who, after sprinkling himself, presented it to Mr. Huntington, President of the Congress. The Calvinist paused a considerable time, near a minute, but, at length, his affection for the great and good ally conquered all scruples of conscience and he too besprinkled and anointed himself with all the adroitness of a veteran Catholic, which his brothers of the Congress perceiving, they all, without hesitation, followed the righteous example of their proselyted President. Before the Company, which was extremely numerous, left the chapel, curiosity

induced some persons to uncover the Bier, when they were highly enraged at finding the whole a sham, there being no corpse under the cloth, the body of the Spanish gentleman, having been several days before interred at Morris Town. The bier was surrounded by wax candles and every member of the egregious Congress, now reconciled to the Popish Communion, carried a taper in his hand. The Royal Gazette, May 20, 1780

Sometimes, were today's reader to lay British and American accounts of the same battle side by side, he could not determine which army had won the battle. For example, the Battle of Princeton, when General Washington had won with the clever feint, earlier described, has always been considered an American victory and was reported a such by the American press:

About seven hundred British troops [leaving Princeton] saw our army about a mile and a half distant. They returned to the town and made ready to receive us. General Mercer's Brigade did not fire until they [the enemy] advanced within forty yards. The enemy received the brigade with charged bayonets. General Mercer was wounded (it is said by a ball flred but it is a fact that he was afterwards wounded in the belly by a bayonet). I fancy the enemy found it impossible to escape, as our troops all began to rally and join in the pursuit. They all dropped their packs and flew with the utmost precipitation and we pursued with great eagerness. The town surrendered and about sixty, including fourteen officers, surrendered. We have taken in the whole about three hundred, about thirty killed and fifty wounded. I have no doubt that others will be brought in. We lost about thirty killed and thirty wounded. We took three pieces of brass artillery. The Pennsylvania Evening Post, January 16, 1777

The *New York Gazette,* under editor Rivington, gave a different account of the same battle[74]:

Several skirmishes between the King's troops and the Rebels have lately happened in the Jersies. But the most distinguished rencounter occurred on the 3d instant, near Princeton. The 17th Regiment consisting of less than 300 men fell in with the Rebel army of between 5 and 6,000, whom they attacked with all the ardor and intrepidity of Britons. They received the fire of the Rebels from behind a fence, over which they immediately leaped upon their enemies, who presently [fled and] left their very cannon behind them. The soldiers immediately turned the cannon and fired at least twenty Rounds upon their rear. . . This has been one of the most splendid actions of the whole campaign and has given a convincing proof that British valor has not declined from its ancient glory.. . . The loss was about twenty killed and eighty wounded of the troops; of the Rebels, above 400 killed and wounded. Among their slain were eleven officers. Mr. Mercer (one of the wounded Rebel officers, since dead) when he was taken up by our people, asked how many the numbers were, who had thus attacked him, and, upon being told, he cried out with astonishment: "My God! Is it possible? I have often heard of British courage, but never could have imagined to find such an instance as this!"

Another Account says, that the 17th Regiment, just before they charged the Rebels, deliberately pulled off their knapsacks and gave three cheers and then broke through the Rebels, faced about, attacked and broke through a second time. Col. Mawhood then said it would be prudent, as they were so few, to retire upon which the men, one and all, cried out" No! No! Let us attack them again." And, it was with great Difficulty that their Colonel could get them to retreat, which at length they performed in the utmost order.

To the Honor of this brave Regiment, both as soldiers and as men, not one of them has ever attempted to plunder or to encourage others to do it.

In the several Skirmishes, the Rebels have lost above 700 Men. Rivington's New York Loyal Gazette, January 13, 1777

The newspapers even allowed - again probably for the first time - the chiefs of state to publicly engage in verbal skirmishes. The American papers reported those duels, usually in the form of letters, in which their champion had the last word. The Loyalist Press, of course, did the same. The first bit of correspondence between Governor William Livingston of New Jersey and James Robertson, the Civil Governor of British occupied New York City. Robertson wrote to Livingston to complain about the treatment to be inflicted upon some British subjects:

> New York, January 4, 1778
>
> Sir
>
> I am interrupted in my daily attempts to soften the calamities of prisoners and reconcile their case with our security, by a general cry of resentment, arising from an information that officers in the king's service, taken on the 27th of November, and Mr. John Brown, a deputy commissary, are to be tried in Jersey for high treason and that Mr. Iliff and another prisoner have been hanged.
>
> Though I am not authorized to threaten or to sooth, my wish to prevent an increase of horrors, will justify my using the liberty of an old acquaintance to desire your interposition to put an end to, or to prevent measures, which, if pursued, on one side, would tend to prevent every act of humanity on the other...
>
> I need not point out to you all the cruel consequences of a such a procedure. I am hopeful you will prevent them and excuse this trouble, Sir, from
>
> > Your obedient humble servant
> > James Robertson

Livingston's reply dripped with sarcasm and scores one for the newborn American propaganda machine:

> Sir, Having received a letter under your signature, dated the 4th instant, I sit down to answer your inquiries concerning certain officers in the service of your king, taken on Staten Island, and one Browne who calls himself a deputy commissary and also respecting one Ilif and another prisoner (I suppose you must mean John Mee, he having shared the fate you mention), who have been hanged.
>
> Boskirk, Earl and Hammel[75], who are, I presume, the officers intended, with the said Browne, were sent to me by General Dickinson as prisoners taken on Staten Island. Finding them all to be subjects of this State and to have committed treason against it, the council of safety committed them to the Trenton goal. At the same time, I acquainted General Washington, that if he chose to treat the three first, who were British officers as prisoners of war, I doubted not that the council of safety would be satisfied. General Washington has since informed me that he intends to consider them as such and they are therefore at his service, whenever the commissary of

prisoners shall direct concerning them. Brown, I am told, committed several robberies in this State before he took sanctuary in Staten Island and I should scarcely imagine that he has expiated the guilt of his former crimes by committing the greater one of joining the enemies of his country. However, if General Washington chooses to consider him also a prisoner of war, I shall not interpose in the matter.

Iliff was executed, after a trial by a jury, for enlisting our subjects, himself being one, as recruits in the British army and he was apprehended on his way with them to Staten Island. Had he never been subject to this State, he would have forfeited his life as a spy. Mee was one of his company and had also procured our subjects to enlist in the service of the enemy.

If these transactions, Sir, shall induce you to countenance greater severities to our people, whom the fortune of war has thrown into your power, than they have already suffered, you will pardon me for thinking that you go farther out of your way and find palliatives for inhumanity, than necessity seems to require. And, if this be the cry of murder to which you allude as having reached your ears, I sincerely pity your ears for being so frequently assaulted with cries of murder much more audible, because much less distant -- I mean the cries of your prisoners who are constantly perishing in the goals of New York (the cruelest and most deliberate kind of murder) from the rigorous manner of your treatment.

I am will due respect, your most humble servant
William Livingston

P.S. You have distinguished me with a title which I have neither authority nor ambition to assume. I know of no man, sir, who bears sway in this state. It is our peculiar felicity, and our superiority over the tyrannical system we have discarded, that we are not swayed by men. In New Jersey, sir, the laws alone bear sway. The New Jersey Gazette, January 14, 1778

Another exchange was between Governor Livingston of New Jersey again and Sir Henry Clinton, Commander in Chief of British forces in America, who was headquartered in New York City. In it, Clinton is the clear winner but, in the war of propaganda, there will be another battle soon:

SIR

I beg leave to acquaint you that I am possessed of the most authentic proofs of a General Officer of your Command having offered a large sum of money to an inhabitant of this state to assassinate me, in case, he could not take me alive; this, sir, is so repulsive to the character which I had heretofore formed of Sir Henry Clinton that I think it highly improbable that you should either countenance, contrive at or be privy to a design so sanguinary and disgraceful. Taking it for granted, however, that you are a gentleman of too much spirit to disown any thing you think improper to abet, I give you this Opportunity for disavowing such dark proceedings, if undertaken, without your Approbation, assuring you, at the same time, that, if countenanced by you, your Person is more in my Power than I have reason to think you imagine.

William Livingston

To which, Sir Henry replied:

SIR,

As you address me on a grave subject, no less than life or death, and your own person concerned, I condescend to answer you, but will not be troubled with any further correspondence from Mr. Livingston.

Had I a soul so capable of harboring such an infamous idea as assassination, you, Sir, at least, would have nothing to fear, for, be assured, I would not blacken myself with so foul a crime to obtain so trifling an end.

Sensible of the power you have of being able to dispose of my life by means of intimates of yours, ready to murder at your command, I can only congratulate you on your amiable connections and acknowledge myself

Your most humble servant

H. Clinton

The New York Gazette, April 19, 1779

CHAPTER 6

The War: 1777

In the latter half of 1776, England had seized New York City. Later that year, in pursuit of a retreating Washington, the British army crossed the Hudson River and invaded New Jersey to the west. Meeting no sustained resistance from the rebels, the British decided to winter there, waiting until spring to finish off the dwindling, deserting Continental Army. British camps were set up all across the state, from Trenton to Bergen.

The American army had indeed been on the run. Since the Battle of Long Island, the prior summer, Washington had had a succession of defeats that eventually forced him to withdraw from New York, retreating across New Jersey, to Pennsylvania, with a slow moving British Army in pursuit. However, at Christmas time 1776 and in early January, 1777, General Washington miraculously had turned the tide, if only temporarily, engineering splendid victories at Trenton and Princeton. General Howe, stung by Washington's unexpected counter punch against these British outposts, united his forces into a single winter camp at New Brunswick, New Jersey on the Raritan River, some few miles slightly southwest of Staten Island. In response, Washington moved his forces from Valley Forge, Pennsylvania to Morris Town, New Jersey, where, in crude huts and ill supplied, they spent an uncomfortable winter, watching the enemy and wondering what it planned for the spring.

The major war activity during this winter was at New Brunswick and its nearby towns. Some had familiar names like Piscataway, Rahway, Woodbridge and Perth Amboy. Others had names strange to us today, -- Spanktown and Squabble or Quibble Town. The story of the war in New Jersey during the winter of 1777 is told in a series of news accounts, often extracts of letters from soldiers home. There were dozens of skirmishes between the hungry British, looking for food in the rebel New Jersey countryside, and the American sharpshooters, eager to inflict some punishment on their enemy. First, the Americans attempted to win back some of the towns where the British still had a presence:

I am just arrived with Major Mifflin from an expedition in the lower parts of the Jerseys, a place called Monmouth Court House. We arrived there Thursday evening. We were informed of a party of men consisting of about 200, under the command of Col. John Morris. We then formed our party (120 in number) in proper order and intended to attack them that night. Col. Morris, it seems, got notice of our arrival, had his baggage loaded and his men formed to draw off for Middletown, about 18 miles from the Court House. We came up about a quarter of an hour before dark and engaged them; a very heavy fire was kept up by both sides and the enemy stood us about eight minutes, then gave way and retreated precipitately; at this time, it was quite dark and we could not see what loss the enemy sustained. On our side, we had none killed. Next morning, we sent a party out to the field we had engaged in; they brought back four dead bodies which we buried. We took, during the engagement, 23 prisoners and brought them to this place. We also took seven wagon loads of stores &c. and twelve horses. The Pennsylvania Journal, January 29, 1777

By letters from General Washington's army of the eighth, tenth and eleventh instant, we have the following authentic intelligence viz. that our army marched from Pluckemin and arrived at Morristown on the sixth; that Gen. Maxwell, with a considerable body of Continental troops and militia, advanced and took possession of [Elizabeth] town and made prisoners fifty Waldeckers and forty Highlanders who were quartered there and made prize of a schooner with baggage and some blankets on board. At about the same time, one thousand bushels of salt were secured by our troops at a place called Spanktown, about five miles from Woodbridge. When a party of our men attacked the troops there, they sent for reinforcements but the Hessians absolutely refused to march, having heard we were very numerous in that quarter. The English troops at Elizabeth Town would not suffer the Waldeckers to stand sentry at the out posts; several of them have deserted and come over to us.

The main body of the enemy is at Brunswick; they also have some troops at Amboy, where some men of war and transports are collected, it is supposed, to take off the baggage. The Pennsylvania Evening Post, January 16, 1777

The Americans tried to contain the British at New Brunswick and Amboy and whacked them whenever they sought forage in the countryside. It proved to be quite a successful and satisfying tactic throughout the winter, as the following collection of news items from central New Jersey skirmishes suggests:

Within these three or four days, there have been several skirmishes in East Jersey, in which our troops have always beaten the enemy. About three miles up the Raritan from Brunswick, a party of our enemy attacked a large body of the enemy and took near six hundred head of cattle, upwards of fifty wagons, and a number of English horses, of the dray breed, which were so excessively emaciated that they were scarce able to walk. The Pennsylvania Evening Post, January 23, 1777

We have hemmed the enemy and are beginning to pinch them. On the 23d ult., we trimmed two regiments, near to Woodbury, killed thirty privates and some officers. Had Col. ---, who commanded, behaved well, we should have destroyed one regiment. He is now under arrest. We lost no men that day.
On the first instant, three thousand of the enemy, under the command of Sir William Erskine, came out of Brunswick to

forage. They had eight pieces of cannon. Several of our scouting parties joined to the amount of six hundred men, under the Command of Col. Scott of the Fifth Virginia regiment. A disposition was made to attack the enemy. [After some fighting] superior numbers at last, prevailed. Our troop retreated about a quarter of a mile, formed again, and looked the enemy in the face until they retreated. The enemy had thirty six killed, that the country people saw, and upwards of one hundred wounded. We have lost three officers and twelve privates and have as about as many wounded. The Pennsylvania Gazette, March 5, 1777

The officer who commanded the two thousand British troops going as a reinforcement from Amboy to Brunswick, we hear, is now under arrest for undertaking, like Don Quixote, to do impossibilities and get himself a great and immortal name. For this purpose, instead of marching directly to Brunswick, which he might have done, must needs go fourteen miles out of the direct road to take prisoners General Maxwell and his party at Spanktown and to make his triumphant entry into Brunswick, leading his captives in chains, like an old Roman General, in which he found his fatal mistake too late to remedy, for he found he had surrounded a nest of American hornets, who soon put his whole body to flight, pursued them to Amboy and obliged them to get back on the ships again, since when they have never ventured a second time to reinforce their cooped up brethren in Brunswick. The Pennsylvania Evening Post, March 15, 1777

General Maxwell attacked the enemy on Saturday last, near Quibble or Squable Town[76], as they were penetrating into the Country for provender, most kinds of which are most wanted among them. We had three men slightly wounded, none killed or taken; the enemy left four dead on the field and carried off numbers as usual, which, by accounts of witnesses, were twenty and numbers wounded also. Their rear was so closely pursued that they left one wagon behind; the three prisoners are just arrived and they say the 42d or Highland Watch, suffered greatly in the last action.

By accounts from New Jersey, we learn that deserters daily come over from the enemy, who are penned up in Brunswick, so that they never peep out, but our people have a knock on them, which as often turns out in our favor. One of which skirmishes happened on Tuesday the 18th instant, where we took several wagons, 8 prisoners and found four or five dead in the field. The Pennsylvania Evening Post, March 25, 1777

On Sunday the 22 ult., the enemy came out from Amboy, to bring in the property of one Barnes, who had gone over, when our people stationed near Woodbridge, attacked them and had a pretty smart shooting match, while they were retiring with the effects. About the same time, the enemy attempted to land from some boats on Woodbridge Neck and at Smith's Farm, to take off some cattle and hay, but, in this they were disappointed, as our people distributed them and took the cattle and burnt the hay. The Pennsylvania Journal, April 2, 1777

A Gentleman from Head Quarters in the Jerseys acquaints us, that when he came away, both Armies seemed disposed to remain quiet. That the enemy were lurking within the scanty confines of Brunswick and Amboy, surrounded by detached corp of our troops, whose advantageous situation enabled them to discover and to repel any plundering party that hunger could force to sally out. Scarce a day passed without an attempt to forage and plunder, but the vigilance and bravery of our troops obliged the enemy to return, commonly without plunder and often with a very great loss of their men. The enemy too well know the fate that must attend their passing the woods and mountains which leads to Morris County, to hazard such an expedition. He further acquaints us that 200 Hessians were lately disarmed upon a repeated refusal to obey orders when commanded to annoy and attack some of our advanced parties.

The Gentleman further remarks that he could not believe it was within the power of any events to have made so great of an alteration in the sentiments and spirits of the people in so short of a time. The repeated failures of [the British] military operations have cast such reproach upon their arms, that those who were frightened with General Howe's successes and begged his pardon and protection have almost to a man returned to the cause and are now fighting for the defense of their country. The Pennsylvania Gazette, April 9, 1777

Although the Americans kept the British penned up and starving, the enemy fought back, on occasion with some success - that is, if you could believe James Rivington and his "lying" Gazette:

On Saturday the 8th instant, one of our foraging Parties surprised a Body of the Rebels at Quibble Town, about six Miles beyond Brunswick, and took the whole Magazine of Forage, which they had collected at that Place. They killed about 12 of the Rebels and took one of their Captain and 5 others prisoner.

Last Wednesday in the Night, a Detachment of the Troops, under Major Gordon, passed over from Staten Island to the Cedars beyond Sandy Hook and surprised a Party of Rebels which had for some time infested Shrewsbury and the adjacent Country. They killed 25 of them and took 70 Prisoners, with the loss of only one man. The whole rebel Army in the Jerseys we hear, does not exceed 6,000 Men[77]. *The New York Gazette, February 17, 1777*

General Cornwallis, who was commanding the British army in New Jersey, appeared content, having roared once or twice, and retired into his cave at New Brunswick all winter, not to engage in the spring the American reinforcements rushing to the scene. Of late, the British seemed to be doing all sorts of strange things:

Philadelphia. A gentleman from camp informs that the British Troops at Perth Amboy, in number about three thousand, last Tuesday morning, embarked on board several transports and sailed out of Sandy Hook, under convoy of three men of war, but, in the evening, they returned and disembarked, under the cover of the night, on Staten Island. This maneuver, it is supposed, was intended to make the appearance of a reinforcement from Europe and which the Tories have industriously reported to be real. The Pennsylvania Evening Post, April 5, 1777

Actually, the British did have a plan afoot. It was to split New England off from the rest of colonies by controlling the Hudson River from its mouth in New York City, all the way north to loyal Canada. General Burgoyne was to go south down the river from Canada to Albany, where he would meet up with General Howe and his army who were to have marched and sailed up the Hudson from their base in New York City. What would help this plan was to have the Americans believe that the British objective was still Philadelphia, as it had appeared to have been the prior winter. If he thought this, then Washington might re-deploy his troops further south and away from the Hudson. Indeed, in consequence of the very fear that the next campaign would focus upon Philadelphia, Washington, at the end of May, 1777, had in fact moved his army somewhat south, away from the Hudson River and toward Philadelphia to Middlebrook, in the Wachung mountains above Bound Brook:

We can with pleasure inform our readers that General Washington has now received such supplies of men &c. that he has removed from his head quarters from Morris Town to Middle Brook, on the east side of the Raritan, within seven miles and a half of Brunswick, where his army (which is not composed of soldiers, whose time of service is continually expiring but of those enlisted for the war) are now encamped and make a show that must please every person who is not a Tory.

From our posts near Middle Brook, we are able to see and watch the movements of the enemy, who are encamped on Brunswick Hills, the west side of the Raritan. *The Pennsylvania Gazette, June 4, 1777*

Rather than expanding their hold in New Jersey, the British seemed indecisive, sometimes acting as if they were considering withdrawal from the state altogether:

Philadelphia. By advices this day from the East Jerseys, we learn that the enemy are abandoning Brunswick, having sent some of their cannon and stores to Staten Island and that Cortland Skinner had sent all his furniture from Amboy to New York. Sickness among the Hessian Soldiers and the excessive fatigue of the British is said to be the occasion of this maneuver; however that may be, we have another incident of Howe's declining a general engagement with Washington. The Pennsylvania Evening Post, May 3, 1777

Skirmishing throughout eastern and central New Jersey, of course, continued, while all awaited Lord Howe's next move:

Post, Bonham Town, May 11
I have the pleasure to inform you that yesterday afternoon, part of Gen. Stevens division attacked the Royal Highlanders and six companies of light infantry. It was a bold enterprise, they being posted within two miles of Bonham town and about the same distance from Brunswick. The action continued about an hour and a half. The Continental troops behave well; drove in the pickets at Bonham, attacked and drove the Highlanders out of a wood they had taken possession

of near Piscataqua town. The enemy were reinforced but again compelled to give way. They were reinforced a second time and it was advisable to retire. The retreat was made in excellent order and our loss is inconsiderable.

The Highlanders, obstinately brave, were too proud to surrender, which cost many of them dear. We are told that the enemy allowed that they had one Major and one Captain mortally wounded and since dead, two Lieutenants wounded and 65 privates killed and wounded. The Pennsylvania Journal, May 21, 1777

Last Saturday week General Stephens ordered eight hundred men, from different regiments, to muster at Col. Cook's quarters, about nine miles from Matuchin meeting house. In the afternoon, they marched over Dismal Swamp and advanced to the place where the enemy kept their picket and, where the enemy, having observed our motions had collected some three hundred men. [A battle ensued] which was pretty warm for some time. By the best accounts from the inhabitants since come out of Brunswick, the enemy had near a hundred killed and many wounded. This may seem very extraordinary but when you consider we had a number of good riflemen and many excellent marksmen well posted in the woods and other suitable places, the enemy in the open field and frequently in confusion, I think you will be reconciled to their losses so far exceeding ours [2 killed, 23 wounded and/or captured]. This action was conducted by General Maxwell and the troops were Jersey men, Pennsylvanians and Virginians. The Pennsylvania Evening Post, May 24, 1777

In the course of this week, we have had between twenty and thirty deserters. A few days ago, we sent out a scouting party, from which a Lieutenant Martin, with ten men, was dispatched as an advance scout, who soon fell in with and engaged a party of Hessian and British light horse, fifteen in number. At the first fire, he killed the commander of the gang, but they spurring up, our men gave way and left the Lieutenant on the field, who was soon surrounded and, although calling out for quarter, was butchered with the greatest cruelty; seventeen wounds were plain to be seen, most of which, it is said, were sufficient singly to prove mortal. The Pennsylvania Evening Post, June 14, 1777

For a short while, it looked as if a major battle were shaping up between some 11,000 British troops and almost twice that many Americans. The British took up positions at Middlebush and Millstone and appeared to dare Washington to attack. The stand off is described by General Benedict Arnold, at the time, still a loyal American officer:

Corell's Ferry, June 17, 1777 -- 11 o'clock at night
Dear General Mifflin,
I have received no intelligence from General Washington since four o'clock last evening, at which time the enemy were encamped at Somerset Courthouse, supposed to be eleven thousand in number, under the command of Generals Howe and Cornwallis. This is doubtless their main body. Their first design seems to have been to have cut off General Sullivan's retreat and possess themselves of this place. Finding Gen. Sullivan had frustrated their intentions by a forced march, they appear to have given over their first design and now wish to draw Gen. Washington from his stronghold, which, if they effect, probably a body from Brunswick would take possession of, Gen. Washington will doubtless disappoint them as he remains quiet in his encampment. The militia turned out in great numbers in the Jerseys. Gen. Sullivan has gone to Flemming Town, twelve miles from this. The troop that arrive here are immediately sent after him. I am very fearful that the enemy will retire to Brunswick before you arrive with your reinforcements and oblige us to attack them at a disadvantage; for fight them we must, when all our reinforcements are in; we cannot avoid it with honor. Our men are in high spirits and, in

a few days, we shall have upwards of twenty thousand. Gen. Putnam has eight thousand with him. Gen. Washington has wrote three days since for four thousand to be sent immediately to him.

I expect to hear every minute from our army and the enemy.

I am &c
B. Arnold
The Pennsylvania Evening Post, June 17, 1777

When Washington did not bite, the British changed their strategy dramatically, withdrawing to New Brunswick and then to Perth Amboy. The fleeing British, burned and plundered along the way out of the state:

Philadelphia, June 24. By an express arrived yesterday afternoon from New Jersey, we have the important intelligence of the enemy's having retreated from Somerset Court house to Brunswick and were in their march from that place to Amboy, destroying many valuable houses along the way and exercising the usual barbarity to the inhabitants in their power, that a part of our army has taken possession of Brunswick, while a large number were in pursuit of the enemy and had engaged some of their rear guard. The Pennsylvania Packet, June 24th, 1777

Gen. Wayne with his brigade pushed the enemy so close that they retired from redoubt to redoubt, without having time to form. All the troops that came in pushed forward with vigor. The enemy seems to retire to Amboy in haste. They were pushed to Piscataway by Col. Morgan's Rifleman (a fine corps) and the troops under Gen. Green and must have suffered considerably. Our loss is three or four killed and as many wounded. They have burnt numbers of houses and their whole possessions show what they must have suffered last winter. Indeed, their waste exceeds all that I could fancy, tho' often described to me. They have lost their reputation, their troops dispirited, their plans subverted, a new scene of action to commence and, of course, one half of the campaign lost to them.

Our troops are in good health, high spirits and ready to pursue the blow. The Pennsylvania Packet, June 24th, 1777

General Washington issued reports to the Continental Congress, sitting in Philadelphia, regarding the British departure from the state. As was his custom, he was generous in his praise of his fighting men, especially the New Jersey militia:

When I had the honor of addressing you last, I informed you that the main body of the enemy had marched from Brunswick and extended their van as far as Somerset Court House. I am now to acquaint you they changed their ground yesterday morning and returned to Brunswick again, burning as they went several valuable dwelling houses.

I must observe, and with particular satisfaction I do it, that, on the first notice of the enemy's movements, the militia assembled in the most spirited manner, firmly determined to give them every annoyance in their power and to afford us every possible aid. This I thought it my duty to mention in justice to their conduct and I am inclined to believe that General Howe's return, thus suddenly made, must have been in consequence of the information that he had received that the people were in and flying to arms in every quarter to oppose him. The Pennsylvania Packet, June 24th, 1777

What did this withdrawal by the British mean? Would Howe concentrate his forces on the Hudson or try a second assault on Philadelphia?

A great part of [the British] force has passed the [Raritan] River and are stationed between it and Amboy and, from every circumstance, there is the strongest reason to believe, have given up all hopes of passing to the Delaware [River] by land. . . What their design might be is, as yet,

uncertain, whether to push up the North [Hudson] River to New England, or, southward, to the Delaware; but, this I am confident, that they have no chance of considerable reinforcements or making any capital stroke, unless by a sudden removal, they may surprise some part of the continent.
The Pennsylvania Journal, June 25, 1777

[The enemy] has retired to Amboy, where we now hear their main body has reached and their advanced guard about four miles between Woodbridge and Bonham Town. The enemy has thrown their bridge (destined for the Delaware) across the Sound from Amboy to Staten Island, by which it is clear they design to retreat if closely pushed. The weather last night and this morning has been so wet that nothing could be done otherwise. . . Their retreat has been attended with such a destruction of property that marks their despair of possessing this country. The Pennsylvania Journal, June 25, 1777

The British were indeed abandoning their positions in New Jersey, which they had invaded the prior November. And they left with little about which to brag:[78]

Last Sunday, we discovered the enemy ferrying over from the Amboys to Staten Island and this morning we took four Tories who were coming over to throw themselves on the mercy of their country. They related that they went as wagoners with the British army from Brunswick to Somerset and expected that they were coming to Philadelphia; that they retreated with them to Brunswick, from thence to Amboy and then to Staten Island; that, as far as they could learn, General Howe retreated because he did not think proper to attack General Washington or to leave him in his rear, while he should attempt a march to Philadelphia; that some said in the army that they were going to England; others, that they were going up the North River; others, up the East River; but that they were all in great confusion. They have pitched their tents upon Staten Island. The Pennsylvania Evening Post, June 26, 1777

Since our last, we have certain intelligence, that soon after he skirmish with Lord Sterling's division[79] the enemy filed off from Westfield to Amboy and, from thence, to Staten Island and left us in the entire possession of New Jersey, in a small part of which they had been penned up for six months, unable to do any great matters, except stealing a few cattle and making Whigs of the wavering and diffident.
The Pennsylvania Journal, July 9, 1777

Surprised at Trenton and Princeton, "penned up" at New Brunswick, and chased out of Amboy, the British never accomplished their planned overland route to Philadelphia. New Jersey had proven too stubborn an obstacle:

The people of England are in daily expectation of receiving the news of Philadelphia's being in the hands of their General. Every ship that arrives, they are looking for important intelligence. With what surprise, will they hear that General Howe has thrice undertaken the expedition, twice by land and once by water; that his heart has both times failed him and that he has not dared to put the matter to the trial; that less than three thousand men insulted him in New Jersey and confined his whole army in New Brunswick; that, when he dared to march a few miles from that place, our brave countrymen chased him from the state; and, when his fleet and army, changing their route, arrived at the mouth of the Delaware, the very report of our preparations melted their hearts and they shrunk back, baffled in their so long boasted enterprise. The Pennsylvania Evening Post, August 2, 1777

But Howe was adamant and would seek again to get his army to Philadelphia. While this fixation was to adversely affect Pennsylvanians and New Jerseyans on both sides of the

Delaware for some months to come, it proved, in the long run, to be a godsend for the Americans. By choosing to attack Philadelphia, Howe had abandoned Burgoyne, in their plot to take the Hudson, to his own devices in northern New York. Encountering more resistance from the Americans than anticipated and without Howe's assistance, Burgoyne was badly beaten at the Battles of Bennington and Saratoga. These victories encouraged France, Britain's ancient enemy, to join the American cause, thus radically changing the course of the war.

Chastened by his attempt to move across New Jersey, Howe chose to conquer Philadelphia by water. He sent his fleet of warships and troop transports south to the Delaware, a prospect those in Philadelphia greeted with concern:

The fleet is standing in again. Forty five sail in sight. The wind at E. which is more favorable for them. It appears to me that they are bound up our [Philadelphia's] bay. The Pennsylvania Evening Post, July 31, 1777

At eight this morning, the fleet stood off, steering E. N. E. and are now out of sight and have been these three hours. This morning, I was, with many others, of the opinion that they were bound up the Delaware, but, as they could have got in this morning, but did not, I am now of the opinion they are making a feint. If so, they have a fresh wind at S. S. W., which will carry them to the eastward very fast. I believe their whole fleet was in sight, although I could count only one hundred and ninety sail. I shall send off an express if the fleet appears. The Pennsylvania Evening Post, August 2, 1777

Instead of coming up the Delaware directly, Howe landed in the Chesapeake Bay and marched his troops to Philadelphia. Washington challenged them at the Battle of Brandywine and Germantown but was soundly beaten. Howe continued on to Philadelphia. At his approach, the Continental

Congress fled to York, Pennsylvania. On September 26, 1777, the British took control of the American capital.

Occupying Philadelphia meant that the Delaware River had to be brought under control or, otherwise, the troops holding Philadelphia could not be supplied. Two American forts, Fort Mercer at Red Bank, below Glouster on the Jersey side of the Delaware, and Fort Mifflin, on Mud Island, near the opposite shore, threatened the British supply line. Hence, the British had to remove them, which it did through intense cannonading. The Americans fought back with galleys, commanded by Commodore John Barry[80], which set afire some of the British war ships:

Yesterday morning, about a quarter after seven o'clock, the enemy began a heavy cannonade on Fort Mifflin, from five batteries they had erected on Province Island, which continued until night. On the whole, [the British fired] I think not less than eight or nine hundred shot and shells, and, from accounts there last night, after the firing had ended, they had not killed one of our men. Many shot had gone through one of our blockhouses, which dismounted a piece of cannon and also damaged the stockade a great deal. This morning, at a quarter past seven, they began the attack again and continue it while I am writing and I suppose they will be at it all day.

I shall now give you an account of the enemy's repulse at Red Bank and the destruction of the Augusta and Merlin. The 22 ult. [October 22, 1777], about fifteen hundred Hessians, under the Command of Count Donop, came down to Red Bank in order to take the fort there, under the command of Colonel Green of Rhode Island. About for o'clock in the afternoon, the attack was begun by a most furious cannonade, which held a quarter of an hour; they then rushed in to storm the fort and got into the old part of the works, where they thought it was all their own and gave three cheers, but were soon obliged to retreat out of it in the utmost hurry. The galleys at the same time kept up a constant fire on them, which did great execution and in three quarters of an hour's attack, they ran off with the greatest precipitation, leaving behind them dead about ninety persons. From good authority, we are assured that the enemy buried one colonel and twenty one privates between this fort and Cooper's Ferry and carried off not less than two hundred wounded.

While the enemy were attacking the fort, the Augusta of sixty four guns, the Roebuck of forty four, two frigates of thirty two, the Merlin of eighteen and their large galley came through the lower chevaux de frize and kept up a great firing in order to draw off the galleys from giving any assistance to the fort, but they were mistaken. The Augusta, in going down that evening, got aground and, the next morning early, all the galleys and floating batteries began the attack, [with] an incessant fire [being] kept upon both sides so that the very elements appeared to be on fire. At eleven o'clock the Augusta was set on fire and at twelve she blew with an astonishing blast. One of our people was killed in a galley by a the fall of a piece of timber and we were so near that some of our powder horns took fire and exploded. The Merlin of eighteen guns [also] ran aground and, at three o'clock, the enemy set fire to her.

Thus ended two glorious days. The Commodore, with his boats, went on board the wreck and took out much plunder and brought off two of their cannon, one an eighteen and the other a twenty four pounder. The New Jersey Gazette, December 5, 1777

In my last I gave you an account of the defeat of the enemy at Red Bank and the destruction of the Augusta and Merlin. I shall now proceed to give you some account of the enemy's proceeding against Fort Mifflin

About the 12th of October, the enemy erected a battery near the mouth of the Schuykill in order to prevent our boats going into that river and then landed a large body of troops on Province Island, opposite to Fort Mifflin, with the intention to erect batteries against the fort. In the night, they threw up one battery within point blank shot directly opposite to the fort, which was attacked the next day by the galleys, who kept so warm a fire on them for two hours that one Captain, one Lieutenant and Ensign, with about eighty men came on the bank with a flag, clubbed their muskets and surrendered themselves prisoners. The enemy now threw up another battery at Hospital Wharf, from which they fired red hot shot, but to very little purpose, having from their first firing to the 9th of November, killed but two men and wounded a few. From all of these [batteries], about seven o'clock in the morning, they began a most furious cannonade with shot, shells and carcasses, not throwing less than 1500 a day. Tuesday morning they began in the same manner. Wednesday and Thursday the cannonade of shells &c. was kept up most violently, which tore up the stockades, barracks &c. all to pieces and dismounted and broke up many of our guns. Friday the fire was also very hot. In the afternoon, the Vigilant Galley, which had been cut down and carried sixteen twenty four pounders, got through close up to Fort Mifflin and fired most furiously at it and such a cannonade, I believe, was never seen in America, which continued until evening. Fort Mifflin lay by this time tore all to pieces having scant a stockade standing, the block house almost entirely beat down and every gun dismounted or broken. It now being found impossible to defend it any longer, Major Thayer, who for some days had so bravely defended it, about eleven o'clock at night, set fire to the remains of the barracks and brought off his garrison. The New Jersey Gazette, December 5, 1777

The destruction of the American forts on the Delaware marked the end of the 1777 Campaign. Washington removed his army to Valley Forge where they passed a difficult winter. He had much to consider. Both New York City and Philadelphia were now occupied by the enemy. Yet, the British had been prevented from occupying the region --i.e., New Jersey -- between those two cities. In addition, the British plan to take the Hudson and cut off New England had been frustrated by the victory at Saratoga. If only Benjamin Franklin could convince France to come to the assistance of the United States. Victory then might be possible.

CHAPTER 7

Life in the War Zone

Life went on, despite the conflict. Some weeks, a patriot, reading his weekly newspaper, might wonder where this terrible war was. Surprisingly, society functioned somewhat as it had before the hostilities. If it were not business as usual, then it seemed pretty close to it. Take, for example, the marketplace. Commerce continued and a variety of most everything the consumer needed was still available, the hostilities notwithstanding:

To be sold, wholesale and retail, by the subscriber at Heights-Town, a quantity of fine wool and cotton cards, linens, handkerchiefs of various sorts, good tea and sugar, French indigo of the best quality, pins, earthenware of various kinds, snuff and tobacco, ribbons, men's silk jackets and breech patterns, womens fans, buttons, mohair, silk and fine threads.
William Sloane
The New Jersey Gazette, June 10, 1778

Peter Crolius has for sale at his store in Trenton: tea, sugar, coffee, chocolate, indigo, snuff, nutmegs, pepper, chintzes, calicoes, black calimancoes, flowered aprons, lawns, cambricks, gauze, catgut, skeleton wires, sattin pelongs, corded dimitty, Barcelona handkerchiefs of different colours and many other articles to be sold for cash or country produce. The New Jersey Gazette, July 22, 1778

TO BE SOLD BY PHILEMON ELMER
Elizabeth-Town, Westfield, New Jersey
the following medicines

Jesuits Bark[81], of an excellent quality, Rhubarb, Calomel, Opium, Spanish Flies, Glauber's Salts, Purified Nitre, Myrrh, Aloes, Tartar, Emetic, Glass Antimony, Corrosive Sublimate of Mercury, Elixir Vitriol, Compound Spirit of Lavender, Salt of Tartar, Salt of

Wormwood, Camphire, Spirit of Turpentine &c, &c. The New Jersey Gazette, September 16, 1778

Conveniences, even luxury items, were also available and advertised, especially to the fairer sex or the more affluent:

Richard Norris
Stay-maker, from London, begs leave to inform the public that he makes all kinds of stays and jumps, turned and plain, either French or Meckleburgh, after the newest and neatest fashion. He prevents by a new and approved method, the appearance of any cast or rise in the hips or shoulders, or other defects in the shape of the body which method has been established by the society of stay makers of the city of London. Ladies that reside at any distance, by sending their measure, may be supplied, on the shortest notice and at as reasonable prices as the times can afford.
The New Jersey Gazette, December 16, 1778

John Dennis
Intends to prosecute the HAT MAKING business, as he formerly did in New Brunswick, where proper encouragement will be given to good journeymen and the highest price for all sorts of FURS. He thanks his former customers in particular, and the public in general, for past favours. Those that are pleased to continue in their custom shall be served with good hats and in a punctual manner. The New Jersey Gazette, February 18, 1778

A market still existed as well for industrial products:

TO BE SOLD
By Public Vendue, at the house of Mary Middleton, at Crosswicks, on Thursday, the 19th instant, an assortment of HARDWARE, such as handsaws, large and small hammers, hatchets, augurs, pitch and small ladles, brass and iron rimmed locks, with brass knobs, 12, 9, and 6 inch H-L and H hinges, dovetail and chest hinges, japanned pistol hooks with screws, fire steels, spike and nail gimblets, japanned handles for doors and chests, large gouge, inch and a half sprigs, scupper nails, sail needles and palms, fish hooks,

best rope traces, a large scale beam and sundry other articles not inserted. The New Jersey Gazette, February 18, 1778

Nor did the war appear to curtail the American public's tastes for tobacco and spirits:

Fine Saffron, Pigtail, Plug and Square Cut Tobacco, to be sold wholesale and retail, by Isaac Heulings, at his tobacco manufactory in Burlington. The New Jersey Gazette, April 1, 1778

William Inness
Returns his most grateful thanks to his friends for past favors and solicits the continuance of their custom. He acquaints them that he has a quantity of beer to deliver at current prices. He begs the favor of those who have casks of his to return them; others, who gave money as a pledge for the casks, are requested to let him have them again and the money shall be returned.
N.B. Those who have sold said Innes their grain are desired to forward it as soon as possible. He gives the current prices for barley. The New Jersey Gazette, February 3, 1779

Plenty of work was available. The flow of indentured servants from abroad had ended with the commencement of the fighting. Ships bound from Ireland and England to America now carried troops and provisions, not more workers. In addition, many native born Americans, attracted by either patriotism or the bounties offered for enlistment, were out of the job market, thus heightening the need for some trades. Advertisements were frequent for book keepers, clerks, school masters, tailors, wheelwrights, watchmakers, silversmiths, wood cutters and stocking weavers as well as the following:

Any person, properly recommended, who understands the business of Riding Chair Maker and would be willing to work in the capacity of a Journeyman, may meet with good encouragement by applying to Frederick King at the Post Office in Morristown, who carries on the business. Said King would be willing to take a young lad of a good character as an apprentice. The New Jersey Gazette, March 4, 1778

Any person who understands distilling rye spirits, may find encouragement by applying to the subscriber at his own house
Kenneth Hankinson
The New Jersey Gazette, April 23, 1778

WANTED IMMEDIATELY
A good tempered, active girl about ten years old. Any person having such a one to bind out, may hear of a good place, where she will be well used, taught to read and write and learned the Mantua Making [82] business if required, by applying to the Printer of this Paper. The New Jersey Gazette, June 3, 1778

A WET NURSE
A healthy, sober woman, living in the Jerseys, about 20 miles from Philadelphia, having a fine breast of milk two weeks old, would be glad to take a child from a reputable family. She can be well recommended. Apply to the printer. The Pennsylvania Evening Post, February 1, 1779

Wanted immediately, a middle aged Woman, who can be well recommended, to attend children in a small family. Enquire of the Printer hereof. The New Jersey Gazette, June 10, 1778

Wanted at Mountholly iron works, a number of Forgemen and Nailors, to whom the best wages will be given and constant employ. None need apply but those who can bring good character with them. A few Woodcutters are likewise wanted to whom three shillings and nine pence per cord will be paid for cutting; the wood is chiefly pine and maple. For further information, apply to Colonel Cox in Philadelphia or the subscriber at the works.
Richard Price
The Pennsylvania Evening Post, May 27, 1777

A Gardiner and Dairywoman is wanted to whom constant employ will be given. New Jersey Journal, April 5, 1780

WANTED IMMEDIATELY
One or two Chimney Sweeps, of small stature. The New Jersey Gazette, March 1, 1780

WANTED

Two experienced Harponiers in the whaling business, to enter the first day of November next, to whom good encouragement will be given by Henry Guest in New Brunswick.

N.B. None need apply without having proper vouchers of their dexterity in the business. The New Jersey Gazette, September 20, 1780

WANTED IMMEDIATELY

A Person that can come well recommended, to keep the Gaol in Burlington. For further particulars apply to
Jacob Phillip, Sheriff
The New Jersey Gazette, August 30, 1780

Indeed, much of life in New Jersey seemed unaffected by the war. The young continued to be educated and graduate, although the war was always in the background:

Princeton, March 24, 1778. The Grammar School at this place is again to be opened on Monday, the 13th of April. Those who have children to begin Latin are desired to be as punctual as possible in having them there on time.
John Witherspoon
The New Jersey Gazette, March 25, 1778

Princeton, October 2. On Wednesday last was held the annual commencement of the College at this place. The Governor, Council and Assembly met the Trustees at the President's house and the company went in procession to the College Hall...
After prayer, the exercises were performed in the following order:
1. Salutary oration by John Scudder on civil discord;
2. Oration by William Boyd on the strength of human passions;
3. Oration by Joseph Scudder on contentment;
4. Oration by Joseph Morton on the horrors of war;
5. Oration by Belcher Smith on eloquence.

The whole was concluded with an exhortation by the President to the graduates, containing advices for the prosecution of their studies and direction of their conduct in future life.

The winter session of this College begins on the 10th of November. The grammar school continues without vacation. The New Jersey Gazette, October 21, 1778

Romance continued despite the war. With all the younger men fighting, some senior citizens had to fill in:

We hear from Somerset County that on Friday the 20th ult, Mr. John Gordon, in the 83rd year of his age, was married to Miss Sukey Lane, a young lady of 18.[83] *The New York Gazette, April 1, 1778*

Couples continued to marry and, some of them would have been better served to have joined the army and done their fighting there.

Whereas the subscriber has great reason to believe that his wife Hannah is determined to run him into debt, as she has long been guilty of many lewd practices and has bedded with another woman's husband for a considerable time. This is to forewarn all persons from trusting her on my account as I am determined to pay no debts of her contracting from this date forward.
LEVY GARDNER
The New Jersey Journal, April 13, 1779

Whereas a most malicious and infamous advertisement, signed Levy Gardner, hath been published, greatly to the prejudice of his wife Hannah Gardner. This is therefore to inform the public that said Gardner eloped from his bed and board, left his wife with five small children, and cohabited with other women, and, as he is a man addicted to all kinds of vices, she forewarns all persons bedding or boarding with him. Any person take will take up Gardner and secure him in any gaol, so that his wife may have restitution made her, shall have thirty dollars reward and all reasonable charges paid by
HANNAH GARDNER
The New Jersey Journal, April 13, 1779

Whereas my wife Elizabeth, with the advice of her mother and by the assistance of James Shotwill, of the Scotch Plains, has

eloped from my bed and board and sundry times swore she would destroy both my left and my estate, this, therefore, is to forewarn any person harboring or trusting her on my account, as I will not pay any debts of her contracting after this date.
William Willis

Since it was my fortune to be join'd
To such a wretched mate,
I've strove to reconcile my mind
To my unhappy fate.
I've born insults and threats likewise,
I've strove for to persuade,
But them that's hardened so to vice
Regard not what is said.
Without a cause she left my bed,
And broke her marriage vow,
So basely from me she has fled,
Who can blame me now?
Then pity my unhappy fate,
Beware of woman's arts,
For oft within a snowy breast
Lurks a deceitful heart.
New Jersey Journal, June 8, 1779

Sometimes, the extremes of the weather were the most important topics in the news, the war scarcely mentioned:

For two days past, the weather has been so intensely cold that the Delaware, opposite to this City [Philadelphia] is frozen over. The Pennsylvania Packet, January 21, 1778

Princeton, July 14. On Thursday, the 9th inst. at two o'clock in the afternoon, the Mercury in Fahrenheit's thermometer rose to 98 3/10; on Friday at the same hour to 97 9/10 [84] *and on Saturday at the same hour to 97 7/10. The New Jersey Gazette, July 15, 1778*

The late storm ["a heavy northeaster"] has destroyed many of the saltworks on our shore, with all the salt in them. The night tide were several feet higher than ever has been known before. A considerable number of horned cattle were drowned on Long Beach and other places.[85] *The Long Beach is almost completely leveled all [and] little more of it than a sand bar [is] left. The furniture has floated out of the lower rooms of some houses that stood low on the waterside. The inhabitants never saw so distressing a time.* The New Jersey Gazette, April 8, 1778

The weather having been remarkably warm and pleasant for about a month past, has occasioned the buds of some early fruit trees to vegetate to a greater degree than has been remembered at this season by the oldest men in the neighborhood. The New Jersey Gazette, February 24, 1779

The navigation is now open from this place [Trenton] to Philadelphia after having been stopped for near to three months with the ice. The New Jersey Gazette, March 8, 1780

Even extra-planetary phenomena were reported:

Mr. Collins,
Walking through my entry on Sunday evening last, my eye was caught by a meteor of a very uncommon size, in the south west. It appeared to me to be as large as a man's hand, very luminous and descended with great rapidity from the height of about 15 degrees above the horizon, which was the place I first saw it in. But what rendered the thing still more remarkable was that a crooked crack or luminous stroke appeared immediately afterwards in the sky, which seemed to have described the path of the meteor and continued for about 10 or 15 minutes.
This phenomenon was altogether extraordinary and it would afford me great pleasure to have the thoughts of the learned and philosophical on the subject.
Creon
The New Jersey Gazette, November 10, 1779

But, the war could not be forgotten for very long, even by those who wanted to block it out. It certainly never seemed to leave New Jersey alone. For three straight winters, Washington wintered his troops at Morristown and Middle Brook. Both New York City and Philadelphia were occupied by the British and neighboring New Jersey was almost daily raided by the armies stationed in both cities. Its cattle, crops and citizens were taken for forage or ransom. During some campaigns, the British themselves tried to winter their troops, occupy or pass through the region and significant battles like those at Trenton, Princeton, and Monmouth resulted. The British occupied New Brunswick under siege by the Americans. For months and months, central Jersey, Rahway, Woodbridge, the Amboys and surrounding towns became a war zone. With their Iroquois allies, the English also threatened the western and northern frontiers. British troops and loyalists refugees from bases in Staten Island and Sandy Hook harassed the people from Elizabeth Town, all the way down to Monmouth County. Along the Delaware, there was similar skirmishing and raiding. British war ships patrolled the coast seizing American shipping and, in turn, American privateers, nested along the South Jersey shore at Egg Harbour and other places, menaced British trade, coming from the Caribbean and Europe.

Danger to the lives and limbs of the inhabitants of New Jersey, either as civilians or as combatants in the militia, was the most obvious effect of the war, but, as will be seen, there were many others. For the average citizen, the war permeated everything, even when the major military campaigns were being conducted elsewhere. Neighbor against neighbor, brother sometimes against brother, it was a painful experience:

To the Freeholders and other Electors for the County of Cumberland, New Jersey
GENTLEMEN
As the Time is near at Hand for electing a Sheriff in the county for the ensuing year, I beg the favor of not being set up as a Candidate for said office as I entirely decline standing any longer, even were I sure of every vote in said county, it being so very disagreeable to me to distress poor people in these times of public calamity; therefore, please to elect some other person to serve instead of, Gentlemen,
Your Friend and Humble Servant
David Bowen, present Sheriff
The Pennsylvania Gazette, August 14, 1776

The war was there, in countless ways, in everyone's life, even in the ordinary events. The same job ads that seemed so benign before, now had an undercurrent of the war about them:

Extraordinary Wages and an exemption from serving in the militia -- and still higher wages without an exemption -- will be given to a few choice wood cutters and laborers, to be employed at the independent salt works [86] *about eighteen miles southward of the forks of Little Egg Harbor and two miles north of Absequean River. Apply at the said works to*
Nathaniel Pettit
The New Jersey Gazette, January 7, 1778

Notice is hereby given to all persons capable of driving a team, who are willing to enlist for carters, to serve for three years, that they have twenty dollars bounty, six pounds per month from the time of their enlistment, a suit of new clothes every year and a great coat (if possible) and shoes and boots, by their producing a certificate from their wagonmaster of their good behavior. All persons willing to enlist on the above terms are desired to meet me at my quarters in Trenton.
Samuel H. Sullivan, D.Q.M.G.
The New Jersey Gazette, February 25, 1778

I understand the business of mould making in all of its branches to perfection. I can make moulds in the best method for manufacturing cannon balls and in such a way that is both profitable to the iron master and myself and grape shot in a method that the iron master can make a ton per day. Any person wanting such a man may apply to the printer thereof. The New Jersey Gazette, April 23, 1778

WANTED IMMEDIATELY
A Number of good TRADESMEN, that are single, such as Carpenters, Smiths of all branches, Armourers, Gun Stockers or Wheelwrights. Any of the above tradesmen that are willing to serve themselves and Country, shall by applying to Capt. Wylie, at the grand continental works at Carlisle, receive Twenty Dollars bounty, Thirty Dollars each man per month pay, one suit of clothes per year

and a ration and a half each man per day and good quarters. The New Jersey Gazette, June 17, 1778

A Man well acquainted with blowing the Trumpet and capable of teaching the Horse Duty of that instrument, will meet with good encouragement by applying to Major Bland, commandant of the first regiment of Light Horse, at Morris Town, or at the Headquarters of the Continental Army. The Pennsylvania Packet, April 1, 1777

The obituaries of fallen soldiers, published in the patriot papers, made all Americans aware of the price that was being paid for this new born concept of "liberty":

Tears like the dew shall fall on the memory of heroes. In the action at Monmouth on the 28th day of June last, fell Lieutenant McNair of the Artillery, an officer who deserves the tears of his country. Born in North Britain, he came to America and early embarked in the cause against the tyrant. He served as a private in the first campaign in Boston and, in the course of the war, rose gradually through the intermediate offices from a private to a lieutenant, without the least solicitation to obtain that promotion and without the interest of one friend, but what his merit gave him. He was humble in spirit, modest in manner and steady in his conduct. His Captain, in a letter of the 25th of August from the Camp at White Plains, writes of him as follows. "I cannot help but lament the death of so valuable an officer. He was cool, attentive to his duty, intrepid and brave, undisturbed in the hottest engagements and commanded with the firmness and courage of a Roman. He was loved and esteemed by the officers and loved and feared by the soldiers. He was humane and extremely charitable. He was possessed of the highest sense of liberty and wished to establish the independence of his country. He had a warm sense of duty to God and lived regularly and religiously. He died fighting bravely for his country against slavery and tyranny. Not less than a cannon ball separated his noble soul from his body. The New Jersey Gazette, September 16, 1778

The 23rd of June last died of lail fever, in New York, Mr. John Gibbon, having been a prisoner of war there six months. He was descended from a very ancient and honorable family in the west of England who became early adventurers to America, were some of the original proprietors of New Jersey and from whom he had derived a very large and valuable landed estate. An ardent love of Liberty and an anxious desire to preserve the freedom and independence of America, induced him, at a time when the enemy was overrunning New Jersey and our affairs wore the most unfavorable aspect, voluntarily to turn out and oppose, with his musket and bayonet, those cruel invaders of his country and the rights of mankind. On the retreat of the New Jersey Militia from Mountholly the 23rd of December last, he was unfortunately taken up prisoner and conveyed to New York, where he has remained closely confined until his death.

He supported his cruel and severe confinement with a firmness and resolution that does honor to his memory, and to the glorious cause in which he suffered. The Pennsylvania Evening Post, August 5, 1777

In the morning of the 25th ult. died at Camp, of wounds he received in bravely doing his duty before the Block House, near Bull's Ferry, on the 21st, Lieutenant Jacob Morris DeHart, of the 2d Pennsylvania regiment, aged nineteen years. The emulation and fire necessary to warm a soldier's breast soon kindled in this young, but manly, officer, having entered into the service of his country at sixteen, from which time his sweetness of disposition and attention to duty, gained him the affection of officers of every rank. At five o'clock in the afternoon he was buried with the honors of war, attended by a large concourse of officers from the different lines of the army. The New Jersey Gazette, August 2, 1780

Obituaries also told the story of how the Loyalists similarly suffered for their support of the King and Parliament. Tragedy was not the domain of the Americans alone, as the following brace of news items show:

Last Wednesday died of Small pox in her 48th year, Mrs. Barton, wife of Lieutenant Colonel Joseph Barton of the 5th Battalion of the New Jersey raised Corps; she had been driven with 7 small Children from their Estate in Sussex County where she had endured every sort of Persecution from the Rebels, who also stripped her of all her Property while the Lieutenant Colonel was a Prisoner at Weathersfield in Connecticut. She was a valuable Member of Society and her Death is greatly regretted. The Children are under the Protection of a Person in Town until their Father can be removed from his Durance. The New York Gazette, January 12, 1778

Died since our last, John Barton aged 15 years and Joseph Barton aged 6 years, both sons of Colonel Barton, now a Prisoner in Connecticut. Since the Colonel's Confinement, he has lost his Wife and three Sons. The New York Gazette, January 26, 1778

The war had disrupted all education in New Jersey. Rutgers sought to get things back to normal.

The Faculty of Queens College [Rutgers] takes this method to inform the Public that the business of said College is still carried on at the North Branch of Raritan, in the county of Somerset, where good accommodations for young Gentlemen may be had in reputable families, at as moderate prices as in any part of the state. This neighborhood is so far distant from Head-Quarters that not any of the troops are stationed here, neither does the army in the least interfere with the business of the College.
The Faculty also take the liberty to remind the Publick, that the Representatives of this state have enacted a law by which Students of Colleges are exempted from military duty. The New Jersey Gazette, January 27, 1779

It was a little more difficult for Princeton, then the College of New Jersey, which had been occupied as a hospital for the Americans

Philadelphia, June 24. The Undergraduates of the College of New Jersey are desired to return to Princeton without delay, as college orders will begin on Tuesday, the 8th day of next month. They are desired to take all possible pains to provide themselves with books, according to their standing and future studies, which are already known to them. It is hoped that all of them have been pursuing separately their studies as well as their circumstances would allow and that they will now apply themselves with extraordinary diligence to recover the ground that has been necessarily lost. The seniors in particular are requested to come prepared for continuing at Princeton through the end of September, as the examination for Bachelor's degrees will not be this year as formerly, in the middle of August, but immediately before commencement.

John Witherspoon
The Pennsylvania Evening Post, June 26, 1777

Nassau Hall, Princeton, New Jersey. April 23, 1779. The many inquiries that have been made by gentlemen at a distance, render it necessary to give information to the public of the past and present state of the College here. Every promise in former advertisements has been fulfilled. In the summer of 1777, as soon as the enemy left the state, the instruction, agreeably to notice, was begun, the Trustees having empowered the President to employ such Teachers occasionally as should be necessary. Accordingly, such of the scholars, as conveniently could, returned and were carried on according to their standing and the Seniors of that Year received their Degree of Bachelor of Arts at Commencement as usual. The same was the case during the winter following and the summer of 1778, when there was a private commencement, but the attendance was difficult and inconvenient, the college being occupied by the Public as a barrack or hospital and the recitations [were made] from necessity in a room of the President' house. Last summer, the College was entirely given up to us but in so ruinous a state as to be very unfit for accommodating the scholars. Several, however, lived in it all the winter session and the recitations were in College. Now, we have the pleasure of acquainting the Public that tradesmen have been have been at work for some time repairing the fabric, that a good part of the windows have been put in, that we expect the roof will be made entirely sound in a few days, and that the chambers will be fitted up sufficiently, it is supposed, to receive those who may come for the summer sessions, which begins on the 10th of May. As to boarding, it is not yet practical to get a Steward for the College but boarding for those who lodge in the College may be had with families in town at such rates as the times will admit. . .

The Grammar School which was begun in April of last year, has continued ever since and is in a thriving condition, there being near thirty boys in it. The school, after a vacation of two weeks, nearly elapsed, will be opened on Monday next, the 26th instant. Great care is taken in this school to make the scholars accurate in the grammar and syntax and by frequent periodical exercises to perfect them in reading, spelling and pronouncing the English language, a branch of education of the first importance, but often neglected.

To encourage the early and punctual attendance of the Students, the same rule will be observed as in former times at the end of every vacation, viz, that after the first day of meeting, no regard will be paid to the standing of the scholars in the distribution of the chambers but those who come first will have their choice of such as are vacant.

John Witherspoon
William Ch. Houston

The New Jersey Gazette, May 5, 1779

One certainly did not need the newspapers to tell him or her that a war was in process. Those that reside in a nation in strife know well the regulations that control and restrict their normal civil liberties. Both rebellious New Jersey and occupied New York and Philadelphia necessarily had their own sets of martial law:

PROCLAMATION

I do hereby, in concurrence with the magistrates of the police, order and direct that no Ferry whatsoever from the City of Philadelphia or from no other place within the environs thereof, to the Province of New Jersey, be allowed, save those ferries called and known by the names of the New and Old Ferries of Water Street, near Arch Street and that no person or persons whatsoever presume to cross the river to New Jersey or land from thence at any other places than the above mentioned ferries, nor cross by those ferries but by virtue of a pass under the hand of one of the magistrates, of which the ferryman and all the others are hereby directed to take notice and govern themselves accordingly, on pain of imprisonment.

Given under my hand at Philadelphia the 15th day of January in the 18th year of his majesty's reign

Jos. Galloway, Superintendent general[87]
The Pennsylvania Evening Post, January 15, 1778

Head-Quarters, Philadelphia, 7th May, 1778
GENERAL ORDERS

Whereas a number of fields near this City and Glouster Point have been lately enclosed by the several departments of the Army, and by many of the inhabitants, with the intention to preserve the sufficiency of grass for use of the government and its friends, and it being complained of that many of the fence rails. enclosing said fields, have been wantonly broken down and carried off and that several trespasses are committed by horses and other cattle belonging to the Army and inhabitants being put in during the night, to graze in said fields.

This is therefore to inform the public that any person or persons, who shall, after the date of this publication, be detected in either pulling down or carrying away any parts of the rails, posts or gates now inclosing the above mentioned fields, under any pretence whatsoever, will be punished with the utmost severity and in the most exemplary manner and that such horses or other cattle as shall be found trespassing in any of the said fields will be seized for the use of the public.

J. Patterson, adjutant general
The Pennsylvania Evening Post, May 8, 1778

By Major General Valentine Jones, Commandant in New York

PROCLAMATION

Whereas there is great reason to believe that there are many evil practices by persons passing and repassing to and fro from this city and the Jersey Shore in small craft. In order therefore the more effectually to prevent such practices in the future, I have thought fit to issue this proclamation, hereby declaring, if any boat or small craft whatever, shall be found in passing or repassing as aforesaid, without having first obtained a regular pass for doing so, that the persons found in such small boat or craft shall be subject to confinement and the boat or craft subject to seizure and confiscation and that all persons going from this City without proper passes will be seized and confined. And I hereby do strictly forbid all persons passing from this City to the Jersey Shore after sun setting and before sun rising under pain of military execution. The New York Gazette, August 11, 1777

Both George Washington and New Jersey's Governor Livingston appealed directly of the people of that state to help feed the Continental Army that occupied New Jersey. They were there as a defense to the British who were in New York and, at the time, Philadelphia:

To the inhabitants of New Jersey, Pennsylvania, Maryland and Virginia

Friends, Countrymen and Fellow Citizens!

After three campaigns, during which the brave subjects of these States have contended, not unsuccessfully, with one of the most powerful kingdoms on earth, we now find ourselves at least upon a level with our opponents, and there is the best reason to believe that efforts adequate to the abilities of this country, would enable us to speedily conclude the war and to secure the invaluable blessings of peace, liberty and safety. With this view, it is in contemplation, at the opening of the next campaign, to assemble a force sufficient, not barely to cover the country from a repetition of those depredations, which it hath already suffered, but also to operate offensively and to strike some decisive blow.

In the prosecution of this object, it is to be feared that so large an army may suffer for the want of provisions. The distance between this and the eastern States, whence

considerable supplies of flesh have heretofore been drawn, will necessarily render those supplies exceedingly precarious. And, unless the virtuous yeomanry of the States of New Jersey, Pennsylvania, Maryland and Virginia will exert themselves to prepare cattle for the use of the army, during the months of May, June and July next, great difficulties may arise in the course of the campaign. It is therefore recommended to the inhabitants of those States, to put up and feed immediately, as many of their stock cattle as they can spare, so that they may be driven to this army within that period. A bountiful price will be given and the proprietors may assure themselves that they will render a most essential service to the illustrious cause of their country and contribute, in a great degree, to shorten this bloody contest. But, should there be any so insensible to the common interest, as not to exert themselves upon these generous principles, [then] the private interests of those whose situation makes them liable to become immediate subjects of the enemy's incursions, should prompt them at least to a measure which is calculated to save their property from plunder, their families from insult and their own persons from abuse, hopeless confinement or, perhaps, a violent death.
G. Washington
The New Jersey Gazette, February 25, 1778

To the Inhabitants of New Jersey
Gentlemen,
Considering the noble ardor that this state has uniformly manifested to the common cause, I am confident that our Farmers will take a particular pleasure in complying with his Excellency's, the General's, request. They will disdain in the close of our struggle to sully the honor which New Jersey has deservedly acquired by affording all possible aid during the whole contest. 'Tis hoped the next campaign will make the enemy repent their execrable purpose of enslaving a free people and teach even British stupidity, wisdom. For liberty's sake, gentlemen, let not our expectations of this campaign be

disappointed, for want of the supplies we can so easily furnish. I know you will exert yourselves and want neither arguments to convince, nor exhortations to rouse you. Your country calls and, to the call of your country, you were never deaf.
William Livingston
The New Jersey Gazette, March 4, 1778

Most of the citizens of New Jersey did not need laws to force them to support the Revolution. The help sought by General Washington and Governor Livingston, as well as similar aid sought by the British generals, was forthcoming from many charitable souls on both sides:

The following donations were lately received at the hospital at Princeton viz from the Rev. Mr. Hardenburg's congregation in Raritan, 180 pairs of stockings, 62 good shirts, 43 shirts part worn, 20 pair linen trousers, 5 linen breeches, 2 linen jackets, 50 woolen jackets, 25 woolen breeches, 17 coats, 4 blankets, 5 pairs of shoes, besides a quantity of old linen and woolen for hospital use. And from the Rev. Mr. Chapman's congregation in Newark Mountains, 10 blankets, 19 sheets, 45 shirts, 9 coats, 40 vests, 27 pair breeches, 105 pair of stockings, 2 pairs of shoes, 3 surtouts, 3 watchcoats and a quantity of old linen. The donors of the above, and those who before contributed and may contribute in the same way, are hereby informed that a proper assortment of all kinds of clothing will be kept in the hospital for the entertainment and the refreshment of the sick and wounded soldiers in general of the Continental Army, who shall be sent to this hospital, and the residue will be distributed to them who are fit for service, paying a particular attention to the regiments of this state, whether in hospital or camp. The New Jersey Gazette, March 18, 1778

From Princeton, we learn that charitable donations from the congregations of Newark, Elizabeth Town,

Connecticut Farms, Turky and South Hanover, Springfield, Morris Town, Scotch Plains and Bound Brook, for the sick soldiers in the hospitals &c. were lately sent to that place, consisting of the following articles viz 68 sheets, 9 pairs of new shoes, 46 blankets, 347 pairs of stockings, 243 shirts, 200 breeches and trowsers, 200 jackets, 76 coats, 39 yards of new cloth, 5 coverlets, sewing thread, yarn, buttons, several new garments cut out but not made up, new linen and a large quantity of old, suitable for lint &c &c   The New Jersey Gazette, April 8, 1778

Last Monday, a handsome collection of clothing and linen were sent up to the hospital at Princeton, for the use of the sick and wounded, being the seasonable and charitable donation of the Rev. Mr. Green's Congregation in Hanover, Morris County. The New Jersey Gazette, February 25, 1778

The active and humane part you have taken to procure Watch Coats for the Jersey Volunteers, demand our warmest Acknowledgments. You will also please to return our Thanks to the Loyal Inhabitants of New York, whose generous and seasonable Donations have contributed so much to the Comfort of the Troops, under our Command, and the Good of his Majesty's Service.
We are with Great Respect
Your much obliged,
And Very Humble Servants
Abraham Buskirk, Lieut. Col.
Commandant 4th, Bat. N.J.V.
Isaac Allen, Lieut. Col.
Commandant 6th, Bat. N.J.V.
Robert Drummond, Major
Commandant 3rd, Bat. N.J.V.
Thomas Millridge, Major
Commandant 5th Bat. N.J.V.
   The New York Gazette, February 2, 1778

The Ladies of Trenton in New Jersey, emulating the noble example of their Patriotic Sisters of Pennsylvania, and being desirous of manifesting their zeal in the glorious cause of American Liberty, having this day assembled for the purpose of promoting a subscription for the relief and encouragement of those brave Men in the Continental Army, who, stimulated by example, and regardless of danger, have repeatedly so suffered fought and bled in the cause of virtue and their oppressed country, etc. The New Jersey Gazette, July 5, 1780

Failure to sacrifice for the cause was considered treasonous to the new nation. It threatened the Revolution, which, in turn, put every patriot's life and liberty in jeopardy. From the distance of more than two hundred years, some might find it ironic that the American rebels, espousing liberty and a desire to be left alone by those with whom they did not agree, nevertheless displayed, as a mob, the same "bully" personality they detested. To insure that all supported the insurrection, they inflicted reprisals against any who did not. The reprisals varied from requiring public apology, shunning, tar and feathering to much worse:

In the Provincial Congress of New York
The Memorial of Robert and John Murray, on the subject of the breach of the Association of the late Continental Congress, whereby they pray to be restored to their former commercial powers. . . and it appearing that they, the said Robert and John Murray, have published a printed hand bill, expressing their contrition for their offense and their resolution for the future strictly to adhere to the said Association. . . RESOLVED therefore that the said Robert and John Murray shall be and hereby are restored to their commercial purposes and declared to be entitled to the forgiveness of the public. The New York Gazette, June 12, 1775

The Committee of the County of Cumberland, in New Jersey, having, from time to time, received information as to the inimical conduct of Richard Cayford, with respect to the present unhappy disputes between Great Britain and America, met on the 21st day of July instant, and, having sent for the said Cayford, informed him of the charges that lay against him and, by the testimony of unexceptionable evidence examined before the Committee in his presence, made it appear that he had repeatedly acted in opposition to the general measures pursued by the united American colonies and endeavored to instill in others his own pernicious principles; that he has repeatedly impeached the first military characters in America and dissuaded the unwary from learning the military art, branding those who had executed themselves in these laudable exercises with the epithets of rebels, rascals, &c., names which Americans detest! And it did not appear to the Committee, by any confession of Cayford, that he thought he had done amiss; therefore, agreeable to their duty, they do in this manner hold him up to the public, that every person may break off all dealings with him and avoid him as an enemy of the rights of America.

By the order of the Committee, Thomas Ewing, Clerk

The 6th December, Quibble Town, Middlesex county, Piscataqua Township, New Jersey:

Thomas Randolf, cooper, who had publicly proved himself an enemy to his country, by reveiling and using his utmost endeavors to oppose the proceedings of the Continental and Provincial Convention and Committees, in defense of their rights and liberties, and he, being judged a person of not consequence for a severer punishment, was ordered to be stripped naked, well coated with tar and feathers and carried in a wagon publicly round the town, which punishment was accordingly inflicted; and, as he soon became duly sensible to his offense, for which he earnestly begged pardon, and promised us to atone, so far as he was able, by a contrary behavior in the future, he was released and suffered to return to his house in less than half an hour. The whole was conducted with that regularity and decorum that ought to be observed in all public punishments. The New York Journal, December 28, 1775

I, Ezekiel Beach, of the township of Mendham, in the county of Morris, have heretofore, by my words and conduct, been guilty of opposing the good people of the country in the measures, by them adopted, in preserving American Freedom, particularly saying "I had rather the Ministerial troops would conquer the Continental," and further declared that "the Parliament of Great Britain had a right to levy the oppressive taxes and acts upon America, particularly the act for changing the government of Massachusetts Bay" and further declared that "I would assist the Ministerial troops with provisions and other necessaries, provided that they would pay for same"; and, having thus on the most mature deliberations, considered of such my conduct, do most heartily disapprove of the same and do hereby promise that for the future, I will observe, as far as within me lie, the rules and regulations of the honorable Continental Congress and the Provincial Congress of New Jersey, and will use my best endeavors to promote and to carry into execution every measure adopted already or that may be hereafter adopted by said Congress for preserving the rights and liberties of this country, and I will most cheerfully sign the Association adopted by said Provincial Congress, when thereunto required, and do hereby desire that in the future the good people of this country would consider me as a friend to the same, which I hope to manifest by my conduct.
Ezekiel Beach
The New York Journal, December 28, 1775

Last Tuesday, about four hundred of the militia of this county [Sussex], under the command of Colonel Ephraim Martin and Mark Thompson, assembled and proceeded in good order and regularity in quest of Tories, a considerable number of whom, (inhabitants of this county) had entered into a combination and agreement not to comply with any of the Congress measures; about forty, we hear, are taken, most of whom have recanted, signed the Association and professed themselves to be true sons of liberty, being fully convinced of their error; and that two or three that remain incorrigible are to be sent to the congress to be dealt with. The New York Journal, December 28, 1775

Those who were caught disobeying the rules and actually assisting the enemy were dealt with more harshly. Penalties for minor infractions ranged from fines to property forfeitures:

A correspondent informs us that one William Pace of Schoolie's Mountain and Thomas Van Camp of Somerset county, both bound for Staten Island, the latter with a quantity of flour and the former with four quarters of beef which had been stall fed for two years and was intended for a British General were apprehended and brought before the president and the council of safety the 28th day of January last. It not fully appearing to the Board that their respective cargoes were to have been transported into the enemy's lines, which would have been high treason, Van Camp was adjudged to forfeit his flour and to pay the fine prescribed by law for asking more than the regulated price and to pay the fine for asking a higher price in continental currency than in specie, and Pace to forfeit his fat beef and to pay the fine for asking for it more than the regulated price, and both being bound over, they were dismissed.

Evidence being produced the day after that one Jacob Fitz Randolph, who lives at the Blazing Star, had met with them at Spanktown [Rahway] and engaged to take their cargoes if they would bring them to is house and to convey them to Staten Island as soon as the ice would permit. The said Pace and Fitz

Randolph have since been committed to gaol for procuring provisions for the enemy and a warrant is issued to apprehend the said Van Camp. The New Jersey Gazette, February 11, 1778

At the Court of Oyer and Terminer lately holden in the County of Monmouth, the Grand Jury found a bill of indictment against Cyrenus Van Meter, for giving information to the enemy and therefore being the cause of their taking Richard Stockton, Esq. and John Covenhoven, Esq. in the month of December, 1776. Van Meter put himself upon his trial and the Jury found him guilty. The Court thereupon sentenced him to pay a fine of 300 pounds and to suffer six months imprisonment. We hear that the enemy, in their late passage through the county, released Van Meter, who, having piloted them through his neighborhood, went off with them to New York, leaving a large real and personal estate behind him, which, we presume, will be forfeited for his crimes. The New Jersey Gazette, July 8, 1778

For some crimes, imprisonment was the penalty for such perfidy:

"The Council of Safety" says a correspondent, "has committed six of the inhabitants of Bergen, who were apprehended upon their return from New York, where they had traded with the enemy. . . [T]he degenerate sons of that county make it a common practice to carry refreshments to the British troops. As this infamous commerce, and even going into the enemy's lines without permission, is declared by one of acts [a] felony without benefit of clergy, it is hoped that the government will make terrible examples of some of these miscreants to prevent the like criminal and felonious intercourse in the future. The New Jersey Gazette, December 5, 1777

We have certain intelligence from New Jersey that the governor and council of safety of that state have confined

James Parker, Esq. and Walter Rutherford, Esq, both gentlemen of very large landed estates, which they seem determined to secure by such a neutrality of conduct as to stand equally fair with both contending parties in the final result of the conflict; having evinced their disaffection, or least want of affection, to the present government by repeatedly refusing to take the oaths of abjuration and allegiance proscribed by law, as a test to try all suspicious and doubtful characters. They are to be kept in durance until the honorable John Fell and captain Wynant Van Zandt, a young gentleman of great magnamity and merit (both kidnaped by the Tories in the county of Bergen and carried to New York and there imprisoned) shall be set at liberty. Our correspondent further informs that the said governor and council of safety has confined a number of other disaffected citizens, chiefly of Bergen county, to be released for an equal number of honest citizens stolen and imprisoned in like manner, being determined for the future thus to retaliate till the enemy shall think proper to discontinue that infamous part of their infamous system. The Pennsylvania Evening Post, August 26, 1777

The ultimate punishment for treasonous conduct was execution:

Trenton, December 16. The Courts of Oyer and Terminer and General Gaol Delivery for the County of Glouster were opened at Glouster on the 17th of November last and ended on the 5th of this month. During the session, Benjamin Bartholomew was convicted of Burglary and Jonathan Chew, Harrison Wells, William Hammett, John Dilks, John Franklin, Joseph Prat, Joseph Dill, James Birch, Daniel Fusman, Abraham Fennimore, David Lloyd, Lawrence Cox, Gideon Urine, Joshua Dilks, Charles String, Thomas Nightingale, Paterson Cook, and Isaac Lord, were convicted of High Treason. On Saturday se'nnight sentence of death passed against the above offenders. The New Jersey Gazette, December 16, 1778

We hear that at the Court of Oyer and Terminer and General Gaol Delivery held in Monmouth on June last . . Ezekiel Forman,[88] John Polhemus and William Grover were tried for and convicted of high treason, who, it is said, are to be executed on the 18th of August next. The New Jersey Gazette, July 22, 1778

Leniency for those convicted of treason was not encouraged. Indeed, such laxity in enforcing the law was the subject of a Proclamation from the Governor of the State of New Jersey:

By His Excellency
WILLIAM LIVINGSTON, ESQ.
Governor, Captain General and Commander in Chief in and over the State of New Jersey and territories thereunto belonging, Chancellor and Ordinary in the same

PROCLAMATION
WHEREAS, some of the Justices of the Peace of this State have been too remiss in discharging the duty required of them, by a certain law, entitled "An Act to punish traitors and disaffected persons". . . I have therefore thought fit, by and with the Advice of the Council of this State, to issue this Proclamation, hereby strictly charging and commanding all Justices of the Peace, within the same, to carry out the said act into execution so far as to them it doth appertain.
William Livingston
GOD save the PEOPLE
The Pennsylvania Packet, February 11, 1777

Despite the ravages of war, physical and psychological, the Americans placed their hopes in their God and the righteousness of the cause for which they fought:

Head-Quarters Camp, Valley Forge, May 5th, 1778
GENERAL ORDERS
"It having pleased the Almighty, Ruler of the Universe, propitiously to defend the cause of the United American States and finally by raising up a powerful Friend among the Princes of the Earth,[89] to establish our liberty and independence upon a lasting foundation, it becomes us to set a day apart for gratefully acknowledging the Divine Goodness and celebrating the important event which we owe to his benign interposition."
The New Jersey Gazette, May 13, 1778

CHAPTER 8

The War: 1778

As the new year 1778 rang in, the British were in control of New York and Philadelphia, two of the principal cities of the rebels, but not much more. Their grip did not extend far beyond the city limits of either. That was not enough acreage to permit their troops "to live off the land" and, of course, it was not feasible to supply the troops from Britain, an ocean voyage of a dozen weeks away. Consequently the British troops were compelled to look to the neighboring countryside for forage. For both Philadelphia and New York, that meant principally New Jersey. Poor Jersey was destined to be both the battle and the feeding grounds of the 1778 campaign.

The winter in 1778 was a horrible one. General Washington and his ill, hungry and half naked troops spent it across the Jersey border in Pennsylvania, at Valley Forge. It was another test of the grit and endurance of the Continental soldier. However, two good things occurred during that winter of suffering. Each would advance the American cause. First, France, encouraged by the American victory the prior summer at Saratoga and anxious to renew hostilities with her old enemy England, signed a Treaty of Allegiance with the United States. It had been at the urging of Benjamin Franklin, America's representative to its Court. Second, Baron Frederick Von Steuben, a Prussian military adviser, arrived at Valley Forge and, through constant drilling and training, turned the Continental soldiers into an army rather than a sometimes rag tag collection of brave irregulars on a holy mission for Liberty.

While the American soldiers trained in the snow of Valley Forge in February and March 1778, the British Lion, wintering in Philadelphia, made an occasional swipe of its paw at the American troops across the Delaware River in New Jersey. When they did, the Americans chased them out:

On Wednesday last, the enemy landed about 3000 men at Billingsfort and marched down the road towards Salem, and, on intelligence received, that another body intended to land at Cooper's Ferry [now the northern part of the city of Camden], in order to surprise General Wayne (who had lately landed in New Jersey with 500 Continental Troops) and Col. Ellis, who commanded a detachment of Jersey Militia at Haddonfield. Our troops not being sufficient to make a stand, it was thought most advisable to move towards Moorestown, to prevent being surrounded, which was accordingly done a few hours before the enemy landed. Our men marched to Mount Holly to wait for reinforcements. The Governor, upon receiving the above intelligence, ordered out a proper number of the Militia to join those under Col. Ellis, who are now collecting with great alacrity, and, unless the enemy retreats before they are attacked by the united vigor of General Wayne's troops and our Militia, we doubt not that they will repent their rash visit to this State. Last Friday, Brigadier General Count Pulaski, of the Cavalry, left this place [Trenton], with a body of horse in excellent order, to join the Continental Troops under General Wayne, and, who, from the former exhibitions of his valor and alertness, will give a good account of the enemy's horse, if they do not deprive him of that pleasure by a precipitate flight. The New Jersey Gazette, March 4, 1778

By accounts from Salem County, we learn that a number of the British troops, supposed to be between fifteen hundred and two thousand, landed last Tuesday at the Town of Salem, with whom our militia has had some skirmishes, but with no great loss on either side. Orders are issued for a large reinforcement of the militia to join Col. Ellis in Glouster County and Col. Shreve, with his battalion of Continental troops, has crossed the Delaware and is on his march to oppose the enemy. It is reported that the militia of Cumberland have turned out with the most laudable spirit and it is expected that the British rovers will not be able to leave this State without great loss, unless they decamp with the hurry and confusion that marked their last visit -- or, rather, visitation. The New Jersey Gazette, March 25, 1778

The British were more interested in gathering forage from the Jersey side of the Delaware River for their hungry comrades in Philadelphia than they were in engaging in any decisive battles. They were helped in those attempts by West Jersey Loyalists, who had sought refuge in British occupied Philadelphia from their former neighbors on the Jersey side of the Delaware. As a result, there were countless skirmishes between scavenging parties and the local citizenry. Most of them never were reported in either the loyalist or rebel press of the time, or, if they were, accounts of the engagements have not survived. A few have and they are illustrative of the border warfare along the Delaware River during the winter of 1778:

Philadelphia. Yesterday about twenty West Jersey loyalists crossed the Delaware, from this city, in order to assist some of their friends, who had expressed a desire of taking refuge here to avoid the horrid tyranny and implacable persecution of the rebels. At the mouth of Mantua Creek, they fell into a party of the enemy in ambuscade, whom they soon repulsed, advanced four miles into the country, and took one Wilson prisoner, who was a committee man, and, it is said, very active in distressing friends of government. They returned this day with their prisoner and their friends. The loyalists had one man killed but what the rebels suffered is not known. Wilson is in confinement. The Pennsylvania Evening Post, February 3, 1778

About ten days ago, a report was spread in this town [Trenton] that a party of the enemy had penetrated into Bucks County as far as Newtown. The intelligence [was] received this place this afternoon and [by] the evening, a respectable number of Militia were assembled at the different ferries. The next morning a party was preparing to cross the river in quest of the enemy, when intelligence was received that they were to return to Philadelphia, having plundered many of the inhabitants and carried off with them two loads of lumber from the house of Joseph Galloway, Esquire, Superintendent General In Philadelphia. The New Jersey Gazette, March 4, 1778

About three weeks ago, a number of cattle, having been sent from this State, intended for [Valley Forge], the enemy gaining intelligence thereof, and by the assistance of the Tories, way-laid them and took them, with several of the guard, in Pennsylvania, about sixteen miles from Philadelphia. The New Jersey Gazette, March 18, 1778

Philadelphia, March 11. On Friday, Capt. Wigstaff with part of his New Jersey independent volunteers [i.e.,loyalists], went down to Penn's Neck, where they were attacked by two armed boats from Christeen and, having nothing but musketry on board, were obliged to run her ashore after exchanging several shots. After Capt. Wigstaff had quitted her, the rebels took out the provisions and burnt the sloop. Capt. Wigstaff proceeded nine miles into the country and came down to Raccoon Creek, where he and his men got on board a sloop and returned to town with a quantity of provisions. During the excursion of this party of this Captain Wigstaff's company, another small party of them went over to Billingsport, marched ten miles into the country, surrounded the house of Capt. Cousins[90] of the militia, took him and his guard prisoner and brought them to town. Rivington's New York Loyal Gazette, April 1, 1778

While the British and American outposts raided each other along the Delaware, there were skirmishes aplenty between them in other parts of New Jersey. Rivington in his Loyal Royal Gazette reported or some of them, in his usual, one sided, distorted fashion that so infuriated the "rebels":

We have a Report that there has been a Skirmish between a Party of the King's Troops and the Rebels, at or near Coryell's Ferry, in New Jersey, in which the latter were very severely handled. Rivington's New York Loyal Gazette, April 6, 1778

New York, April 8. Last Sunday Morning a Party of about 200 of the King's troops landed at a Place called Squam, 40 Miles to the southward of Sandy Hook, in New Jersey, and destroyed the Rebel Salt Works at that Place and, next Day, also destroyed some of the same Kind of Works lately set up at Shark River near that Neighborhood. Rivington's New York Loyal Gazette, April 8, 1778

We are informed that on Wednesday morning last, a party of about seventy of the Greens [Loylists] from Sandy Hook, landed [91]near Major Kearney's, headed the Mill Creek, Middletowne Point [Matawan][92] and marched to John Burrow's, made him prisoner, burnt his mills and both his storehouses, all valuable buildings, besides a great deal of his furniture; also took Lieut. John Smock,

Captain Christopher Little, Mr. Joseph Wall, Capt. Jacob Covenhouse and several other persons; killed Pearce and Van Brockle and wounded another man mortally. Having completed these and several other barbarities, they precipitately returned the same morning to give an account of their abominable deeds to their bloody employers. A number of these gentry, we learn, were former inhabitants of that neighborhood. The New Jersey Gazette, June 3, 1778

New York, June 15. The Rebels last Tuesday Night at about one o'clock, began a heavy Cannonade from their works at Elizabeth Town Point and, soon after, attempted to land in a number of flat boats, upon Staten Island, between the Blazing Star and Burnt Island, but finding the Provincial troops stationed there were alarmed and prepared to give them a proper reception, they returned to the Jersey Shore and remained quiet until about four o'clock of the same morning, when they again made their appearance in ten boats, each supposed to contain a hundred men; and attempted to land in the same place under cover of their Batteries and a continued discharge of small arms from their boats, but they were so vigorously opposed by General Skinner's Brigade that they were obliged to make a final and disgraceful retreat.[93] Rivington's New York Loyal, June 15, 1778

By May, 1778, the speculation was that the British were going to evacuate Philadelphia. General Henry Clinton had replaced Lord Howe as Commander of the British forces in America. London had recognized that Howe's seizing the rebel capital, Philadelphia, had been a dalliance that did little to defeat Washington or his increasingly strengthening army, an army soon to be aided by the French. The rumor mill that the British were going to evacuate Philadelphia was fueled by reports such as the following:

We have accounts by various persons that the enemy have dismounted many of their cannon, and put them on board, that their transports are taking fresh forage board and 'tis suspected that they are preparing for a retreat. I am of the opinion, however, that they will not leave Philadelphia until they cannot possibly hold it any longer and perhaps the forage being put on board is only to accommodate the horses of Gen. Howe's family and the refugees who go with him, for I am informed by a gentleman who has been down with a flag, that General Howe will sail in a few days time for England. The Jersey Journal, May 20, 1778

The new commander, Clinton, indeed had ordered the evacuation of Philadelphia and it was not a trick. The British destroyed all the fortifications they had erected rather than have them fall into American hands:

I have just returned from the enemy's lines, where I have learnt that they were actually destroying their works, that all the ships, except the Vigilant and four transport ships and as many smaller vessels, were fell down, that the eight remaining were ordered to drop down as last night, that a number of boats, mounted on carriages, and a body of sailors to attend them, were at Cooper's Ferry, which boats were to transport the enemy across the creeks in Jersey, in case the bridges should be taken up or destroyed. The prisoners in Philadelphia will be exchanged in a few days when the enemy will probably move off immediately. They have knocked the trunnions off the iron cannon in the city and drove the broken pieces in the muzzles.

From good authority, we learn that the enemy have, during the fortnight past, impressed a great number of wagons and horses, belonging to the farmers near their lines in Pennsylvania, for the purpose of conveying part of their baggage through this state to New York, to which place a movement is daily expected. The New Jersey Gazette, June 10, 1778

The British ships would sail down the Delaware and disappear out in the Atlantic, beyond the ken of the landsmen. However, the cavalry, artillery and foot soldiers could not fade away from Philadelphia as effortlessly. They marched off in formation, in full battle regalia, followed by a train of supplies and civilian camp followers, a dozen miles in length. The Americans were at their heels, both the rebel and loyal press reported.

The British army early last Thursday morning completed their evacuation of Philadelphia, having before transported their

Stores and most of their artillery into the Jerseys, where they had thrown up some works and several of their regiments were encamped. They manned the lines the preceding night and, retreating over the commons, crossed over to Glouster Point. It is supposed that they will endeavor to go to New York. A party of the American light horse pursued them very close and took a great number of prisoners, some of whom were Refugees. The Pennsylvania Evening Post, June 20, 1778

The Royal Army, under the command of Sir Henry Clinton, left Philadelphia the 18th Inst. and [by] the 26th, a Division of them was at a Place called the Cross-Roads, Monmouth County, about 22 Miles S.E. from South Amboy; The Center was at Crosswicks and the Rear at Allen's Town, the last two mentioned places 5 Miles apart and halfway between Amboy and Philadelphia, a very plentiful Country.

Three fourths of the Militia of New Jersey are going to oppose the Royal Army by breaking up the Roads &c. Rivington's New York Loyal Gazette, June 29, 1778

At the same time as the American horse soldiers were chasing the British troops across the Delaware, the Jersey militia was attempting to slow the British advance through New Jersey by throwing obstacles in their path. The main American army -- now well fed, well trained and equally strong in number and led by General Washington -- planned to intercept the vulnerable British line of march in its week long march through Jersey. Washington sent Lafayette, the French volunteer to the cause of Liberty, ahead to harass the British and even further impede them.

Clinton halted his army near Monmouth Court House, now Freehold, in central New Jersey, not quite two thirds the way from Philadelphia to New York City. This is where Washington would battle the British. He sent General Charles Lee ahead with a strong advance force to engage the enemy sufficiently to permit Washington to come up with the main body of troops. Lee's forces attacked at 10 o'clock in the morning of Sunday, June 28th and, at first, were successful. However, British reinforcements soon pushed the attackers back. Lee, out of cowardliness or panic, ordered a general retreat. As he approached the line of battle with his own troops, ready to crush the British, Washington was suddenly overrun by the fleeing Americans. He and Lee exchanged heated words on the battlefield. Washington assumed command, personally rallied the troops and attacked the British. The events that followed were succinctly summarized the next morning by General Washington to his then trusted adjutant, General Benedict Arnold:

"I have the honor to inform you that, at about seven o'clock yesterday morning, both armies advanced on each other. About twelve, they met on the grounds near Monmouth Courthouse, where an action commenced. We forced the enemy from the field and encamped on the ground. They took a strong post in our front, secured on both flanks by morasses and thick woods, where they remained until twelve at night and then retreated. I cannot at this time go into a detail of matters. When opportunity permits, I shall take the liberty of transmitting to Congress a more particular account of the day." The Pennsylvania Post, June 30, 1778

Other contemporary accounts, all published in the American press, elaborate on the Battle of Monmouth:

His Excellency General Washington, having early intelligence of the intended movement of the enemy from Philadelphia, detached a considerable body of troops under the command of Major General Lee. These troops were intended to harass the enemy on their march though this state to Amboy and to retard them till General Washington, with the main body could get up.

The march of the enemy being thus impeded the main army on the 27th overtook the enemy at Monmouth Courthouse. Two field pieces, covered by two regiments, commanded by Colonels Livingston and Stewart, were advanced to check the enemy's approach, which they performed with great spirit and with considerable loss on both sides. In the mean time, strong detachments marched and attacked the enemy with small arms, with various success. The enemy were finally obliged to give way and we took possession of the field, covered with dead and wounded. The intense heat of the weather and the preceding fatigue of the troops, made it necessary to halt them and rest for a time. The enemy in the meantime, presenting a front of about one mile, advanced beyond the seat of action. They left on the field the honorable Col. Monckton, with several other officers and a great number of privates, which cannot be ascertained yet with precision. About 12 o'clock on Sunday Night, they moved off with great precipitation towards Middletown, leaving at the Courthouse five wounded officers and above forty privates.

On our side, Lieut. Col. Bonner of Pennsylvania and Major Dickinson of Virginia are slain; Col. Barber of this State is wounded by a musket ball which passed through the right of his body, but it is hoped will not prove mortal. Our troops behaved with the greatest bravery and opposed the flower of the British army. Our artillery was well served and did amazing execution. Before, during, and after the action deserters came over in great numbers and still continue so to do. Of the enemy's dead, many have been found without any wound, but being heavily clothed, they sank under the heat and the fatigue. We are well assured that the Hessians absolutely refused to engage, declaring it was too hot. Their line of march from the Court house was strewn with dead, with arms, knapsacks and accouterments, which they dropped on their retreat. They had the day before taken fifteen prisoners, whom in their haste, they left behind. Had we possessed of a powerful body of cavalry in the field, there is now doubt the success would have been more complete. The New Jersey Gazette, July 1, 1778

The Battle of Monmouth had proved inconclusive. The British fled during the night across Monmouth county to Sandy Hook Bay where they boarded transports back to New York City. It was the last time that the two main armies would meet in battle. The remainder of the war would involve conflicts between lesser commands or battles between the northern or southern armies. The Battle of Monmouth also provided for the legend of Molly Pitcher[94], who, while bringing water to the artillery gunmen, saw her husband wounded and jumped into his place and kept his gun firing.

Washington, still enraged at what he considered the cowardliness of General Charles Lee, ordered a court martial. According to his report to Congress, published in the press, he had ordered Lee and his men to make the initial assault upon the enemy but:

"to my great surprise and mortification, I met the whole advanced corp retreating and, as I was told, by General Lee's orders, without having made any opposition. The peculiar situation of General Lee at this time requires that I should say nothing of his conduct. He is now in arrest. The charges against him, with such sentence as the court martial shall decree, shall be transmitted for the approbation or disapprobation of Congress, as soon as it shall be passed.[95] *The New Jersey Gazette, July 8, 1778*

During 1778, an old threat, in new form, revisited the western border of New Jersey. The settlers there, as well as in the eastern Pennsylvania and the lower Hudson River regions, had, from the first days of colonization, been plagued by periodic Indian attacks. Usually they had been incited by the French in Canada. The Indians were not the native, peaceful New Jersey Leni Lenape, who, by 1758 numbered fewer than a hundred and were contained on a tiny reservation near Burlington. They were the fierce Iroquois from the north, warriors of the Confederate Nations, and their allies, the Mohawks, Onondaga, Senecas, Oneidas, Cayugas, Tuscaroras, Nanticokes and Conoys.

Everyone thought that the threat of hostilities with the Indians had ended in 1763, when the French departed North America. The British took over the lucrative Indian trade of the French which created better relations. Sir William Johnson, his son John and nephew Guy Johnson were the Crown's representative to these Indians. Sir William, in fact, married Mohawk princess Molly Brant and took into his household her brother, Joseph. Now, faced by the insurrection of its colonists, Britain quickly used the relationship created by Johnson to their benefit, recruiting the Iroquois to incite fear along the frontier.

The British/ Indian alliance was headed by two New York Loyalists, a father and son team, John Butler and son Walter, a major. Their regiment, known as Butlers Rangers, were frontier troops recruited among the Loyalist refugees. About 500 strong, and accompanied by as many Indians, one detachment of Rangers, led by John, marched into the Wioming Valley of Pennsylvania and attacked the settlement at Forty Fort. They killed all but 60 of the Americans who had sought protection there. The survivors were tortured and then slaughtered by Butler's Indian allies. Queen Ester, a half breed woman chief, had a dozen Americans formed into a circle and, while dancing and jumping, tomahawked them to death one by one. This slaughter came to be known as the Wioming Valley Massacre among the patriots.

A few months later, another detachment of Rangers, led by the younger Butler and a body of Indians, under Molly Brant's brother Joseph, a Mohawk of considerable intelligence and education, surprised the Cherry Valley settlement of New York, killing almost all the soldiers and about 30 of the settlers, including all the women and children that they had caught outside the walls. This came to be called the Cherry Valley Massacre.

The terrorism had the desired effect. The rumor of an Indian attack struck fear in the hearts of those along the Jersey, Pennsylvania, New York frontier.

Several Indians on the frontier of Pennsylvania have informed many of the inhabitants of that Province that, as soon as they have their corn planted, they intend to take up their hatchets in order to aid the Great King over the water, in consequence of which, several families had removed from Wyoming and Shamokin into many parts of New Jersey. Rivington's New York Loyal Gazette, May 18, 1778

We are well informed that Col. Butler's Party, now on the Frontiers of Pennsylvania, New Jersey and this Province, amounts to at least 5 to 6000 men and daily increasing, that the Settlers, back from Carlisle in Pennsylvania, to the City of Albany, are in the greatest tribulation and daily retiring. Rivington's New York Loyal Gazette, August 17, 1778

Meanwhile, things were looking a lot better on the eastern portion of New Jersey. The American forces, confident after Monmouth and well manned, crossed the Hudson, back to Westchester County, north of New York City. They had been chased from there two years before. Moreover, the French had arrived. For those in New Jersey, the first manifestation of this new alliance came in the form of a fleet suddenly appearing in Sandy Hook Bay. It immediately threw up a blockade of New York City, forcing starvation to those loyalists and British soldiers living there:

We are informed that the French Fleet are drawn up in a line just without Sandy Hook, so as to prevent even a pilot boat from getting out of New York Harbor; that the East River is also blocked by two French seventy-fours; that General Washington with the grand American Army, crossed over the North River last week and will unite with General Gates above Kingsbridge. Thus are the enemies of America surrounded on all sides by the forces of the Magnanimous and Most Christian King and the virtuous citizens of America. It is therefore more than probable that the destruction of the emissaries of Britain had concerted for the free and independent sons of America will, ere long, fall with tenfold misery on their own heads.

Since our last, a number of American prisoners, being lately exchanged, arrived here from New York. They left that place on Thursday last and report that the British Army, as well as the citizens, are under great apprehension on the appearance of the want of bread in that city, it being very scarce already. The New Jersey Gazette, July 22, 1778

If the French Fleet should preserve its present position, a famine must, I think, (and very soon) ensue in the enemy's army, as all their supplies must be cut off. Nothing but rice, instead of bread and flour, has been dealt out to the soldiery since their arrival in New York. A loaf of bread that used to cost 4 pence now sells in the city for a dollar. In short, it appears to me, not at all impossible, that if they should be thus kept hemmed in on the sea and land side, they will be reduced to the necessity of surrendering the city in less than a month, without any enterprise of General Washington against them. The Pennsylvania Packet, July 25, 1778

Despite being still at war, the Americans had much about which to be happy two years after their Declaration of Independence. Their toasts - one for each of the states in rebellion - illustrate the patriots' thanks:

Last Saturday, being the Anniversary of the Declaration of our Independence, was commemorated at Princeton with the greatest demonstration of joy for our happy deliverance from tyranny and arbitrary power and the glorious prospect of transmitting freedom and happiness to our latest posterity. At six o'clock in the afternoon (a signal gun having been previously fired to collect the inhabitants) the solemnity commenced by the discharge of thirteen rounds of cannon, being some of the brass field pieces having been previously taken from General Burgoyne. The discharge of the cannon was preceded by three huzzas from a large concourse of people, all exulting in the opportunity of expressing their congratulations in being delivered from the yoke of a merciless tyranny and his execrable minions. After this, His Excellency the Governor, with such of the Members of the Legislative Council and General Assembly as were in Town, with the Officers of the Army and Militia, repaired to the Governor's Quarters, where they passed the rest of the day with great festivity and decorum and drank the following toasts:

1. The Honorable Congress
2. The Free and Independent States of America
3. His Excellency General Washington
4. The American Army and Navy
5. May our Independence endure while the sun shall shine or the rivers flow
6. His Most Christian Majesty, our illustrious Ally and the magnanimous Protector of the rights of mankind[96]
7. May the Confederated States of America be ever supported by the same public virtue and patriotism by which they were established
8. Our Ambassador at the Court of Versailles[97]
9. The State of New Jersey
10. Our brave and patriotic Militia
11. All our officers and privates engaged in the battle at Monmouth Court House in which we obtained a complete victory over the choicest and most veteran of the enemy's troops

12. The memory of all the heroes who have fallen in defence of American liberty during the war
13. May our example excite the oppressed in every part of the world to resist the outrages of tyranny and may they be equally as successful in asserting the natural and unalienable rights of mankind.[98]

In the evening the inhabitants testified their joy by a general illumination of the village. The New Jersey Gazette, July 8, 1778

Indeed, everywhere there was a spontaneous love for this new born babe America, which made grown men act as infatuated and giddy youths. Witness this citizen's (known to us only by the name Adolphus) "throwing together a few lines" on "The future Glory of America" and sending it along to The New Jersey Gazette, together with the optimistic prediction that "[s]hould America continue to be the Land of Liberty, it will probably be the happiest country the sun ever saw. The contemplation of this must animate every generous mind in the cause of freedom". The poem tells what a circling lark sees at daybreak in the America of the Future and is worth re-reading a score of times until we can understand, and thereby recreate, the exhilaration of our birth as a nation:

She sees the time when this New World shall show
The giant strength she bears and crush the foe
When tyrant kings shall vex her realms no more
But haughty Britain trembles at her power
When mad Bellona shall forget to rage
And smiling peace recalls the Golden Age
When Angel Freedom hastens to our shore,
She calls it hers, nor be an exile any more.
See! peaceful hamlets deck the rural scene
and towns arise by many a distant stream.
I see them rise beside's Ontario's flood,
where once huge oaks and ancient poplars stood,
I see them glittering in the Ohio's tide
I see them deck the Mississippi's side

I see the time when Industry explores
the desert thro' and meets the ocean's shores
What millions swarm (call'd forth by Freedom's ray)
From Georgia's groves to Baffin's frozen bay,
From where the huge Pacific laves her shore
To where the wild Atlantic surges roar
To bless the millions, Art exhausts her powers
And lavish Nature empties all her stores;
While Commerce lays her treasures at their feet
And rifles different lands to make them great.
Here Governments their last perfection take,
erected only for the People's sake.
Founded no more on Conquest or in Blood,
But on the basis of the public Good.
No contests then shall mad ambition raise
No chieftains quarrel for a sprig of praise
No thrones shall rise, provoking lawless sway
And not a King to cloud the blissful day
But FREEDOM, universal FREEDOM, reigns
Nor sees a slave in all happy plains
The New Jersey Gazette, May 20, 1778

As the summer progressed, General Washington's troops remained north of New York City in Westchester. The French fleet patrolled the coast and the bottled up British army and the civilian Loyalists of New York City became increasingly hungry:

(Extract of a letter from camp at North Castle, dated July 21, 1778)
The army has at length joined the troops under General Gates and is encamped at this place, a few miles from White Plains. How long we shall continue here is uncertain, but I hope we shall soon move down to Kingsbridge and add to terrors and distress which is said to reign among the enemy's troops and the numerous tribe of Tories which is collected in New York from all parts of America. Deserters who come out to us daily say that their army is already distressed for want of flour but they look for

relief from the Cork fleet, which is expected daily. But this I hope will fall in the hands of the French fleet, which now lies at the Hook, braving the British flag which once waved in triumph along the coasts of France. The New Jersey Gazette, July 29, 1778

While there was overall calm in the Jersey countryside during the summer of 1778, there were still the usual forays and skirmishes along the Hudson and Jersey shorelines. For example:

Last Saturday morning a small Boat from Kings Bridge, going too near the Jersey Shore at Hoebuck, was fired upon by a Body of Men that lay in Ambush in the Meadows and 'tis supposed that some of the People in the Boat got hurt. The Boat immediately made to the Shore, when the Crew were made Prisoners and the Boat burnt. Rivington's New York Loyal Gazette, September, 7, 1778

We are informed that on Friday the 18th instant, two armed ships and two brigs, belonging to the enemy, came to anchor close to Tom's River Inlet, where they lay all night and next morning between seven and eight o'clock, they sent into the inlet seven armed boats with between 20 and 30 men in each, who retook the Ship Washington, formerly called the Love and Unity and two sloops which were near the bar, with most of their crews. The Captain of the Ship, his Mate, Boatswain and three sailors made their escape in one of the Sloop's boats. Soon after they got ashore, a certain Robert M'Mullen (who sometime since was condemned with William Dillon, to be hanged for burglary in Monmouth, and both having been reprieved) took the boat and made off to the enemy, huzzaing as he went. Dillon, who also joined them some time before, was supposed to pilot the British vessels in the inlet. The New Jersey Gazette, September 30, 1778

We hear that on Wednesday last, the enemy left Egg Harbor, after having destroyed several vessels and the houses of a few gentlemen, who had distinguished themselves by their attachment to the American cause. They have, it is said, bent their course towards Tom's River in order to destroy our salt works. The New Jersey Gazette, October 14, 1778

Among the officers who fell into the hands of the enemy in Col.'s Baylor's late disaster, at Old Tappan, were Captain Swan, Doctor Evans, Junior, surgeon, Lieut. Randolph and three Cornets. Capt. Stith, being suddenly surrounded by the enemy's horse and foot and seeing no probable way of getting off, called out for quarter, but they contrary to the rules of war and every sentiment of humanity, refused his request, called him a damn'd rebel and struck him over the head with a sword -- which fired him with such indignation, that he bravely fought his way through them, leaped over a fence and escaped into a morass. Lieut. Barret got off on horseback; Lieut. Morrow, with a number of others badly wounded and left on the field as dead, were next morning brought off by a party of the regiment. The New Jersey Gazette, October 21, 1778

We hear that a certain George Zabriskie was a few days since shot on the Road near Paramus in New Jersey by a Person unknown. The day before he had been busy in pressing wagons to carry the Grain from the Farmers in that Neighborhood, agreeable to an order of Congress.[99]
The New York Gazette and Weekly Mercury, June 29, 1778

To the patriots, it seemed as if some major British troop movement were afoot. The feeling lasted all summer, yet nothing ever happened. Clues and rumors abounded that Britain was going to move its main army out of New York. Peculiar preparations were being made and strange ships (which later proved to be British) appeared on the horizon:

We have certain information that the enemy is getting water on board their shipping with the utmost industry. The New Jersey Gazette, August 5, 1778

Yesterday, the British fleet, under Lord Howe, sailed from the Hook for Rhode Island, as 'tis said. We are also informed that a number of transports are taking troops on board at New York, but are uncertain as to their destination. The New Jersey Gazette, August 12, 1778

About 7 o'clock last Saturday Evening, seven large Ships, Two Deckers, came to an Anchor off Sandy Hook, 6 of them were black sided, the other bright. One of them had a red flag at her Main Top Mast Head. Rivington's New York Loyal Gazette, August 17, 1778

A gentleman from Cape May informs us that a fleet of ships approached the coast of New Jersey, somewhat southwesterly of Little Egg Harbor, on Thursday and Friday last. A large ship and five smaller vessels only were seen but it was manifest there were several others in company by signal guns fired in the offing. The weather was hazy. The Pennsylvania Evening Post, August 18, 1778

A little more than a month later, British troops invaded the rich farms of the neutral Dutch of northern New Jersey, raiding the countryside for provisions with which to fill these ships.

(Extract of a letter from Springfield, New Jersey, dated October 6, 1778)
Since I came home, I snatched a moment to give you a small account of the enemy's proceedings. They possess the ground between the North and Hackensack Rivers, near the half of Bergen County, which they were very busy stripping. Upwards of one hundred vessels, some pretty large, went up to bring off their forage; several have returned, of these we burned four; they were loaded with forage and the petticoats of old women. The hay was pressed and stalls made and, to appearance, ready to put directly to sea. Yesterday, they crossed the Hackensack River and possessed the heights on the east side of the Passaic River, driving and carrying off with great industry till near night, when they returned to their old quarters over Hackensack. Which way they intend to stretch their course next is uncertain. Great preparations were made at Staten Island to invade us at Elizabeth town and Woodbridge and Vaughn,

the firebrand who has command of the Island, swears by the Eternal God that he will burn every house in Elizabeth town. Our comfort is that he, as well as the other devils, has his chain, beyond this he cannot go. Our militia here seems to manifest their usual spirit. The distance of our grand army leaves us indeed much exposed, but, if we are invaded, we are determined to yield our country but by inches and to sell every inch dear and slow. The Pennsylvania Evening Post, October 9, 1778

Would the British attack Elizabeth and central New Jersey? What exactly were they up to? Sometimes, during that October of 1778, it appeared as if they were abandoning New Jersey, not assaulting it:

The enemy has embarked ten full regiments and the vessels have fell down with them to [Sandy] Hook. We have information by deserters this day that the enemy has evacuated Paulus Hook and Hoobuck; if so, they have no outpost left in New Jersey. They were also evacuating Fort Washington. Fort Independence and their other works without Kingsbridge, they had abandoned some days ago. We observed them moving off from their encampment nearest us on Staten Island this morning, whether with intent to leave the Island or set down on some other part of it, is not yet certain. The New Jersey Gazette, October 21, 1778

We hear that on Monday last about 100 sail of transports with troops on board, under convey of several men of war, sailed from the Hook, supposed for the West Indies. The New Jersey Gazette, October 21, 1778

We hear a few only of the enemy's troops remain on Staten Island and those are commanded by General Skinner. They have no provisions or stores of any kind, it is said, but what are drawn from New York. The New Jersey Gazette, October 21, 1778

In early November, the British fleet in fact sailed away. General Clinton had abandoned New York, except for a garrison on the always loyal Staten Island. The Americans would have to wait to learn their enemy's destination.

All things considered, the year 1778 had turned out to be pretty successful. There had been a lot of apprehension but, aside from the Battle of Monmouth where the Americans displayed their mettle against Britain's best, no other major engagements had taken place in the Middle Atlantic region. Content, the Americans spread out their forces across Dutchess County, just above Westchester, New York and in northern New Jersey and settled in for the winter:

General Washington's Head Quarters, about 20 Days ago, was at Pauling's Purchase, in Dutchess County and we hear his Army was cantoned as far as Hartford Eastward and West to Short Hills, in Morris County, New Jersey. Rivington's New York Loyal Gazette, November 30, 1778

It is reported that the American Army is about to go into winter quarters. For this purpose, part of it has already crossed the North River and head quarters, we are told, will shortly be established at Lord Stirling's Seat, at Baskenridge, in this State.
The New Jersey Gazette, November 25, 1778

CHAPTER 9

The Soldiers of the Revolution

The American Revolution so altered the manner in which men governed themselves that it is uniformly depicted in epic terms, with its leaders described more like gods than humans and its ordinary soldiers shown as possessing extraordinary courage and endurance. And those descriptions are indeed appropriate. No revisionist could suggest that Washington truly was not a genius at the bold use of out numbered, ill equipped and independent irregular forces. Or that he could have been more patient at their faults, or quicker to take advantage of their strengths. Nor can the modern historian deny that the soldiers themselves at times displayed super human strength in both their accomplishments and in the sufferings they endured. Imagine thousands of poorly clothed soldiers, many of them bootless, with feet wrapped in rags, crossing an ice clogged Delaware River, in the teeth of a winter storm and then marching miles on frozen rutted roads in below freezing weather to attack the Hessians entrenched in Trenton. Would the citizen of today even contemplate such an ordeal? Can he even fully appreciate it? Or does he merely skeptically dismiss it as a patriotic fable?

Just as the Revolutionary War period - the era during which our nation was born and our natural rights as citizens forged - has been relegated to being just another chapter of the many in the book of American history, like the Roaring Twenties or the Great Depression, so too has the role of George Washington as leader been neglected or even devalued by those unschooled in his remarkable achievements. No man was more indispensable, than was General Washington to the ultimate American victory in the War for Independence. A decade later he would be equally heroic as President of the Convention that drafted the Constitution and, after that, as President of the Republic itself for two terms.

Virtually all first hand accounts of Washington express awe at his impressive carriage and the dignity with which he presented himself. Physically, he was a large man, taciturn, with a regal bearing. He was also one of the wealthiest men in America, especially after his marriage to the widow Martha Custis. He had supported the principles of the Revolution from the very first, including serving as a delegate to the First and Second Continental Congresses. The former commander of the Virginia militia and experienced in fighting the French west of the Alleghenies, Washington had become the obvious choice of the Continental Congress in June, 1775 to be the Commander in Chief of the American forces, a selection which even the always independent New Englander quickly accepted.

It became Washington's responsibility to quickly organize, form and command an army of citizen soldiers to combat the greatest military force then known to mankind, that of Great Britain. And, if that were not sufficient challenge, he would then have to keep his army together through eight years of war in the face of many difficulties, often with only slight support from Congress or the countryside. Opportunistic and decisive, Washington excelled in fighting the defensive war, using to his advantage, as each particular situation required, the unfamiliar thickly wooded American terrain and his highly independent irregular force -- described by one historian as a force "in which every man was his own company commander, if not his own colonel". As we shall see later, Washington was also a spymaster extraordinaire, controlling a ring of American agents that helped even the odds against him and America. Clearly, Washington's leadership was well regarded, by those who risked their necks and properties to follow him, as is evidenced in an humorous exchange appearing in the colonial press.

BONMOT
A British officer in New York, being in company with a lady whose sentiments were favorable to the cause of liberty, was making some severe remarks upon the American troops.
"However, Madam" said he, "I think you have a Howe and a Clinton in your Army[100]."
"We have, Sir," replied the Lady, "but you have not a Washington in yours." The New Jersey Gazette, November 11, 1778

Without doubt, there was something about Washington that commanded respect. His bravery was unquestioned. So was his dedication to the cause. Maybe, oddly enough in the popular concept of a military leader, it was the humanity in Washington that set him apart from the professional military commanders:

> *After the battle of Princeton, on the third of this instant, General Washington, perceiving a wounded soldier belonging to the enemy laying on the field, came up to him and, after enquiring as to the nature of his wound, commended him for his gallant behavior and assured him that he should want for nothing that his camp could furnish him. After the General left him, an American soldier who thought he was dead, came up in order to strip him; the General, seeing it, bid the soldier begone and ordered a sentry to stand over the wounded prisoner till he was carried to a convenient house to be dressed. The Pennsylvania Packet, January 22, 1777*

The contemporary press described General Washington as a "wise and able leader whose prudence, firmness and attention to his great charge, have procured him the most unlimited confidence both of those who direct the public counsels and of those who are in arms under his command."[101] He certainly enjoyed the respect and trust of the officers and men who served under him, as the following account suggests:

> *Agreeably, to the above orders, His Excellency George Washington, his amiable lady and suite, Lord Stirling, the Countess of Stirling, with other General Officers and Ladies, attended at nine o'clock at the Jersey Brigade, and, after prayer, a suitable discourse was delivered to Lord Stirling's Division, by the Rev. Mr. Hunter.*
> *At half past eleven, the whole army repaired to their alarm posts, upon which General Washington and the General Officers reviewed the whole army at their respective posts. And, after the firing of the cannon and musketry and [after] the huzzas were given agreeably to the orders, the army returned to their respective brigade parades and were dismissed.*
> *All the officers of the army then assembled and partook of a collation provided by the General, at which several patriotic toasts were given, accompanied by three cheers. His Excellency took leave of the officers at five o'clock, upon which there was universal huzzaing -- Long live General Washington -- and clapping of hands*

until the General rode some distance. The non-commissioned officers and privates followed the example of their officers as the General passed their brigades. Approbation indeed was conspicuous in every countenance and universal joy reigned throughout the camp.
The New Jersey Gazette, May 13, 1778

Perhaps, part of the soldiers' devotion to Washington was due to the manner in which he was quick to share victory with, and to applaud publicly, the efforts of his men:

We hear his Excellency General Washington, having made the necessary disposition of the Continental Army for covering the fort at West Point has, in public orders, thanked and discharged all the militia, who had turned out to his assistance in order to check the further progress of the enemy up the North River. The New York Gazette, June 23, 1779

The Commander and Chief cannot leave this post without expressing the highest sense he entertains of the conduct and bravery of the officers and men of Maxwell's Brigade, in annoying the enemy in their incursions of the 7th instant. Col. Dayton merits particular thanks. He also with pleasure embraces this opportunity of testifying that the behavior of the militia has been such as to do them signal honor and entitles them to the warmest approbation. There never, since the commencement of the contest, appeared a more general ardor, than animated all ranks on this occasion and the spirited opposition given was attended with answerable effects.
The New Jersey Gazette, June 28, 1780

The citizens too viewed Washington as a hero of epic proportions and expressions of the adoration given him can be witnessed in opening verses of a paean composed in his honor by Governor William Livingston of New Jersey, himself an extraordinary leader under the name Hortentius. Can citizens today even imagine the American public showing such affection and respect for one of its leaders?

TO HIS EXCELLENCY GENERAL WASHINGTON

Say -- on what hallow'd altar shall I find,
A sacred spark that can again light up
The muse's ardour in my wane of life
And warm my bosom with poetic flame
Extinguished long --and yet O WASHINGTON,
thy worth unequall'd, thy heroic deeds,
Thy patriot virtues and high soaring fame,
Prompt irresistibly my feeble arm,
To grasp the long forgotten lyre and join
the universal chorus of thy praise.
When urg'd by thirst of arbitrary sway
and over-weaning pride, a ruthless king
Grim, spurn'd us, suppliants, from his haughty throne
And, in the tyrant, all the father lost;
When, to our prayers, with humble duty urg'd,
He, Pharoh-like, his heart obdurate steel'd,
Denouncing dreadful vengeance, unprovok'd
And all the dire calamities of war--
No ray of mercy beaming from his brow,
No olive branch extended in his hand
A sword unsheath'd, or ignominous yoke,
The only sad alternative propos'd --
Then, with one voice, the Country call thee forth,
Thee, WASHINGTON, she call'd --with modest blush,
But soul undaunted, thou the call obeyed,
To lead her armies in the martial field --
Thee, WASHINGTON, she call'd to draw the sword,
And rather try the bloody chance of war
In virtue's cause, than suffer servile chains,
Intolerable bondage! to inclose
The Limbs of those, whom God created free.
                    HORTENTIUS
         The New York Gazette, April 1, 1778

Some idea of the esteem in which General Washington was held by the ordinary American people might be gleaned from the respect accorded his wife, even when the General was not accompanying her.

Wednesday evening last arrived at Newark, in their way of the Provincial Camp at Cambridge, the Lady of his Excellency General Washington, the Lady of Adjutant General Gates, John Custis and his Lady and Warner Lewis Esq. They were escorted from Elizabeth Town by the company of Light Horse and most of the principal gentlemen of that borough and, at their arrival in Newark, the bells were set ringing and Colonel Allan's company of minute men immediately mounted guard. About 10'clock on Thursday morning, Lady Washington and Lady Gates etc., escorted by a company of the Elizabeth Town Light Horse and a great number of ladies and gentlemen form Newark, set out for Dobb's Ferry, in order to pass the North River at that place on their way to the Provincial Camp. The Pennsylvania Gazette, December 6, 1775

General Washington had many excellent officers on whom to depend. Some were from Europe, volunteers to the aid of the American cause for liberty and independence. The Marquis de Lafayette, for example, was only 19 years old when he arrived in America but his amiability and idealism quickly made him a favorite of General Washington's. The Battles of Brandywine, Monmouth and Yorktown matured him and his exploits there and throughout the war also made him a favorite of the American people as well.[102] Another, Johann de Kalb, Bavarian born[103] and French trained, accompanied Lafayette to America. He was to fall, sword in hand and victim of a dozen wounds, in the Battle of Camden, South Carolina. Tadeusz Kosciuszko, from Poland, brought with him important military engineering knowledge (which helped insured victory at Saratoga), as well exemplary fortitude as a calvary commander. Friedrich Wilhelm von Steuben, a former Prussian staff officer, once in the service of Frederick the Great, but down on his luck when recruited in France by Benjamin Franklin, is credited with taking Washington's irregular troops at Valley Forge and transforming them into disciplined military units. Casmir Pulaski, a Polish Count was permitted to raise his own elite corps, which became known as the Pulaski Legion. Most of the enlistees were British deserters and prisoners of war, who might have been attracted by the promise of booty. In fact, plundering proved to be a problem of the Pulaski Legion.

Congress, having resolved to raise a Corps consisting of Infantry and Calvary, to be commanded by General Count Pulaski, all those who desire to distinguish themselves in the service of their country, are invited to enlist in that corps which is established on the same principle as the Roman Legions were. The frequent opportunities which the nature of those services will offer to the enterprising, brave and vigilant soldiers as will serve in it, are motives which ought to influence those who are qualified for admission into it, to prefer it to another corps, not so immediately destined to harass the enemy and the many captures which will infallibly be made must indemnify the legionary soldiers for the hardship they must sustain and the inconsiderable sum given for bounty, the term of their service being no longer than one year from the time the corps shall be completed. Their dress is calculated to give a martial appearance and to secure the soldier against the inclemency of the weather and the season. The time for action approaching, those who desire to have an opportunity of distinguishing themselves in that corps are requested to apply to Col. Kowatch, at Head Quarters at Easton, to Major Julius, Count of Mont -Fort, at Head quarters or at Major Beltkin's quarters at Trenton. The New Jersey Gazette, April 23, 1778

Pulaski was to die of wounds received, leading his Legion, in an attack against the British in Savannah in 1779.

General Washington even had a general in his command who claimed to be a member of the British nobility, Lord Sterling:

Bad news from New York this morning. A man who calls himself Lord Sterling (I believe one of his family has a right to the title, but passed eldest, and this gentleman plays alone) put himself at the head of three thousand men, in conjunction with that arch rebel (Lee) and has driven all the well effected people from the Town of New York. The Pennsylvania Evening Post, September 21, 1776

Born in New York City of well to do Scots Jacobite emigrant parents, William Alexander spent may years in England and increased the fortune left him.[104] He claimed the title of "Lord Stirling" from an ancestor, the Scottish Earl of Stirling, but the House of Lords disagreed and denied it to him. Nevertheless, he continued to use the title and it was how his American compatriots, including General Washington, referred to him. He fought in the Battle of Long Island, where he was captured, then exchanged. He was also involved in the various New Jersey campaigns, where his bravery was only outshone by his daring. His battlefield coolness is attested to in the following account:

> *I must not omit to mention a little affair that happened in the late engagement. The fire growing hot and our men beginning to retreat, a British officer singly rode up to a cannon that was playing on the enemy, and with his pistol and hanger, forced every man from it; then, seeing Lord Stirling, he cried: "Come here, you damned rebel, and I will do for you."*
>
> *Lord Stirling answered him by directing the fire of four marksman upon him, which presently silenced the hardy fool, by killing him on the spot. Our men recovered the field piece which their want of small arms obliged them to surrender. The Pennsylvania Journal, July 2, 1777*

Washington also had many brave and capable officers in his command who were American born or bred. As with Washington's own battle record, they were not always victorious, but, taken together, performed the job for America. "Mad Anthony" Wayne of Pennsylvania, for example, captured the British fort at Stoney Point in the Hudson and fought bravely at Brandywine, Germantown and Virginia's Green Spring. "Light Horse" Harry Lee was commander of Lee's Legion, an elite force of mounted dragoons and light infantry units that effectively specialized in quick hits upon the enemy. He won an important victory at Paulus Hook, on the Jersey shore, opposite the southern tip of Manhattan Island, but most of his combat was in the south.[105] Benjamin Lincoln, born in Massachusetts, was a hero at Saratoga, surrendered Charlestown to the British, then redeemed himself at the crucial battle of Yorktown. Horatio Gates secured a giant victory in Saratoga but was soundly defeated at Camden. Israel Putnam began the war as one of America's most experienced veteran of the prior conflicts with France, was a hero at

Bunker Hill but a major cause in the patriot defeat in the Battle of Long Island.

Even under the leadership of men like Washington, the American army would have accomplished nothing without the courage and endurance of the rank and file. Wars are fought by ordinary soldiers, the front line troops. These are men who suffer the hardships of little pay, not enough food, boredom and poor shelter, miss their families, worry about the wisdom of their actions and necessarily fear the next morning's battle.

Happily, the newspapers of the period, like snapshots, preserve for posterity some of the ordinary soldier's life that have not been romanticized by history. Indeed, some of these accounts also saved, like dirty family secrets, evidence of conduct by both our and British troops that might better have been forgotten.

When hostilities began in Massachusetts in 1775, the "United Colonies" were still forming the Continental Army, the forebear of our army of today.[106] The following resolution of the Continental Congress, dutifully published in the newspapers, provides us a sketch of those first recruits:

Province of New Jersey in Congress, February 5, 1776.

WHEREAS, by a Resolution of the Continental Congress, a third Battalion is recommended immediately to be raised in this Colony, for service and at the expense of the United Colonies, consisting of eight companies and each company of seventy eight privates and officered with one Captain, two Lieutenants, one Ensign, four Sergeants, and four Corporals, which recommendations this Congress being desirous fully to comply with, do therefore resolve, that Officers of said Battalion be immediately recommended for Commissions and that the Captains and Subalterns be appointed and warrants issued for enlisting the aforesaid compliment of men,

Resolved, that agreeable to the recommendations of the Honorable Continental Congress, the recruiting officers enlist none but healthy, sound, and able bodied freemen, not under sixteen years of age. The form of the enlistment to be in the following words:

"I, ----, have this day enlisted myself as a soldier in the American Continental Army for one year, unless sooner discharged,

and do bind myself to conform in all instances to such rules and regulations as are or shall be established for the government of said army."

Resolved, that no apprentice whatsoever be enlisted within this colony, without the consent of his master or mistress first obtained in writing and that every person under the age of twenty one years, enlisting himself as aforesaid, within twenty fours hours after their parents or guardians have notice of said enlistment, obtain his discharge, by refunding the money received from the recruiting officer and returning such necessaries as may have been supplied him by the officer or the value thereof in money.
That it be recommended to the officers of said battalion, to pay the strictest attention to the behavior of the troops in quarters or on their march that they give no reasonable cause of complaint.
The New York Gazette, February 19, 1776

The Continental Army, of course, needed more than the traditional foot soldier. A mobile, well armed fighting force required support troops of every description, as the following advertisements suggest:

NOTICE IS HEREBY GIVEN to all persons capable of driving a team, who are willing to enlist for carters, to serve for three years, that they have twenty dollars bounty, six pounds per month from the time of their enlistment, a suit of new clothes every year and a great coat (if possible) and shoes and boots, by their producing a certificate from their wagon master of their good behavior. All persons willing to enlist on the above terms are desired to meet me at my quarters in Trenton.
Samuel H. Sullivan, D.Q.M.G.
The New Jersey Gazette, February 25, 1778

WANTED IMMEDIATELY
A Number of good TRADESMEN, that are single, such as Carpenters, Smiths of all branches, Armourers, Gun Stockers or Wheelwrights. Any of the above tradesmen that are willing to serve themselves and Country, shall by applying to Capt. Wylie, at the grand continental works at Carlisle, receive Twenty Dollars bounty,

Thirty Dollars each man per month pay, one suit of clothes per year and a ration and a half each man per day and good quarters. The New Jersey Gazette, June 17, 1778

A Man well acquainted with blowing the TRUMPET and capable of teaching the Horse Duty of that instrument, will meet with good encouragement by applying to Major Bland, commandant of the first regiment of Light Horse, at Morris Town, or at the Headquarters of the Continental Army. The Pennsylvania Packet, April 1, 1777

At the beginning of the war, while the Continental army was still forming, the militia from each state had to respond to the immediate need for fighting men. These militias, the ancestors of our state chartered National Guard of today, were comprised of citizen/soldiers, formed on a local level, who, while living at home, periodically drilled together, very often on a casual and irregular basis. Initially, a protection against Indians and then used as a supplement to regular British forces in England's North American struggles against France and Spain, most of these troops had seen little or no action since the cessation of hostilities with France in 1763. But they were excellent riflemen, especially with their own weapons, which went with them. Their assistance proved invaluable throughout the war, frequently instrumental in the victories. By war's end, they had developed into an impressive military force, whipped into shape by the likes of Von Steuben and other European professional military men:

New York, June 17th. We hear from Morris Town that, in obedience to orders from General Dickinson, Colonel Ford drew up his Regiment in order to draught one quarter of them for immediate Service, who, to the Honor of their Country and the Cause in which they are engaged, immediately turned out as Volunteers. It is hoped that these spirited people will meet with the Applause they deserve and encourage others to imitate their noble Example. The New York Gazette, June 17, 1776

New York, June 22. The Militia of the Province of New Jersey are divided into two Brigades as follows, viz, Sussex, Morris,

Bergen, Essex, Somerset and Middlesex to be commanded by General Wind; and Salem, Cumberland, Cape May, Glouster, Monmouth, Hunterdon and Burlington under the command of General Heard. The New York Gazette, June 22, 1778

Major General Dickinson set off from this place [Trenton] yesterday morning to take command of the Jersey Militia in order to cooperate with the Continental Army in rebelling the incursions of the enemy, who have taken post on Elizabeth Town Point.
It must give the most heartfelt pleasure to Friends of Liberty and Independence of our country, to observe with what unanimity and resolution, the militia hase turned out for the support of the common cause and gives a happy presage to our final success.
The New Jersey Gazette, June 14, 1780

The militia continued to improve and, by war's end, was certainly a competent military force.

On Friday last, the Camp which had been formed at Trenton by the Militia of this state, by orders of his Excellency General Washington, broke up in consequence of a countermand by him. It consisted of 1500 infantry, two companies of artillery, with four pieces of cannon and a troop of Light Horse. During their encampment, they daily practiced the manoeuvres and disciplines introduced into the Continental Army by Baron Steuben and made very great progress. The greatest harmony and good order prevailed. They were well provided with tents and all other necessaries for actual field service. In a few days more, the whole, with the addition of Lancaster, York and Cumberland, would have made a corps of 3400 men, all under the Command of his Excellency, the President of the State, ready to cooperate with the Continental army, if their services had been immediately necessary. The Pennsylvania Packet, September 5, 1780

Discipline is part of a soldier's life and essential to an army's performance on the battle field. It was no different during the Revolution:

GENERAL ORDERS

Head Quarters, Morris Town, April 8, 1777

HIS Excellency, the Commander in Chief orders, in the most positive terms, that all the Continental Officers, who are absent without leave in writing from himself, or some Continental General Officer, or are not upon any special command or not on the recruiting service (the two last by proper authority) do immediately join their respective corps, without the least hesitation or delay. The time for which they have written furloughs cannot be exceeded by a single hour. Such as have been sent upon particular commands or are engaged in the recruiting service, must pay the utmost attention to their orders. No excuse can be admitted for idleness or dissipation, at a time when their own honor and their country's interest call them to the field.

His Excellency does not wish to convey these orders through the channel of a newspaper, but the difficulty, indeed, impracticability of transmitting them in time in any other way, render it indispensably necessary.
By his Excellency's Command.
G. Johnston, A.D.C.
The Pennsylvania Packet, April 15, 1777

All Recruits belonging to the third New Jersey Regiment, whose Furloughs are out, are required to rejoin their Regiment at Head Quarters at Morris Town, on or before the 25th of this month. Those who neglect this NOTICE will be deemed deserters and treated accordingly.
Joseph Bloomfield
Major, 3d Jersey Regiment
The Pennsylvania Gazette, April 16, 1777

Head Quarters, Morristown, May 8, 1777
GENERAL ORDERS
As few vices are attended with more pernicious consequences in civil life, so there are none more fatal in a military one that of gaming, which often brings disgrace and ruin upon officers and injury and punishment upon the soldiery. And reports prevailing that this destructive vice has spread its baneful influence in the army the Commander in Chief, in the most pointed and explicit

terms, forbids all officers and soldiers playing at cards, dice or any games except those of exercise for diversion.
Morgan Conner, Ad. Gen. pro tem
The Pennsylvania Evening Post, May 17, 1777

A soldiers lot includes the possibility of capture, wounding and even death and the news press of the period contains accounts of each. In modern warfare, when soldiers are captured, they are detained as prisoners of war until the end of hostilities. In the warfare of the 18th century, however, prisoners were periodically recycled, returned to the enemy in exchange for the release of the soldiers it had captured. Until they were exchanged, some of the captured officers would be allowed "parole", a non custodial captivity, based on an officer's honor, which even allowed them to remain armed:

Trenton, Sunday last, Brigadier General Thompson, Colonels Magaw and Reynolds, having been sometime past out of New York on parole, passed through this town on their return to captivity, in conformity to Requisition of our Commissary General of Prisoners. The New Jersey Gazette, January 13, 1779

[We learn] that Capt. Armstrong, with several other officers taken at Fort Lafayette, contrary to the articles of capitulation, were stripped of their side arms upon their arrival at New York. The New Jersey Gazette, June 23, 1779

However, many prisoners of war, officers among them, were imprisoned and there mistreated. Notorious were the British prison ships, mastless hulks lying in New York Harbor, into the lower decks of which were crammed thousands of captured Americans. Each morning at the most notorious the Jersey, the day began by the British guard shouting "Rebels throw out your dead"! They were never disappointed with the number of corpses. Over eleven thousand Americans died in this and the other prison hulks anchored in New York Harbor.[107] Incidents of mistreatment of prisoners resulted in rebel threats of retaliation:

Last Night, Capt. Nathaniel Fitz Randolph of Woodbridge, with a party of 15 volunteers, landed on Staten Island, surprised and made prisoners 13 of the militia of the Island who were on guard; also Col. Christopher Billop Farmer, Lieut. Daniel Winants and one more not on duty, without firing a musket shot or any accident happening to him or his party. It ought to be mentioned in connection with this worthy officer and his brave followers that, although the law of retaliation would have justified their marking their route with devastation and ruin, they were careful not to do the least injury to any peaceable inhabitant. But, O ye destructive, butchering British Monarch, beware! We are not obliged to delay retaliation any longer! Therefore, as you value the safety of your friends on the island, do not set such another example as that of Middletown, for the consequences may be fatal to the Tories of the island, in spite of all your efforts to protect them. The New Jersey Gazette, June 10, 1778

Not to be outdone, James Rivington also accused the Americans of mistreating captured British soldiers:

Staten Island, May 18, 1780
Mr. Rivington,
Yesterday, a number of exchanged British Naval Prisoners were arrived here from Elizabeth Town. In Lieu of Fat Beef, the poor fellows have had thirteen dried Clams, per day, for a considerable time. A Ration (if the expression can subsist on it) or a man's allowance of those testaceous animalulae, for twenty four hours, you have inclosed and may hang up in your Store, a specimen of the expiring emanantions of the Rebel Cornu Copia. The Royal Gazette, May 20, 1780

Eventually an exchange of prisoners would be negotiated between the British and the Americans:

Headquarters, Valley Forge, February 18, 1778. We hear that an exchange of prisoners is soon to take place between General Washington and General Howe, the latter having consented to give up the point so long in dispute about the prisoners sent out last winter on parole. Most of them were treated so hardly that they died soon after their arrival among us or were rendered forever unfit for service and, consequently, were not proper objects for an exchange. The New Jersey Gazette, February 25, 1778

Ironically, like all discussions between enemies, reaching an agreement would be a long, drawn out process:

Last Wednesday, the Commissioners who met at Amboy, for the purpose of setting up a cartel for the exchange of prisoners, broke up, having effected only the partial exchange of a few civil staff officers. It is hoped, however, that their negotiations will lead to the general release of all prisoners now in the hands of the enemy, although the powers of the British Commissioners were inadequate to the forming of a permanent cartel. The Jersey Journal, March 29, 1780

Chatham, September 27. We hear that General Phillips and General Lincoln, who met at Elizabeth Town last week as commissioners from the two armies, for the purposes of effecting an exchange of prisoners, have done nothing towards bringing about so desirable an affair. They are to meet again on Long Island. The New York Gazette, October 9, 1780

Last week, forty of our officers who have been in captivity with the enemy, were exchanged and came over to Elizabeth Town and, on Sunday last, one hundred and fifty privates. The New Jersey Journal, November 8, 1780

In addition to the risk of capture and incarceration in the dreaded prison ships, the soldier had to fear being wounded in the battle. As sometimes happens in war, the damage was accidentally inflicted by the soldiers upon their own comrades:

This morning as detachment of about 300 of the enemy, under the command of Col. Boskirk, made descent into this country. Their object was manifestly to murder and carry off the militia. They divided themselves into two parties, each going upon a scout. They met at the house of J. Zabriskie at about one o'clock A.M. and, mistaking one another for the rebel guard (as they call it) fell upon each other in a most furious manner, and by the discharge of their muskets and the use of their bayonet, they appear to have made a dreadful slaughter, the ground round the house being in a measure covered with blood, and in some places, the clotted gore lay in heaps when we arrived at the spot, which was at five o'clock. After this, they, finding their mistake, retreated over and took up the bridge to prevent our men from pursuing them. 'Tis said they had seven or eight killed on the spot, besides wounded. All were carried off. The New Jersey Gazette, June 14, 1780

Surprisingly, while it scrimped in providing the Continental Army soldier with many of the necessities of life, the Congress did do all it could to provide adequate medical care to the American wounded:

The liberal provision made by Congress in the new medical arrangement, joined with a humane desire to prevent the repetition of the distresses which afflicted the brave American soldiers the last campaign, have drawn men of the first abilities into the field to watch over the health and to preserve the life of the soldiers, many of them from very profitable and extensive practices and every species of domestic happiness. None but gentlemen of the best education and well qualified are employed as senior Physicians, Surgeons, &c. The Eastern and Northern Departments are filled with gentlemen of the first character in those countries and the public may depend on it that the greatest exertion of skill and industry shall be constantly made, and no cost spared, to make the sick and wounded soldiery comfortable and happy. As a consequence of the above liberal arrangement of the Honorable Congress, we do, with great pleasure and equal truth, assure the public (notwithstanding the many false and wicked reports propagated by the enemies of American liberty and only calculated to retard the recruiting service) that all the military hospitals of the United States are in excellent order and that the army shall enjoy a degree of health seldom seen or read of. W. Shippen, jun. Director General of the American Hospitals, and John Cochran, Physician and Surgeon General of the Army in the Middle Department The Pennsylvania Evening Post, June 5, 1777

Trenton, December 23. It is with pleasure that we can inform the public that, of a thousand sick and wounded, admitted into the general hospital of this place, since the departure of our army from Valley Forge, only forty three have died and not above fifty convalescents and inoculated patients) remain in the charge of the surgeons. The New Jersey Gazette, December 23, 1778

We hear from Brunswick in New Jersey, that out of upwards of 1,500 sick, who were admitted into the military hospital in that place, since November last, only 22 have died. This extraordinary success in the management of the sick has been justly ascribed, next to the diligence and care of the Surgeons, to the plentiful and punctual supply of stores and necessaries of all kinds for the sick, by the present Purveyors of the hospitals. The Pennsylvania Packet, June 17, 1779

The worse fate, save dishonor, that a soldier could suffer was, of course, death in battle or in the prison ships. The obituaries of fallen soldiers made all Americans aware of the price that was being paid for this new born concept of "Liberty" and gave fresh meaning to Horace's "Dulce et decorum est pro patria mori"[108]:

Tears like the dew shall fall on the memory of heroes. In the action at Monmouth on the 28th day of June last, fell Lieutenant McNair of the Artillery, an officer who deserves the tears of his country. Born in North Britain, he came to America and early embarked in the cause against the tyrant. He served as a private in the first campaign in Boston and, in the course of the war, rose gradually through the intermediate offices from a private to a lieutenant, without the least solicitation to obtain that promotion and without the interest of one friend, but what his merit gave him. He was humble in spirit, modest in manner and steady in his conduct. His Captain, in a letter of the 25th of August from the Camp at White Plains, writes of him as follows. "I cannot help but lament the death of so valuable an officer. He was cool, attentive to his duty, intrepid and brave, undisturbed in the hottest engagements and commanded with the firmness and courage of a Roman. He was loved and esteemed by the officers and loved and feared by the soldiers. He was humane and extremely charitable. He was possessed of the highest sense of liberty and wished to establish the independence of his country. He had a warm sense of duty to God and lived regularly and religiously. He died fighting bravely for his country against slavery and tyranny. Not less than a cannon ball separated his noble soul from his body. The New Jersey Gazette, September 16, 1778

Deaths--Col. Philip Johnson of New Jersey. This gentleman, we hear, in the late action on Long Island, behaved with remarkable intrepidity and fortitude. By the well directed fire from his battalion, the enemy were several times repulsed and lanes were made through them, until he received a ball in his breast, which put an end to the life of as brave an officer as ever commanded a battalion. General Sullivan, who was close to him when he fell, says no man could behave with more firmness during the whole action. As he sacrificed his life in defense of the invaded rights and liberties of his country, his memory must be dear to every American who is not insensible to its sufferings. The Pennsylvania Evening Post, September 12, 1776

Sadly, atrocities and war are inseparable companions and, while neither the American nor Britisher of today is eager to admit it, the Revolutionary War had its share of such repulsive conduct.

Atrocities were committed by both sides and, although narratives of these events have disappeared from the popular histories of the war, the press accounts of the time preserve their existence. Some accounts might be explained by the discovery by editors like James Rivington of the Royal Gazette and Isaac Collins of The New Jersey Gazette of the propaganda value that exaggerated or distorted news could contribute to a war effort. Yet, the large number of claims reported and contemporaneous official reaction to them give some credence as to their existence. For example, the British charged the rebels with assorted atrocities:

One of the many instances of barbarity exercised by Joseph Hedden of Newark, in East New Jersey, a Rebel judge and justice, who, in the heat of the summer of 1777, issued his mandate to banish a helpless woman and her children for no crime except for her husband being a friend to His Majesty's Government and, accordingly, sent a rebel guard to execute his order, who, when they came to the house of this disconsolate woman (six miles from Newark) found her very weak and unable to travel, having been delivered of twins about fourteen days before, which excited so much compassion in the guard as to cause them to forego their orders and return without the woman, which only produced a new and absolute decree from Hedden to bring her in at all hazards to Newark, and from thence to be sent to Bergen and, when the rebel captain remonstrated to Hedden that executing his order would be the death of the woman, Hedden relied "Let her die. There will be one damn'd Tory less" and accordingly the guard was sent a second time and brought her and her children in a wagon to Newark, although she fainted (through weakness) on the wagon; when the woman arrived at Newark, her deplorable case drew tears even from the eyes of the rebels and the kind office of some friends of the same sex enabled her to go through the next day the last stage of her journey to Bergen, where, soon after her death and the death of her two innocent babes, closed the dismal tragedy. The Royal Gazette, March 18, 1780

A Specimen of Rebel Humanity, experienced at Newark, New Jersey, by the Wives of Thomas Longworth, Isaac Longworth, Uzal Ward and some others whose Husbands left that Place last January and took Refuge in this City. The Committees of Newark ordered that the Wood be cut off their Land, their Grass and Hay to be destroyed and their Persons insulted and they were not permitted to remain in this Province longer than the 26th ult. , when Guards were placed around their Houses and their Effects secured. To expostulate was needless, as the Guards told the Women, if they refused to obey, Violence would be used. The Cries of Mothers, Women and Slaves, obliged to leave their Homes, for differing in Sentiment from their Neighbors, would have999999 Pity in the Breast of any but Savages. The New York Gazette, July 7, 1777

We hear from Shrewsbury that a young Man, very inoffensive in his Behavior, except being a Friend to Government, was last Week hung up at his Father's Door, without Ceremony, by one Forman who calls himself a Major, for no other Crime than an attempt to bring off from that Place, a few Cheeses to this Town, where he had been forced to take his Abode. After he had hung for several Hours, it was with the utmost Difficulty that the relentless Murderer could be prevailed upon to indulge his afflicted Father so far as to permit him to bury the Body. Does not this (to use a Phrase of William Livingston's, the Usurper of the Government of New Jersey) "Out barbarize all the Barbarities in History!" The New York Gazette, October 27, 1777

On the 13th of March, 1777, I was seized early in the morning by a rebel sergeant named Post and twelve others, all armed, and brought to the Town of Newark, fifteen miles from my own house, through mud and dirt the whole way, near knee deep,(my persecutors being allowed to ride). I was arraigned before Hedden, Burnet and the rebel Major Hays. Many speeches being made by Hedden and Hays and three witnesses sworn against me. Hedden said that, if I would make an ample confession, it would be better for me. I told him I head none to make; he repeated the same words with this addition, that, if I did not, he would find proof to hang me at the next court, being the second Tuesday in April following. I again told him I had no confession to make; he then wrote a mittimus and committed me to the main guard, where I was treated with the greatest indignity till the 18th, at night, when I made my escape and got to Staten Island, and during the time he had me in confinement, being from the 13th to the 18th inclusive, there was no refreshment allowed me, but water, and very little of that.

A JERSEY REFUGEE
The Royal Gazette, March 11, 1780

The Americans accused the British of similar barbarity:

In Congress, April 18, 1777
The Committee appointed to inquire into the conduct of the enemy beg leave to report that in every place where the enemy has been, there are heavy complaints of oppression, injury and insult, suffered by the inhabitants from officers, soldiers and Americans disaffected to their country's cause. . . [The Committee] now briefly state what they found to be the truth upon each of the [four parts of their inquiry]:

First, the wanton and oppressive devastation of the country and destruction of property

The whole tract of the British army is marked with desolation and a wanton destruction of property, particularly through Westchester county in the State of New York, the towns of Newark, Elizabeth Town, Woodbridge, Brunswick, Kingston, Princeton and Trenton in New Jersey. The fences destroyed, houses deserted, pulled in pieces or consumed in fires, and the general face of waste and desolation spread over a rich and well cultivated and well inhabited county, would affect the most unfeeling with compassion for the unhappy suffers. . . Places and things, which by their public nature and general utility should have been spared by a civilized people have been destroyed, plundered or both. But, above all, places of worship, ministers, and other religious persons of some particular Protestant denominations seem to have been treated with the most rancorous hatred and, at the same time, with the highest contempt[109].

Second, the inhuman treatment of those who were so unhappy as to become prisoners

The prisoners, instead of the humane treatment which the prisoners taken by the United States experienced, were in general treated with the greatest barbarity. Many of them were kept near four days without food altogether. When they received a supply, it was both insufficient in point of quantity and often of the worse kind. They suffered the utmost distress from cold, nakedness and close confinement. Multitudes died in prison. Sometimes the common soldier expressed sympathies with the prisoners and the foreigners, more than the English but this was seldom or never the case with the officers; nor was any charitable assistance given them by the inhabitants who remained in or resorted to the city of New York.

Third, the savage butchery of those who had submitted and were incapable of resistance

The Committee found it to be the general opinion of the people in the neighborhood of Trenton and Princeton that the enemy, the day before the battle of Princeton, had determined to give no quarter. Officers wounded and disabled, some of them of the first rank, were barbarously mangled and put to death. A minister of the gospel at Trenton, who neither was nor had been in arms, was massacred in cold blood, though humbly supplicating for mercy.

Fourth, the lust and brutality of the soldiers in abusing of women

The Committee has authentic evidence of many instances of the most indecent treatment and actual ravishment of married and of single women.

On the whole, the Committee are sorry to say the cry of barbarity and cruelty is but well founded.

The above report received, approved and ordered to be published with the proofs.

Charles Thomson, Secretary
The Pennsylvania Evening Post, April 24, 1777

The British army burnt, stripped and destroyed all as they went along. Women and children were left without food to eat or raiment to wear. Three hundred barrels of flour were sent down toward Westfield and Ash Swamp, by order of his Excellency, to be distributed among the poor sufferers. The enemy even destroyed all the bibles and books of divinity they came across; this I assert as fact. The Pennsylvania Evening Post, July 10, 1777

I had almost forgot to mention that our brigade was just in the rear of the British Army, during part of their late excursion into New Jersey, and do assure you that, till then, I had no idea of the inhumanity and acts of cruelty these people can be guilty of. Barbarity and the most wanton destruction of private property, marked their footsteps throughout their whole tour; were I to attempt descending into particulars, it would far exceed the bounds of a letter. The Pennsylvania Evening Post, July 12, 1777

From a correspondent, we have received the following Intelligence:
"On Saturday, the 21st ultimo, about break of day, our guard posted on Hancock's Bridge on Alloways Creek, in Salem County, consisting of about twenty men, were surprised by those of the enemy called Jersey Volunteers.[110] They, from their acquaintance with the country, had found means to cross the creek and came upon the guard from some unsuspected quarter and, being undoubtedly led by some person well acquainted with the disposition of the sentries, opened the guard house door and came in, many of the guards being asleep, without giving the least alarm. Nay, so far from it, that it is said that some of them shook hands in a friendly manner with some of the guard, with whom they were intimately acquainted, as indeed they were with most of them and -- O Tempora! O Mores![111] -- immediately began bayoneting them, with our people not making the least show of resistance, not only reeking their fury upon the guard but also on some of the peaceable inhabitants who were slumbering in their beds. One Bacon, of the people called Quakers, was inhumanly murdered in his own house and bed; Old Mr. Hancock, beside his being of that society, was a cripple in both his arms, was stabbed in his bed and is since dead of his wounds. Another of that

society is also dead of his wounds and the life of a fourth person is despaired of. The New Jersey Gazette, April 8, 1778

We hear Col. Baylor's regiment of horse, having taken post at or near Old Tappan were surprised in the night by means of a Tory giving the enemy information and who conducted them along by-roads into the rear and between our our sentries. These horrible murderers consisted of two regiments of British Light infantry, a regiment and two troops of horse, who made a joint attack, the British Officers ordering their men "to give no quarter to the rebels". A considerable portion of [the American troops] unavoidably fell a sacrifice to those cruel and merciless men. Several of our men were murdered after they had surrendered.[112] Colonel Baylor, Major Clough and Dr. Evans were dangerously injured [and] taken prisoner; the Major, we hear, has since died of his wounds; 20 others were killed on the spot, the like number left for dead and near 30 wounded and taken off by the enemy. *The New Jersey Gazette, October 7, 1778*

As soon as they [the British soldiers] came to Connecticut Farms, seven miles from the place of their landing, they began the exercise of their awful cruelty. They first set fire to the house of Deacon Wade and then to the Presbyterian church, but soon advancing to the house of the Rev. Mr. Caldwell, they had an opportunity to reach the summit of that cruelty after which they have been climbing for so many years. Mr. Caldwell could not remove all his property or his family. His amiable wife, with a babe of eight months, and one of three years old, with the housekeeper and a little maid, were left. Mrs. Caldwell, having dressed herself and put her house in order, retired with them to the back room, which was so situated that it was secure from transient shot from either party, should they dispute the ground near her house, which happened not to be the case. The babe was in the arms of the house keeper, the other child the mother held by the hand, all sitting on the side of the bed, when the barbarians, advancing around the house, took advantage of a small space, through which the room was accessible, and fired two balls into that amiable lady, so well directed that they ended her life in a moment. From some circumstances, this does not appear to be the act of one rash inconsiderate villain, but the effect *of deliberate orders given before their coming to the place that she should be murdered. She was stripped of part of her clothes but her corpse was preserved from the flames by two or three of the enemy whose humanity was not yet extinct. This was murder without provocation and most opposite to humanity. Not satiated by this horrid deed, after stripping the house, they set fire to it and eleven more dwelling houses in the neighborhood.*

Thus has British cruelty been led to perfection by the hirelings of Hesse. Six widows are burned out, some very aged and some others with small families and almost all the houses in the neighborhood, which were not burned out, were torn to pieces and entirely plundered...

Their brutality to some women at the Farms would even make Savages blush and we are informed, from undoubted authority, that the same line of conduct has been pursued in Elizabeth Town toward some of the first characters. New Jersey Journal, June 7, 1780

The British Troops are now on the point below Elizabeth Town. Their flanks are secured by the water which makes them unattackable. They advanced, on landing to Connecticut Farms, burning and pillaging, but on the appearance of our army retreated under cover of a heavy shower of rain before midnight and took their present position. The distress occasioned by their devastations is too shocking to reflect on. An American who could have beheld the scene and not sworn vengeance against the savage enemies, ought to have a mark set on him as a curse to the human species.

On my arrival at the Farms, immediately after they had left it, the first object that presented itself to my view, was a handsome young country girl in the most affecting distress and anguish of mind, who had the night before, been forcibly subjected to the brutal violence of seven or eight different officers of that army. When we questioned her, she could only answer in broken accents of the most excessive grief -- that she was ruined and wished never again to be spoken to.

The situation of poor widows and numbers of other women flying almost naked for protection, having lost their houses and nearly everything in them, was considered comparatively happy [by the British]. If there is justice to be dispensed in this world from above, it must surely visit these sons of cruelty, ere long, whose scarlet crimes are daily filling up the measure of their iniquities.

I never saw soldiers pant more for revenge than ours do, not a deserter from us since we came to the ground, but all anxious for the happy hour when they shall receive orders to engage an enemy who has with coward violence only desolated the weak and unprotected. The New Jersey Gazette, June 21, 1780

Mercenaries, especially from the German state of Hesse,[113] were also responsible for atrocities against the civilian population of New Jersey:

It appears from an orderly book found with the Hessians who were taken at Trenton last December, that the following letter was given out in the general orders on the 29th of August last, signed Van Heister, who says it was sent to him by General Howe.

(copy of a letter from a Gentleman in Long Island to General Howe):

"I was this morning an unwilling spectator of outrages as I never believe could have been committed in a Christian country. The Hessian Troops have plundered this place entirely and without distinction of persons. They have driven every poor person out of their houses and robbed them of their property, which I believe will have the most unhappy consequences.

I am sure the commanding general will not permit such dreadful havoc and I entreat you to acquaint him with it that we may be freed of our misery as quickly as possible."

In consequence of the above letter, the General issued his orders, forbidding such conduct in the troops under his command but it seems that similar complaints were repeatedly made and no effectual means taken to prevent them.

The British recruited Indians to terrorize the frontier population. The Cherry Valley and Wioming massacres of 1778, where British commanders watched while their Indian allies ritually tomahawked white captives to death, were sad examples. The following letter from an Indian chief to King

George and the gifts he sent him are graphic evidence of the cruel times:

> *(Extract of a letter from Captain Griffith of the New England militia, dated Albany, March 7, 1782)*
> *The peltry taken in the expedition will, as you see, amount to a good deal of money. The possession of this booty at first gave us pleasure, but we were struck with horror to find among the packages eight big ones, containing scalps of our unhappy country folk, taken in the three last years by the Seneca Indians from the inhabitants of the frontiers of New York, New Jersey, Pennsylvania and Virginia and sent by them as a present to Colonel Haldimand, Governor of Canada, in order to be transmitted by him to England. They were accompanied by the following curious letter to that gentleman.*
>
> *Tioga, January 3, 1782*
> *May it please your Excellency,*
> *At the request of the Seneca chiefs I send herewith to your Excellency, under the care of James Boyd, eight packs of scalps, cured, dried, hooped and painted with all the Indian triumphal marks of which, the following is invoice and explanation.*
> *No. 1. Containing 43 scalps of Congress soldiers, killed in different skirmishes. These are stretched on black hoops, four inches diameter. The inside of the skin is painted red with a small black spot to note their being killed with bullets. Also 62 of farmers killed in their houses; the hoops red; the skin painted brown and marked with a hoe; a black circle all around to denote their being surprised at night; and a black hatchet in the middle, signifying their being killed with that weapon*
> *No. 2. Containing 98 scalps of farmers killed in their houses; hoops red; figure of a hoe to mark their profession; great white circle with sun to show they were surprised in the day time; a little red foot to show they stood their defense and died fighting for their lives and families*

No. 3. Containing 97 scalps of farmers; hoops green to show they were killed in the fields; a large white circle, with a little round mark on it for the sun to show that it was in the day time; black bullet marks on some; hatchets on others

No. 4. Containing 102 scalps of farmers mixed of the several signs above; only 18 marked with a little yellow flame, to denote they being of prisoners burnt alive after being scalped, their nails pulled out by the roots and other torment. One of these latter supposed to be a rebel clergyman, his band being affixed to the hoop of his scalp. Most of the farmers appear by the hair to have been young or middle aged men, there being but 67 very grey haired heads among them, which makes the service more essential

No.5. Containing 88 scalps of women; hair long and braided in the Indian fashion to show they were mothers; hoops blue; skin yellow ground with little red tadpoles to represent, by way of triumph, the tears of grief occasioned among their relations; a black scalping knife or hatchet at the bottom to mark their being killed with those instruments; 17 others, hair very gray; black hoops; plain brown colour; no mark but the short club or caffetete, to show they were knocked down dead or had their brains beat out

No. 6. Containing 193 boys scalps, of various ages; small green hoops; whitish ground on the skin, with red tears in the middle and black bullet marks, knife, hatchet or club, as their deaths happened

No. 7. Containing 211 girls scalps, big and yellow, small yellow hoops, white ground; tears, hatch, club, scalping knife &c.

No. 8. This package is a mixture of all the varieties above mentioned to the number of 122; with a box of birch containing 29 little infant scalps of various sizes, small white hoops, white ground, no tears and only a little black knife in the middle to show they were ripped out of their mother's belly

With these packages, the Chiefs send to Your Excellency, the following speech, delivered by Coneiogatchie in council, interpreted by the elder Moore, the Trader, and taken down by me in writing.

Father,

We wish you to send these scalps over the water to the great King, that he may regard them and be refreshed and that he may see our faithfulness in destroying his enemies and be convinced that his presents have not been made to ungrateful people.

Father, attend to what I am now going to say. It is a matter of much weight. The great King's enemies are many and they grow fast in number. They were formerly like young panthers. They could neither bite nor scratch; we could play with them safely; we feared nothing they could do to us. But now their bodies have become big as elk and strong as the buffalo. They have also great and sharp claws. They have driven us out of our country for having taken part in your quarrel. We expect the great king will give us another country, that our children may live after us and be his friends and children as we are.

Father, we have only to say further that your traders exact more than ever for their goods and our hunting is lessened by the war, so that we have fewer skins to give for them. This ruins us. Think of some remedy. We are poor and you have plenty of everything. We know you will send us powder and guns and knives and hatchets but we also want shirts and blankets.

I do not doubt but that your Excellency will think it proper to give some further encouragement to those honest people. The high prices they complain of are the necessary effect of the war. Whatever presents might be sent to them through my hands, shall be distributed with prudence and fidelity. I have the honor of being Your Excellency's most obedient and most humble servant
JAMES CRAUFURD

Indeed, despite claims that looting and other atrocities were sometimes encouraged by the military commanders, it appears that more often the leaders attempted to prevent it:

> *It is said that several of the Hessian Officers, from a just sense of Honor and Conviction of the Meanness of suffering a soldier to plunder, are resolved to discourage it entirely. Perhaps, the best means of discouraging it in the future would be to burn all that the Soldiers have collected before their faces and to assure them they must expect the same Attention to real military Discipline hereafter.* The New York Gazette, January 13, 1777

> *His Excellency General Washington strictly forbids all officers and soldiers of the Continental Army, the militia and all recruiting parties, plundering any party whatsoever, whether Tories or others. The effects of such persons will be applied to public uses in a regular manner and it is expected that humanity and tenderness to women and children will distinguish brave Americans contending for liberty from infamous mercenary ravagers, whether British or Hessians.*
> G. Washington
> The Pennsylvania Evening Post, January 14, 1777

> *By His Excellency, WILLIAM LIVINGSTON, ESQ. Governor, Captain General and Commander in Chief in and over the State of New Jersey and territories thereunto belonging, Chancellor and Ordinary in the same*
>
> PROCLAMATION
> *WHEREAS, it has been represented to me that several detachments of the Militia of this State have, at different times, seized and carried away the goods and effects of their fellow inhabitants, on pretense that the owners thereof were inimical to the liberties of America. [It is] a practice which is not only repugnant to the laws of the land, whereby every man's property is secured and protected until it is declared forfeited by judicial process, but hath a manifest tendency to inflame the minds of the sufferers, to excite jealousies and contentions between the inhabitants, at*

a time when we should be peculiarly studious of cultivating unanimity and concord, to disuse amongst the soldiery a spirit of licentiousness and plunder and to relax, or rather to abolish, all discipline in the military, as well as in the civil department, I have therefore thought fit to hereby strictly charge and command all the officers and privates of the militia to desist for the future from all such depredations and violence.

Given under my hand and seal at arms of Haddonfeld, this fifth day of February, in the Year of Our Lord One Thousand Seven Hundred and Seventy seven
William Livingston
By his Excellency's command
Charles Pettit, Secretary
GOD save the PEOPLE
The Pennsylvania Packet, February 11, 1777

Camp, Middle-Brook, February 6th,
The Commander in Chief approved of the orders issued by Major General Lord Stirling, during his command at this Camp, and thanks him for his endeavors to preserve order and discipline, and the property of the farmers in the vicinity of the Camp. He doubts not but the officers of every rank, from a just sense of the importance of securing to others the blessings they themselves are contending for, will use their utmost vigilance to maintain those privileges and prevent abuses, as nothing can redound more to their personal honor and the reputation of their respective corps.
ALEX. SCAMMELL, Adjt.. Gen
The New Jersey Gazette, February 17, 1779

It is an ugly side of the Revolution and one upon which history books understandably rarely dwell. Civilized men acted as animals. The following account of a British demand for American surrender, under threat of the most dire alternatives, even singling out specific individuals for retaliation, certainly proves the truth of Churchill's assertion that civilization has a very thin veneer. On the other hand, the American response to the threat should warm every patriot's heart. First, the challenge:

> *Colonel Mawhood, commanding a detachment of the British army at Salem, induced by motives of humanity, proposes to the militia of Quintin's Bridge and the neighborhood, as well officers and private men, to lay down their arms and depart each man to his home. On that condition, he does solemnly swear to re-embark his troops without delay, doing no further damage to the country and he will cause his commissaries to pay for the cattle, hay and corn that have been taken, in sterling money.*
>
> *If, on the contrary, the militia should be so far deluded and blind to their true interest and happiness, he will put the arms which he has brought with him into the hands of the inhabitants well affected, called Tories, and will attack all such of the militia as remain in arms, burn and destroy their houses and other property and reduce them, their unfortunate wives and children, to beggary and distress and to convince them that these are not vain threats, he has subjoined a list of the names of such as will be the first objects to feel the vengeance of the British nation.*
>
> C. Mawhood, Colonel
>
> *Edmund Keesby, Thomas Sinnickson, Samuel Dick, Whitten Crips, Ebenezer Howell, Edward Hall, John Bowen, Thomas Thomson, George Trenchard, Elisha Cattle, Andrew Sinnickson, Nicholas Keen, Jacob Hufty, Benjamin Holmes, William Shute, Anthony Sharp and Abner Penton*

And the American response:

SIR,
> *I have been favored with what you say humanity has induced you to propose. It would have given me great pleasure to have found that humanity had been the line of conduct to your troops since you came to Salem. Not only denying quarters, but butchering our men who surrendered themselves prisoners in the skirmish at Quinton's Bridge last Thursday and bayoneting yesterday morning at*

Hancock's Bridge, in the most cruel manner in cold blood, men who were taken by surprise, in a situation where they neither could, nor did, attempt to make any resistance, and some of whom were not fighting men, are instances too shocking for me to relate and I hope for you to hear. Your proposal that we lay out arms, we absolutely reject. We have taken them up to defend rights that are dearer to us than our lives and will not lay them down, 'till either success has crowned our cause with victory, or like many ancient worthies contending for victory, we meet with an honorable death. Your threats to wantonly burn and destroy our houses and our property and reduce our wives and children to beggary and distress, is a sentiment that my humanity almost forbids me to recite and induces me to imagine I am reading from a cruel order of a barbarous Attila and not a Gentleman, brave, generous and polished, with a genteel European education. To wantonly destroy, will injure your cause more than ours. It will increase your enemies and our army. To destine for destruction the property of our most distinguished men, as you have done in your proposals is more like a rancorous feud between two contending Barons, than a war carried on by one of the greatest powers on earth, against a people nobly struggling for Liberty. Be assured that these are sentiments and determined resolution, not of myself only, but of all the officers and privates under me.

Elijah Hand, Colonel
The New Jersey Gazette, April 15, 1778

CHAPTER 10

The War: 1779

According to the European fashion of war, wintertime normally was not the season for major troop engagements, Washington's surprise attack on the British at Trenton on Christmas, 1776, being an exception. Instead, armies retired into secured camps for the colder season, content on resting, re-supplying and retraining the troops and preparing for the next campaign that would begin late the following spring. Washington had chosen Middle Brook in New Jersey, about seven miles further up the Raritan River from New Brunswick for his camp for the 1778-79 winter. He sent some troops there, towards the end of November, to build huts and fortifications for their comrades, who would be coming in during December.

It was a mild winter, compared to the one before at Valley Forge and, what, obviously unknown to them, would be the horrors and suffering that awaited them at Morris Town the next winter, 1779/80. At least during the 1778/79 winter, there was sufficient food and supplies and the enemy was remote enough in New York to make things comfortable.

The Americans were aware that the British had a stratagem in mind, but not what it was. Intelligence gathered by Washington's agents[114] suggested that the British were focusing their attention to the south and redeploying much of their main army to Georgia and the Carolinas. They thought the South to have more Loyalists who might stage a counter revolution. The intelligence Washington received turned out to be accurate, although it would be months before news from the southern front would reach the general public. Savannah was captured on December 29, 1778 and Augusta on January 29, 1779. Meanwhile, the Americans in the Jerseys watched ship movements and listened to gossip from New York in an attempt to guess where the war was headed next:

By a Gentleman who left New York on Saturday last, we learn that the enemy there, are very busy in preparing for another embarkation, but the place of their destination remains a profound secret. The New Jersey Gazette, February 17, 1779

> *Tuesday last 28 sail of square rigged British vessels put to sea from Sandy Hook.* The New Jersey Gazette, April 28, 1779

> *We learn that on the 5th instant, a fleet of about 70 sail of British vessels put to sea from Sandy Hook, with troops on board, said to be bound to the southward.* The New Jersey Gazette, May 12, 1779

Do not think that because the main action had shifted to the south and the resident American and British armies were comfortably holed up in their winter quarters that everything was quiet in New Jersey. There were many skirmishes, guerilla warfare, with quick forays by both sides designed to seize or destroy enemy supplies and take hostages.

British shipping was a frequent American target:

> *A gentleman from Jersey informs that some row boats, about a fortnight ago, went from Jersey to Sandy hook, where, in the night, they boarded and took four sloops, one of which was armed. In carrying them to a place of safety, three of them, by the unskillfulness of the pilots, ran ashore, and were burnt. The other, with nineteen prisoners, got safe to New Jersey. It is farther said, the persons concerned will share about four hundred pounds, each man.* The Pennsylvania Evening Post, January 23, 1778

> *Last night about twelve o'clock, a small party, commanded by Cap't Craig, consisting only of adjutant Nixon and eight privates belonging to our regiment, boarded and took the sloop Neptune of ten carriage guns, four swivels and two cohorns, with 21 men, commanded by Cap't Palfry of Boston, with his two mates; his lady was also on board who is a prisoner with him.*
> *In bringing the sloop to the Jersey shore, he unfortunately ran aground and, finding it impossible to get her off, our people got out what stores were on board her, which consisted of beef, pork and rice, with some powder and shot, two cohorns, four swivels and nineteen stands of arms; likewise a considerable quantity of spare rigging, viz. sails ropes &c. We had scarcely got the vessel unrigged when the enemy sent a number of armed boats to retake her. They*

came upon us so fast that we were obliged to leave her, without setting fire to her, when they boarded her, and, at high tide, carried her off. The New Jersey Gazette, October 20, 1779

The British were more aggressive in their raids. Elizabeth, Amboy and Woodbridge, convenient to the British camp on loyalist Staten Island, were favorite targets. Very often, the British were aided by loyalist ex-residents of New Jersey who had fled to the British in New York City for protection:

Last Tuesday about 3 o'clock in the morning, a party of New Levies from Staten Island, came over into Woodbridge, and marched up into the town undiscovered, to the house of Charles Jackson, in which there happened to lay that night a scout of Continental troops from Bonham Town, consisting of twelve men. The sentinel did not discover them 'till they had well nigh surrounded the house, it being very dark, when he fired and ran off, making his escape; the rest being unfortunately asleep, were taken by surprise without making any resistance. Their principal object was Captain Nathaniel Fitz Randolph, who lived at this house. He had just returned from Staten Island, having been over there with a small party [most] of the night, and was but a few minutes in the house before he was alarmed by the firing of the sentinel, when they instantly rushed into the house and seized him and Mr. Jackson, with the scout as above. The party were gone before the inhabitants had time to collect, without doing any other damage except plundering the house of a few trifling articles. The New Jersey Gazette, February 17, 1779

A body of the enemy consisting of the 42d and 33d regiments and the light infantry of the guards, in number about a thousand, commanded by Lieut. Colonel Stirling, attempted to seize the troops and inhabitants of Elizabeth Town, on the morning of Thursday last. They embarked on Long Island the evening before, about seven o'clock, and landed on the salt meadows better than a mile to the left of Crane's Ferry, between two and three in the morning. From thence, they were conducted through a very difficult marsh to Woodruff's farms, which lies directly to the left of the town.

The guard at Crane's Ferry, having discovered their landing, immediately dispatched the intelligence to town, where the alarm being sounded, the troops were afforded an opportunity to collect. The number and movements of the enemy remained doubtful by reason of the darkness, our troops were marched to the rear of the town where the Whig inhabitants likewise retired.

Finding themselves completely disappointed in every expectation, they made their visit to the town very short; however, during their small halt, they set fire to the barracks, the school house (in which were stored some few articles of provision) and a blacksmith's shop. So soon as they began their retreat to the boats, General Maxwell marched against their rear. About halfway between the town and the ferry, the enemy, perceiving their rear in danger, faced about and paraded, as if for action. A few well directed shots from our artillery induced them to renew their retreat, leaving two dead on the field.

Our loss, exclusive of a few aged inhabitants, whom they took with them but have since sent back, are one private killed, two officers --to wit, Brigade Major [Aaron] Ogden and Lieut. [John] Ruecastle, with four privates wounded and seven privates missing.

The enemy's loss we cannot ascertain, besides the two killed whom they left behind, two made prisoners and one boat taken. Mr. Remington allows them seven wounded in one company. Cornelius Hetfield, Smith Hetfield and Capt. Luce, late of this town, were their principal guides. They had collected a considerable number of horned cattle and horses, but their retreat was so precipitate that they were obliged to leave them behind. The New Jersey Gazette, March 3, 1779

Last Tuesday a detachment from his Majesty's 37th regiment, with a party of Colonel Barton's, went over from Staten Island to a place called Woodbridge, Rahway, where they surprised a party of rebels in a tavern, killed their commander officer, Captain Skinner of a Troop of Light Horse and another man and took the following prisoners: Capt. Samuel Meeker, Christopher March, Joseph Stephens, Benjamin Willis, David Craig, Stephen Ball, Lewis March, Jotham Moore, Jesse Whitehead, John Tharp, Thomas Bloomfield, Jeremiah Corey and David Hall. The New York Gazette, July 5, 1779

On Tuesday last a party of about fifty of the Greens came over to Amboy early in the morning and had collected upwards of a hundred head of horses and cattle, before any of our troops were alarmed; but, at about ten o'clock, a small detachment of our regiment marched down and attacked them so briskly that they were obliged to fly and leave the greatest part of their booty, taking off only twenty head. Cap't Davis, who commanded our party, had reason to think that several of them were wounded in the attack but no one of his men received the least hurt. The New Jersey Gazette, October 20, 1779

The British would also raid in north and west New Jersey, especially in Bergen County:

On Sunday night, the 28th ult. a party of about 30 men belonging to Col. Van Buskirk's corp of Tories and embodied refugees, stationed at Hoebock in the County of Bergen, who came out as far as Closter, for the purpose of stealing horses, and of robbing the inhabitants, were attacked and put to flight by nine of the militia, commanded by Lieut. J. Huyler, leaving their plunder behind them and one of their officers, the noted, Peter Myer, Ensign in Capt. David Peak's company, dead on the field. Another of the officers was wounded in the arm and the infamous Weart Banta, so notoriously known for his complicated villainies, thefts and robberies, was shot through the knee and it is supposed will, by the amputation of a limb, be disabled from kidnaping and plundering loyal subjects of this state in the future. The New Jersey Gazette, April 28, 1779

On the 12th instant, a detachment of the enemy, consisting of about 60 men, belonging to Bushkirk's corps, commanded by a Capt. Van Allen, by taking a circuitous route, surprised one of our guards posted at Little Ferry, near New Barbadoes in Bergen county. It consisted of two non commissioned officers and 10 Privates of the Carolina Brigade and one of our militia; two of the former escaped; the others were made prisoners and carried to New York. The New Jersey Gazette, April 28, 1779

This day about 100 of the enemy came by way of New Dock, attacked the place and carried off Cornelius Tallman, Samuel Demarest, Jacob Cole and George Bushkirk; wounded Hendrik Demamrest, Jeremiah Veestervelt, and Dow Tallman &c. They burned the dwelling houses of Peter Demarest, Matthias Bogart, Cornelius Huyler, Samuel Demarest, Jacob Cole and George Bushkirk; wounded Hendrik Demamrest's house and barn, John Banta's house and barn and Cornelius Bogart and John Vestervelt's barns. They attempted to burn every building they entered, but the fire was in some places extinguished. They destroyed all the furniture &c in many houses and abused many of the women. In their retreat, they were so closely pursued by the militia and a few continental troops that they took off no cattle. The New Jersey Gazette, May 12, 1779

The detachment of the enemy that landed in Bergen county on Monday, the 17th instant, consisted of about 1,000 men, composed of several different corps, under the command of Col. Van Bushkirk. Their path in this incursion was marked with desolation and unprovoked cruel murders. Not a house within their reach, belonging to a Whig inhabitant, escaped. Mr. Abraham Allen and Mr. George Campbell fell a prey to these more than savage men. Two Negro women who were endeavoring to drive off some cattle belonging to their masters, were also murdered. Mr. Joost Zabriskie was stabbed in 13 different places. Col. Van Buskirk, although he was formally acquainted with these barbarities, yet he did not think it proper to take the least notice of the perpetrators. Having in some measure satiated their appetite for blood and plunder, and dreading the vengeance of our militia, which by this time was collecting in considerable numbers, the enemy predictably retreated to their boats and went off to New York. The New Jersey Gazette, May 26, 1779

Monmouth county, to the south along the shore from New York, also was raided frequently by the British in 1779:

Tuesday se'nnight, a party of Tories from Staten Island landed in Middletown in Monmouth, plundered several houses and carried off four or five of the inhabitants prisoners. The New Jersey Gazette, June 9, 1779

On Monday last, the 26th inst, about break of day, a detachment of British, consisting of seven hundred men, were discovered by a scouting party of Col. Ford's coming up the North

River[115], about half a mile below Red Bank, who immediately gave the alarm. The Enemy directly landed four hundred men at Painter's Point and about forty of them marched up to Shrewsbury. The remainder went about a half a mile to the Westward and came about William Wardill's place, with a view to cut off the retreat of some three hundred of our people posted at that station. Col. Ford's party (uncertain of the size of the force) retreated and got about four hundred yards ahead of them. The enemy pursued them to the Falls, firing all the way, but could not overtake them. They then set forth to High Sheriff Van Breenck's house and a small house, the property of and adjoining to, Col. Hendrickson's dwelling house, which were burnt to the ground. They also fired the houses of Capt. Richard McKnight and John Little. But they were extinguished by the activity of the inhabitants, before they had suffered much damage. The enemy then returned to Shrewsbury plundering all the way to Col. Breeze's whom they robbed of all his money and most of his plate and to Justice Holmes where they plundered and destroyed every thing they could lay their hands on and then retreated to their boats, a few militia firing on them. Then, they went to Middletown where they joined the three hundred which had crossed over there, when the four hundred had marched to Shrewsbury and stayed to evening, burning a house and barn and plundering some of the inhabitants. Col. Holmes, had by this time assembled one hundred and forty of the militia, who drove them to their boats near the gut that separated the Highlands from Sandy Hook. One of the enemy was killed and another taken prisoner. The enemy carried off with them Justice Covenhoven and his son, likewise several others. They got off by sunset and returned to New York, taking away some cattle and some horses. The Pennsylvania Evening Post, April 30, 1779

Last Thursday Night, a Party of Loyal Refugees landed at Shrewsbury, in New Jersey and brought off Cols. Hendrickson and Wycoff; Maj. Van Brunt, Captain Chaddock, Capt. McKnight (who broke his parole here some time ago), one of the Militia and a Continental Soldier. About 9' o'clock on Friday Morning, in returning to their Boats, they were attacked by a Body of Militia, whom they repulsed, after killing three and wounding 14. They then brought off their Prisoners and a considerable Number of Cattle,

Sheep, &c, the Particulars of which we intend to insert in our next.
The New York Gazette, June 14, 1779

James Rivington, editor of the *Royal, Lying Gazette*, whose misrepresentations and exaggerations so infuriated the patriots, reported, in his usual fashion, on one such attack in Monmouth County. Sandy Hook was the rendezvous for a group of Refugees, led by the notorious runaway mulatto slave, Titus, who had been rechristened himself Colonel Ty. These refugees would row, by evening, the several miles from Refugee Town on Sandy Hook to Black Point on the tip of Rumson, secure their crafts, march, in the dead of night along what was part of the Burlington Path, to the Falls at Tinton Manor and further to Colt's Neck, ten miles from their place of first landing. There, they would plunder homes, kidnap rebel leaders for exchange or hostage, raid livestock and return the way they had come to their vessels waiting for them at Black Point. Inevitably, the inhabitants, who had been raided, would quickly gather in pursuit of the bandits and their booty. Often they would catch up to them as they loaded their plunder on board for the return trip to Sandy Hook. Indeed, a number of skirmishes took place at the tip of the stubby peninsula of Rumson, the news account one of which follows:

On the ninth day of June instant, a party of Volunteers went down to Sandy Hook, where they were joined by a small detachment of Colonel Barton's regiment of New Jersey Volunteers, from whence they proceeded to the Gut, about four miles distant, but as the wind blew very hard, the boats that were provided did not come up, and they were obliged to return to the lighthouse. On the 10th, being ready to cross the Gut, it was agreed by the party that Lieut. Okerson, who was perfectly acquainted with the country, should give them directions. They advanced undetected with 56 men as far as Tinton Falls, about ten miles from the landing, where they halted just about as day appeared, near the rebels headquarters at the back of town, but not knowing the house where the main guard was kept, they determined to surround three houses at the same time. Captain Hayden of General Skinner's proceeded to the house of Mr. McKnight, a rebel Captain; Ensign Moody to the house of Mr. Hendrickson, a colonel; and Lieutenant Throckmorton to one

Shadwick's, a rebel captain. The three parties came nearly at the same time to the same place, where the main guard of the rebels was kept, but missed them, they being out on a scout. They made Colonel Hendrickson, Colonel Wickoff and Captains McKnight and Shadwick, with several privates, prisoners and, after proceeding one mile further took a Major Van Brunt. They had collected about three hundred sheep and horses belonging to the rebels and were returning when attacked by a party of about thirty, who harassed them in their retreat, till they got down to the water side at Jumping Point Inlet[116], through which they drove the sheep and all except fifteen of the Volunteers, who were left to secure a passage, over on the other side. A warm engagement then ensued and continued an hour, when they heard the captain of the guard swear by God that he would give them no quarter, and, soon after he received two balls. Upon his falling, the Volunteers charged their bayonets and took possession of the ground where the dead and wounded lay. When they crossed the river, they observed a man with a flag riding down from the rebels, who asked permission to carry off the dead and wounded, which was immediately granted. The man with the flag informed him that the whole of their party who were engaged were killed or wounded. They returned to Sandy Hook that evening with their prisoners. The New York Gazette, June 21, 1779

The skirmishing along New Jersey's eastern border would not win the war. In June, the main armies began to stir from the winter camps, although in what direction and to what end was anyone's guess. Clues abounded and suspicion turned to the American fort at West Point, the sentinel of the Hudson River. If it fell, so too would the Hudson River at and, with it, maybe, the new born America:

It is reported that a number of the enemy's ships, with troops on board, went up the North River and that a considerable body of them have landed as far up as King's Ferry, but their intention in this movement is not certainly known. The New Jersey Gazette, June 2, 1779

We hear that the greatest Part of Washington's Army have left their Camp at Middlebrook and are marching toward Tappan and Haverstraw, on the West Side of Hudson's River. *The New York Gazette, June 7, 1779*

As the summer of 1779 began, General Washington selected a site -- an alpine retreat -- on the west side of the Hudson River, above Tarrytown, to await a British move:

Mr. Washington, by our latest accounts, was on the 8th instant still serenely embowered at Smith's Clove, most of his artillery at Ringwood and about 300 of his dragoons at Kakiate, his Magazines only at Trenton, from whence, with incredible fatigue, and difficulty, subsistence is lugged up to about 4,000, of all sorts, that are now with him in his Alpine retreat; the rout for his provisions is through Morris Town, where there is a considerable store of camp equipage. The Royal Gazette, June 23, 1779

The British remained on the eastern side of the Hudson, amassing at White Plains in Westchester county an army twice the size of the American forces. Capturing the American fort at West Point appeared to be their goal. To accomplish this they began building their own fort across the Hudson at a place called Stoney Point:

The latest account of the enemy at New York is that the whole force, supposed to be about 8,000 men, collected at White Plains; two sloops loaded with fascines lay in the harbor opposite the White Hall. Yesterday, all the wagons and horses in Staten Island were pressed into service and sent to New York. The 26th, 37th, and 1 foreign regiment and Barton's are on Staten Island. General Clinton is in New York, Gen. Vaughn and Sir W. Erskine at White Plains.
In consequence of the movement of the main body of the enemy's troops up the North River, our army marched the latter end of last week from their late encampment in Middlebrook towards Fort Clinton, which, it is supposed, is the enemy's principal object, from whence we hourly expect important intelligence. This fort is situated in the Highlands, on the West side of the North River, at a place called West Point. The New Jersey Gazette, June 9, 1779

The last accounts from the North River mention that the enemy is very busy fortifying at a place called Stoney Point, on the hither side of the River, near King's Ferry. It is supposed by this maneuver that they have two objects in view, the one to make a stronghold in order to enable themselves to send out detachments into Jersey to plunder and forage, the other by committing those depredations, to draw the attention of our army from covering the fort at West Point and thereby facilitating an attack against it, which, it is said, is the enemy's main object. But, in this, we flatter ourselves, they will be disappointed. The New Jersey Gazette, June 16, 1779

Victory to the Americans! Again, General Washington surprised the British. The fort they were building at Stoney Point was taken by "Mad" Anthony Wayne in a surprise attack, expertly planned and executed. The victory was a great boost to American morale, especially in view of the large number of the enemy captured and the few Americans lost in the effort.

Stoney Point was taken last night by surprise, by General Wayne with the light infantry of the line. The garrison, consisting of 500 men, are prisoners. We lost only four men. General Wayne is slightly wounded. The prisoners are on their march and were expected at Boon Town last night. New Jersey Journal, July 20, 1779

This American victory was followed by another, in August at Paulus Hook, today the tip of Jersey City, across the harbor from New York City. Henry Lee[117], under the command of Lord Stirling, led a force of 400 on a surprise raid on the fort at Paulus Hook, Britain's last toehold in New Jersey. The British had more than 50 killed and wounded and lost 158 prisoners to the Americans. Lee's losses were two killed, three wounded. General Washington, in his characteristic style of applauding the efforts of his soldiers and men, reported to Congress on America's second victory in as many months:

Head Quarters, West Point, August 23, 1779

Sir,

I have the honor to enclose your Excellency's Major Lee's report of the surprise and capture of the garrison at Powles-Hook. The Major displayed a remarkable degree of prudence, address, enterprise and bravery upon this occasion --- which does the highest honor to himself and to all the officers and men under his command. The situation of the post rendered the attempt critical and the success brilliant. It was made in consequence of information that the garrison was in a state of negligent security, which the event justified.

I am much indebted to Major General Lord Stirling for the judicious measures he took to forward the enterprise and to secure the retreat of the party.

Lieut. M'Callister, who will have the honor of delivering these dispatches, will present Congress with the standard of the garrison which fell into his possession during the attack. Mr. Lee speaks of this gentleman's conduct in the handsomest terms.

I have the honor to be with perfect respect and esteem
Your Excellency's most obedient servant
G. Washington
The New Jersey Gazette, September 21, 1779

Yet, despite Major Lee's daring at Paulus Hook and General Anthony's like boldness at Stoney Point, the 1779 summer campaign, for both combatants, was relatively uneventful. Respites from the war provided the Americans the opportunity to celebrate victory of another sort. The victory at Saratoga in 1778 and Ambassador Franklin's efforts as a diplomat had allowed Washington to capitalize on one enemy's long hatred for another. France, which had been loaning the United States funds with which to finance its revolution against Britain, had officially joined the war against its foe of many centuries, England. King Louis provided first a fleet and then, it was hoped, ground forces to support the small American force. The hope of victory that France offered the American cause of liberty was immense and the alliance was elaborately celebrated:

The anniversary of our Alliance with France was celebrated on the 18th ultimo at Pluck'emin[118], at a very elegant entertainment and display of fireworks given by General Knox and the officers of the corps of artillery. It was postponed to this late day on account of his Excellency General Washington's absence from the camp.

General Washington, the principal officers of the Army, Mrs. Washington, Mrs. Greene and Mrs. Knox, the gentlemen and ladies for a large circuit around the camp were of the company. Besides these, there was a vast concourse of spectators from every part of the Jersies.

About four o'clock in the afternoon, the celebration of the Alliance was announced by the discharge of thirteen cannon, when the company was assembled in the academy, to a very elegant dinner. The room was spacious and the tables very prettily disposed both as to prospect and convenience. The festivity was universal and the toasts descriptive of the happy event, which had given certainty to our liberties, empire and independence.

In the evening was exhibited a very fine set of fireworks, conducted by Colonel Stevens, arranged on the point of a Temple of one hundred feet in length and proportionally high. The Temple showed thirteen arches, each displaying an illuminated painting in the following order:

The 1st Arch on the right represented the commencement of hostilities at Lexington, with this inscription: the scene opened.

The 2d [Arch], British Clemency, represented in the burning of Charlestown, Falmouth, Norfolk and Kingston.

The 3d [Arch], the separation of America from Britain. A magnificent arch broken in the center, with this motto: "By your tyranny to the people of America, you have separated the wide arch of an extended empire."

The 4th [Arch], Britain represented as a decaying Empire, by a barren country, broken arches, fallen spires, ships deserting its shores, birds of prey hovering over its moldering cities and a gloomy setting sun.

The 5th [Arch], America represented as a rising Empire, prospect of a fertile country, harbors and rivers covered with ships, new canals opening, cities arising among woods and a splendid sun emerging from a bright horizon.

The 6th [Arch], a grand illuminated representation of Louis, the sixteenth, the encourager of letters, the supporter of the rights of humanity, the Ally and Friend of the American People.

The 7th [Arch], the center arch. The fathers in Congress.

The 8th [Arch], the American Philosopher and Ambassador extracting lightning from clouds.

The 9th [Arch], the battle near Saratoga, 7th October, 1777

The 10th [Arch], the Convention of Saratoga

The 11th [Arch], a Representation of the Sea Fight off Ushant, between Count D'Orvillers and Admiral Kepple.

The 12th [Arch], Warren, Montgomery, Mercer, Wooster, Nash and a crowd of heroes who have fallen in the American contest, in Elisium, receiving the thanks and praises of Brutus, Cato and those spirits who in all ages have gloriously struggled against tyrants and tyranny. Motto: "Those who have shed their blood in such a cause shall live for ever."

The 13th [Arch], Represented Peace with all her train of blessings. Her right hand displayed an olive branch; at her feet lay the honors of harvest; the background was filled with flourishing cities, ports crowded with ships and other emblems of an extensive empire and unrestrained commerce.

When the fireworks were finished, the company returned to the academy and concluded the celebration by a very splendid ball. The whole was conducted in a style and manner that reflects great honor on the taste of the managers. The New Jersey Gazette, March 3, 1779

To learn firsthand what the participants in the war, on both sides, thought were the principles for which they were risking their lives, one should listen to the toasts they gave at celebrations of various sorts. For example, the toasts at the "going away" party given by the townspeople of Newark for the regiment of Continental soldiers that had wintered there, provides some insight as to what was in the mind and heart of the common man:

The 2d New Jersey regiment, commanded by Col. Israel Shreve, which has been quartered at Newark since last Fall, having received orders to hold themselves in readiness to march at a moment's notice, and it being supposed that they will soon be ordered away from this station, a number of the principal inhabitants of the town gave an elegant entertainment to the officers of the regiment. After Dinner, the following patriotic toasts were drunk and the day was spent with agreeable festivity and mutual satisfaction and joy:

1. *The United States of America*
2. *The Congress*
3. *His Excellency George Washington*
4. *The army and navy*
5. *The King and Queen of France and all our foreign allies*
6. *Dr. Franklin and our ambassadors at foreign courts*
7. *The Governor and State of New Jersey*
8. *The memory of all those worthies who have gloriously fought and bled in defense of their country*
9. *The glorious minority of the British Parliament*
10. *The Friends of Freedom throughout the World*
11. *May the glorious example of the first asserters and defenders of American Freedom be always hallowed by their posterity*
12. *A speedy, honorable, lasting peace*
13. *May the American fair never give their hands or hearts to any but those who have virtue and courage to defend them; New Jersey Journal, June 8, 1779*

Similarly, the toasts at a birthday party for the King, held in New York City, reveal a British soldier's priorities:

Yesterday being HIS MAJESTY'S BIRTHDAY, and an elegant Entertainment was given by his Excellency General Tyron, at which were present the Governors of New Jersey[119] and North Carolina and members of his Majesty's Council for the Province of New York, the Judges and other Officers of Government. The following toasts were drank on the Occasion:

1. *The KING*
2. *The QUEEN and Royal Family*
3. *The LANDGRAVE of Hesse*
4. *The Foreign Powers in amity with Great Britain.*
5. *The Army and Navy*
6. *The Commander in Chief and Success to his Majesty's Arms.*

7. His Majesty's Ministers
8. Governor Tyron and the speedy Restoration of Government to New York
9. Governor Franklin and the speedy Restoration of Government to New Jersey
10. Governor Martin and the speedy Restoration of Government to North Carolina
11. Unanimity and Firmness to Great Britain
12. The Navy and Army of St. Lucia
13. General Haldimand and our Friends in Canada
14. General Knyphausen and the Hessian Corps under his Command
15. General Prescot, Garrison and our Friends in Rhode Island
16. General Prevost and our Friends in Georgia
17. General Campbell and our Friends in Florida
18. General M'Lean and our Friends in Halifax
19. The COMMANDANT of New York
20. Mr. MATTHEWS, the Mayor and LOYAL CITIZENS OF NEW YORK
21. The LOYALISTS of the Continent of America
22. Success to the Exertions of the Refugees
23. JOSEPH AND HIS BRETHREN
24. A speedy suppression to rebellion
25. A happy restoration of Civil Government in is Majesty's Colonies
26. A speedy arrival to Admiral Arbuth not and the Fleet under his Command
27. CHURCH AND STATE

The Royal Gazette, June 5, 1779

The summer ended as it had started with both sides poised to defend against attacks each feared from the other. In addition, all awaited a battle between the English and French fleets, perhaps as a prelude to an invasion of New York or New Jersey, a confrontation that never occurred. Rumors abounded nonetheless.

The following series of news items suggest the sense of anticipation and dread under which both sides found themselves:

The militia of this state are directed to hold themselves in readiness to assemble on the shortest possible notice and to be attentive to the signals and the persons appointed to fire the beacons are to have everything in readiness to give the alarm on a moment's notice. The New Jersey Gazette, August 25, 1779

By a person directly from New York we learn that Admiral Arbuthnot's fleet arrived at that place consisting of 70 sail, among which are two 74's and five frigates, the remainder transports with about 3,000 troops, 1,000 of whom are said to be Hessians, 1,000 Highlanders, the remainder British newly raised. This fleet we heard has brought an immense quantity of British goods. The New Jersey Gazette, September 1, 1779

A French Fleet may be momentarily expected upon this coast, having been spoken with at sea. All the pilots in this state, we hear, are engaged to hold themselves on readiness to go on board, should they make this coast. The New Jersey Gazette, September 21, 1779

By authentic intelligence from Long Island, we learn that General Clinton has demanded a number of men from every county to fortify the island, being apprehensive of a visit from our illustrious ally. The New Jersey Gazette, October 6, 1779

We are informed that the enemy, to be of about the number 1,500 or 2,000, are upon Staten Island and have collected a considerable number of flat bottomed boats at Billop's Point, in order, it is said, to make a descent into this State. But, from the disposition of several detachments of the Continental Army, as well as our militia, we flatter ourselves they will be frustrated in their predatory designs.

Suddenly, it seemed as if the British were not attacking New Jersey, but pulling out:

We have just now received an account of the enemy's embarking a number of troops from Staten Island, their destination not yet known. The New Jersey Gazette, October 20, 1779

> *We learn that Verplank's and Stoney Points were evacuated a few days ago by the enemy, who have retired to New York, from whence a considerable embarkation, it is said, will soon take place.* The New Jersey Gazette, October 27, 1779
>
> *We also learn that a letter is received by Congress from General Gates, that the late movements of the enemy in Rhode Island indicate a speedy evacuation and that he, with the army under his command, are marching toward New York.* The New Jersey Gazette, October 27, 1779
>
> *A gentleman from Elizabeth Town informs us that the enemy, to the number of 8000, have embarked and part of them have sailed, supposed to be bound for South Carolina or the West Indies.* The New Jersey Gazette, November 10, 1779
>
> *By several corroborating accounts, we learn that the enemy at New York is preparing for a large embarkation, but their destination is not yet certainly known.* The New Jersey Gazette, November 10, 1779

But while the arrival of the French fleet and the Battle of New York proved to be non events, there were the usual attacks, during 1779, on the settlers on the Jersey/New York/Pennsylvania frontiers from Butler's Rangers and his Indian allies, led by Mohawk chief, Joseph Brant. The accounts from Rivington's *Gazette* continued his practice of belittling the "rebels":

> *The rebels, greatly alarmed at the successful operations of the Loyalists and Indians, under young Mr. Butler and Mr. Joseph Brant, upon the back settlements, have occasioned, we are informed, three brigades to be detached from Jersey to Cherry Valley to defend, if possible, the townships in that district.* The Royal Gazette, January 23, 1779
>
> *From two men who on Saturday last from the Minisinks, we learn that a number of Indians have lately committed some depredations on a small settlement at Cuhichtun on the Delaware since, carried off one prisoner and a number of horses and other*

cattle from the neighborhood of Wyoming. The New Jersey Gazette, April 7, 1779

By Persons of Credit lately arrived from the Enemy's Country, we learn that Colonel Joseph Brant, had sent a flag into Sussex county, in New Jersey, to inform the inhabitants of his having been apprized that many of them, who last year had pretended Friendship and Attachment to the Cause for which he had taken Hostilities, had since taken up Arms; he now gave them Notice that no longer any Regard for Professions of that Kind would be attended to, for that every Man that did not join him upon his approach to their Country, should be deemed and treated by him as an Enemy and that he should soon lay the Country waste as low as Mushankunk. His troops had been again at Wyoming, drove off all the Cattle and every Thing else without the Fort that was moveable, where several of the Rebels had been killed and taken Prisoners. *The Royal Gazette, April 12, 1779*

By several persons from Sussex and Elizabeth town we learn that, during the latter end of May, some hundreds of continental troops and militia, consisting of Hand's and Spencer's Corps, left East town [Easton, Pa.] to cut a road for the passage of artillery through the great swamp to Wioming. These were, in this employment, somewhat molested by a large number of Indians, laying in ambush for that purpose, who slew the greatest part of the rebels. The few survivors owed their escape to a precipitate flight. We are told Colonel Spencer was among the wounded. A large detachment under Mr. Maxwell, who were following the chastised battalion, to cut up the Indians upon the Susquehanna and proceed to attack Fort Niagara, came to a sudden halt, a very prudent pause truly, after the loss of so many of their fraternity, ere they marched against an enemy ever terrific, but now becoming immensely formidable because of their alarming numbers. By a late letter from a dispirited Rebel officer, Col. Brailey, at East town, we are assured that the body of loyalists and Indians, in motion on the Susquehanna, amounts to upwards of four thousand. To oppose them Mr. Maxwell was ordered up from East town yesterday, with one Virginia, two New Jersey and two New England battalions, four three pounders and two howitzers. *The Royal Gazette, June 12, 1779*

Last Friday night, we had a small alarm, our out sentries perceiving the approach of two savages, fired upon them, but the savages made their escape. On Saturday, between this and Easton, a family was routed, three women taken prisoner and a lad of 14 years of age was scalped and tomahawked. The few scattering inhabitants still out there are moving in great distress to Brinker's Mills within 19 miles of Easton.

"The Rebel press call the acts of the British and their ardent attacks "depredative" which history has to acknowledge."
The Royal Gazette, July 21, 1779

General John Sullivan was dispatched with a large force to teach the Iroquois the folly of their alliance with the British, an objective he sought to accomplish by destroying most of the Indian villages of New York:

By a letter from Tioga, dated the 15th instant we learn that General Sullivan with his army arrived at that place on the 11th instant, without molestation. On his way, he burned an Indian town called New Kittanning. On the 12th at night, the whole army moved to Chemung, 12 miles distant, in order to surprise a number of Indians there, but they, having previous notice, evacuated the town, which our army destroyed, with all the corn etc. in the vicinity. While the town was on fire, a detachment of light infantry was ordered to move forward, who were fired upon by the savages, by which 6 were killed and 9 wounded. Our men bravely returned the fire, then rushed in with fixed bayonets which immediately put the enemy to flight. A party of our troops who were ordered to cut up the corn, were fired upon which, by which one man was killed and five wounded. The enemy's losses in these skirmishes was not known. Our army having completed their business at Chemung, returned to Tioga. The New Jersey Gazette, August 25, 1779

General James Clinton's army, we hear, have joined Major General Sullivan at Tioga. From thence, the whole body is to move in to the midst of Indian Country in order to chastise the deluded savages and Tories, for their unprovoked, wanton and cruel depredations on our innocent and defenseless frontiers. The New Jersey Gazette, September 1, 1779

The number of Indian villages which have been destroyed by our army under the command of General Sullivan, in the Western Expedition, including those burned by General Clinton previous to the junction, amounts to 14, which, with the destruction of all their corn, beans etc. in the vicinity of those towns, will, we flatter ourselves, somewhat frustrate the savages during the remainder of the campaign in their predatory schemes against our frontier inhabitants. The New Jersey Gazette, September 22, 1779

Since the action of the 29th of last month, the Indians have fled the approach of our army and left their settlements to our mercy. [They] are now great heaps of ruin; besides we have burnt a number of scattering houses and destroyed as large country of corn, pumpkins, cymblines, cucumbers, watermelons, peaches and apples. This day we shall set out for Genesee and lay that country in ashes. The enemy having retreated to Niagara, we expect no opposition as we advance, but expect an attack as we return. The New Jersey Gazette, September 29, 1779

General Sullivan's expedition was a total success. Not only were the Indians chastised, the burning of their crops and farms forced thousands of them to converge that winter on Fort Niagara in Canada where the British had to feed them.

The war in New Jersey in 1779 sparked two times toward the end of the year. One was a sneak attack on Newark that accomplished little. The second was a bolder long range attack into central New Jersey by the British under the command of 27 year old John Simcoe of the Queens Rangers:

Just as this paper was going to press, we were informed that a party of the enemy's light dragoons, consisting of about 100, landed on Tuesday night last at Sandy Point, above Amboy, and proceeded on to Bound Brook, where they burnt some stores; from thence they went up to Van Veghter's bridge and burnt 18 boats; and from thence to Somerset Courthouse, which they likewise burnt; and then returned, by way of Brunswick, to South Amboy. The militia turned out and annoyed them very considerably. They killed the horse of the commanding officer, a colonel [Simcoe], and made him prisoner and also one private, beside two or three horses. 'Tis thought some of the enemy were wounded. The New Jersey Gazette, October 27, 1779

Next week's paper contained additional details:

A party of the enemy that came up to Van Vegher's bridge, to burn the boats, suffered much more considerably than was first imagined; the militia killed three of them, made six prisoners and wounded a considerable number; they pushed them so closely that they dropped a number of their caps, coats and other articles; and, if it had not been for a large body of foot [soldiers] that were landed at South Amboy, to cover their retreat, every one of them would have fallen into our hands. Their commanding officer, who was made prisoner, is Lieutenant Colonel Simcoe, of a new corps called the Queen's American Rangers.

It is to be observed that Simcoe is one of the enemy's principal partisans and that his exploits have generally been marked with acts of the most inhuman barbarity. In this expedition, Capt. Peter Voorhees, of the first Jersey regiment, unfortunately fell into their hands near Brunswick and was massacred in the most shocking manner. Dr. Ryker and Mr. Polhemus were made prisoners by the covering party with several others. The New Jersey Gazette, November 3, 1779

This successful strike by the British to the center of New Jersey ended the 1779 campaign on a sour note. Washington decided to set up his winter quarters in Morristown, New Jersey and at nearby Jockey Hollow:

Advices from the country that all the Army, but a Garrison of 1,200 left at West Point, are marching down the Country in Divisions under their proper Generals, supposed for Morris County and, 'tis conjectured, that they will hut this winter either at Morris Town, the Notch below Passaic Falls[120], or the Mountain in the Rear of Mr. Kimble's. The New York Gazette, December 6, 1779

It would not be a pleasant winter. A constant shortage of supplies and the coldest snowiest winter in memory would combine to make the 1779/80 winter worse for Washington's troops than even the infamous one of Valley Forge, two years earlier.

CHAPTER 11

Banditi

Colonial laws were harsh and their enforcement strict. Inherited from an England, still feudal in many ways, was the insistence upon an orderly society in which each citizen had his proper place and role. Little leniency or sympathy was extended to those who broke the order or the rules which regulated it. Although crime was present -- a number of colonists had come from jails of London on prison transports -- it was not tolerated by the authorities or the law abiding majority.

The Revolutionary War would change all that. With soldiers from both sides plundering, loyalists raiding their former hometowns and rebels, in turn attacking Tory strongholds for provisions and plunder, a confusion and lawlessness soon prevailed that permitted gangs of villains and bandits to freelance against any likely victim.

Once the Revolutionary War commenced, society lost the abilities to investigate, detect, prosecute, or punish, and thereby regulate, crime. Local and state authorities, now made up of the rebels rather than appointees of the Crown, were more focused on funding and fighting a war, than in maintaining local order. Gangs of criminals popped up in different parts of New Jersey. *Banditti*, as they were popularly called, they preyed on the citizenry of both sides. One such gang was known as the Pine Robbers and used the Pine Barrens of Jersey as its lair. These freebooters, nominally espousing the Tory cause, were in actuality nothing more than highwaymen and villains of the worse kind, whom even the British were not anxious to accept as their own. Many were from the Shrewsbury area of Monmouth County and some were from old line, prosperous families. Their conduct was so obnoxious that the Governor of the State of New Jersey, William Livingston, issued a Proclamation, offering rewards for their capture:

Whereas it has been represented to me that a Number of Persons in the County of Monmouth, and particularly those hereinafter mentioned, have committed diverse Robberies, Violences,

Depredations on the Person and Property of the Inhabitants. I have therefore thought proper to issue this Proclamation, hereby promising the rewards herein mentioned to any Person or Persons who shall apprehend and secure in any Goal of this State the following persons and offenders, to wit: For Jacob Fagan and Stephen Emmons, alias Burke, Five Hundred dollars each and for Samuel Wright, late of Shrewsbury, William Vannote, Jacob Vannote, Jonathan Burdge and Elijah Groom, one hundred dollars each. The New Jersey Gazette, October 7, 1778

Fagan was killed by a force led by Captain Benjamin Dennis of the Monmouth County militia, an incident celebrated by the local citizenry and the press alike:

About ten days ago, Jacob Fagan, who having previously headed a number of villains in Monmouth County, that had committed divers robberies and were the terror of travelers, was shot. Since which his body has been gibbeted on the public highway of that county to deter others from perpetrating the like detestable crimes. The New Jersey Gazette, October 14, 1778

So detested was this "monster in wickedness" as he had been called, that his death was not enough. His body was dug up from the grave, tarred, chained and hung from a chestnut tree on the road to Colt's Neck, near the Monmouth Courthouse. "Finally, the birds picked the flesh from the skeleton and the bones fell to the ground."

Later, thanks to the bravery of an undercover agent of the Americans, other members of the same gang were slain in a gun battle:

The Tory Free Booters, who have their haunts and caves in the pines, and have been for some time past a terror to the inhabitants of this county, have, during the course of the present week, met with a very eminent disaster. On Tuesday evening last Capt. Benjamin Dennis, who lately killed the infamous robber Fagan, with a party of his militia, went in pursuit of three of the most noted of the Pine-Banditti, and was so fortunate as to fall in with them, and kill them on the spot. Their names are Stephen Bourke, alias Emmans, Stephen West and Ezekiel Williams. Yesterday they were brought up to this place, and two of them, it is said, will be hanged in chains. This signal piece of service was effected through the instrumentality of one John Van Kirk, who was prevailed upon to associate with them on purpose to discover their practices, and to lead them into our hands. He conducted himself with so much address that the robbers, and especially the three above named, who were the leading villains, looked upon him as one of their body, kept him constantly with them, and entrusted him with all their designs.

Van Kirk, at proper seasons, gave intelligence of their movements to Capt. Dennis, who conducted himself accordingly. They were on the eve of setting off for New York, to make sale of their plunder, when Van Kirk informed Capt. Dennis of the time of their intended departure, (which was to have been Tuesday night last) and of the course they would take to their boats, in consequence of which, and agreeable to the directions of Van Kirk, the Capt. and a small party of his militia planted themselves at Rock-Pond, near the sea shore, and shot Bourke, West and Williams in the manner above related. We were in hopes at first of keeping Van Kirk under the rose, but the secret is out, and of course he must fly the country, for the Tories are so highly exasperated against him, that death will certainly be his fate, if he does not speedily leave Monmouth. The Whigs are soliciting contributions in his favor, and from what I have already seen, have no doubt that they will present him with a very handsome sum. I question whether the destruction of the British fleet could diffuse more universal joy through the inhabitants of Monmouth, than has the death of the above three most egregious villains. A certain John Gilbertson, of the same group of villains, was killed about three weeks ago, by a party of the Militia near Tom's-River. The New Jersey Gazette, February 3, 1779

Another group of *banditti* operated in north New Jersey. Their headquarters was atop a mountain, at Smith's Clove, near the border between New York and New Jersey

On Saturday night, the 6th instant, were taken at the house of Nathan Miller, in Smith's Clove, James Smith (son of Claudius Smith, a notorious offender, who was executed at Goshen the 22d ult.) and one Benson of Long Island. These villains, in connection with

Claudius, had committed many daring robberies. They are now safely lodged in jail. *New Jersey Journal, February, 16, 1779*

On Friday, the ninth instant, as Captain Trapp was on his way from Boston to this City, between six or seven o'clock in the evening, he was met by two men in the road from New Windsor to Morristown, in the Clove, when one of them, with a musket, stopped him and swore that, if he did not immediately dismount, he would blow his brains out. Capt. Trapp asked by whose authority. He replied, if he did not get off, he would show him. By this time, the other one came and took the horse by the bridle and took a pistol out of his pocket. Capt. Trapp then alighted and they tied the horse and took off his saddlebags, in which there was upwards of Eight Thousand Eight Hundred Pounds, lawful money, and all his clothes and ordered him up the mountain, where they stopped and demanded the key. He told that he had lost it, when with a knife, he cut them open. One of them guarded him to almost the top of the mountain, when seeing his opportunity, he ran and made his escape from them and came to the first house from the place, where he found some rifle men who went in pursuit of them. He found his horse where they had left him the next morning but could find nothing of the robbers. The night before they broke opened and robbed a house near the same place. One Cole, and one Straw who belonged to the same party, were executed the same day at Hackensack. There have [been] thirteen of them seen about but it is supposed that there are between forty and fifty now on the mountain, near the same place. *The Pennsylvania Packet, April 17, 1779*

Last week, six daring villains in Smith's Clove, had the audacity to fire upon two of our light horse, as they were passing in the rear of the army, one of which they wounded in the body and broke the thigh bone of the other. They were immediately pursued by a party from the army, taken and one hanged. The five were conducted to head quarters and, a court martial being held upon them, they were found guilty and received the sentence of death, pursuant to which four were hanged. It was insinuated to the fifth, that, if he would discover his accomplices, he would be pardoned which offer of clemency he eagerly embraced and conducted a party of our people to a cave in the mountain, the depository of all their plunder, where lay concealed five more, whom they secured. Various *items of plunder were found in their den. New Jersey Journal, June 15, 1779*

Last Friday night, two wagons belonging to Mr. Gamble, Commissary, on their way from Fishkill to Morristown, were stopped in Smith's Clove by a party of the enemy from New York and robbed of most everything that was of value in them. In one of them was a trunk of hats for some officers in our army, a trunk of books belonging to Capt. Granger of the Artillery, together with a collection of book, the property of Samuel Witham Stockton, Esq, who arrived about six months ago from Holland. A few days ago, the last two mentioned gentlemen with a party of continental troops, scoured the mountains in that quarter and searched all the disaffected houses in that neighborhood of the clove, suspected of harboring those infamous refugee robbers, but met with little success in making any important discoveries. Instead of the enemy's discouraging these villains, I am informed that they stimulate and endeavor to protect them from the immediate punishment due their crimes, by putting commissions in their pockets as officers, thus providing against an incidental capture. The New Jersey Gazette, June 8, 1780

Still another gang, headquartered on Sandy Hook, and led by a runaway slave from John Corlies of Shrewsbury, named Titus. He had adopted the title of Colonel Ty and afflicted Monmouth county with his night time raids:

Ty, with his party of about twenty blacks and whites, last Friday afternoon took and carried off prisoners Capt. Barnes Smock and Gilbert Vanmarter, at the same time spiked up the iron four pounder at Capt. Smock's house, but took no ammunition. Two of the artillery horses and two of Captain Smock's horses, were likewise taken off.

The above mentioned Ty is a Negro, who bears the title of colonel and commands a motley crew at Sandy Hook. The New Jersey Gazette, June 14, 1780

Numerous other accounts of acts of lawlessness, perpetrated under the guise of the war, were also reported in the press of the day:

Saturday night last, the house of the widow Boellisfelt, near the Great Swamp in Amwell, was attacked by several armed Tories painted like Indians, who cruelly robbed her of 700 dollars, threatening that, if she made the least noise, or resistance, they would put her to immediate death. We doubt not but that the gentlemen in authority will exert themselves to bring those daring villains to exemplary and condign punishment. The New Jersey Gazette, September 2, 1778

A particular account of the robbery, committed at Hibernia Iron works, mentioned in our last. On Tuesday night, the 27th ult. a party of robbers and well armed villains surrounded the dwelling house at Hibernia furnace, three of whom entered when the family was at dinner, about 9 o'clock in the evening and stayed two hours. They entered before the family discovered them, clapped a pistol to each of their breasts, ordered them to give up their arms and surrender themselves prisoners in the King's name or they were dead men. They were obliged to submit, having only three workmen about the house and they in bed. The villains fixed a sentry at each door and then proceeded to plunder the house of everything valuable, to a very considerable amount, with which items they loaded five horses, which they took off with them also. They went from there to Dr. Jonathan Chuver's house, near Charlotburg iron-works, with an intent to murder him, having discovered them some time before, having met them in the wood between there and Long Pond. While they were surrounding his house, he made his escape out of a window; they fired at him, but missed him; he ran six or seven miles with no clothes on other than his shirt and alarmed the country as he went. They plundered his house, threatened to kill his wife, made her go down twice to her knees to beg her life. There are parties of the militia in quest of them and it is hoped that the spirited true sons of liberty, will turn out and scour the woods 'till they are detected, that they may get their just deserts. The New Jersey Journal, May 11, 1779

On Friday the 16th instant, a little after sunset, six armed villains came to the house of John Chamberlain, Esq., in Windsor, Middlesex County. Three of them entered the house and three stood as guards. Putting their bayonets to his chest, they demanded his *money, and after much abuse and many threatenings, they went off, taking with them about 6 pounds and five shillings sterling and about a 1000 pounds Continental money, three pairs of silver shoe buckles, three pairs of silver buttons, half a dozen tea spoons and a variety of the family's wearing apparel. The New Jersey Gazette, June 28, 1780*

New York City was identified as the lair of these *banditti* and the British appointed ruler of the City, James Robertson, as the ultimate general of this warfare of terror and cruelty upon the non combatants of New Jersey:

About three weeks ago, a gang of robbers stole twenty horses from the neighborhood of Pompton, in New Jersey. Some young men pursued them so closely that they recovered eleven of the horses, the others were carried off to the original den of the thieves, at New York. It is now publicly known that, in New York, an office is erected for licensing robbers and conveyers of counterfeit money into the country. Was ever such a species of business and malevolence to men, reduced to a system, before the present royal disturber of the peace introduced it? The New York Journal, May 3, 1779

At a Court of Oyer and Terminer, held in Bergen County on the 12th ult. William Cole and Thomas Welcher, alias Straw, were convicted of a felony and executed on Friday, the ninth ult.
They were worthies, by Mr. Robertson of New York in his Royal American Gazette of the 15th instant, called loyalists. They were famous all over the county for robbery, housebreaking, pocket picking and horse stealing and few so eminent in that vocation. Americans may perhaps wonder, but they will be pleased to know these are recommending qualifications in a loyalist. The New Jersey Gazette, April 28, 1779

Yesterday evening Captain Jonathan Hopper[121], a brave and spirited officer of the militia of this county, was basely murdered by a party of ruffians from New York. He discovered them breaking open his stable door and hailed them, upon which they fired and wounded him. He returned to the house; they followed, burst open the door and bayonetted him in upwards of twenty places. One of them named

Stephen Rider, had formerly been one of his neighbors. The New Jersey Gazette, May 12, 1779

We hear that a few nights ago, eight horse thieves from New York, where the enemy keeps a considerable number of that profession in employment, stealing horses from the inhabitants near the lines, came up to the neighborhood of Hackinsack and took off with them sixteen horses. They had engaged boats to meet them at a certain place on the North River and carry over their booty, at which place they arrived safely, but no boats appeared. In the meantime, twelve or fourteen of the Bergen militia collected and pursued them closely. The enemy having no inclination for contest, skulked and hid themselves among some tall thick weeds, to which the Bergen lads, form the sake of expedition, setting fire, the contents came out and very submissively surrendered. They are lodged securely at Morris Town. The militia also brought back the horses. The New Jersey Gazette, December 13, 1780

The citizenry was warned in the newspapers about the tricks and guises utilized by the *banditti* to gain entrance into the homes of their victims:

It is truly to be wished that travelers and housekeepers would be more on their guard than they generally have been. Several robberies have lately been committed on both sides of the Hudson's River and New Jersey by the malignant murdering Tories. Some days since, in the forepart of the evening, a number of villains came to a house, pretending they were friends and used flattering speeches to get in. One of them counterfeited a person who lived a few miles distant, saying he had a letter for the man of the house, upon which he inadvertently opened the door. They abused the family and robbed the house of cash to a considerable amount. The Pennsylvania Evening Post, May 15, 1779

Newtown Township, Glouster County
ONE HUNDRED AND FIFTY DOLLARS REWARD
WHEREAS three men came to the house of the subscriber at about one o'clock last night, pretending to be Continental soldiers and demanded entrance to search for some of their men and, being let in,

asked for a candle and searched the house, when finding no one about the house but myself, they presented their bayonets to my breast and threatened to take my life, unless I delivered my money and also threatened to break open the drawers whereas myself and my wife, through terror, unlocked the drawers from whence they took about One Hundred and Fifty Pounds in old Paper money, Four Hundred and Forty Pounds in Continental money of those two emissions called in, a bag of ten or twelve Pounds in Spanish Pieces of Eight and a Bag containing about 10 shillings in pennies. One of the said men was of a low stature, wore a blue coat turned up with red and the others were of a middling size; one of them had a red jacket and a pair of trousers, the other wore brown or blue turned up with red.
        AQUILLA JONES
        The Pennsylvania Packet, April 17, 1779

On at least one occasion, a trap was set to catch these brigands in the act of their depredations:

On Thursday last a Mr. Van Meter was knocked off his horse on the road to Longstreet's Mill, in Monmouth County, by Lewis Fenton and one Debow, by whom he was stabbed in the arm and otherwise much abused, besides being robbed of his saddle. In the meantime, another person coming up, which drew the attention of the robbers, gave Mr. Van Meter the opportunity to make his escape. He went directly and informed a sergeant's guard of Major Lee's light dragoons, who were in the neighborhood, of what had happened. The sergeant immediately pressed a wagon and horses and ordered three of his men to secrete themselves in it under some hay. Having changed his clothes and procured a guide, he made haste thus equipped to the place where Fenton lay. On the approach of the wagon, Fenton (his companion being gone) rushed out to plunder it. Upon demanding what they had in it, he was answered a little wine and spirit. These articles he said he wanted and, while advancing toward the wagon to take possession of them, one of the soldiers, being previously informed who he was, shot him through the head, which killed him instantly on the spot. Thus did this villain end his days --which, it is hoped, will at least be warning to others, if not induce them to throw themselves on the mercy of their injured country. The New Jersey Gazette, September 29, 1779

There is some indication that some of these *banditti* included American soldiers, who specialized in robbing Loyalists. One might have been John Lozler. Was he a bandit, terrorist or a patriot? That might depend on whose side you were or which paper you read. The Loyalist papers pictured him as a murdering thief:

On Thursday Afternoon, on his way to gratify an ardent Desire to see his Family, who were ill of the Small Pox, Mr. John Richards of New Barbados Neck, was taken near Bergen by two armed Men and on the Road between them and The Three Pigeons, was shot dead by one of them, as he was preventing the other from robbing him of his watch. He was a Man universally known and as universally beloved, warmly attached to his Friends, humane and candid to his Enemies, benevolent and hospitable to all Men and has now fallen a Sacrifice to his unsuspecting and generous Temper, for, when warned of the Danger of his intended Visit, his Answer was "that his Countrymen, even if they should take him, would never injure him".

Mistaken man to trust to the Generosity of those who have involved their Country in Ruin.

The Names of the Monsters who perpetrated this horrid Tragedy are Brower and Le Sheair [Lozler]. The New York Gazette, February 2, 1778

The following, however, is the American version of the same incident. Richards was "shot while trying to escape":

"On the 29th ult. Major Goetschius, who commands a party of rangers in Bergen county, had dispatched John Leshier [Lozler] and Abraham Brower, two of his men, to reconnoiter the enemy's position at Paulus Hook. As they lay in ambush at Prior's Mill, within sight of the enemy's sentry, they were passed by John Richard, with a Negro man belonging to himself and another to Cornelius Van Vorst, upon a wagon. John Richard had a pass from Col. Trumbull to go to Bergen. Maj. Goetschius's men thought it was their Duty to carry Mr. Richard and the two Negroes to their commanding officer for examination. Upon the road, about six miles from the place where they were taken,

Mr. Richard and his Negro, took hold of Leshier's musket (they being in the wagon and Brower at a little distance on horseback) with design, as Leshier thought, to kill him. Upon this, he called to Brower to come to his assistance. As Brower came up, the Negro took hold of Leshier and Richard turned to seize Brower, but Brower, to prevent him, shot him dead on the spot and the Negroes were carried to Maj. Goetschius's." The New Jersey Gazette, February 11, 1778

As the war progressed, Lozler would be in other heroic assaults, or "atrocities", depending on the source, against the British and would be captured, exchanged and captured at least one more time:

A Detachment form the Garrison at Paulus Hook, of which Major Sutherland is Commandant, on Friday Morning last took Prisoners, the noted John Loshier and David Ritzema Bogert. A third of the Banditti escaped very narrowly by throwing away his Arms and swimming the Hackensack. Loshier is safely lodged. The New York Gazette, July 26, 1779

Early yesterday morning, a party of the fourth battalion of the New Jersey Volunteers, were ordered out by their Lieutenant Bushkirk under Capt. Van Allen to intercept a gang of rebels, who paint themselves black and commit murders and thefts in Bergen county. Three of them were met at a small distance from the town of Bergen carrying off an inhabitant, but being briskly pushed, two of them were made prisoners, one named David Ritzema Bogert, the other the noted John Loshier, who was concerned in the murder of honest Capt. John Richards and whose repeated instances of villainy had rendered him among the rebels deserving their earliest attention for exchange, when lately taken by a battalion of the same regiment, who have a second time spared his life.
The Royal Gazette, July 21, 1779

CHAPTER 12

The War Years: 1780

For the third time in the four year old war, General Washington selected New Jersey as the site for his winter camp. Morristown, located in an ancient mountain chain about 35 miles northwest of British occupied New York City, had been a wise choice. The hilly terrain provided protection against any British sneak attack. There, the Americans could sit securely, while outposts watched the British movements across the Hudson River. If the British were to decide to advance unexpectedly up the Hudson or south toward the Delaware, Washington could intercept them, by sending his troops, through a back country corridor of friendly territory.

What no one bargained for was the frigid weather of the winter of 1779-1780. It was a severe one, the worse since 1755. Fortunately, Washington had ordered an advance party in November to construct huts for their soon to arrive comrades, because, by the time the main force arrived at nearby Jockey Hollow in December, there was already two feet of snow on the ground. January would bring a number of more storms and drifts of snow, six and seven feet high, lay across countryside.

The snow had cut the supply line for fresh provisions from the south. The capacity of the local market to ease the shortage was further reduced by hoarding among some residents, especially the more neutral citizenry of Dutch descent. Smuggling to New York City where the food drew a higher price, paid in British gold and silver, not Continental IOUs, made matters worse. The streams of the country were frozen solid by the cold, thus preventing grist mills from grinding the soldier's grain into useable flour. The suffering was great, worse than that at Valley Forge. Yet, the veterans had warm huts and they kept their humor about themselves:

(Extract of a letter from Baskenridge, December 18, 1779)
I rode out today on purpose to take a view of our encampments. I found it excessively cold, but was glad to see most of our poor soldiers were under good roofs. The encampments are

exceeding neat; the huts are all of a size and placed in more exact order than Philadelphia; you would be surprised to see how well built they are without nails. Head Quarters is at Morristown and the army extends from thence along the hills nearly to this place. *The New Jersey Journal, February 2, 1780*

(Extract of a letter from Baskenridge, January 22, 1780)
We had a fast lately in camp, by general constraint of the whole army, in which we fasted more sincerely and truly, for three days, than ever we did from all the resolutions of Congress put together. This was occasioned by the severity of the weather and the drifting of the snow whereby the roads were rendered impassable and all supplies of provisions cut off, until the officers were obliged to release the soldiers from command and permit them to go, in great numbers together, into the country to get the provision where they could find it. The inhabitants of this part of the country discovered a noble spirit in feeding the soldiers and, to the honor of the soldiery, they received what they got with thankfulness and did little or no damage. The New Jersey Gazette, January 26, 1780

The Loyalists and British in New York City were faring as badly, if not worse. At least the soldiers at Jockey Hollow had the timbered hills to supply fuel for their warming fires. Fuel in the burned out New York City was scarce:

By a gentleman from New York, we learn that the inhabitants are so necessitated for fuel that near 100 of them have perished during this inclement seasons for want thereof. The New Jersey Journal, January 25, 1780

From Mr. Ludlow, who has left New York and thrown himself on the mercy of this state, besides others from that same state, we learn that the situation of the Refugees is more doubtful than ever. No supplies have arrived from Europe since the forepart of the fall of any kind, nor of any intelligence of the troops since their departure, except what has been conveyed to them through our hands. The high toned Loyalists sing small and hang their drooping guilty heads. The New Jersey Gazette, March 8, 1780

The Continental soldier had much besides the harshness of the winter to dampen his spirits. His pay, meager as it was and dispensed in depreciated Continental paper, was in serious arrears. Many of the soldiers, cold, hungry and risking their lives as sentinels for a more comfortable Congress in Philadelphia, thought themselves and their sacrifices forgotten by the folks back home. Some troops from Pennsylvania even mutinied and marched off to the Congress in Philadelphia to protest their condition.

The arctic weather, the gloom at camp and the need of the troops for provisions inspired Washington to send Lord Stirling - the American general who claimed an English title - to attack Staten Island. He planned to cross the frozen Arthur Kill, which separated that loyalist island from New Jersey, on horse driven sleighs. Washington describes the result in a letter to the Continental Congress and attached Lord Stirling's own report:

The severity of the weather having rendered a descent upon Staten Island practicable by the ice and, it being also imagined by the ice that the communication between New York and the Island was interrupted by the same cause, a favorable opportunity of striking the enemy stationed there (who amounted by report to 1000 or 1200 men) seemed to present itself. A detachment of 2500 men, including the troops under General Irvine, was accordingly made for that purpose and the Command given to Major General Lord Stirling. It was originally intended to have attempted the execution of the matter by surprise, but there being good reason to suppose that the enemy, by their emissaries or by other means, had got notice of our designs, little hope remained for effecting the business in that manner. As the attachment was assembled near Elizabeth Town, it was thought advisable to proceed at all events, upon a consideration that no bad consequences could possibly result and that we might find an opportunity of reaping some advantage. We were, however, disappointed in our expectations, as Congress will perceive by the enclosed report from Lord Strirling."   Lord Strirling's Report
Sir,

I have the honor to inform your Excellency, that early on yesterday morning, the corps under my command crossed the Sound at De Hart's Point and proceeded toward the watering place. The enemy having received previous reports of our movements, a surprise was out of the question and, as their works were well situated and appeared otherwise strong, an assault was deemed unadvisable, as it would probably have caused us more than we could have gained by success. We found too, contrary to our expectation, that communication between the Island and New York was open.

Immediately upon our arrival in front of the enemy's works, they sent a boat off to the city and, in the evening, several boats came down thence to the Island. As from this circumstance, there was no hope of reducing them from want of provisions or fuel [and] a reinforcement might have rendered our continuance dangerous, we determined to march off this morning. The retreat was effected in good order and with very little loss. A party of the enemy's horse charged our rear guard under Major Edwards but was immediately repulsed. The Major had three men killed, killed one of the light horsemen and took his horse. Some few of the men were frost bitten, and though we took all the pains in our power to have all those unable to march, transported in sleighs, yet I imagine a very few were left behind. Immediately after crossing, a party was detached, under Lieutenant Willet, to Decker's House. The corps there had been alarmed and barely made its escape. The house as a garrison place and 8 or 9 small vessels, were burned. A considerable quantity of blankets and other stores were found.

While the troops were upon the Island, a number of persons from this side took advantage of the occasion to pass upon the Island and plundered the people there in the most shameless and merciless manner. Many of them were stopped on their return and their booty taken from them. In addition to which, I have sent an order for publication, requiring those who have eluded the search to restore the articles in their possession and exhorting the good people, at large, to assist in detecting them. All the soldiery, on re crossing the ice, were searched and the little plunder they had, taken from them and their names noted, that they might be brought to punishment. The articles recovered are and will be deposited with the Rev. Mr. Caldwell, who is exerting himself in this affair, to be returned to the owners. I am happy to inform your Excellency that a very inconsiderable part indeed of the troops dishonored themselves by participating in these enormities. The officers and men in general showed a good disposition, and I only regret there was no opportunity of turning it to advantage.

The Pennsylvania Packet, January 25, 1780

Despite the raid's failure and the pilfering by American soldiers, the patriot press found some reason a success to acclaim:

We hear that on Friday evening last a detachment from the American army, commanded by Major General Lord Stirling, went in sleds from Morristown with several pieces of light artillery, in order to surprise the British troops upon Staten Island and to bring off the stores which might fall in their hands. They went upon the Island on Saturday morning, but the enemy, it is said, having had information of the design, retired, with most of the principal inhabitants to the forts on the east side of the Island, carrying with them a considerable part of their valuable effects. Our troops, after scouring the Island, came off on Sunday, bringing with them several prisoners, horses, a number of tents and other valuable effects.

This may serve to show the British mercenaries with what zeal and alacrity the Americans will embrace an opportunity, even in a very inclement season, to promote the interests of their country, by harassing the enemies to their freedom and independence. With pleasure, we inform our readers that our army, which, through the unexpected inclemency of the season, winter setting in much earlier than usual, and the roads becoming almost impassable, had suffered a few days for want of provisions, are, from the spirited exertions now making, likely to be well supplied. The New Jersey Gazette, January 19, 1780

The protection and isolation that the frozen weather afforded souls brave enough to use it to their advantage encouraged more forays by both sides. The British attacks against Newark and Elizabeth, although considerably smaller than Lord Strirling's, were said to be in retaliation for his attack upon Staten Island. The patriots were not intimidated:

A party of the enemy, consisting of about 300 infantry, under the command of Col. Van Bushkirk of the new levies and about 60 dragoons, said to be under the command of Capt. Steward of the 17th light dragoons, with several refugees, the whole, in number, near 400, crossed on the ice from Staten Island to Trembley's Point, about three miles from Elizabeth Town, last Tuesday night. From thence, they were conducted by Cornelius Hetfield, Job Hetfield and Smith Hetfield, their principal guides, the nearest and most retired route to Elizabeth Town. They entered the Town in two divisions before the alarm was sounded. As soon as the troops who were in town (consisting of about sixty men) perceived their danger, they retreated. However, they took a major, who was commandant of the place, and two to three captains that lodged in town that night and a few troops. They then set fire to the presbyterian meeting and court house, which were consumed, plundered, insulted and took off some of the inhabitants and retreated, with great precipitation, by the way of De Hart's Point, whose house they like wise consumed.

The same night another party of the enemy, consisting of draughts from the different regiments stationed in New York, passed over the North River in sleighs, to Powles Hook, from thence through Bergen, the nearest way to Newark. They entered the town in three divisions and immediately proceeded to the academy, where they surprised and took about 15 men, being all the troops that were on duty in the town. A lieutenant, notwithstanding he was twice a prisoner of the enemy, by his vigilance, effected his escape. They then set fire to the academy which they consumed, during which time a party was dispatched to several of the inhabitants' houses, which they rifled of the most valuable effects; that which was not portable, they destroyed. They took off Justice Hedden and Robert Neill, jun., two of the inhabitants. The former gentleman was taken out of his bed and without any other clothes on except his shirt and a pair of stockings and carried off, notwithstanding the strong solicitations of Mrs. Hedden, to the officers, for permission for her husband to dress himself, who received two wounds with a bayonet, one in her face, the other in her breast, by those mighty veterans of fallen Majesty.
They continued in town about fifteen or eighteen minutes. A few militia, being hastily collected, pursued their rear, by which means five of the enemy fell into their hands. Two of them died a short time later with the intense cold.

We are informed that Justice Hedden is so frost-bit that he will lose both his legs.

Last Sunday evening about 8 o'clock, a party of the enemy landed at Rahway and carried off near a dozen of the inhabitants.

The Church in Town, not discouraged or intimidated by the barbarous impiety of the enemy met last Sabbath and sung the following verses:

*With Flames, they threaten to destroy
The Children in their Nest
"Come, let us burn at once" they cry
"The Temple and the priest"
And shall the Sons of earth and dust
That sacred power blaspheme
Will not thy hand that formed them first,
Avenge thine injured name?
Think of the cov'nant thou has made
And all thy words of love;
Nor let the birds of prey invade
And vex thy mourning dove.
Our foes would triumph in our blood,
 And make our hope their jest;
Plead they own cause almighty God,
And give thy Children rest.
The New Jersey Journal, February 2, 1780*

The British occupied Sandy Hook, then an island and probably two thirds of its present size. Sandy Hook guarded the entrance to the Hudson River and New York City and its lighthouse[122] was critical to the safe navigation of ships arriving from Europe with men and supplies. Sandy Hook was an inviting target because of its isolation and importance:

We are informed that on Thursday se'nnight, Capt. Rudolf of Major Lee's rangers, a sergeant, corporal and eight men landed on Sandy Hook, within a half mile of the Light house, surrounded a house and made seven of the enemy prisoners; they also brought off 45,000 counterfeit continental dollars, a quantity of hard money and several parcels of dry goods of different kinds, without any loss. The New Jersey Gazette, January 19, 1780

On the morning of the 15th [of January], Major Lee, detached from Burlington, forty men under the command of Captain Patten, in sleighs, who, before the next morning, were alongside the guard ship, laying froze in the ice around Sandy Hook, but, finding, that the ice, for several yards around her, was cut so that they could not board her, they retired to a small distance unperceived, where they surprised two schooners and a sloop, made the men prisoners, burnt the vessels and then returned without the least loss, bringing with them the prisoners and what plunder they thought proper. The New Jersey Journal, February 2, 1780

The British also crossed the Hudson and struck the northern towns lying along it on the Jersey side. Who won? Contemporary accounts differ. As was to be expected, Rivington's *Royal Gazette's* accounts of one of these British attacks was at odds with that given by the *New Jersey Journal*:

New York, March 29. On Wednesday night, the 22d inst. two detachments of the army were passed over the Hudson's River into Jersey, one from Kingsbridge consisting of three hundred men from the Brigade of Guards under the command of Lieut. Col Howard, the other from New York of equal force, composed of the British and German Troops in Garrison, under the command of Lieut. Colonel Macpherson, of the 42 regt.

Lieut. Col Howard's detachment landed at Kloster, several miles north of Fort Lee; the troops from the city at Weehawk. The former were to penetrate into the country north of Hopper's Town and destined to attack the rear of the rebel cantoonments of that place. The latter, taking their route by the little ferry upon Hackensack, where boats were sent to transport them across, were to have surprised the town of Hackensack, in which a company of militia were quartered and, pushing forward, to have fallen upon the front of the Paramus cantoonments. These services were not effected owing to unavoidable delays, till several hours later than intended. Lieut. Col Howard arrived near Hopper's Town, two hours after daybreak in the morning of the 23rd, and, continuing his march, surprised two pickets and pressed one of their cantoonments so closely as to oblige the officer and his command to leave their arms behind them, which to the amount of above thirty stand were destroyed. Their main body, consisting of between two and three hundred men, made a show of defense at the church, but finding that they would be instantly attacked, they retired with precipitation, were pursued for above a mile and several prisoners taken. Lieut. Colonel Macpherson's detachment at this time upon its march through the cantoonments, which were found abandoned, made its appearance upon the road near the church, having taken a few prisoners.

Every further attempt to come up with the enemy being impracticable, both detachments returned to Zabriskie's Mills, where being joined by the party left at Hackensack, which had taken several prisoners, the troops retired by New Bridge and the English Neighborhood, Lieut. Col Howard's detachments embarking near Fort Lee, Lieut. Colonel Macpherson's detachment, with the prisoners, continuing their march to Weehawk, where boats were waiting to receive them.

One man of the Guards was killed, Capt. Anstruther of the 42 regt. and a few men were wounded upon the march toward the English Neighborhood, the rebels in loose parties, keeping up an irregular fire upon the rear and some men dropped behind because of fatigue.

In the course of the march, a Clergyman with another inoffensive inhabitant (taken prisoners by mistake) were dismissed and are reported to have been accidentally shot by the rebels.

Sixty four prisoners were brought from Jersey, of those twenty four belonged to the Continental troops and a captain and twenty three were militia men. Thirteen deserters also, who were part of the Paramus command, came off with their arms. The loss of the rebels in killed and wounded cannot be ascertained. The Royal Gazette, March 29, 1780

Last Thursday evening, a party of the enemy came out and penetrated into the country as far as Paramus. In their route, cruelty and devastation, the characteristic of the tyrant's troops, marked their steps. At Hackensack, they burned the court house and two dwelling houses and almost tore the house of Mr. Cambell, inn keeper, to pieces, after plundering him of a very considerable sum of specie and continental money. In short, they plundered indiscriminately, both Whig and Tory. Their cruelty and barbarity to the women was unparalleled. Some they most inhumanely choked to make them tell where all their money was, and one, we hear, was so unfortunate as to have her arm broke by them. The militia of the county turned out spiritedly, and forming a junction with a few continental troops, that lay at Paramus, pushed them on their retreat very hard, took a few prisoners and killed and wounded several, whom they carried off in wagons. Remember, apostate Britons, that your towns, during the last summer, have been in the power of our fleets and that perhaps may be the case the ensuing one, when taught by your example, we may retaliate ten fold! The Jersey Journal, March 29, 1780

British raids against northern New Jersey continued throughout the spring:

On the 16th ult. a detachment of two hundred continental troops, under the command of Major Byles, of the Pennsylvania line, stationed at Paramus, was suddenly attacked by a party of the enemy, consisting of about two hundred horse and 400 foot. The attack commenced a little after sunrise. Major Byles, besides his morning patrols, had that morning sent out two parties, each with a commissioned officer, but such was the situation in that country, intersected with roads and inhabited chiefly by disaffected people, that all precautions failed. His parties and patrols were eluded and the sentinels near his quarters were the first to give notice of the enemies approach. He had just before that paraded and dismissed his men. The advance of the enemy was so rapid that there was no time to reassemble them. The Major had no resource but the defense of the house he was in. This, therefore, with only a small quarter guard, he resolved to defend, although from the smallness of his forces, he could have no prospect of success, but chose rather to fall in a brave, though hopeless, resistance than to save himself by a dishonorable surrender. He immediately made the best disposition, the hurry of the moment would permit and animated his men by his exhortation and example. A brisk fire ensued on both sides. The house was so surrounded on every part and no effort of the little party, seemed capable of hindering the enemy from forcing their way. Some of the men, intimidated by so threatening a scene, began to cry for quarters; others, obeying the commands of their officers, continued to fire from the windows. The enemy without, upbraided them with the perfidy of asking quarters and persisting in resistance, desiring them to come out and they would quarter them. Major Byles, exclaiming in a determined tone, denied his having asked for quarters; but his resolution could not avail; a surrender took place and, in the act[123], the Major took a mortal wound to his left breast from which, two days after, he expired, a victim of his gallantry and refined sense of duty. So distinguished and enviable fall must endear his memory to his fellow soldiers and fellow citizens. The New Jersey Journal, May 17, 1780

Most of the engagements were quick hitting forays:

Thursday evening, a party of about 30 refugees from New York, landed at Stoney Point on the Raritan River and from thence went to Woodbridge, where they made Justice Freeman, Mr. Edgar and six other white men and two Negroes prisoners, and carried off to New York. The Pennsylvania Journal, June 7th, 1780

Early on Sunday morning last, Major Van Emburg of Bordentown, with eight or nine others, being at Tom's River on a fishing party, were surprised, while a-bed, by a number of armed Tory refugees and put on board a vessel bound for New York, but they found means to make their escape. The Pennsylvania Journal, June 7th, 1780

Thursday last, a party of about thirty of the enemy landed at Closter, in Bergen County, in order to plunder cattle from the inhabitants, but, while they were collecting them, they were attacked by a party of our militia under the command of Col. Blanch, who retook the cattle, killed one and wounded two of the plunderers and drove them to their boats, without any loss on our side. The New Jersey Gazette, June 14, 1780

The attacks on Jersey by the British during the spring were meant to occupy General Washington and his army, still at Morristown. On Christmas Eve, 1779, the British had sent transport after transport filled with troops from the New York harbor southward and the mysterious movement continued throughout the first part of 1780. Their destination? No one was certain. Perhaps, the Chesapeake or the Virginias; maybe, Charlestown:

By an express from Shrewsbury, we learn, that on Sunday last upwards of a 100 transports, conveyed by three ships of force, sailed out of Sandy Hook and, it is said, General Clinton is on board. The Pennsylvania Journal, January 5, 1780

I have just received intelligence of the sailing of the British fleet out of Sandy Hook yesterday morning. They consisted of ten ships and seven brigs. There is not one horse gone aboard. They are convoyed by the Rainbow, the Delight and the Swift Brig and it is said that they expect to meet at sea with the Galatea and Thames Frigates, which left New York last week with the packet. It is reported that General Clinton had all his effects on board. The New Jersey Gazette, April 12, 1780

Soon, it was learned that Charlestown, South Carolina had been the British target and, on May 12, 1780, General Henry Clinton and an army of 14,000 easily captured the city, together with many Continental soldiers, vast armaments and provisions[124]. It was a crushing blow and reported in the press more in the funeral tone of an obituary than as a late breaking news account:

We are sorry to inform our readers that the garrison at Charles Town, consisting of 2,571 continental troops, including officers of every rank, surrendered prisoners of war on the 12th ult., but the particulars coming late to hand and being very lengthy, are deferred to our next. The New Jersey Gazette, June 21, 1780

Meanwhile, the British remaining in New York seemed to be preparing for an invasion of New Jersey and the appearance of sails on the horizon was interpreted by many Americans as the return of the British from Charlestown to begin that invasion:

On Saturday last, 35 sail of square rigged vessels came up to Decker's ferry, opposite Bergen Point. Their design is certainly not known. The New Jersey Gazette, May 17, 1780

Last Sunday, twenty six sail of vessels went up Hackinsack River. Time will develop their intentions. The New Jersey Journal, May 17, 1780

It is reported that part of the British Troops is arrived at Staten Island from South Carolina. The Pennsylvania Packet, June 17, 1780

We hear that a fleet of upwards of a one hundred sail arrived a few days ago at the Hook, supposed to be from Charles-Town South Carolina, with a reinforcement. The New Jersey Gazette, June 21, 1780

As it turned out, the British also had their eyes on the horizon. But they were not awaiting the return of their own ships but were watching for the arrival of the French fleet, coming to the assistance of its American allies. In fact, the British had begun making preparations for the defense of New York City, including a plan to sink ships in the channel leading to the harbor.

The British had been correct. The French fleet indeed was coming!

A gentleman from Middletown Point [Matawan] informs us that there certainly is a fleet of our allies on the coast and that several of the officers have been ashore. 'Tis said they consist of nearly one hundred sail. New Jersey Journal, May 24, 1780.

We are happy to be able to inform the Public from the best authority, that a French Fleet, with a large body of troops, is expected hourly off the American coast. The enemy in New York know this to be a fact and therefore are exerting themselves to put all their works in and near that city in as good a condition for defense as lies in their power. For some time past, they have had parties out cutting fascines, stealing fence rails and other materials for use [in] their fortifications. The New Jersey Gazette, May 24, 1780

We hear that a large ship from London for New York was captured off the Hook, on Sunday sennight, after an obstinate action of four hours by two New England privateers and carried into an eastern port, laden with dry goods, said to be valued at 60,000 pounds sterling. During the engagement several frigates were dispatched from the Hook to reconnoitre the vessels, but after they had gone some distance, were, by a signal form the British ship of 74 guns, ordered to return lest the firing should prove the decoy of the French fleet, which they daily expected on the coast and, in consequence thereof, have ordered a number of vessels to be got ready to sink in the channel on short notice.
The New Jersey Gazette, May 17, 1780

Suddenly, like the hurricane that veers off its target at the last minute and strikes unexpectedly elsewhere, the French Fleet sailed past the fortified New York City. Its aim was on Rhode Island and the northern theater of the war in New England:

Preparations are making to land the expected French army at Rhode Island and a variety of circumstances contribute to brighten our expectations of the ensuing campaign. The Pennsylvania Gazette, June 7, 1780

On Monday the 10th inst. Mons de Ternay arrived at Newport, Rhode Island, with a very formidable fleet of ships and a large body of land forces, sent to the relief of these United States by his most Christian Majesty, with whose assistance we hope very soon to extirpate from our territories those invaders of our rights, the apostate Britons. New Jersey Journal, July 19, 1780

Now that the storm had passed by harmlessly, Washington in New Jersey and the British in New York City nervously lashed out at each other again. The British had secured a foothold, in Elizabeth, just across the Arthur Kill from Staten Island. What were the British plans for the main American army under the command of George Washington?

We are informed that the enemy still continues at Elizabeth Town Point inactive, except scouting parties which are every day skirmishing with our militia, in several of which the militia has fought with great spirit and been successful. Our loss is computed to be about 30 killed and wounded, Capt. Reves being included among the former. The enemy's loss it is said to be 150 killed and as many wounded. The Pennsylvania Packet, June 17, 1780

By a letter from an officer of rank dated the 15th, at Springfield, we learn, the enemy are fortifying, on both sides, the water at Elizabeth Point and have nearly completed their bridge; that, by taking this position, they meant to try the complexion of the country and the temper of our army, in both of which they have doubtlessly been greatly deceived -- the militia worked to a charm and but very few desertions from the continental army; that the enemy intended to penetrate further into the country as soon as their works were finished, to secure a retreat. The New Jersey Gazette, June 21, 1780

The British appeared to be moving in two directions at the same time. One body of troops sailed up the Hudson towards the key fort of West Point. The continued control of the Hudson was crucial to the Americans and the fortress at West Point was its most important defense. Another body of British troops, led by the Hessian general Knyphausen was attacking central New Jersey with particular cruelty:

We have no accounts, from authority, since our last, of the motions of the enemy. The common report (for which we cannot vouch the accuracy of) is that the body of them that lay entrenched at Elizabeth Town Point, have divided, one part marching further back into the country [New Jersey], the other up the [Hudson] river to our fort at West Point; that General Washington had also divided his army and, with one division was proceeding to the fort, where he was expected to arrive this day; that the other division, under the command of Marquis Lafayette, had been attacked by the enemy and, after a severe engagement, repulsed them; that a number of their ships to the number of 70, 80 or 90 sail, were coming up the river and had proceeded as far as Tarrytown and Teller's Point, where they had landed considerable bodies of troops on each side of the river and it was expected would attack the fort, where the garrison had lately been reinforced by General Clinton's brigade and that the militia was assembling fast from every quarter. The New York Journal, June 26th, 1780

The enemy from New York, have lately made an excursion which, to judge from the force employed it must have had some very important object, although not having succeeded in the attainment of it, what they had in our view is not quite apparent.

Our accounts of their proceedings are that at before day on Wednesday morning, the 7th instant, a body of about 5,000, under the command of General Knyphausen, Tryon and Governor Robertson, crossed the river from Staten Island to Elizabeth Town Point and proceeded to the town where, met with no opposition, they were employed mostly as news carriers, in distributing plentifully Rivington's new handbills (published by authority) giving an account of the surrender of Charlestown to the British invaders. They then advanced four miles further to Connecticut Farms, where they burned fourteen houses, among them, the Presbyterian church, and murdered Mrs. Caldwell, the minister's lady. They then moved on to Springfield, but, on the way, were met by General Maxwell with a small body of continental troops, and a few of the militia hastily collected, who, at the bridge, near the town, attacked them and stopped their further progress. Skirmishing, however, continued until that part of the Continental troops stationed at Morris Town, and a body of Jersey militia who assembled with their normal alacrity, had time to come up and oppose them, which was done so effectually that, suffering much from the well directed fire of our people, the enemy took advantage of the opportunity of a heavy rain in the night, to retire to Elizabeth Town Point, where on Saturday (the 13th), when out last advances came away, they lay encamped in our old entrenchments and, it has been said, have been joined by 2,000 troops and 200 light horse from New York. It is also said that the Generals and some of the officers have sent for their carriages and ladies, as if they intended to make some considerable stay. The loss on either side was unknown. We had upwards of 40 prisoners and a number of deserters, among whom were six Hessian light horse, well mounted and completely equipped. The British General Stirling is said to be badly, if not mortally, wounded.   The New York Journal, June 19th, 1780

The initial attack on New Jersey was followed by a second one some days later:

The Commander in Chief has for several days been extending the left wing of our army towards the north, so as to prevent the enemy from outflanking him on the right.
This morning early General Knyphausen, with thirteen regiments consisting of 5000 troops, exclusive of New Levies, advanced upon our right, which was commanded by Major

General Green. *The progress of the enemy was slow, at least six hours advancing from the Point to Springfield and did but little damage on their march. When they arrived, they were checked by the spirited conduct of a few Continentals and some militia, who gave them so warm a reception, they thought proper to halt and burn every house, except two or three, in the Town of Springfield.*

6:00 P.M. The enemy retired to Elizabeth Town; 11:00 P.M., their main body are at the Point below the town.

24th. It is reported that Clinton has gone up the North River with all the force he can make, exclusive of Knyphausen's division.

The loss of killed and wounded on both sides must be very considerable. Col Angel's and Col. Dayton's regiments have suffered much; a Capt. [Thomas] Thompson, of Col.'s Lamb's regiment is killed; further particulars I have not been able to gain. The Pennsylvania Gazette, June 28, 1780

It is said that [the enemy's] object in coming out at this time was to subjugate the state of New Jersey, having had intelligence from their friend that the majority of the inhabitants were so distressed that they would not take up arms again to oppose them and that the army was so pinched for want of provisions that the soldiers were much disposed to desert. Others say it is the consequence of an express order from Sir Henry Clinton to facilitate some future operation. If they came on the report of their friends, they have found the circumstances very different, for no militia ever turned out with more cheerfulness and behaved with more intrepidity and no troops could make a more gallant resistance. If upon the orders of Sir Henry, we may expect a very active campaign and the expense of much blood. Friday morning, we made prisoners of a British Lieutenant and six privates who came a small distance from their picquets to steal poultry and, before day break the same morning, on the mountain near Scotch Plains, a party of villains who came from Staten Island to steal horses, were discovered by Mr. Casterline, an officer of the militia, who killed one Inslee and took three others, Lesegh, Hutchinson and Closson. A court martial is now sitting for the trial of the latter. New Jersey Journal, July 5, 1780

The enemy still remains on the Point. We have continuous skirmishes; last night, they attacked our picket, were thrown back with loss, and one Hetfield, their pilot, badly wounded. We are assured that the enemy's loss is near 300 men from their attack at the bridge, numbers of them are daily found in the woods. Yesterday, 13 were found dead in a rye field. General Stirling's wound is thought to be mortal as his thigh must come off. They are very angry at being deceived by the Tories, who assured them that the militia would not fire but would join them. Count Donop's son was wounded in the action on Wednesday last. The New Jersey Gazette, June 21, 1780

Last week about 90 sail of great and small vessels appeared in the North River, nearly opposite Col. Philips', from whence it was concluded that Sir Harry intended to attack West Point, in consequence of which the militia was called out, who appeared at the respective places of rendezvous with great alertness. We have since heard that most of the vessels have fallen down the river. 'Tis thought the manoeuvre was made in order to facilitate their burning plan in New Jersey. Though they burnt the small town of Springfield, they paid dearly for it, having lost in killed and wounded, by the best accounts we can collect, from 500 to 700 men. The New York Packet and the American Advertiser, June 29, 1780

But the British had a pleasant surprise for the Jersey men braced for an attack. The British decided to withdraw from New Jersey, apparently with an intent to concentrate on an expedition against West Point on the Hudson. While skirmishing and forays would continue on her soil for the remainder of the war, Knyphausen's attacks were to prove to be the last invasion suffered by New Jersey:

This morning some of our horsemen have been down to Elizabeth Town and find that the enemy went over to Staten Island last night, took up their bridge and bid us farewell. Deserters and prisoners agree that their expedition will be carried up the North River. The New Jersey Gazette, June 28, 1780

By accounts from Jersey we are informed that General Knyphausen made a moonlight retreat out of that state on Friday night last and left his works at Elizabeth Town to be leveled by the Militia, which was soon effected. The Pennsylvania Journal, June 29, 1780

Since our last, returned to this place [Trenton], Major General Dickerson. The enemy having evacuated the state, the General, at the request of his Excellency, the Commander in Chief, marched the militia to Elizabeth Town and destroyed those works which the enemy had erected at and near the old Point, which service having been performed, he dismissed them with great reputation. The New Jersey Gazette, July 5, 1780

The news that the French fleet and ground forces had come to the assistance of the Northern Division of the Continental army and that Britain had seemingly abandoned her designs on New Jersey were events to celebrate on the fourth anniversary of the signing of the Declaration of Independence. The sentiments expressed are no less poignant or apt now, more than two centuries later, than when they were uttered:

Yesterday being the anniversary of the Declaration of Independence, the President and Faculty of the College [Princeton], with the students, the officers and soldiers of the army and militia and other inhabitants, assembled at six o'clock, afternoon, when thirteen guns were fired, before each of which one of the following sentiments was publicly read by Major Egbert and, after it, the whole company gave three cheers, in testimony of their approbation.
1. The United States of America -- May they prosper and flourish to the latest ages.
2. The Congress -- May that body always preserve the dignity, the integrity and the power necessary to govern so great a republic
3. The Kings of France and Spain and all our Allies-- May they be rewarded for their friendly aid to America.
4. General Washington -- May he ever vanquish the enemies of America and live to enjoy the honors of a grateful country.

5. *The army of the United States -- Blessings crown their bravery and may Providence reward, and their country never forget, their great and generous services.*
6. *Our brethren and countrymen in captivity --May they support their fortitude in that unhappy state and be speedily restored to us by an equitable exchange.*
7. *General Lincoln and the Garrison at Charles Town -- Thanks to them for their gallant defense -- May they never, like General Burgoyne, experience a cruel ingratitude because they wanted success.*
8. *General Gates and the southern army -- May Carolina, like Saratoga, see British confidence, raised by undeserved success, humbled by the same leader.*
9. *The Liberties and Independence of America -- May they be forever secured from the hands of oppression and tyranny.*
10. *The Confederation of the United States -- May it be completed upon just and lasting principles, so that no divisions may ever disturb the happy union.*
11. *May Virtue, the sure basis of free governments, ever be the cement and support of the American union.*
12. *The Governor, Assembly, Judges of New Jersey -- May they always have the wisdom and integrity that is necessary to make us happy citizens and this state distinguished in the confederacy.*
13. *May this destructive war speedily terminate in a lasting and honorable peace.*

Afterwards the company adjourned to the College Hall, where a discourse was delivered by the President, in which he considered: 1. The importance and necessity of independence at the time it was declared; 2. The events of Providence in the course of the contest; and, 3. The duty of all ranks in the present crisis. After sunset, the college and town were illuminated and the whole was concluded with the greatest good order. The New Jersey Gazette, July 12, 1780

The echos from celebrations had not died before there was a report of additional skirmishing in New Jersey. Colonel Ty, the runaway slave, led one of the expeditions, a joint Refugee and regular British army venture:

Yesterday morning a party of the enemy, consisting of Ty with 30 blacks, 36 Queen's Rangers and 30 refugee Tories, landed at Conascung. They, by some means, got in between our scouts undiscovered and went up to Mr. James Mott's plundered his and several of his neighbors' houses of almost everything in them and carried off the following persons, viz. Mr. James Mott sen., Jonathan Pearse, James Johnson, Joseph Dorset, William Blair, James Walling, son of Thomas, Philip Walling, James Wall, Matthew Griggs, also several Negroes and a great deal of stock, but all the Negroes, one excepted, and all the horses, horned cattle and sheep were, I believe, retaken by our people. We had wounded Capt. Walling slightly, a Lieutenant Henderson had his arm broke, two privates supposed to be mortally and a third slightly, in a skirmish we had with them on their retreat. The enemy acknowledged the loss of seven men, but we think it much more considerable. New Jersey Journal, July 5, 1780

On Monday evening last, five loyal Refugees under the command of Lieut. Eben. Ward, went from this city in a small boat to the Jersey shore, when they proceeded to the town of Newark and made prisoners Major [Samuel] Hayse, Thomas Canfield (a justice of the peace and a commissioner for the selling the estates of the Loyalists that have taken protection within the British lines) Job Canfield and Zophar Lyon, all atrocious rebels. These four prisoners were brought to town yesterday morning and safely lodged in the sugar house. The Royal Gazette, July 19, 1780

On the 24th, the light camp, which you know is commanded by Major General Marquis de la Fayette, took up its line of march from the place of its encampment in the vicinity of Fort Lee and moved on the road to Bergen. We arrived near the town at 1 o'clock at night where we halted and fixed our picquets and patrols. Col. Steuart with his regiment took post within about a musket of Paulus Hook, the place where our friend Lee so very deservedly gained such reputation.

In the morning, the light camp took a position on the high ground between Bergen town and Paulus Hook. The city, the shipping, Long Island and the harbor lay exposed to our view. The troops in New York, of course, had an opportunity of seeing us and I make no doubt felt themselves injured by our near approach.

All this day the infantry were employed in foraging as low as the Kills. The enemy fired a number of shot upon those of Bergen Neck from Staten Island but they were too ineffectual either to disturb the wagoners who were loading with grain or to drive off any of the foragers. I cannot say the amount of cattle and dry forage collected, but certificates were given to the people that they might have as little room as possible for complaint. These will procure them at some future date compensation; they should consider that they have contributed heretofore very little to support of this war and that what was taken for the use of the army and to prevent it from becoming a source of subsistence to the enemy does not amount to the value of their taxes. In this light we have only assisted them to liquidate a tax cheerfully paid by their fellow citizens and which they could not have paid in any other manner, owing to the particular situation.
But a business of this kind is seldom unattended with more or less of injury to the household property of the inhabitants. The soldiers will find occasion to pilfer, however, watched by the officers. It is impossible to exclude every practice of this nature. All the officer can do in this case is to punish the offender when discovered and restore the goods. This was done in every instance and one of the soldiers hung on the spot. The New Jersey Gazette, September 6, 1780

The British appeared ready to launch, from the north shore of Long Island, an assault on the French in Rhode Island. Washington countered by putting his troops into a position to be able to swoop down into New York City, once the British had departed for Rhode Island. As a result of Washington's strategy, the uneasy British abandoned their plans:

This morning at three o'clock, the whole army, except the Jersey Brigade, marched from this place, as we imagine, for King's Ferry and how much further is very much uncertain. It appears from accounts from New York that Sir H. Clinton, with all the troops he could muster, are embarked upon transports and gone up the East River; it is also said by good authority that Admirals Arbuthnot and Graves, with all their ships and little boats, are now lying before Rhode Island. You will readily conjecture from these circumstances that our good friends and allies will soon have an opportunity of discovering to every political infidel or Tory their attachment and zeal for this country and their high sense of honor of their Prince. The New Jersey Gazette, August 2, 1780

We are told there are few or none of the Continental army from Newark to Amboy or in the vicinity of East New Jersey. They have been called away by General Washington, who we hear has crossed Hudson's River at King's Ferry and in now in the neighborhood of the White Plains and about 30 miles from this city. The New York Gazette, August 7, 1780

We hear that two brigades of light infantry of the continental Army, consisting of near 2000 men, are at the White Plains, under the command of Marquis de Lafayette. New Jersey Journal, August 2, 1780

Certain intelligence having been received that Sir Henry Clinton had embarked the principal part of his force and had proceeded to Huntington bay, on his way to Rhode Island, to make a combined attack upon the fleet and armies of our allies there, His Excellency George Washington marched from his camp at Prackness the 29th of July, and crossed the North River on the 31st, where a junction was formed with the troops under the command of Major General [Robert] Howe. His Excellency had resolved, in case the enemy should continue their course to Rhode Island, to march immediately to New York and to attack it. All the necessary preparations were made for this purpose, when intelligence had arrived that the enemy had put back the 31st instant. It is regretted that they did not go with their intended expedition, as our allies were well prepared to receive them and they could have met with nothing except disgrace and defeat in that quarter, while, in this [attack on New York] we had every reason to expect, from the spirit and number of our troops, the most decisive and glorious success. Sir Henry, no doubt, relinquished this project in consequence of this movement of our army and, it must be confessed, he abandoned it with much more prudence than he undertook it. The object for which the army crossed the river having ceased, the whole re crossed the 4th instant and are marching towards Dobbs Ferry, in prosecution of the original plan formed for the campaign. The New Jersey Journal, August 9, 1780

George Washington, the General, had to share the credit for this stratagem with George Washington, the Spymaster. A little known fact about Washington was that he was personally involved in the espionage side of the War. One of his key aides in this endeavor was Major Benjamin Tallmadge of the Second Continental Dragoons, which were squads of horsemen scattered along the perimeters of British controlled territory. Under the pretense of checking his outposts, Tallmadge would move from place to place, meeting with agents from the half dozen spy networks he had set up, on Washington's instructions, in New York City. One network came to be known as the Culper Network. It was comprised of Samuel Woodhull in Setauket, on the north shore of Long Island, a Robert Townsend of New York City, co-owner of the British Coffee House where confidential information was obtained from indiscreet British officers and even, perhaps, a Mata Hari type female agent, about whom little is known. It was they who discovered British plans of the invasion of Rhode Island. They passed the information along in invisible ink on the bottom of trading documents from Townsend to Woodhull. Woodhull then arranged the laundry on the clothesline in such a manner as to trigger a night time visit from an American agent in Connecticut, who rowed across the Long Island Sound, picked up the message, rowed back again to the Connecticut shore, and delivered it to one of Tallmadge's horseman. From there, the information regarding the planned invasion of Newport went directly to General Washington. He reacted with a campaign of disinformation He arranged for some of his double agents "to intercept" some secret American documents that revealed that Washington was himself planning an attack against New York and that he had twice the number of soldiers that the British thought he had. When Clinton read these, he re-thought the attack on Rhode Island, which had not been his idea any way.

The British attack on Rhode Island thwarted. The principal American army maintained its defensive posture, its attention focused on the Hudson and the key fort of West Point. News was received from the south of a second American defeat at the hands of the British. It was at Camden, South Carolina, on August 16, 1780. There the American troops, a mixture of Continental soldiers and state militia, under the command of Horatio Gates, the hero of the Battle of Saratoga, was defeated by General Cornwallis:

By intelligence from the southward, we learn that our army in South Carolina, under the command of General Gates, has lately been repulsed by the loss of upwards of one thousand men killed and taken prisoners and that General Gates, with difficulty, escaped sharing the fate of the latter; that Baron DeKalb, who commanded the Maryland Line of the Continental troops, was wounded and taken; that the two armies met one another at night, both endeavoring to gain a certain piece of ground; that to the pusillanimous behavior of the militia, the disaster may be attributed. The New Jersey Journal, September 6, 1780

Then, suddenly, came the loudest explosion heard yet in the Revolution, created not by pyrotechnics, but by the treachery of one man, Benedict Arnold. Arnold, a hero at the attempt at taking Quebec and at the important American victory of Saratoga which encouraged the French to join the fight against Britain, was the commander of West Point, having been formerly military Governor of the City of Philadelphia. West Point, a post for which Arnold had solicited Washington, was a key one to the American defense. The fort commanded the Hudson River and many thought that controlling the Hudson River was Britain's best way of winning the war. If Britain could rule the Hudson as it claimed to rule the seas, then the northern colonies could be cut off from the others and Britain, having divided its enemy, could then conquer it.

By chance, it was discovered that Arnold had agreed to surrender the fort to the British. His plan was to send as many of the garrison as possible into the country side, thus reducing the number of defenders. Good Fortune smiled on Arnold. General Washington, on his way back to his main army in New Jersey from Hartford, Connecticut, where he had been meeting with the French, was going to stay at West Point the very night appointed for the surrender. Had both West Point and General Washington fallen into British hands, then it is more than likely that the war would have ended in favor of the English, not the Americans:

Fishkill, September 28. On Monday last his Excellency General Washington passed through this town on his way from Hartford, and his arrival at West Point was announced by the discharge of thirteen cannon about eleven o'clock the same day.

About the time of his Excellency's arrival at the fort, a most horrid plot was discovered, the infamous General Arnold at the head of it, who, it is supposed, has been corrupted by the influence of British gold, having agreed to deliver up the fort at West Point, for which purpose he drew up a plan of all the works at West Point and gave it to a spy, Major John Andre, Adjutant General of the British Army and First Aid to Sir Henry Clinton. Arnold on Thursday last, early in the day came to Mr. Joshua Smith's (brother of the honorable William Smith) at Haverstraw. Smith, who is now in custody says that Arnold told him that there was a person on board the Vulture, a British frigate then in the river, whom he greatly wanted to see; he mentioned Colonel B. Robinson who he said was coming under pretense of serving the British, to make interest to obtain his estate and return. Arnold proposed to Smith to go on board the Vulture. Smith accordingly, at night, went on board, where he saw Colonel Robinson and Major Andre. Col. Robinson refused to come ashore but Major Andre did. They found Arnold waiting for them on the shore and they had a long private conference, after which Arnold went to Smith's house with Andre and Smith secured the barge. Next day, Arnold requested Smith to supply Andre with a suit of clothes, lest he should be suspected as his were British regimentals, which he did. They were prevented from going on board the frigate the next day as our gun boats being in the river, on which they agreed to go by land and Arnold supplied Andre and Smith with passes to conduct below our lines. Having provided horses they set off on Saturday morning and Smith conducted him past our guards and, as he thought, out of danger and then left him[125]*; but a* party of our militia soon after met and secured him and notwithstanding his large offers of cash and goods, to let him pass, which they nobly disdained, [and] brought him to Head-Quarters and on Tuesday last he was removed to West Point in order to have his trial with Joshua Smith, his conductor, who was secured on Monday night.

Arnold, hearing of General Washington's approach, seemed greatly confused, called for his horse and rode immediately to the landing where he ordered the barge to set off with him, who carried him to the Vulture, where he now remains. 'Tis said he sent a letter to George Washington to assure him that neither his wife nor his aid were in on this nefarious conduct.

This hasty narrative contains all the particulars we have heard of this tragical affair. We expect in our next to give our readers a more correct account of it. *The New Jersey Gazette, October 4, 1780*

As the public curiosity and anxiety must naturally be raised by the providential detection of the perfidity and treachery of a late distinguished general officer of the United States, we shall endeavor to give our readers such particulars as have come to our attention and are well authenticated.
On Monday last, Congress received a letter from General Greene, inclosing one from Col. Hamilton, one of General Washington's aides, informing him that a scene of the blackest villainy has just been disclosed: that Arnold has gone off to the enemy; Col. Andre, General Clinton's principal aide and confidant, was apprehended in disguise in our camp; that West Point, where Arnold commanded, was to be the sacrifice and that all the dispositions were made for delivering it up last Monday night; that he had pursued Arnold as far as Verplank's point, from which the letter was dated, but without success; that tho' it was not now probable that the post would fall, yet it was possible and especially as the wind were fair; therefore, he recommended to General Greene (who commands the army in General Washington's absence) to put it under marching order and detach a brigade immediately.

As soon as these letters were read, the contents were delivered to the Vice President and Council, of this State who directed an immediate seizure of all Arnold's papers, which was made, and, although no direct proof of his treachery found, the papers disclose such a scene of baseness and prostitution of office and character as it is hoped this new world cannot parallel. His participation in the plunder of this city after the evacuation of the enemy, is now found by the agreement, signed between himself and his accomplices to share the profits of this shameful business. It appears that he and some others whose names will probably in time be made known, now have subsisting contracts with persons in New York for merchandise.

In making an estimate of his estate, he estimates the value of the sloop Active, tho' he found witnesses to swear in front of the grand jury that he had no share in her. In short, his whole command appears to have been a scene of the basest traffic and public plunder. In August last he directs his wife to draw all she can from the commissaries and to sell it or store it, although at the that very time the army was destitute of provisions. In the private correspondence between his family and himself are contained the most sarcastic and contemptuous expressions of the French nation and of an eminent personage of that country, whose hospitality and politeness they are at that time experiencing. The illiberal abuse of every character opposed to his wicked and fraudulent transactions exceeds all description. The New Jersey Gazette, October 4, 1780

(Extract of a letter from Camp Tappan, September 26)
Lost to every sentiment of honor and disgraced by the inordinate thirst for gold, General Arnold has gone over to the enemy. He was to have surrendered the important post of West Point and entrapped the Commander in Chief, who lodged at the post on the intended night of execution. The plot was providentially discovered and the whole mystery unraveled. Major Andre... was taken by three militia men and delivered to Col Sheldon's regiment of horse.[126] In the bottom of one of his boots were discovered letters and plans which unfolded the hellish scheme. It soon took wind and was reported to General Arnold and just before his Excellency [General Washington]

arrived at the place, [Arnold] made his escape to the Vulture sloop of war. Tom Smith's brother was an accomplice and has gone off likewise. Mrs. Arnold is at West Point, or Robinson's house, in a very distressed situation and Major Parkes is with her. The enemy's whole force, except a garrison, had embarked yesterday and the plan was to have been executed last night. The New Jersey Gazette, October 4, 1780

The year 1780 ended with some encouraging news from the southern front. At the Battle of King's Mountain in North Carolina, the Americans killed or captured an entire Loyalist Regiment of over a thousand men. Locally, there were only the continual skirmishing and kidnaping expeditions:

On Saturday night last Smith Hetfield, Cornelius Hetfield, Cornelius Blanchard and some others came over from Staten Island to Elizabeth Town, where they were informed that Col. Ogden of the first Jersey regiment and Capt. Dayton of the third, were to lodge that night at William Herd's, at Connecticut Farms, to which place they hastened, made them both prisoners and carried them off unmolested to Staten Island. New Jersey Journal, November 8, 1780

Yesterday morning about daybreak about a hundred of the enemy under the command of Captain Ward, entered the Town of Newark, on a picarooning expedition. They collected a number of hogs, cattle and sheep but out people having collected pursued them so close that they retook 89 head of the cattle and most of the hogs and sheep; also ten prisoners. The enemy burnt a house belonging to Mr. Robert Niel. The New Jersey Journal, November 22, 1780

We are informed that the enemy are in force upon Staten Island and, from the number of boats they are collecting opposite Elizabeth Town, it is apprehended that they intend to make a descent into this state. In consequence of which the militia of several of the counties are ordered to hold themselves in readiness and such other orders given as will, we flatter ourselves, frustrate their nefarious plans. The New Jersey Gazette, November 29, 1780

The year ended with Washington again electing New Jersey as his winter headquarters, at New Windsor, near Princeton:

About a fortnight since the grand American army went into winter quarters on the North River and in the eastern parts of this state. Head Quarters is established at New Windsor. The New Jersey Gazette, December 20, 1780.

CHAPTER 13

The War at Sea

Fortunately for us, the American Revolution was fought predominately on land and not at sea. Had it been otherwise, America's hopes would have been quickly snuffed out. England's Royal Navy dominated the seas. Hers was the greatest naval force known to history, her sailors proven masters of the ocean. The newborn America had nothing in comparison.

Ironically, the strategic value of Britain's naval power -- especially her fast frigates and formidable ships of the line, the battleships of her day -- was diminished, especially at the onset of hostilities, by America's not having any vessels with which Britain could do battle and crush. Instead, her fleet's use was limited to broadsiding land positions and blockading the coast, neither one of which contributed very heavily to the war effort. The battles were inland, far beyond the range of the mighty cannon. Stores could be landed at too many rivers, bays, and inlets along the long American coastline to be effectively policed. Nor, even later in the war, could the British employ its fleet against an American fleet. The patriots took to the sea in single ships, either privateers or frigates commissioned by Congress. As a result, the naval portion of the Revolution, from the American standpoint, was one of attacks on British shipping and of duels between individual ships.

Particularly at the war's beginning before Congress had commissioned any warships, privateers had to serve as the American navy. Specially fitted and privately owned, these vessels concentrated on capturing enemy commerce. Motivated by profit as well as patriotism, the ships were given licenses by the Government, called letters of marque and reprisal, to attack the British. They were often successful, causing disruption in British supply lines that necessarily had to stretch thousands of miles from England or the Caribbean all the way to New York City.

> *Lately retaken and brought into Great Egg Harbor, by the privateer sloop Cornet, Capt Yelverton Taylor, the Schooner Carolina Packet, Capt. Walter Belt, from St. Ubes, with 1600 bushels of coarse salt. Also the sloop Lucy, Capt. Thomas Grandle from South Carolina, with 112 tierces and 30 half tierces of rice, one tierce and a half ditto indigo.*
> *The Sloop Lark, Capt. John Laing, was lately taken and sent into a safe port. Her cargo consists of 77 hogsheads of rum, one ditto dry goods, 18 kegs of nails, 3 tierces and 1 case joiners and carpenters tools, door locks, hinges &c. The schooner Phoenix, Captain Robert Gilbert, from Bermuda, for New York with 30,000 oranges and lemons and a considerable quantity of onions. And a schooner from Antigua with rum, brandy &c.*
> *Retaken and brought to Little Egg Harbor, by two New England Privateers, in Company with Capt. John Rice, a brig and sloop loaded with tobacco. New Jersey Gazette, August 5, 1778*

Privateers were not the only scourges of British shipping. Local militia, keen to the chance to strike a blow against the enemy, took advantageous of any unprotected trading vessels.

> *On Tuesday last, the schooner Little Hope, with part of her cargo consisting of rum, sugar, coffee, tea and a number of blankets, drifted from Philadelphia with the ice above Point-no-point. The day following, Major Edwards with eight men, boarded her, after having, with much difficulty, worked their way through the ice. Previous to their having boarded her, the captain of the schooner, with five sailors, paraded as if they were going to dispute the matter, but, their hearts failing them, they saved further trouble by a ready surrender.*
> *The same day (several vessels drifting with the ice between Philadelphia and Glouster Point) Capt. Robert Quigley, with twenty four of the militia, boarded and took the transport brigatine John and the armed schooner Industry, with thirteen English seamen, among whom are two captains. The brigatine had several hogsheads of Rum &c. on board and the schooner some tobacco. After taking out the valuable articles and stripping them of their rigging, sails &c., they were burnt.*

Another party of our militia, on the same day, made prize of the transport Lord Howe, which was also stripped and destroyed and, on the day following, a sloop, on her way from Chester to Philadelphia, was taken with about twenty barrels of flour on board. In these little expeditions, thirty four British seamen and soldiers were taken and, on Friday last, they passed through this city [Burlington] on their way to a place of security. New Jersey Gazette, January 7, 1778

We hear that on Thursday sennight the ship Love and Unity, from Bristol, with 80 hogsheads of loaf sugar, several thousand bottles of London porter, a large quantity of Bristol beer and ale, besides many other valuable articles, was designedly run on shore near Tom's River, since which, by the assistance of some of our militia, she has been brought into a safe port and her cargo properly taken care of. New Jersey Gazette, August 12, 1778

Last week a brig bound from the West Indies to New York was brought into Tom's River. She had on board 150 hogs heads of excellent rum and spirit. Her water and provisions, having fallen short on her passage, and mistaking the land for the coast of Long Island, sent her boat ashore with four hands for a supply of those articles. Our militia getting information secured the tars and, manning two boats, went off and brought the vessel in without opposition. The New Jersey Gazette, December 27, 1780

The captured vessels, their rigging and cargoes were prizes of war and sold by Courts of Admiralty:

To be Sold by Public Vendue on Tuesday the 28th instant, at the Forks of Little Egg Harbor, the following vessels and their Cargoes, viz. Brig Industry, burthen about 150 tons, with her tackle &c per inventory and cargo consisting of 1700 bushels of best Turk's Island Salt; the Sloop Speedwell, burthen fifty tons and her cargo consisting of sixty tierces of rice and several hogsheads of tobacco; the Polly's Adventure, a sloop of about thirty tons burthen and her cargo consisting of one hundred and sixty barrels of flour.

The above vessels are completely sound and ready for sea. It is expected that the money will be paid on delivery of vessels or cargo.

Joseph Ball and Nathaniel Nichols
The Pennsylvania Packet, July 21, 1778

By order of the Court of Admiralty of New Jersey will be sold at public vendue, on Tuesday the fifth instant (August) at the Court House in Freehold, in the County of Monmouth, the sale to begin at ten o'clock, the cargo of the prize Brigatine William and Anne, lately taken by a detachment of troops in the Continental service, consisting of fine white sugars, in boxes and casks, sweet oil in barrels, lemons in boxes, ground sumac in sacks, figs in baskets, wine vinegar in casks, corks cut and uncut, almonds in casks, lees of wine for clothiers &c. &c. Also the anchors, cables, sails and running rigging and hull of the said brigatine as she now lies on shore at Long Branch.

The Pennsylvania Evening Post, August 2, 1777

TO BE SOLD BY
PUBLIC VENDUE

At the House of Garrit Schank, in Middletown, county of Monmouth, on Thursday the 27th instant at 10 o'clock in the forenoon, viz. Irish Beef, pork, bread, coffee, sugar, sweet oil, powder, lead, muskets, swords, water casks, and sundry other things too tedious to mention; also the hull of the Brig Britania now laying near Cheesequake Creek in the county aforesaid. And, on Monday, the 31st inst. at 10 o'clock in the forenoon, will be Sold by Public Vendue in Bordentown, in the County of Burlington, the following articles viz. 16 six and 12 four pounders, 4 swivels with all the necessary apparatus, also a quantity of shot of every kind, and all the sails and rigging late belonging to the brig aforesaid.

By order of his honor the Judge of Admiralty
Zachariah Rossell, Marshall.

The Pennsylvania Journal, January 26, 1780

To all whom it may concern.
NOTICE *is hereby given that at a Court of Admiralty, will be held at the Court house in Burlington, on Wednesday the 22nd day of May next, at 10 o'clock in the forenoon of that day, there and then to try the proof of the facts alleged in the bill of Adam Hyler, commander of the privateer armed boat Revenge against certain Negro men to wit: John Holland, Charles Jackson, Harry Jackson, John Brown, Plato Williams, Samuel Creighton, Francis Chambers, John Richards, John White, Peter Peters and Frank Oatman and sundry goods wares and merchandises taken at sea from aboard the British Cutter Alert, commanded by Robert White on her voyage from New York to Bermuda, brought into this state, and libeled by the said Adam Hyler, to the end that the owner or owners of said Negroes or merchandise or any other person or persons interested therein may appear and show cause, if any they have, why the same should not be condemned to the captors and a decree of the court thereon pass, agreeably to the prayer of the bill aforesaid*
    By the Order of
    Joseph Bloomfield
    New Jersey Gazette, May 8, 1782

A portion of the monies received from the sales of the cargoes were split among the crew:

Notice is hereby given to all Seamen and Landsmen that were on board the armed sloop Chance, when she captured the ship Venus and made a prize of her, that they meet the subscriber at Richard Westcott's at the Forks of Little Egg Harbor then and there to receive their respective dividends of the prize money, and like wise, all those who purchased shares from such sailors are requested to meet at the same place, on Thursday, the second day of April next.
    DAVID STEVENS ,Capt.
  The Pennsylvania Packet, March 27, 1779

Despite having few ships and none of size, the American rag tag naval force, aided by the privateers and then the French fleet had some successes:

The following is a list of ships lost by his Britannic Majesty, since the war with America:

No. of Guns
24   The Mercury on the Chevaux-de frise in the North River.
64   Augusta, In Delaware River
32   A Frigate.   "
28   Liverpool, on Long Island
32   Juno, burnt and sunk in Rhode-Island
28   Cerberus   "
32   Orpheus   "
32   Lark   "
20   Rose   "
32   Grand Duke   "
14   King Fisher   "
16   Swan and a galley 20   Drake, taken by Capt. Jones, in the Ranger
32   Syren, cast away on Point Judith
44   Actaeon, at Carolina
28   A Frigate   "
20   Merlin, drove ashore by Count d'Estaing
32   Minerva, and Tenders carried into Cape Francois
32   Active,   "
18   Thunder Bomb, Taken by Count d'Estaing
16   Senegal   "
28   For, taken and carried into Brest
22   Lively   "
14   Alert   "
64   Somerset, cast away at Cape-Cod, Captain and crew taken.

A Galley cast away near Egg-Harbor.
Hotham tender cast away at Cape Henlopen.

A guard ship, mounting eight 12 pounders, and one 32 pounder, taken in second passage, and carried into Grotan, by Major Talbot, in a small sloop of two guns. New Jersey Gazette, January 13, 1779

The details of some of these naval engagements have been preserved in newspaper reports that were based on first hand reports. For example, the American schooner *Hunter,* Captain Douglass of ten guns, from Egg Harbor, fell in with the Brig *Bellona,* Capt. Buchanan, of sixteen guns, belonging to New York. The engagement lasted almost two hours.

(extract of letter from Captain Douglass of the Schooner Hunter, to his owners, dated Egg Harbor, February 9.)
"Being at sea, about ten leagues from Egg Harbor, we saw a sail to the southeast and gave chase, wind at southwest. Finding her to be a brig of force, we immediately got clear for action. She then took in her topgallant sails, hauled down her flying jib and hoisted an English ensign instead of a Continental one that was flying before. We gave three cheers and poured in a broadside, being on her lee quarters. The Captain of the brig called out to board us. I immediately ordered the pikes to be got ready and luffed to for boarding. He luffed too likewise but found out he was not for boarding. We lay alongside him for two glasses and heard the men screech and cry several times and the Captain stamp and swear at the men for leaving the rammers in the guns. At length, they found that we had warmed them so that they lacked their main topsail and we shot ahead, the sea running so high that we could not sight our lee guns and, springing our mainmast, prevented our making sail, when they departed. She was called the Bellona, Capt. Buchanan, of sixteen six and four pounders and 12 swivels. We lost our second lieutenant and one private killed, two men mortally wounded, and the second mate and three men wounded, but like to do well. The schooner Hunter has only 8 four and three two pounders, 12 howitz and 60 men. We cannot give too much applause to the officers and men in general and in particular to Rufus Gardiner, our second lieutenant. The Pennsylvania Gazette, February 17, 1779

John Paul Jones, the Scottish born captain enjoyed the greatest fame among the American naval heros. In September 1779, while commanding the *Bon Homme Richard*, Jones defeated the British *Serapis* far out at sea. It was here that Jones refused an offer of surrender by the immortal words "I have not yet begun to fight". There were a number of dramatic engagements, however, nearer the shore, in the waters of New Jersey. One of them put on the American stage the man later to be known as the Father of the American navy, John Barry. Born in Ireland and an immigrant to America in the early 1770s, he was commissioned a captain in the Continental Navy in 1776. Given the command of the brigantine *Lexington*, Barry captured the British tender *Edward*--the first British ship to be taken at sea by the Americans.

In 1778, Barry commanded a flotilla of small vessels on the Delaware and tried to prevent the British at Philadelphia.

*We learn that on the 12th instant, a fleet of transports, under convoy of several vessels of war, arrived at Philadelphia from Rhode Island. On their passage up the Delaware, two of the transports viz. the Katy and Mermaid, with forage, one of which was mounting six four pounders, being at some distance ahead, were attacked by eight of our armed boats under the command of Captain Barry, who, after a smart but short engagement, obliged both of the boats to strike. Soon after the armed schooner Alert, mounting eight four pounders and ten howitz, came up, another action commenced and the Alert, notwithstanding that she bravely defended herself, was also obliged to submit. The other armed vessels, which were convoying the remaining part of the fleet, observing at a distance the fates of the ships and schooner, made haste to their assistance, but our people, having taken out the passengers and stripped the ships, set fire to them, by which they were destroyed. Captain Barry intended to have run the schooner into Christiana Creek [Delaware] but finding himself too closely pursued by the enemy, he put her ashore near Hamburg, a little below Newcastle, where he got out most of her valuable articles.
New Jersey Gazette, March 18, 1778*

Barry's subsequent commands were the *Effingham*, the *Raleigh*, and the *Alliance*; in the last, he captured two British ships in 1781 and fought, on March 10, 1783 the final naval engagement of the war, against the British *Sybil*.

There were a number of American heroes who operated in the waters of New Jersey. One was John Symmes, an Associate Justice of the Supreme Court of New Jersey and a member of the Provincial Congress, who participated in the war for liberty as a colonel in the New Jersey militia:

By a gentleman from the eastward, we are informed, that the week before last, Colonel Symmes[127] of New Jersey, with four men in a whale boat, crossed over from Guilford to Long Island. When understanding a number of vessels were cast a way on the Island, they formed a design to seize some of the goods belonging to one of them. Accordingly, the five, with fixed bayonets in the dark of night, surprised the house where the freight of one of the vessels was stored, made the master, mate, three sailors and two tories prisoners and loaded their whale boat with part of the vessel's cargo. They took 9 gold and 9 silver bound hats, 60 pair of English shoes, a chest of medicine, a box of glass and earthen ware, 24 steel plate cross cut saws, a barrel of coffee, another of rum, 1 doz. silk handerchiefs, 1 doz. buckskin gloves and many other valuable articles and returned safe to Guilford with their prize. New Jersey Gazette, March 25, 1778

Another was New Jersey waterman who harassed the enemy was William Marriner, a resident of New Brunswick who sailed from Middletown Point, now Matawan, and raided the Long Island shore.

William Marriner, a volunteer, with eleven men, and Lieut. Schanck, of our militia, went last Saturday evening from Middletown Point to Long Island in order to take a few prisoners from Flatbush and returned with Major Montcrieffe and Mr. Theeophilus Bache (the worshipful Mayor and Tormentor General, David Matthews, Esq., who has inflicted on our prisoners the most unheard of cruelties, and who was the principal object of the expedition, being unfortunately in the City) with four slaves and brought them to Princeton to be delivered to his Excellency the Governor. Mr. Marriner and his party left Middletown Point on Saturday evening and returned at six o' clock the next morning, having traveled by land and water above fifty miles and behaved with the greatest bravery and prudence. New Jersey Gazette, June 17, 1778

On Tuesday, third instant, Captain Marriner of Brunswick, with seven men belonging to Lord Stirling's division, landed from the Jersey shore at New Utrecht, on Long Island and brought off Simon and Jacques Cortelyou, two famous tories in the enemy's lines and in specie and other property to the amount of 5000 dollars. The two prisoners are on parole in New Brunswick and to be exchanged for two citizens of this state in captivity with the enemy. New Jersey Gazette, November 11, 1778

A third American, Adam Hyler, also pestered the British to distraction. Like Marriner, Hyler was from New Brunswick and used Great Egg Harbor as his lair until the British closed it down. That did not stop Hyler, however, who merely moved his site of operations elsewhere. He was quite successful as evident from the following handful of accounts of his different missions against the enemy, both in New York and in New Jersey:

On the 5th instant Captain Adam Hyler went from New Brunswick in an armed boat to Long Island, marched three miles and a half into the country, and made Captain Jeromus Lot, a Lieutenant Colonel of the militia, and one John Hankins, a Captain of a vessel, prisoners and brought them safe to New Brunswick. New Jersey Gazette, August 15, 1781

"On Friday night last Capt. Adam Hyler, from New-Brunswick, with one gun boat and two whale boats, within a quarter of a mile of the guard ship at Sandy-Hook, attacked five vessels, and after a smart conflict of fifteen minutes, carried them away; two of them were armed, one mounting four six pounders, and one six swivels, and one three pounder. The hands made their escape with their long boats, and took refuge in a small fort, in which was mounted twelve swivel guns, from which they kept up a constant firing, notwithstanding which he boarded them all without a loss of a man. On board of one of

these was 250 bushels of wheat and quantity of cheese belonging to Capt. Lippincott, bound to New-York; he took from them 50 bushels of wheat, a quantity of cheese, several swivels, a number of guzes, one cask of powder, and some dry goods, and stripped them of their sails and rigging, not being able to bring the vessels into port, in consequence of a contrary wind and tide; after which, he set all on fire save one, on board of which was a woman and four small children, which prevented her from sharing a similar fate." New Jersey Gazette, October 10, 1781

On Monday last, Capt. Hyler, of New-Brunswick, with a gunboat, and a small party of men, went to the Narrows, where he captured a ship with 14 or 15 hands, and brought her off, with an intent to run her up Raritan River, but near the mouth she unluckily go aground, where as the enemy approached in force, he was obliged to set her on fire. She was loaded with rum and pork, several hogheads of the former he got out and brought off with the prisoners. New Jersey Gazette, November 14, 1781

We are informed that on Friday night last, Capt. Hyler with a one gun boat and a barge went on an expedition to the Narrows, were he surprised and captured a British cutter, mounting six 18 and ten 9 pounders; but the wind being unfavorable for bringing her off, and having landed her crew, about 50 in number, and taking out such articles as he thought proper, set her on fire. He also took a sloop at the same time, which he ransomed for 400 Dollars. The prisoners are properly secured. New Jersey Gazette, April 24, 1782

The evening of the 25th instant, Captain Hyler, with his armed boats, being in Shrewsbury River, a party of British troops, consisting of 25 men under the command of Captain Schaak, of the 57th regiment, were dispatched to intercept him in passing through the gut. As soon as Captain Hyler discovered them, he landed 13 of his men with orders to charge, in doing which 4 of the enemy were killed and wounded and the Captain and 8 others were prisoners; and, by the firing of the gunboats, it is supposed, several others were killed, as a number *were seen to fall. Captain Hyler, previous to this recounte , accidentally met with a hurt, otherwise it is probable he would not have let a man escape. The New Jersey Gazette, June 5, 1782*

On the 24th instant, Captain Hyler of this place went down in one gun boat to surprise the refugee town near Sandy Hook, where the horse thieves report. He landed with three-quarter mile of the lighthouse but found that they were out in the county of Monmouth, stealing horses. The Captain, however, fell in with six other noted villains, whom he brought off and they are now lodged in a safe place. New Jersey Gazette, November 7, 1781

When the France joined the war, her formidable fleet became a factor in it. It fought the British fleet in the Caribbean and elsewhere. For example:

Letters from New-Jersey say, that on Wednesday and Thursday last, 25 sail of ships of war out of 30 which sailed some time ago, returned to the Hook, and by prisoners which were landed at Monmouth, the letter-writer says, they were informed that the British had an action with the French, in which the London, of 98 guns, had received considerable damage, and the Intrepid, of 74 guns, had been so well handled, that she sunk on the passage, and with difficulty the people and a few stores were saved by the rest of the fleet. New Jersey Gazette, September 26, 1781

The French fleet also patrolled the New England waters and blockaded New York harbor, causing the British army headquartered there (and the Loyalists huddled next to them for protection), no small amount of deprivation. The fleet's greatest aids to the cause of liberty would come in 1781, in the Chesapeake when it sent the English back to New York and then weeks later off the Virginia coast, when it prohibited any rescue attempt of the British army, trapped at Yorktown.

Chapter 14

The War: 1781

The year 1781 started off badly for General Washington, with two mutinies, albeit reluctant ones, by some of his soldiers wintering in New Jersey. Pay seemed to have been at the heart of the problem, with recent enlistees earning more than those who had signed up earlier and, consequently, had been at the business of war longer, seen more action and suffered greater hardships. However, the mutinying soldiers shortly agreed to return to camp and a general pardon was given them for their insubordination. There was little violence and, when it was all over, the mutineers were praised for their restraint and their obvious loyalty. For example, when approached by messengers from the British to cross over to their side, the mutineers captured the envoys and turned them over to the American authorities

The public may depend upon the authenticity of the following brief account of the disorders that have lately taken place among the soldiers of the Pennsylvania line and which are now happily settled.
A discontent arose among them on the first of this month about the periods of their enlistments which many of them contend have expired. Some invidious comparisons were also made between the large bounty given to enlist those who were engaged during the war. Endeavors were used by the officers to quiet them, but without success. One officer was unfortunately killed and a great part of the soldiers marched off from their encampment toward the Delaware. They were under the conduct of their sergeants but General Wayne and some other officers were determined to follow and keep with all the events, though the General could not prevail upon them to stop till they came to Princeton. They marched through the country with great regularity and good conduct, perhaps with less damage than is

common on the passing of troops. While they continued at Princeton, a sergeant with the British army with one Ogden, an inhabitant of this state as a guide, came to them and made proposals from General Clinton. These they rejected with so much honor and indignation that they seized the messengers and delivered them to General Wayne, who put them under guard. Soon after this, a Committee of the Council of Pennsylvania came to meet the soldiery and a Committee of Congress came to Trenton. Their grievances were redressed, particularly by giving an interpretation favorable to the soldier of the enlistments which were for three years or during the war, declaring them to expire at the end of three years. They marched from Princeton to Trenton on Tuesday the 9th. On Wednesday the 10th, the two spies were tried and executed the next day at the cross roads near the upper ferry. Commissioners were appointed to hear and settle the claims of the soldier who are now going through them with all possible dispatch and, on Monday, the Committee of Congress returned to Philadelphia.

Upon the whole, this affair, which, at first, appeared so alarming, has only served to give a new proof of the inflexible honor of the soldiery and their inviolable attachment to American Liberty and will teach General Clinton that, although he can bribe a mean toad eater like Arnold, it is not in his power to bribe an American soldier. *New Jersey Gazette, January 17, 1781*

On Saturday evening, the 20th instant, about 150 privates of the New Jersey brigade, who were quartered at Pompton, left their tents and, under the conduct of some of their sergeants, marched toward Chatham. The proceedings of the Legislature, at their last sitting, at which commissioners were appointed to inquire into the claims of the soldiers of the brigade, who conceived themselves entitled to a discharge on account of the expiration of their enlistments, had not them been communicated to these troops. The Commissioners went to Chatham on Monday and, having read and explained to them the resolutions of the Legislature, they immediately agreed to return to their duty. The Commandant of the brigade, in consideration of their being unacquainted with the measures *taken on their behalf and of their acknowledgments of the offense, granted their request for a general pardon. The commissioners, having appointed a time for settling their claims, they returned to their officers. A small part only of the brigade was involved in this matter, the greater part disapproved of it and all regret that it happened. To the honor, however, of those brave men we mention it with pleasure, that, when they left their quarters, they adopted a solemn resolution to put to death anyone who should attempt or even propose to go to the enemy's lines and hang up without ceremony every tory who should presume to say a word tending to induce any of them to do so. New Jersey Gazette, January 31, 1781*

Some of the returning mutineers, however, encouraged by the effect they had had on the Command, immediately resumed their mutinous talk and began challenging anew some of the conditions to which they had agreed in exchange for their pardons. At this point, there could be no second chances. Punishment had to be inflicted upon the recalcitrant, which had the desired effect upon the other troops.

But after the arrival at the huts, a few of the ringleaders encouraged by emissaries from Sir Harry, and perhaps by the too great clemency of granting them a full pardon , again became insolent and mutinous. A detachment from the main army under the command of General Howe, which had been sent on to quell the mutineers, arrived about this time, when those who had forfeited the pardon, by not performing the conditions, were apprehended by order of the General and David Gilmore, sergeant in the 2d. regiment and John Tuttle, private in the 1st, were tried, found guilty and immediately executed. Every mark of penitence and respect for order was manifested by the others who had offended and entire order and subordination took place in the brigade. New Jersey Gazette, February 7, 1781

Washington could be cheered, however, with the good news coming from the South. The British expedition under Lord Cornwallis to subdue the Southern states was faltering, after initial successes at Augusta, Savannah, Charleston and Camden.

Bands of rebel guerrilla fighters had made British pacification of the back country, all but impossible. Nor was the countryside proving to be of loyalist sentiments, as had been predicted. To the contrary, the militia, disappointing the summer before at Camden, South Carolina, now had been revitalized. The previous fall, rebel frontiersmen, mainly from settlements in eastern Tennessee, had wiped out a thousand Loyalist troops at King's Mountain on the border of the Carolinas. It had been Britain's first reversal on its two year march north, from Georgia to hopefully northern Virginia.

While the American guerrillas harassed Cornwallis, a new American army in the South was being formed under General Nathaniel Green. The American plan was to keep Cornwallis and his larger army off balance, and eventually run it ragged, by a series of rapid troop movements through unfamiliar terrain, its flanks constantly assaulted by the guerrillas, led by rebels such as the legendary Swamp Fox, Francis Marion and Thomas Sumter of South Carolina. The British began 1781 with a stinging defeat at Cowpens of one of its prize units, Col. Banastre Tarleton's mounted legion of British regulars and Loyalist veterans. Cornwallis reacted by madly chasing the Americans through the mountains of North Carolina, as the Americans had hoped he would. Sir Henry Clinton, aware that Cornwallis was acting like a stupid dog chasing its own tail, tried to order him to stop. It was not Cornwallis' first blunder in the war. It had been Cornwallis who had chased Washington ever so slowly across the Jersey countryside at the end of 1776, allowing the American general to escape across the Delaware for a badly needed winter's regrouping. And it had been Cornwallis who had recommended to Lord Howe that the British troops spread themselves over the Jersey countryside that same winter, giving Washington the chance to sneak back across the Delaware on Christmas night and capture the British post at Trenton. And it had been Cornwallis, who, roused from his New York winter quarters by the Washington surprise attack on Trenton, was fooled by the American general's campfire ruse, which ended up costing the British their troop garrison at Princeton. Cornwallis ignored Clinton, determined to do things he felt best. He was protected. He had more important friends at the Royal Court than did Clinton[128].

Although most of the fighting in 1781 was in the South, Washington kept his main army in New Jersey and Clinton still had a sizeable force in New York City. As in the prior years of the war, the close proximity of two enemies and the richness of the Jersey bread basket that lay between them necessarily resulted in a number of raids by each side against the other. For example, the British seemed keen on sneaking into New Jersey, capturing rebels, soldiers and local authorities, and dragging them to Staten Island for ransom or exchange:

Last week Ensign Fitz-Randolph, with ten or twelve privates of our militia, was surprised in Amboy by a party of the enemy and carried to Staten Island. New Jersey Gazette, January 17, 1781

On Monday last about fifty of the enemy made their appearance in Bound Creek upon which the militia in the neighborhood assembled and obliged them to retire. New Jersey Gazette, March 14, 1781

Thursday last, a party of the enemy from New York attempted to carry off the Honorable Josiah Hornblower, Esq., Speaker of the Assembly of this state. They were in the habit of peasants and impersonated Jersey militia. In this manner, they came to the ferry nearly opposite his house in Essex County and called for the boat, which was carried over to them, the people not suspecting their villainy. The ferryman on their arrival observed "G. R."[129] *on their cartouch boxes and therefore on his return with some address, let the boat fall down stream with the tide, in order to give a hint to Mr. Hornblower's family that all was not right. This had the desired effect; Mr. Hornblower escaped out the back door prior to their coming in the front. Two of the villains pursued him and were taken; the others got off, after making Mr. Hornblower's son in law, Mr. Cape, a prisoner, who has since returned on parole.* New Jersey Gazette, April 4, 1781

On Tuesday night, the 27th, about 200 regulars and refugees from Staten Island, under the command of Major Beckwith, who had eluded by circuitous routes, the vigilance of the different paroles, entered Elizabeth Town in four divisions, where they captured ten of the inhabitants, one lieutenant of the state troop and two Continental soldiers. They stayed about an hour and a half in town and then retreated, with the loss of one man killed and another taken prisoner. They plundered the house of Mr. Joseph Crane to a very considerable amount. New Jersey Gazette, April 4, 1781

On the 21st ult a party of about 70 of the enemy came over to Elizabeth Point from Staten Island. They landed at Halstead's Point and were discovered between that place by O. Hendricks, who was patrolling with about ten of his men, and, though so much inferior in number, he kept up a smart fire on them, which prevented them from penetrating deeper in town than Doctor Winan's. After collecting a few horses and firing through the window of the room where Mrs. Winans was sitting, by which a boy was wounded in the arm, and burning the house of Mr. Ephraim Marsh, they went off to their boats. In this excursion one of the freebooters viz, Elias Mann, late an inhabitant of Elizabeth Town killed and the noted Smith Hetfield wounded in two places.

And on Friday night last, another party of plunderers were over at Elizabeth Town and carried off about 40 head of cattle. New Jersey Gazette, May 9, 1781

The Americans, in turn, made forays into British occupied soil

On Monday night, the 26th ult., a detachment of eight men, from the state troops in Elizabeth Town, went over to Staten Island and brought off a Lieutenant and one private of the militia. They took two more, but with the wind blowing fresh, and their boat small, incapacitated them so much that they could not bring them over. New Jersey Gazette, April 4, 1781

Last Monday night, Capt. Baker Hendricks went from Elizabeth Town to Staten Island and brought off one Lieutenant and a private of the Refugees and one inhabitant. Previous to the above, a party went over and brought off a Captain. New Jersey Gazette, April 25, 1781

Clashes like this notwithstanding, there was considerable uneasiness in New Jersey with Britain's relative lack of aggression. The main body of British troops were camped on Staten Island, doing nothing. Everyone was waiting and getting ready for the British attack – somewhere. Many thought it would come in New Jersey:

General Dickinson desires the Militia of this state will hold themselves in the most perfect readiness to march on the shortest notice, it being probable their services may now be required. He requests the officers will pay the strictest attention to their men's arms and accouterments, that their appearance on the field may reflect honor on themselves and flatters himself, when called upon, they will turn out with the spirit that characterizes the Militia of New Jersey. New Jersey Gazette, March 14, 1781

There was a few attacks in New Jersey, which turned out to be nothing more than a larger than usual foraging party, which the Jersey militia turned back:

From Monmouth county we learn that on Thursday last, a body consisting of about one thousand New Levies, British and Foreign Troops, under the command of Cortland Skinner, made an incursion into that county. By their conduct, it appears that their intention was to plunder a place called Pleasant Valley, where they arrived about 11 o'clock A.M., with little or no interruption; the inhabitants had however exerted themselves in such a manner in driving off their stock of every kind, that they found very little booty.

The militia of the neighborhood were by this time beginning to collect and a pretty smart skirmishing was kept up through the remainder of the day, in which we are informed that our people behaved with great spirit. They began their retreat at around sundown and made no halt till they got to Garret's Hill, where they continued that night, during the course of which one of our gallant officers made a descent upon them and rescued a number of their stolen sheep; the next day they embarked again, having captured and taken off with them about 40 cattle and 60 sheep, with the loss of one man killed and a number deserted; their loss in wounded is unknown. The loss on our side is one killed and three or four wounded. They have burned two houses but it is acknowledged in their favor that they behaved remarkably well to the persons of the people in general.

By their coming out in such force, it was expected that their aim was to penetrate further in the county, to prevent which the militia of the surrounding counties was called upon and it was truly surprising to see with what spirit and alacrity they flew to their arms and were crowding from every quarter to the assistance of their brethren on this occasion, when accounts of the hasty retreat of the enemy rendered their further services unnecessary. New Jersey Gazette, June 27, 1781

Others concluded that the object of the British plans was elsewhere, hopefully very far away, like England

A very considerable movement in New York is taking place, the particulars of which we have not been able to learn, though some people, more sanguine than ourselves, imagine a good embarkation is in on the carpet, as our Commissioner General of Prisoners, a few days ago was ordered to leave the city. New Jersey Gazette, March 14, 1781

By persons from New York, we are informed that a number of troops have embarked on board of transports, their destination said to be Eastward

That last week a very hot press [impressment] took place by which several hundred men of the city were carried on board the fleet and 309 American prisoners were also carried off the prison ship and forced on board their ships of war, among whom were captains, mates and other officers. Such is the unexampled barbarity of the piratical nation against which we

have to contend! They revere neither the laws of GOD or nations.
New Jersey Gazette, May 9, 1781

The uncertainty of the enemy's next move in New Jersey did not stop the Americans from celebrating the fifth anniversary of their Declaration of Independence. Indeed, evident in the celebration, is an excitement and optimism about the new order that was being established around them.

Last Wednesday, being the anniversary of the independence of America, that event was celebrated at this place [Princeton] with great festivity and good order. In the morning, the Ladies discovered their taste in ornamenting the house with greens and flowers. At noon, the principal men of the town met at Mr. Beekman's Tavern, at the sign of the college, where they were honored with the company of his Excellency, the Governor. From thence, after a few draughts of good punch, they repaired to a tree in front of Mr. Beekman's house, from the top of which a union flag was displayed. Here all the inhabitants of the town were collected by the field piece belonging to it, from which thirteen rounds were fired in honor of the states, and, before each round, one of the following sentences was pronounced, expressive of the wishes of the people, upon the occasion.

1st. The United States of America -- May the latest times see them flourishing in independence, happiness, and in union.

2d. The Kings of France and Spain - As the best reward for their friendship to America, may they reign in the affection of their subjects and be deservedly handed down in history as the greatest patriots of their own country.

3d. The Congress -- May that body never want the virtue, wisdom or power necessary to establish the independence of the American Republic, on foundations that shall render it the wonder and the blessing of all times to come.

4th General Washington -- When the greatest and most virtuous commanders of antiquity are named, may they be compared to him and hold only the second rank!

5th. General Greene and the Commanders of the South -- May they compel their enemies not to boast of having conquered countries which they have only passed through as travelers or fugitives!

6th. The American Plenipotentiaries to the Congress at Vienna -- May the have the pleasure of seeing the ministry of Britain as humble before them as they once boasted that they would make America!

7th -- The American Army and Navy -- May they, victorious over all the enemies of their country, live to enjoy, as happy citizens, the blessings of that freedom and independence, for which they have fought as brave soldiers!

8th. The army and navy of France -- May Heaven crown her Generals with success in the defense of America and give her Admirals the glory of humbling the flag of a nation who boast that they are the lords of the ocean.

9th. The States General of the United Provinces --May they remember and revenge Eustatia!

10th. If there are British officers who treat a traitor as he deserves, let their enemies esteem them; but perpetual infamy on the wretches who are not ashamed to consult with or to serve under Benedict Arnold!!!

11th. The confederation of the American States -- May virtue cement and ambition never disturb the union.

12th. The Governor and State of New Jersey -- May this state always hold a distinguished rank in the confederacy, for the wisdom of her institutions and the wealth and industry of her citizens.

13th The College -- May this institution ever serve the most essential interests of the state and of the continent, by extensively disfusing the influence of science and of virtue among the people!

The assembly was then dismissed with three cheers, after which his Excellency and a great number of gentlemen retired to partake of an elegant at Mr. Bergen's, when many patriotic toasts were drank and the officers of the army were particularly remembered. In the evening the whole rejoicing of of the day were concluded with good order and harmony, by parading the students of the college, and the militia of the town, in the presence of the Governor and the Gentlemen of his company. Each corps fired thirteen rounds and gave three cheers and everyman returned peaceably to his own habitation and happy in the memory of this great revolution. New Jersey Gazette, July 11, 1781

Washington moved some of his troops back across the Hudson to northern Westchester and made his headquarters at a river town named Fishkill[130]. Now it was the British turn to wonder what the Rebels were up to. Was an attack on New York City next?

Major Andrew Brown, who made his escape from prison in New York, on Thursday last, and arrived here [Boston] last Sunday evening, has favored us with the following intelligence, viz. That last Tuesday Admiral Hood with 13 sail of the line, 4 frigates and 2 fire ships, arrived at Sandy Hook. That the troops and inhabitants of New York, expect every moment to be attacked by General Washington. That the inhabitants of Long Island and Staten Island, are every man obliged to do military duty. New Jersey Gazette, September 19, 1781

Meanwhile, the forays back and forth continued:

We hear that last Thursday night a party in six whaleboats consisting of 70 men, under the command of Lieut.

Asher Fitz Randolf, of the state regiment stationed at Woodbridge, landed on Staten Island and proceeded as far as Fort Richmond, in which were stationed upwards of 200 tories and refugees. A severe firing commenced about daybreak and continued until 11 o'clock. All that ventured out of the fort were either killed or taken and Lieut. Fitz Randolf brought off several prisoners, without any loss except having three men slightly wounded and Captain Storey who commanded one of the whale boats was wounded in three different places, but none of them mortally. New Jersey Gazette, August 29, 1781

"On Monday, the 15th inst. A party of refugees from Sandy Hook, landed at Shrewsbury, in Monmouth county, and under cover of the night, marched undiscovered to Colt's Neck near 15 miles from the place of their landing, and took six of the inhabitants from their houses. The alarm reached the Courthouse between four and five o'clock in the morning of the 16th, when a small number of the inhabitants who were in the village of Freehold and its vicinity, (accompanied by Doctor Nathaniel Scudder, accidentally in the place that night) went immediately in pursuit of them, hoping either to relieve their friends who had been stolen into captivity, or to chastise the enemy for their temerity. They rode to Black Point, the place where the refugees had landed with all possible speed, fell in with them, attacked the rear of the refugee party, and drove them on board their boat. In which skirmish, to the great grief of our party, Doctor Nathaniel Scudder, whilst he was bravely advancing on the enemy, received a wound by a musket ball passing through his head, of which he instantly expired [131].
The New Jersey Gazette, October 24, 1781

The English fleet was seen returning to New York harbor at the end of September with their proverbial "tails between their legs". Count De Grasse and the French fleet had routed them in a battle in the Chesapeake:

It is no longer a doubt that the British fleet have returned to the Hook from the Mouth of Chesapeake Bay, where it is said they received a severe drubbing from Count De Grasse.

Certain it is that they have come back with several ships less than they took out. The New Jersey Gazette, September 26, 1781

While the reader of this item in the *New Jersey Gazette* could never have guessed it, the defeat of the English fleet by the French was the beginning of the end of the Revolution. Cornwallis foolishly had followed General Greene and his American army, on an exhausting chase through the south, finally catching up to them at Guilford Courthouse on March 15, 1781. After the battle, Cornwallis tired army was battered and limped, first eastward and then northward, finally erecting a base at the port of Yorktown in Virginia to rest. General Greene did not bother pursuing him, but returned to South Carolina, and between April and October had picked off, one by one, every British post except those at Charleston and Savannah.

Clinton immediately recognized that Cornwallis had made himself vulnerable to a land-and-sea blockade, now that the French fleet had displaced the British one, and ordered him to return to New York. Stubbornly, Cornwallis refused to leave, foolishly believing his position to be a beach head in the American South, when, in reality, he had painted himself in a corner from which he could not escape.

Washington saw his opportunity. He raced his 7,000 man army south, taking with a like number of French troops of Count Rochambeau, who were in Rhode Island, and began a siege of Yorktown. Soon, the French fleet under the Comte de Grasse formed off the coast, preventing either a British escape or rescue by sea. Then, began almost two weeks of intense bombardment.

Clinton received a dispatch from Cornwallis. It was obvious from it that Cornwallis was crushed and about ready to capitulate.

(Copy of a letter from the Earl of Cornwallis to his Excellency Sir Henry Clinton, dated York Town, Virginia, dated October 15, 1781)
    SIR:
    My situation now becomes very critical. We dare not show a gun to their old batteries and I expect their new ones will

be open tomorrow morning. Experience has shown that our fresh earthen works do not resist their powerful artillery, so that we shall soon be exposed to an assault in ruined works, in a bad position, with weakened numbers.
The safety of this place is so precarious that I cannot recommend that the fleet and army should run great risk in endeavoring to save us. I have the honor to be with great respect, Sir, &c.

Despite Cornwallis' recommendation to the contrary, Clinton immediately ordered a fleet, with 7,000 of his troops aboard under his own command, to assist the besieged Cornwallis. As they neared Virginia, however, a message from one of his pilot boats informed him that it was already over. Cornwallis had surrendered on October 19th.

Clinton sent one of his vessels, the Sloop *Rattlesnake,* Captain Melcombe commanding, with a dispatch to Lord George Germaine in London, Cornwallis' ally, advising him of the probable capture of Cornwallis and his some 8,000 British troops and that Clinton was returning with his forces to New York.

"Agreeable to the information which I had the honor to give Your Lordship in my last dispatch, the Fleet under the command of Rear Admiral Graves, sailed from Sandy Hook on the 16th instant and arrived off Cape Charles on the 24th, when we had the mortification to hear that Lord Cornwallis had proposed terms of capitulation to the enemy on the 17th. This intelligence was brought to us by the pilot of the Charon who came off from the shore and said that he had made his escape from Yorktown on the 18th and had not heard any shooting since the day before. The Nymph frigate, also arriving the next day from New York, brought me a letter from his Lordship, dated the 15th, the desponding tenor of which gives me the most alarming apprehension of its truth. Since then, we have been plying off the coast with variable and hard gusts of wind to the present hour without being able to procure any additional information, except from two men taken in a canoe, whose report exactly corresponds with the former.
Comparing, therefore, the intelligence received from these people and from others since come in, with the import of Lord

Cornwallis' letter, a copy of which I have the honor to enclose for your Lordship's information, we cannot entertain the least doubt of his Lordship's having capitulated and that we are unfortunately too late to relieve him, which having been the only object of the expedition, the Admiral has determined to return with his fleet to Sandy Hook."

The news of the victory at Yorktown soon reached the ears of the Americans as well.

"With the most unbounded pleasure, we can assure the public, that dispatches have the moment arrived, giving an account of the unconditional surrender of Lord Cornwallis, on the 17th instant, to our great and magnanimous General Washington." The New Jersey Gazette, October 24, 1781

For all practical purposes the war was over. It was evident to all that, were Britain to resume the offensive, it needed a new army to replace the one Washington had captured. And it was equally evident that England would not do that to continue a war, already six years old and from which the British had so little to show - New York City, two southern ports and little more. Worse, the people and merchants of London were demonstrating against the long, expensive war that the British were clearly now losing. In Parliament an opposition party was questioning the continuance of the war and, surprisingly, the mood was changing.

The Americans knew they had won as well. Celebrations were spontaneous, including in Trenton, capital of New Jersey.

On Saturday last the great and important event of the surrender of Lord Cornwallis and his whole army, to the combined forces commanded by His Excellency, General Washington, was celebrated here with every mark of joy and festivity.

The day was ushered in with the beating of drums, and the American colors were displayed in various parts of the town.

At 11 o'clock in the forenoon His Excellency the Governor, the Honorable Council and Assembly, with the inhabitants of the town and vicinity, attended divine service at the Presbyterian

Church, where a discourse adapted to the occasion was delivered by the Reverend Mr. Spencer.

At noon, a proper discharge of cannon was fired by the corps of artillery belonging to the town, in the presence of the Governor, General Dickinson, the Members of the Legislature and the Gentlemen of the town and neighborhood, assembled on the common.

At three in the afternoon, the company repaired to an elegant entertainment, at which the following toasts were drank, and severally accompanied with a discharge of artillery.

1. *The United States of America.*
2. *The Congress.*
3. *The King of France.*
4. *General Washington and the American army.*
5. *The Count de Rochambeau and the French army.*
6. *The Count de Grasse and the French fleet.*
7. *General Greene and the southern army.*
8. *The friends of liberty throughout the world.*
9. *The memory of Generals, Warren, Montgomery, and all the other heroes who have fallen in the defense of the liberties of America.*
10. *Peace on honorable terms, or war forever.*
11. *The great and heroic Hyder Alli, raised up by Providence to avenge the numberless cruelties perpetrated by the English on his unoffending countrymen, and to check the insolence and reduce the power of Britain in the East Indies.*
12. *The Governor and state of New Jersey*
13. *The glorious 19th. Of October, 1781.*

At seven in the evening the company retired, and the rejoicings were concluded by brilliant illumination. Everything was conducted with the greatest good order and propriety; and we mention it with pleasure, that not the least disturbance or irregularity happened during the whole festivity. What greatly added also to the joy inspired by this glorious event, was the pleasing recollection of the advantages already reaped from our alliance now more firmly cemented by the united effusion of French and American blood, in a conquest the more agreeable to both nations, for being obtained by their combined efforts as fellow soldiers and fellow victors in the same triumphant cause. The New Jersey Gazette, October 24, 1781

Princeton, both the town and the college, had been hot beds of Revolutionary thought as well as the scene of an important American victory. Not unexpectedly, they celebrated the news of Cornwallis' surrender at Yorktown with great joy.

On an occasion so glorious and happy for American as the surrender of the greatest of the British Generals, with a numerous garrison to the arms of the continent, every friend of his country must feel the most sincere and lively joy. The inhabitants of Princeton took the earliest opportunity to testify their pleasure in this event, and on Tuesday last celebrated it with the utmost festivity. At twelve o'clock most of the reputable gentlemen of the town and several in the neighborhood, met at Mr. Beekman's tavern, and enjoyed the occasion awhile over some good punch and wine. From thence they repaired to the green in front of the house, where the field-piece was drawn out; and after an address suited to the institution of the day, delivered by one of the Professors of the College, thirteen rounds were fired. The whole company then partook of a public dinner, to which several strangers in the place were invited. The following thirteen toasts were drank, and the company broke up with decency at six o'clock.

1. *United States.*
2. *The Congress.*
3. *The King of France.*
4. *The King of Spain and States General.*
5. *General Washington and the American army.*
6. *The Count de Rochambeau and French army.*
7. *The Count de Grasse and navy of France.*
8. *General Greene and Southern army.*
9. *The memorable 16th and 19th of October, and the action of Eutaw Springs.*
10. *Our Plenipotentiaries at foreign courts.*
11. *The Governor and State of New-Jersey.*
12. *The memory of all who have fallen in this war in defense of America.*

13. *A speedy peace, and the firm establishment of the independence of the United States of America*

In the evening the town was handsomely illuminated, and thirteen rounds from the militia concluded the rejoicings of the day. The New Jersey Gazette, October 24, 1781

So did the citizens of New Brunswick, the town on the Raritan that the British had occupied during the winter of 1777.

This day arrived here official accounts of the surrender of the Earl of Cornwallis, and, as might naturally be expected in a place which so sensibly feels the effects of the present war, occasioned universal joy and satisfaction. In the evening were discharged thirteen cannon, after which a number of gentlemen of the city and neighborhood, and several strangers, of whom were Sir James Jay and Richard Stevens, Esq. convened at Marriner's tavern, in order to spend an hour together in festivity and gladness. After supper the company, for the sake of convenience withdrew into another room, and having appointed Mr. Kirkpatrick their President, the following toasts were pronounced and drank.

1. The Congress and the United States of America.
2. His Most Christian Majesty Louis the XVI.
3. The glorious Washington and the allied army.
4. His Excellency the Count de Grasse and the French navy.
5. His Excellency the Count de Rochambeau.
6. General Greene and the southern army.
7. The friends of American liberty.
8. The memorable 19th of October.
9. The memory of the brave who have fallen in their country's cause.
10. May the present revolution prove a terror to tyranny throughout the earth.
11. May the lilies of France and stripes of American wave in triumph from shore to shore.
12. Liberty.
13. A speedy and an honorable peace.

> *The greatest order and decency was observed throughout the whole --As in the feast of Ahasuerus the King, the drinking was according to the law, none did compel, for it was appointed that they should do according to every man's pleasure. The evening being thus spent, each of the gentlemen drank a good-night to the company in a bumper, and retired.. The New Jersey Gazette, November 7, 1781*

Nor could the Americans missed an opportunity to ridicule James Rivington, editor of the loyal, "lying" *New York Gazette* that had so long misstated the news of the war in a pro British fashion.

Mr. Collins,

> *In your next issue, please to inform Jemmy Rivington that, although he tells us that two ships of Count De Grasse's squadron, attempting to force a passage up the York river, above Gloucester Point and Yorktown, were obliged to return defeated, we hear that our illustrious General Washington is returning north eastward, crowned with laurels plucked from the brow of Lord Cornwallis, victorious.*

> *"When British glory once begins to fade,*
> *Jemmy no more pursues his wonted trade,*
> *Nor post nor pay can now bring out a word,*
> *E'en the Gazette royal submits to the sword;*
> *Tho' brib'd to print, his coward heart misgives,*
> *Invention fails him -- vainly he strives*
> *To forge a falsehood but the authentic tale,*
> *Of hosts subdued, terrifies the pale*
> *Frightened Rivington, whose well told story*
> *Trusts not honest Whig nor hapless Tory.*
> *Cornwallis taken! -- 'tis no more nor less --*
> *Alas! 'tis true -- What think you now of Congress?"*
> *The New Jersey Gazette, November 7, 1781*

After the celebrations and gloating, came the realization that the American Cause had been aided from Above. Governor Livingston of New Jersey issued a proclamation, a "retrospective" of the War that cited many examples of the assistance provided by God to the American Cause at critical times. He fixed December 13, 1781 as a Day of Thanks -- and a public holiday -- giving to be observed by all citizens of New Jersey, regardless of their sects.

BY HIS EXCELLENCY
William Livingston
Governor, Captain General and Commander in Chief in and over the State of New Jersey and the territories thereunto belonging,
PROCLAMATION

WHEREAS it has pleased Almighty God, Father of Mercies, remarkably to assist and support the United States of America in their important struggle for liberty against the long continued efforts of a powerful nation, it is the duty of all ranks to observe and thankfully acknowledge the intercession of his providence on their behalf. Through the whole of the contest, from its first rise to this time, the influence of Divine Providence may be clearly perceived in many signal instances, of which we mention but a few: in revealing the councils of our enemies, when the discoveries were seasonable and important and the means seemingly inadequate and fortuitous; in preserving and even improving the union of the several states, on the breach of which our enemies placed their greatest dependence; in increasing the number of and increasing the zeal of and attachment of the friends of liberty; in granting us remarkable deliverance and blessing us with the most signal successes, when affairs seemed to have the most discouraging appearance; in raising up for a most powerful and generous ally, in one of the first of the European powers; in confounding the counsels of our enemies and suffering them to pursue such measures as most have directly contributed to frustrate their own desires and expectations and -- above all, in making their extreme cruelty to the inhabitants of these states, when in their power, and their savage devastation of property, the very means of cementing our union and adding vigor to every effort in opposition to them.

And as we cannot help leading the good people of these states to a retrospect of the events which have taken place since the beginning of the war, so we recommend, in a particular manner, to their observation, the Goodness of God in the year now drawing to a conclusion, in which the confederation of the United States has been completed; in which there have been so many instances of prowess and success in our armies, particularly in the southern states where, notwithstanding the difficulties with which they had to struggle, they have recovered the whole country which the enemy had overrun, leaving them only a port or two near, or on, the sea; in which we have been so powerfully and effectively assisted by our allies, while, in all the conjunct operations, the most perfect harmony has subsisted in the allied army; in which there has been such a plentiful harvest and so great abundance of the fruits of the earth of every kind, as not only allows us to easily supply the wants of our army, but gives comfort and happiness to the whole people.

IT IS THEREFORE recommended to the several states to set apart the THIRTEENTH of DECEMBER, to be religiously observed as a day of THANKSGIVING and PRAYER; that all the people may assemble that day with grateful hearts, to celebrate the praises of our gracious Benefactor; to confess our manifold sins; to offer up our most fervent supplications to the God of all Grace, that it may please him to pardon our offenses and incline our hearts to the future to keep all his laws; to comfort and relieve all of our brethren who are in distress or captivity; to prosper our husbandmen and give success to all engaged in lawful commerce; to impart wisdom and integrity to our counselors, judgment and fortitude to our officers and soldiers; to protect and prosper our illustrious ally and favor our united operations for a speedy establishment of a safe, honourable and lasting peace; to bless all seminaries of learning and cause the knowledge of God to cover the earth as the waters cover the seas.

I HAVE THEREFORE thought fit, by and with the advice of the Privy Council and from a deep sense of our indispensable duty to celebrate with united hearts, in social worship, throughout the whole continent, the praises of the Great Disposer of all events, who has so often and so conspicuously during the present war displayed His Omnipotent Arm for our deliverance, to appoint the said THIRTEENTH DAY of DECEMBER next to be observed in this state as a day of THANKSGIVING and PRAISE, hereby recommending to the Ministers of the Gospel of every denomination therein, to perform the Divine Service and to the people committed to their charge to attend on public worship on that day and to abstain from servile labor and all recreations inconsistent with the solemnity of the festival.
WILLIAM LIVINGSTON

GOD SAVE THE PEOPLE

The year 1781, begun with a mutiny, closed with victory. The war was not officially over by any means. Sporadic guerilla fighting would continue and a peace treaty was more than a year and a half away. Yet, there were some obvious signs that the worse was over. The enemy was going home.

The London fleet will sail from New York in about eight days. Lord Cornwallis goes home on the Robust, and the traitor General Benedict Arnold and his family on the Edward, a twenty gun ship. The New Jersey Gazette, December 12, 1781

We hear from New York that the Hessians and other German troops are called home by their respective princes. New Jersey Gazette, December 12, 1781

CHAPTER 15

The War's End: 1782 and 1783

It had been seven years since 1775, when Lord North had soundly defeated, 192 to 46, those who objected in the House of Commons to second class citizenship of the colonists. The Revolution that followed had been expensive, however measured -- in the costs to fight it, in the territory surrendered, or, lastly, in the face that the mightiest Empire on earth lost to its upstart colonies. How Britain could terminate this unpleasant mess in which it now found itself was a matter debated in Parliament on March 9, 1782. While Lord North was able to defeat a motion against all future efforts to subdue the American provinces, he was clearly himself defeated.

HOUSE OF COMMONS
Motion made by Sir James Lowther:
That it is the opinion of the House that the war carried on in the colonies and plantations of North America, has proven ineffectual, either for the protection of his Majesty's loyal subjects in the colonies or for defeating the dangerous designs of our enemies."
This the Baronet attempted, in a short speech, to support and was seconded in a declaration against the ministry, by Mr. Powers, which brought up Lord North to reply. H i s Lordship informed the House that the misfortunes and calamities of the war made it necessary for the Government to determine that the mode of carrying on the war internally upon the continent of America, as had been the practice under Lord Cornwallis and other generals, should no longer be followed, but to change the form of the war altogether. This declaration, his Lordship said, had given him some inconvenience; nor would he have made it even then, had not the estimates of his own army declared as much in the most

clear and express manner: to prosecute the war continually, we must assemble a much larger army. Such an idea would have been absurd in the highest extreme, and obviously impractical.

Having made this declaration, the Lordship said, in response to some of the remarks of Mr. Powers, that the war had never been a favorite of his; on the contrary, he had always considered the war a cruel necessity, but yet as a war founded on a truly British basis, a war instituted to support the just rights of the Crown and of the Parliament of Great Britain. In that point of view, and only, should the war be regarded as just in its origins and necessary, however calamitous to the country, as its events had unfortunately proved.

His Lordship went into an examination of the motion, either with regard to peace or war. The words of the seconding motion was to resolve against all future efforts to subdue the American provinces. "All efforts?" asked this Lordship. Great Britain will never covenant to cede what is hers. His Lordship showed that, if the present motion was acceded to, it is, in effect, tantamount to a motion for immediately withdrawing all the troops, in other words, for abandoning the American War and British rights altogether. He asked whether the gentlemen in the house were prepared to go that length. Were they ready to say that New York or its dependencies ought not to be kept, either as a post whence we might annoy the common enemy and offer assistance to our West Indies islands or with a consideration to have something in our hands to make peace with.

His Lordship very forcibly painted the disadvantages in making a peace, which the country would lie under, supposing that the motion was carried. And, then, as forcibly, argued the disadvantages which would befall us on further prosecution of the war.

Mr. Burke made a very long speech in favor of the motion.

Lord North was very ably supported by his colleague in office, Lord George Germain, who replied to Mr. Burke.

The debate continued to two in the morning, when the opposition having exhausted all their force, the House divided and the motion was lost by the following numbers:

Against the motion   220
For the motion   179
Majority   41

Even thought the motion for, in effect, a complete British withdrawal from America did not carry, it was evident that changes were to be made. Lord North was gone, pensioned off. The American citizens learned of the changes from a British newspaper that came on the ship that carried Sir Guy Carleton's, Sir Henry Clinton's replacement.

New York, May 8.
Last Sunday, his Excellency Sir Guy Carleton, Knight of the Bath, Commander in Chief of his Majesty's forces, and commissioner for making peace or war in North America, arrived in this city in good health. The Ceres Man of War, Captain Hawkins, brought his Excellency and his suite in 25 days from Portsmouth.

His Excellency landed in the afternoon under a discharge of the cannon at Fort George and dined with the Honorable General Sir Henry Clinton, K.B. and Admiral Digby.

From the English newspapers brought by Ceres, we have the following advices, viz.

A Dissolution of the late Ministry
On Wednesday the 20th of March, Lord North informed the House of Commons, that his Majesties Ministers were no more. His Lordship then moved that the House should adjourn to Monday, March 23, in order to give the Crown time to form a new arrangement. The House adjourned accordingly.

Appointment of Lord North
Lord North is to be appointed Constable at Dover Castle and Warden of the Cinque Ports, for life, and also a grant of 4,000 pounds sterling a year, payable quarterly for life. Likewise, a grant of 1,000 pounds sterling for life too to

John Robinson, Esq., his Lordship's Secretary. The New Jersey Gazette, May 15, 1782

Peace might be in the air and the armies, more or less, at rest, but the attacks by the Refugees or Loyalists against the citizens of Monmouth county in New Jersey, and vice versa, continued during the winter of 1782

We hear from Monmouth that on Friday evening the 8th instant, about forty refugees, commanded by one Stevenson, a Lieutenant, came over from Sandy Hook, across the Gut, and thence into the country to a place near Pleasant Valley. They visited the houses of sundry persons in the neighborhood, from whence they took off upwards of twenty horses, five sleighs, which they loaded with plunder, and eight or nine prisoners, namely Hendrick Hendrickson and his two sons, Garret Hendrickson, Peter Covenhoven, Esq., Samuel Bowne and son, and Jacques Denice. They then made off with their prisoners and booty. At Garret Hendrickson's, having entered the house and made him prisoner, they went to the barn to take his horses and sleigh. In the meantime, two young men, his son and one William Thomson, who slept in the second story of the house, being awaked by the noise below, secreted themselves till the enemy were gone to the barn, and then came down, escaped and went to the house of Capt. John Schenck, of Col. Holmes's regiment, whom they alarmed about an hour and an half before day. This gallant officer immediately collected a small party, left orders for as many as could be got together to follow him, pursued the refugees on the route they had taken, and arrived at the Gut just as they had got the prisoners, two or three of the horses and a small quantity of the other plunder carried over. He immediately attacked those which were with the remainder of the horses and plunder, and after a few fires, in which unfortunately young Mr. Thomson fell, and a Mr. Cottrel was wounded in the knee, he made them prisoners to the number of twelve, three of them were wounded. Captain Schenck finding it impracticable to continue the pursuit for want of craft to cross the water, was returning with his recapture and who had remained behind to secure the retreat and favor the passage of those who were before. A firing immediately ensued on both sides, but Captain Schenck ordering his men to charge and give the enemy the bayonet, they thought proper to throw down their arms and submit. This encounter being altogether unexpected, eight of the prisoners, first taken, found means to escape. Captain Schenck left Saturday forenoon on his way through Middletown with nineteen horses, five sleighs with the plunder which had been taken from the inhabitants, and one and twenty of the enemy prisoners. The people report that they huzzaed and triumphed as they returned to their boats, boasting of their success, and that the next time they would penetrate as far as Mount Pleasant, several miles further into the country. Among the prisoners are several atrocious villains who have at different times, done much mischief in that part of the country.

We hear that a party of refugees, to the amount of upwards an hundred, under the command of one Ryerson, made an incursion last week in the county of Monmouth, as far as Colt's Neck. We have not yet learnt what mischief was done, but if we conjecture from their former conduct, they have probably, with their usual heroism, surprised some of the inhabitants in their beds, and what is more probable, that they have, with singular bravery and address, made sundry sorties upon the sheep and calves, making great numbers of them prisoners. This, no doubt, will be ushered forth in the Royal Gazette as a most glorious achievement, reflecting the highest honour upon British arms. New Jersey Gazette, March 13, 1782

We are informed that on Friday night last, Capt. Hyler with a one gun boat and a barge went on an expedition to the Narrows, were he surprised and captured a British cutter, mounting six 18 and ten 9 pounders; but the wind being unfavorable for bringing her off, and having landed her crew, about 50 in number, and taking out such articles as he thought proper, set her on fire. He also took a sloop at the same time, which he ransomed for 400 Dollars.-The prisoners are properly secured.. New Jersey Gazette, April 24, 1782

Extract of a letter from Monmouth, March 25. " I am sorry to inform you our guard at Toms river were cut off yesterday morning by about 100 refugees under command of one Davenport. On the Alarm, Capt. Huddy repaired to the block-house, in which some of the inhabitants joined him, and others remained outside: the house was defended till the ammunition was expended when it surrendered. Major Cook, who was out of the house fell; five others were killed and two wounded. - Capt. Huddy, Daniel Randolph, Esq. and several more are carried off prisoners. Davenport was wounded, supposed since dead, and one Negro was killed. The enemy then burnt the village, except the houses of Aaron Buck and Mr. Studson, after which they went off immediately. The unfortunate inhabitants have not saved more than two horses would draw." *New Jersey Gazette, March 27, 1782*

    This last mentioned attack, upon Tom's River, in which Joshua Huddy was taken away as prisoner, was the first link in a chain of emotionally charged events that reached the thrones of England and France, and whose odor still hangs in the air of New Jersey. It had happened at the end of Clinton's command, but it became Guy Carleton's first challenge -- ironically, not in battle, but in diplomacy, his adversary being no other than General George Washington himself.

    The Loyalists in New York City, many of them displaced from New Jersey, had become desperate, realizing that England, on whose behalf they had been struggling for the past eight years, was about to desert them and abandon their properties to the rebels. The anger made a few of them act barbarically. Joshua Huddy, the American officer captured at Toms Rivers, had been the commander of a privateer that had long harassed the British. He was turned over by the English to the Loyalists, so that they might exchange him for one of their own. Instead, Huddy was brought to the shore at Highlands, New Jersey, opposite Refugee Town on Sandy Hook Island, and hung from a tree. A note was pinned to his body, saying the execution was in reprisal for a Loyalist death and promising to hang rebels "while there is still a refugee existing."

> "Last Saturday was brought to this place the corpse of Capt. Joshua Huddy, who was about ten o'clock the day before most barbarously and unwarrantably hanged by a party of refugees. This murder was attended with so much deliberate injustice and wanton cruelty, that the circumstances ought to be preserved, and made public, as a shocking instance of the blackness of that guilt of which human nature is capable.
>
> Capt. Huddy was one of the bravest of men, a fit subject therefore of cowardly inhumanity. He has distinguished himself on a variety of occasions, one instance of which I cannot avoid mentioning: The summer before last alone and unassisted, except by a woman, he defended his house against a party of near seventy refugees for several house, and when it was in a manner riddled with musket balls, and in flames about him, he refused to submit until he obtained from the assailants safe and honorable terms: among the number who were killed in that encounter was the famous Negro Ty, justly much more to be feared and respected as an enemy, than any of his brethren of the fairer complexion. - Capt. Huddy also commanded the troops at the Block-House on Tom's river, when it was lately reduced; he defended it most gallantly against a vast superiority of numbers, until his ammunition was expended, and no alternative was left. The refugees, like their taskmasters, the British, who employ them in every kind of infamous business, are always cruel in success and pitifully mean in adversity. After the little brave garrison was in their power, they deliberately murdered five of the soldiers asking for quarters. From Tom's River, Capt. Huddy, Justice Randolph, and the remaining prisoners were taken to New York, where suffering the various progressions of barbarity usually exercised upon those who are destined to a violent or a lingering death, those two gentlemen, with a Mr. Fleming, were put into the hold of a vessel. Capt. Huddy was ironed hand and foot. On Monday last a certain John Tilton, a refugee, came to him, and told

him, "That he was ordered (by the board of refugees, as we suppose) to be hanged." Capt. Huddy asked "What charge was alleged against him?" Tilton replied, "That he had taken a certain Philip White, a refugee, six miles up in the country, cut off both his arms, broke both his legs, pulled out one of his eyes, and then damned him and bid him run.[132]" To this Huddy answered, "It is impossible that I could have taken Philip White, I being a prisoner closely confined in New York at the time and for many days before he was made a prisoner. Justice Randolph confirmed what Huddy had said, and assured Tilton that he could not possible be charged with White's death; upon which Tilton told Mr. Randolph that "He should be hanged next." This flimsy story, which must have been created by the murderous hearts of the refugees, to cloak their villainy, was the only crime charged against Capt. Huddy, and was the common subject of their conversation. From the sloop, Capt. Huddy, with his fellow prisoners, were put on board the guard ship at the Hook, and confined between decks till Friday morning the 12th inst. when some men, strangers to the prisoners, came below and told Capt. Huddy to "Prepare to be hanged immediately." He again said, "He was not guilty of having killed White," and that "He should die an innocent man, and in a good cause;" and with the most uncommon fortitude and composure of mind, prepared for his end, and with the spirit of a true son of liberty, he waited the moment of his fate, which he met with a degree of firmness and serenity, which struck the coward hearts of his executioners with admiration. He even executed his will under the gallows, upon the head of that barrel from which he was immediately to make his exit, and in a handwriting fairer than usual.

Capt. Huddy was taken prisoner on Sunday the 24th of March, and kept in close custody, with Justice Randolph, out of whose presence he never was for half an hour from the time he was taken, until the hour of his execution, which shows how impossible it was for him to have been concerned in White's death, and that they must have known it was so.

To show their insolence yet further, they left the following label affixed to the breast of the unfortunate Capt. Huddy.

"We, the refugees having with grief long beheld the cruel murders of our brethren and finding nothing but such measures daily carrying into execution, therefore determine not to suffer without taking vengeance for the numerous cruelties, and thus began (and I say may those lose their liberty who do not follow on) and have made use of Capt. Huddy as the first object to present to your views, and further determine to hang man for man as long as a refugee is left existing, "Up goes Huddy for Philip White."

This paper needs no comment. Is it not high time seriously to enquire whether these refugees are owned by, and under the direction of, the British commander at New York? If so, and he should refuse to deliver up the wicked perpetrators of the above murder, ought we no to treat his officers in the same manner until satisfaction be obtained? If, as some say, they are not under his authority, what are they but pirates and robbers? And, why ought they not to be treated as such when they fall into our hands?" New Jersey Gazette, April 24, 1782

It was such a cowardly, cold blooded needless act that the American public clamored for retaliation. General Washington wrote to Clinton, demanding that the parties responsible for this atrocity be surrendered to the Americans or reprisals would result

Sir:

The enclosed representation from the inhabitants of the county of Monmouth, with testimonials to the fact (which can be corroborated by other unquestionable evidence) will bring before your Excellency the most wanton cruel and unprecedented murder that ever disgraced the arms of a civilized people. I shall not, because I conceive it altogether unnecessary, trouble your Excellency with any animadversions on this transaction. Candor obliges me to be specific: to save the innocent, I demand the guilty.

Captain Lippincott, therefore, or the officer who commanded at the execution of Captain Huddy, must be given up, or if that officer were of inferior rank to him, so many of the perpetrators as will, according to the tariff of exchange, be an equivalent. To do this will mark the justice of your Excellency's character. In failure of it, I shall hold myself justified, in the eyes of God and Man, for the measure to which I shall resort.

I beg your Excellency to be persuaded that it cannot be more disagreeable to you to be addressed in the language than it is to me to offer it, but the subject requires frankness and decision.

I have to request your speedy determination as my resolution is suspended but for your answer
I have the honor to be &c
GEORGE WASHINGTON

Carleton had been relieved Clinton of command and, with it, also of the need to respond to Washington. Instead, Sir Guy Carleton answered, blaming the incident on the passions of private, unauthorized individuals and, assuring Washington that Britain sought peace -- he enclosed news clippings of North's ouster -- and that, even if there were no peace, Britain planned to wage war as gently as possible. Carleton also freed some American prisoners as a gesture of England's approach toward what she still considered to be her misbehaving colonists, but he made no mention of Huddy. To this non-responsive olive branch, Washington replied straightforwardly. Washington then sent his exchange of correspondence with Carleton regarding the Huddy situation to the Continental Congress in Philadelphia.

Just as I am enclosing these dispatches, a letter from Sir Guy Carleton is handed me, covering sundry printed papers, a copy of which, with the papers, I now have the honor to enclose to your excellency, together with a copy of my answer to him, and I flatter myself my conduct herein will be agreeable to the wishes of Congress.

Sir,

Having been appointed by his Majesty to the command of his forces on the Atlantic Ocean, and joined with Admiral Digby in the Commission of Peace, I find it proper in this manner to apprize your Excellency of my arrival in New York and acknowledge your letter to Sir Henry Clinton, K. B.

The occasion, sir, seems to render this communication proper, but the circumstances of the present time render it also indispensable, as I find it just to transmit herewith to your Excellence, certain papers from the perusal of such Your Excellency will perceive what dispositions prevail in the government and people of England towards America and what further effects are likely to follow. If the like pacific disposition should prevail also in this country, both my inclination and duty will lead me to meet it with the most zealous concurrence. In all events, sir, it is within me to declare that, if the war is to prevail, I shall endeavor to render its miseries as light to the people of this continent as the circumstances of such a condition will possibly permit.

I am much disturbed to find that private and unauthorized persons on both sides have given way to those passions, which ought to have had the strongest and most effectual control and which have begot acts of retaliation, which, without proper preventions, may be equally calamitous and dishonorable to both parties, although as it should seem more extensively pernicious to the natives and settlers of this country.

How much so ever, sir, we may differ in other respects, upon this one point we must perfectly concur, being alike interested to preserve the name of Englishmen from reproach and individuals from experiencing such unnecessary evils, as have but no effect on a general decision. Every proper measure which will tend to prevent these criminal excesses in individuals, I shall ever be ready to embrace; and, as an advance on my part, I have, as the first act of my command, liberated Mr. Livingston and have written to his father, Governor of New Jersey, upon the subject of such excesses as have passed in New Jersey, desiring his

concurrence in such matters, as, even under the conditions of war, the common interests of humanity require.
  Your Excellency's most obedient humble servant
            Guy Carleton

       [Washington's reply]
 Sir,
  I had the honor last evening to receive Your excellency's letter of the 7th with the several papers enclosed.
  Ever since the commencement of this unnatural war, my conduct has borne invariable testimony against those human excesses, which in too many ways has marked its various progress.
  With respect to a late transaction, to which, I presume Your Excellency alludes, I have already expressed my fixed resolution in the event Captain Huddy's executioner is not delivered to us for justice -- a resolution formed on a most mature deliberation and from which I shall not recede.
  I have the honor to be &c
            George Washington

  When Carleton refused to turn over Lippincott, the man most responsible for Huddy's murder, a young British officer, Charles Asgill, who had been captured at the Battle of Yorktown, was selected to be executed in Lippincott's stead. The boy's mother, Lady Asgill, managed to have King Louis of France and his wife Marie Antoinette petition Washington directly for leniency. It was, of course, a plea a grateful America could not refuse. Lippincott was court martialed by the British, found not guilty and rewarded with half pay for life and land in Canada where he passed a long life.
  The spot of Huddy's execution is marked today in a park in the Highlands, New Jersey. A plaque, erected by the Sons of the American Revolution, still seethes with hatred at the British treachery for Huddy's "execution without warrant", a crime which the British authorities repudiated, but for which, the plaque notes, they did not atone.
  The Loyalists' anger notwithstanding, the war was over. The Board of Loyalists was dissolved. The refugees

were told that a peace treaty was being negotiated, to appoint a few of them to represent them all and to otherwise to conduct themselves as the loyal citizens they were.

Sir Guy Carleton, in consequence of his instructions for discontinuing the offensive war in this country, has broken up the Board of Loyalist Refugees at New York

NOTICE TO NEW YORK LOYALISTS

The inhabitants within the British lines are requested to appoint in their several wards and districts, two or three persons from each to meet and confer on the subject of the following letter communicated by their Excellencies Sir Guy Carleton K.B. and the Honorable Admiral Digby and that the persons so appointed to be empowered to adopt such measures as shall be thought proper on the occasion. The meeting will be held at Rouba tavern, on Friday next, ten o'clock a.m.

It is earnestly recommended to the Loyalists everywhere, to suspend their opinion of the present important occasion and each, in his place, to continue firm in his professions he has made of loyalty and zeal for the re-union of the empire. The Independence of the Thirteen Colonies has indeed been proposed at a conference in Paris, held for the purpose of a general peace, but until a general peace is ratified, we cannot know what is to be the eventual outcome of this country. In the meantime, therefore we are bound, by every consideration of prudence and duty. To wait the issue, with that manly steadiness and cheerful reliance on the abilities and attentions of our commanders, which at present are our surest pledges of safety. By such a conduct, we shall preserve a claim to national regard and protection, which it would be madness to forfeit, since by giving away our suggestions of impatience, we can only disgrace ourselves in the eyes of our enemy, without a shadow of advantage. Rivington's Loyal Gazette of August 7, 1782

However, a few months later, when the armistice was read from the balcony of City Hall, despair was written on every face and all that were heard were groans, hisses and bitter curses hurled at their King for having deserted them.

The British military and naval commanders were in communication with General Washington, regarding the ongoing peace process and arranging for exchanges of prisoners.

(Copy of a letter from Sir Guy Carleton and Rear Admiral Digby to General Washington, New York, August 2, 1782 and written in consequences of direction from England)
SIR
The pacific disposition of the Parliament and People of England has already been communicated to you and resolutions of the House of Commons, the February 27th, have been placed in Your Excellency's hands and intimations given at the same time that further pacific measures were likely to follow.

We are acquainted, Sir, by authority that negotiations of a general peace have already commenced at Paris and that Mr. Grenville is invested with full powers to treat with all the parties at war and is now in Paris in the execution of his commission.

And we are further, Sir, made acquainted that His Majesty, in order to remove all obstacles to that peace that he so ardently wants to restore, has commanded his ministers to direct Mr. Grenville, that the Independency of the Thirteen Provinces, should be proposed by him in the first instance, instead of making it a condition of the general treaty, however, not without the highest confidence that the loyalists should be restored to their possessions or full compensation made them for whatever confiscations may have taken place.

We are further acquainted that transports have been prepared in England for conveying all the American prisoners to be exchanged. A proposition has already been made that all exchanges of men of the same description being exhausted, sailor and soldier shall be immediately exchanged, man for man, against each other, with this condition annexed, that your sailors shall be at liberty to serve the moment they are exchanged and the soldiers so received by us shall not serve in or against the Thirteen Provinces for one year.

We have the honor to be Your Excellency's most obedient and humble servants
        Guy Carleton
        R. Digby

The details took a long time to work out. The treaty was being negotiated in Paris, but there was a lot to do in New York. Loyalists had to be re-located. Three thousand refugees on 14 transports sailed in a single day in June for England. On August 16, more than five thousand displaced souls sailed south to the West Indies. A month later, a record fleet left New York to go north, to the wilderness of Nova Scotia with 8,000. By the end of the year, 29,000 Americans without a country had landed, as colonists in the Province of New Brunswick, Canada, recently carved out of the Quebec province that had been ceded to England by France twenty years before.

New York City was also full of runaway slaves who had come to the City in response to Sir Henry Clinton's promise in his Philipsburg Proclamation of 1779 that "every Negro who shall desert the rebel standard. . . full security to follow [within the British] lines any occupation which he shall think proper." The effects of the appeal, advertised to the slaves under the banner of "freedom and a farm" were formidable. While 5,000 slaves had thrown their lot in with the rebels, accepting their offers of manumission in exchange for joining the American cause, many, many more preferred the British offer of freedom. At war's end, the British, before leaving New York, kept Sir Henry's pledge. From May, 1782 to November, 1783, on every Wednesday morning, Negroes came to the Queens Head Tavern. The building, by then, already a half century old, was owned by Samuel Fraunces. (It still stands today, more than two centuries after that later, on the same corner of Pearl Street and Broad at the foot of Manhattan Island and enjoying the same use as a tavern .and restaurant) Maintained there at Fraunces Tavern by a joint commission of Americans and British was the "Book of Negroes". It determined which Negroes were eligible to be evacuated and which had to be returned to slavery with their American masters. In it were logged details of each black's enslavement, escape and military service. If their stories checked out, the former slave would be given a pass that read:

New York

This is to certify to whomever it may concern that the bearer hereof
[name],
a Negro, reported to the British Lines in consequence of the Proclamations of Sir William Howe and Sir Henry Clinton, late Commanders in Chief in America, and that the said Negro hereby has his Excellency Sir Guy Carleton's permission to go to Nova Scotia or where else [he or she] thinks proper.

By order of the Brigadier General
[Samuel Birch]

Thousands of former slaves were registered in the Book of Negroes and given the choice of relocating in Florida, the West Indies or Nova Scotia. Fearing re-enslavement if they ventured near the plantations of the south or the Caribbean, all elected to sail north to Canada and Nova Scotia, a region that Britain had obtained from France in 1749. It was the northernmost frontier of European settlement in the New World and among the least desirable because of the cold and thin rocky soil.[133]

Finally, the big day came. The British were to leave New York City -- Evacuation Day as it came to be known and celebrated for many decades. At 8 o'clock on the morning of Tuesday, November 25, General George Washington, acknowledging with nods, bows and polite replies, the cheers and praises of the folk that lived on the nearby farms, mounted his white steed at Bowery's Bull Head Tavern and road out at the head of his troops, down Bowery Lane to New York City. Today the route would be from 15th street, south along First Avenue to downtown. On his right, rode Brigadier General Elias Dayton, on his left, Major Benjamin Tallmadge. Both of them had been Washington's adjutants in America's espionage network and had requested the privilege of entering the City first so that they could protect their agents there from the wrath of the Rebels who knew them only as Loyalists and Tory sympathizers. Washington could not deny this plea. These were Washington's agents as well. And he too was conscious that they had one final responsibility to discharge.

The withdrawing British army was fewer than a hundred yards ahead, making their way to the East River where they bordered transports for England. Washington could see the rumps of the horses of the departing dragoon guard ahead of him. After seven years, the British finally were evacuating New York City, their last toehold in the United States. The negotiations in Paris had dragged on for 18 months before the definitive treaty had been signed on September 3, 1783.

New York was a much different place from the one they had fled in the war's beginning. It was an ugly place now, not the quaint Dutch seaport it once was. A village maiden had grown into a hardened bitter woman, never to be innocent again. The Americans, in hopes of defending the city, had chopped down its shade trees and orchards for barricades; trenches had been built across roads to impede invaders. Then, the fire set by the departing Americans had burned down more than a thousand residences and businesses, a third of the City. What the fire had not destroyed was then used by the British army and some 30,000 Loyalist refugees who fled into the City for protection from the rebel countryside. For six years, they lived in burned out, derelict homes, in foundations with ripped sails stretched across them for roofs, and in tents on muddy fields. Everything was scarred and old. The side streets were blocked by earth works. Abandoned defense trenches were now open sewers filled with stagnant water.

Once the British departed, Major Tallmadge did in fact protect his agents. He arranged that General Washington would meet publicly with each of them, shake their hands and embrace them so that all who watched would know that these were friends, not enemies, of American Liberty

Needless to say the citizens were incredulous, upon seeing General Washington greet in that same familiar way, James Rivington, the detested editor of the *Royal Gazette*, whose news was always anti rebel and pro British. Washington had calculated correctly. Rivington's slurs on the American Cause, both fired up the Rebels, and added greatly to the trust that the British high command gave him. Together with Robert Townshend, his partner in the British Coffee House, where many a secret was discovered, Rivington had been a member of Tallmadge's Culper Network.

END NOTES

1. There were some larger farms, especially in Bergen and Somerset counties where the Dutch used more slave labor.

2. *Nova Caseseria* -- the original name of New Jersey -- had an eastern (the civilized) and western (the frontier) division well into the Revolution. Burlington was the capital of the West, Perth Amboy of the East.

3. There had been only 15,000 inhabitants at the beginning of the century. That number had increased to some 60,000 by the middle part of the century and to more than twice that by the War's beginning. Every generation, since 1700, marked a doubling of the New Jersey population.

4. They traced their lineage to lowland Scotland. Their ancestors, a mixture of the Viking, Norman and German tribes that had invaded England in the Dark Ages, thrived on frontiers, where independence was valued and authority challenged.

5. Nor was their influence on America a one time affair. The Scotch Irish were to be the next stage of the American experience, after the colonist. They would be the pioneers, the frontiersmen who tamed the West. Their children and grandchildren were the Texans of a half century later that fought their war for independence.

6. Indeed, for the first years, many of those from the African continent were brought to North America in only temporary bondage. As with the indentured servants from Europe, the Africans, at first, were enslaved for a fixed period of time, and then become free settlers when their indentures were served.

7. *Dunlap's Pennsylvania Packet*, August 7, 1775.

8. *The New York Gazette*, December 6, 1773

9. *The Pennsylvania Gazette*, August 15, 1771

10. This does not include the population of New Jersey College, now Princeton, which lay within the Township of Windsor's borders. It totaled 134, of which 130 were students (college and grammar school) and the remainder faculty.

11. Towns eagerly sought schoolmasters to begin the process of education. There were also rudimentary correspondence courses and even night schools.

12. William Tennent, a Presbyterian minister from a family of famous preachers, was a great supporter of the Revolutionary cause. Reportedly, on his death bed, he asked his Maker, if possible, to let him live "to see a happy issue to the severe and arduous controversy my country is engaged in."

13. The Rev. Charles M'Knight also was a well known Presbyterian preacher in Monmouth County and an avid supporter of the Revolution. His parsonage in Middletown was burned by the British and he was taken prisoner to New York and placed in festering prison ships anchored in the harbor. Eventually released, he was so weakened by the captivity that he soon died. His son and namesake was a captain in the Colonial Army.

14. Dr. Scudder was perhaps the greatest patriot of the three founders of this School. A medical doctor from Freehold, he was a delegate to the Continental Congress and a member of the Committee on Correspondence, part of the network throughout the colonies that served to encourage and support independence. He was also a colonel in the Monmouth militia. In October, 1781, he would be shot at Black Point, in Rumson, New Jersey, by a quasi military band

of British sympathizers/bandits, stationed on Sandy Hook and known as the Refugees.

15. Today, Princeton University

16. The newspapers captured the first important steps in Rutger's life, the notice of a meeting of Trustees in Hackensack where "it will then be taken into consideration where the College should be placed, with other important affairs relating to the said Institution" *(The New York Gazette*, March 18, 1771) and the follow up reports that the Trustees "did fix said College at the City of New Brunswick". It also appointed Mr. Frederick Frelinghousen tutor, to instruct the students in the learned languages, liberal arts and sciences. In New Brunswick, there was promised "good and sufficient board at private houses of said place, and as cheap (if not cheaper) than at any other places where colleges are erected." New Brunswick was a wholesome place as well. "The gentlemen students can be expected to be treated with becoming candor, without any discrimination with respect to their religious sentiments and will also have the opportunity to attend the divine worship of different denominations of said City. *The New York Journal*, October 24, 1771

Three years later, Rutgers had it first graduation ceremony:

New Brunswick, October 14, 1774. On Wednesday last the first Public Commencement of Queen's College was held here. The Rev. J.R. Hardenbergh officiated by appointment of the Board of Trustees as President for the Day. Mr. Matthew Light [Leydt] of New Brunswick, was the only candidate for the degree of Bachelor or Arts, who delivered orations in Latin, Dutch and English with high applause. In the afternoon, Mr. Davis Annan, Mr. Jasper Farmer, Mr. James Schurman, Mr. John Van Dike and Mr. Samuel Vickers, all of the present senior class, spoke with gracefulness and propriety on various subjects. A number of ladies and gentlemen of this town between the exercises entertained the audience with excellent vocal music and the

whole was conducted in a manner that gave satisfaction to a very numerous and respectable assembly. On Friday preceding, the Commencement of the Grammar School here was examined and six of the students were admitted to the Freshman Class in College.
The New York Gazette, October 24, 1774

17. Frelinghuysen only stayed a few years at Rutgers. In 1775, he was elected to the New Jersey Provincial Congress and, when war broke out, joined the state Militia where he fought at the Battles of Trenton and Monmouth. Later, he represented New Jersey in the Continental Congress and, after the Constitution was enacted, was one of New Jersey's Senators to the United States Congress.

18. Orthography is the practice of proper spelling and script.

19. Aaron Burr was the grandson of Jonathan Edwards, a famous religious leader of America's earliest days. His father, who also was named Aaron Burr, had been a president of Princeton as well as being a religious leader. Young Aaron, graduating Princeton at the age of 16, studied law until hostilities broke out with Britain. He volunteered for action immediately and held a number of posts as *aides de camp* to senior Continental Army officers, including Benedict Arnold, Israel Putnam and George Washington. He spent the dreadful winter in Valley Forge and fought in the Battles of Long Island, Manhattan and Monmouth. Later, he became a Senator and Vice President of the United States. He had his dark side too. He killed Alexander Hamilton in the famous duel in Weehawkin, New Jersey, and, after a failed attempt to create a new nation west of the Mississippi, was tried, but acquitted, for treason.

20. Linn, a Jersey native, was also a patriot, serving in the militia against the British and as a member of then New Jersey Provincial Congress. After Independence, he held a number of public offices in the new federal and state

government and was a member of Congress from New Jersey and its Secretary of State for seventeen years.

21. The son of the New Jersey Governor, William Livingston, Henry Brocholst Livingston, joined the Continental Army and rose in rank, after seeing service in a number of battles. Sent to Spain with John Jay in a diplomatic mission to gain that nation's assistance in the war, he was captured by the British upon his return and was forced to sit out the rest of the hostilities. Studying law after the war, Livingston, in 1806, became an Associate Justice on the Supreme Court of the United States.

22. David Witherspoon and John Witherspoon were probably sons of Princeton's President at the time, John Witherspoon, himself a patriot and dedicated member of the Continental Congress.

23. Part of the famous Lee family of Virginia, Henry Lee would come to be known as Light Horse Harry Lee and is considered by many to have been the best cavalry officer in American history. A true hero, he fought with valor throughout the war. Upon independence, he returned to Virginia, where he served several years as Governor of the State. His son, Robert E. Lee, who many consider the greatest American general, commanded the Confederate troops during the Civil War.

24. William Bradford was the grandson of the first colonial printer and the son of the William Bradford, publisher of *The Pennsylvania Journal* and himself, despite his advanced age, a volunteer in the Revolutionary War. He was seriously wounded, ironically enough, at the Battle of Princeton. The youngest William Bradford, who, as an undergraduate, won the prizes here, would join the Continental Army as a private upon his graduation from Princeton, eventually reaching the rank of Colonel. After the War, he was the Attorney General of Pennsylvania and then its Chief Justice.

25. Hugh Henry Brackenridge, the foreign born son of immigrant Scottish farmers who settled deep within the Pennsylvania wilderness, worked his way through Princeton by teaching at its grammar school. He, with his classmate Philip Freneau, authored the revolution stirring poem *"The Rising Glory of America "* which received an enthusiastic response from the graduation audience and which was thereafter widely circulated among the colonies. He was a teacher, a clergyman/chaplain during the War, an author, and a patriot. He was later a member of the Pennsylvania Legislature and appointed a Judge on the Supreme Court of that State.

26. *"Regarding the Human Society"*.

27. *"Lying is always wrong."*

28. McKnight went on to study medicine and served during the Revolution as an army surgeon, accompanying the main army throughout the entire war. He completed his military career as Surgeon General and Chief Hospital Physician and went to New York to teach Medicine at Columbia University School of Medicine. He was considered the most eminent surgeon in New York City.

29. Donald Campbell was later to become a Colonel in the Continental Army.

30. Samuel Spring had a vocation to the ministry and became a Chaplain in the Continental Army. Afterwards, he was an eminent preacher and awarded an Honorary Doctor of Divinity by Princeton in 1806.

31. Known as *the Poet of the American Revolution*, Philip Freneau's verses, essays and political satires of the Royalists stirred the pot of liberty and independence that was brewing in America. He was captured by the British during

the Revolution and placed on one of the notorious prison ships, anchored in New York harbor.

32. Upon graduation, Gunning Bedford, already with a wife and child, returned to his native Delaware to become a lawyer. He was later a Member of the Continental Congress and a member of the Convention which wrote the Constitution of the United States. Later, he was Delaware's Governor and her first federal judge, the position in which he served through his death in March, 1812.

33. After Princeton, Black, originally from South Carolina, was ordained into the Presbyterian ministry.

34. James Madison, of course, was not only President of the United States, but is also considered *the Father of the Constitution*. As a student at Princeton, he reportedly got by on three hours of sleep a night, so hard did he study. He was also an ardent patriot and, like his fellow students, closely followed the rising cry for liberty. In a letter to a former tutor, the Princeton senior Madison described all 115 members of the College and Grammar School as "of American Cloth". Madison studied Hebrew for an additional year at Princeton, but, his interest in theology was becoming re-directed to the approaching revolution.

35. A patriot at first, Skinner would stop short of revolution. Indeed, he would command a regiment of Jersey Loyalist volunteers, to be known, because of the color of their uniforms as "Skinner's Greens". These Loyalists, or "refugees" as they were also called, would inflict great sufferings during the Revolution on the citizens of New Jersey.

36. And not just in the larger cities. For example, Monmouth County records its own Tea Party. In April 1775, Sandy Hook Bay pilots refused to take up a ship that had recently arrived from England until they were assured that she had no tea aboard as were their instruction from the

Committee of Safety. Eight chests of tea were found, thrown overboard and the captain forced to return to England without unloading the rest of his cargo.

37. Captain Chambers returned to London on another vessel. The Tea ship also set sail back to London, but not before her crew attempted to desert her.

38. Staten Island remained Loyalist throughout the War. It and the nearby Jersey coast towns, of Elizabeth, Rahway and Amboy, engaged in a continuous and particularly bitter struggle, until the last British troops departed in 1783.

39. Photography did not yet exist to capture the scene of the battle. Fortunately, Yankee ingenuity did: "It is proposed to print an exact view of the late Battle of Charlestown, June 17th, 1775, in which an advance party of seven hundred provincials stood an attack made by eleven regiments and a train of artillery of the ministerial forces, and, after an engagement of two hours, retreated to their main body at Cambridge, leaving eleven hundred of the regulars killed and wounded upon the field, with a view of General Putnam, a part of Boston, Charlestown in flames, Breeds Hill, provincial breastworks, a broken officer, the *Somerset* Man of War and a frigate firing on Charlestown. It shall be printed on good crown imperial paper and to be delivered to the subscribers in about ten days." *The Pennsylvania Gazette*, September 20, 1775

40. Meanwhile, hoping the colonists of the Canadian provinces would join in the rebellion against England, if properly encouraged, Congress sent an expedition against Montreal, under General Richard Montgomery. Once he had captured that city, he was to join Colonel Benedict Arnold on his mission to capture Quebec. The two American forces combined in an assault against Quebec on New Year's Eve, which closed the year on a disaster. Montgomery was killed, Arnold badly wounded and the assault a failure.

41. The Murrays had hired unsuspecting individuals to remove a shipment of forbidden imports from the *Beulah,* a plot exposed by the Committee of Observation of Elizabeth. Aside from the apologies, necessary to be permitted to trade among the inhabitants again, the Murrays also had to pay certain expenses and to forfeit the offending goods to the Committees for return to England.

42. A company, commanded by a captain, is a subdivision of a battalion. A battalion is a part of a regiment (commanded by a colonel), which in turn is part of the larger brigade.

43. Instructions were given how to find salt petre: *"We hear of a person in New Jersey, having an occasion to pull down an old barn, from the earth under, collected upwards of forty pounds of good saltpeter. As it is proved to a demonstration that the loose dirt and for one or two inches below it, of all the cellars in this City and county, will produce saltpeter, it behooves everyone to try to produce the same. Those who have a quantity of earth fit for the purpose and do not chose to try the same, would no doubt do their country a service by mentioning it to someone on the Committee of the Provincial Saltpeter works in this city who have men employed to remove the same to the works. The Pennsylvania Journal,* November 22, 1775

44. This "flying camp" was comprised of militias from the states surrounding New Jersey and was under the command of General Hugh Mercer. His headquarters was at Perth Amboy, on the Jersey shoreline, immediately across from Staten Island. It was not an easy assignment. The militias were undisciplined, untrained and often poorly led. They appeared to come and go as they pleased.

45. Now Liberty Island, site of the Statue of Liberty.

46. *i.e.*, the side of Staten Island that faced the Americans encamped across the bay at Amboy.

47. Known as *the Fighting Parson*.

48. Lord Stirling was a valiant figure. Claiming to rightfully possess the Scottish earldom of Sterling, William Alexander, as he had been christened, inherited a large fortune, which he compounded, only to lose it. Despite his claim to be a member of the British nobility, Lord Sterling served throughout the war as a high ranking officer in the Continental Army.

49. Colonel John Glover and his fishermen/soldiers from Marblehead Massachusetts were key to successfully evacuating the withdrawing soldiers on a flotilla of small craft across the East River from Brooklyn to Manhattan, thereby saving the army. Later in the year, the same unit would transport Washington and his army across the Delaware on a snowy Christmas night to surprise the Hessian mercenaries at Trenton.

50. The Fire of 1776, as it has come to be known in New York City history, was, like the World Trade Center attack, an intentional act of war. Ironically, the damage on New York City then was inflicted by its own citizens, the American patriots. George Washington, unable to withstand the British attack, was forced to abandon the city, allowing the Sons of Liberty to burn it so as to deny the invaders any sustenance. The first blaze spotted was in a sailor's brothel near Whitehall Slip, at the foot of Broadway, near the tip of the island. Still another conflagration broke out at *The Fighting Cocks Tavern* at the Battery, close by. A third began at the *White Hall Inn*, on Broadway near Bowling Green. Some of those setting the fires were caught red handed, with bundles of sticks wrapped in resin and brimstone. They were strung up by the heels and hung from tavern signs or bayoneted and cast into the fires they had created.

The flames spread to what was known as the Mall, a grove of ancient elms preserved by Peter Stuyvesant more than a century before. Soon, all the lower city was aflame. The cedar shaked wooden buildings were tinder dry and the fire quickly leapt from building to building, from street to street up the island, across and north of Wall Street, burning down the residences and shops in the mercantile area of the city. Another tongue of the fire headed west toward the Hudson, destroying in its path the venerable Trinity Church and the river homes of the wealthy. One third of the City was destroyed, nearly 500 homes.

51. Bowling Green is a small park at the foot of Broadway. It has had a long history -- the spot, for example where Dutch Governor Peter Minuit, in 1626 purchased the island of Manhattan for $24 worth of merchandise. It witnessed the Revolution. On November 1, 1765, the day the hated Stamp Tax became effective, a mob marched down Broadway, carrying an effigy of the Royal Governor. They threw rocks and bricks at Fort George, dared the Governor to come out and warned him not to enforce the tax. Then, it was off to Bowling Green, a few yards away. There, the mob burned the effigies as well as the Governor's coach which it had picked up along the way.

When news was received that the dreaded Stamp Act had been repealed, the colonists thought a bit more kindly of King George III and, in gratitude, the Common Council voted to erect in Bowling Green a statute of him on horseback. In 1770, the statute was dedicated and, a year later, an iron fence built around the park to protect it.

When it became obvious that George III meant to punish the colonists and assert greater control over the colonies, the Mob's gratitude turned to hate. And where to express that sentiment? At Bowling Green, of course.

When, in July, 1776, the newly enacted Declaration of Independence was read to Washington' troops, they reacted enthusiastically, marching with the Sons of Liberty down Broadway to Bowling Green and its six year old monument to the tyrant George III. The fence was knocked town and the statue toppled. George's head was cut off and put on a spike. The rest of him and his horse were chopped up and the pieces shipped by wagon to a foundry in Connecticut to be made into some 40,000 bullets for Patriot use.

52. Fort Paulus Hook was strategically located. It became one of a string of forts, guarding the Hudson River and the rebel held New York City. The fort sat at the crossroads of Grand and Washington streets. The site is remembered today as a park.
The position had to be abandoned when the British captured New York City. For the first time, the British occupied a piece of New Jersey. Three years later, however, it had all come fall circle. By then, Britain had concentrated its forces in New York and Paulus Hook had become Britain's *last* toehold in New Jersey Several hundred patriot troops, under the command of Henry Lee, made a surprise raid on the fort there. The British had more than 50 killed and wounded and 158 captured. American losses were but two killed, three wounded.

53. This does not refer to Bergen County, but to the region today known as Jersey City.

54. Richard Stockton, whose health had been broken in a British prison hulk in New York harbor

55. A likely explanation for the British reluctance to annihilate the Americans is that General William Howe, along with his brother, Admiral Richard Howe, had not only been given the assignment to subdue the Rebels, but to negotiate a peace with them. Both were not unsympathetic to the American cause and General Howe apparently thought that the possibility of peace would be jeopardized by too ardent a crushing of the American army.

56. A hamlet in Burlington County on the road from Mount Holly to Borden Town, four miles north of the former.

57. Now known as Columbus, Burlington County

58. Once again, with the assistance of Col. Glover and his Marblehead sailors, who, fewer than six months earlier, had helped evacuate Washington's troops that had been trapped on Long Island.

59. One of the handful wounded that morning at the Battle of Trenton was a young officer, James Monroe. Fortunately for all Americans, he survived his wound to become one of the principal authors of the Constitution and the President of the United States.

60. Including General Mercer of the Flying Camp

61. It was not the only pro British press. *The Pennsylvania Evening Post* and *The Pennsylvania Ledger* performed the same roles in occupied Philadelphia as did the *Gazetteer* in New York.

62. Charles Rivington had succeeded Richard Chiswell in Paternoster row in 1711 and specialized in religious books. After his death in 1742, the business was then carried on, for the next half century, by his son John. His descendants kept up the business of the House of Rivington at least through the end of the 1800's and perhaps longer.

63. Not the American Constitution, which was still fifteen years away, but the British Constitution

64. A public notice relating to Rivington's son's absconding from an apprenticeship suggests how hated the Loyalist printer was.

Runaway from his apprenticeship, to the shoemaker's trade, James Rivington, jun., son to the notorious James, the royal, alias, lying, printer, in New York. Those who knew the father need no other description of the son, than to be informed, allowing for age and experience, he is, in low cunning, deceit, lying and roguery, equal to the sire and proves, without the wedding knot, that he is the real offspring, full blooded. It is thought probable that this youth, on the rumor of the French Fleet, is gone, agreeable to Tory policy to join the American army that, by dividing the family, part of the breed can be saved, even should the property be lost. Whoever takes up the identical son, shall be weekly entitled to the father's privileged Gazette, except those which may happen to contain aberrations from the truth." New Jersey Journal, July 26, 1780

    65. Apparently, the name of *The New York Gazette* must have been appropriated by another, during the more than a year period that Rivington had returned to London. New York was a "rebel" town during that period and, not surprisingly, so was this *New York Gazette*.

    66. This was written supposedly by Annis Boudinot Stockton and is reported to be the first political communication ever written by a New Jersey woman and addressed to the editor of a newspaper. It would be difficult to find a more knowledgeable and dedicated advocate for the American cause. She was the sister of Elias Boudinot, a leading member of the New Jersey Bar, who quickly became a delegate to Congress and a government official, reaching his highest office in 1782, when, as President of the Congress established under The Articles of Confederation, he was the chief executive of the United States. Her husband Richard Stockton had signed the Declaration of Independence for New Jersey and one of the new State's most prominent men. Annis Boudinot Stockton was not removed, by her social position and wealth, from the sentiments of the suffering women whose voice she purported to speak. She wrote this letter in 1778, after her home had been looted and burned by the British and after her husband Richard Stockton had been captured, imprisoned in New York City and, broken both in spirit and in health, and after he had executed, in exchange for his freedom, an amnesty agreement, a surrender which robbed

him of much of the admiration and respect of the people that he had enjoyed before.

67. More than sixty were to die of small pox that winter in Morristown.

68. Newly enlisted or conscripted troops

69. A contraction for "seven nights" - *i.e.*, a week. It is not unlike a "fortnight" meaning fourteen nights or two weeks

70. A barber.

71. Ossining, New York

72. Peekskill, New York. "Kill" was a Dutch word for stream or river.

73. Don Juan de Marelles who was Spain's representative to the new American government.

74. *The Gazette's* veracity was so suspect that it was known as the *Brussels Gazette of America*, a paper known throughout Europe for its notorious falsehoods. Americans referred to it more simply as *Rivington's Lying Gazette*.

75. All Jersey residents who, as Loyalists, joined the British Army at the war's inception.

76. New Market

77. This might have been an overstatement in favor of the Americans, a rarity with Rivington and obviously unintentional. Washington had probably only two thirds that number of troops at his disposal, the enlistments of many having ended with the last campaign.

78. The last feint alone was expensive to the British:

> *"It is conjectured on good grounds that Howe, in moving back from Brunswick to Somerset, and from thence back to his last embarkation for Staten Island did not lose in killed, wounded and deserted, much short of 1000 men."* The Pennsylvania Journal, July 16, 1777

79. This was another feint by the British that, initially successful, was quickly abandoned:

> *"A great part of our army has left the mountains and General Lord Sterling was posted at the Short Hills with about a thousand men. On Thursday morning, General Howe, having reinforced his army with all the marines that could be spared, began his march again towards us... His numbers were from 12 to 14,000. He met with Lord Sterling's party early in the morning, a smart engagement ensued and our men stood their ground manfully for a considerable time, but the amazing superiority of numbers obliged them to retreat."* The Pennsylvania Journal, July 2, 1777

80. Later to be known as the *Father of the American Navy*

81. Quinine

82. A kind of loose fitting gown, formerly worn by women

83. If you were wondering how this marriage turned out, an article in the same paper, just two weeks later, revealed the suspicious outcome:

> *"We hear that Mr. John Gordon of Somerset County, who lately married Miss Sukey Lane (mentioned in Number 18 of this paper) was, a few days ago, thrown from his horse, by which he was hurt so much that he died in a short time after, in consequence of which, it is said, a considerable*

estate fell to his widow." The New Jersey Gazette, April 15, 1778

84. This is said to be the first weather record published in any New Jersey newspaper

85. Cattle were branded and then permitted to roam on islands along the Jersey shore. Many evolved into "wild cattle" -- Jersey Longhorns, if you will -- which were not extinct in Cape May County until as late as 1880.

86. On e of several salt works established along the Jersey coast which extracted salt from sea water via evaporation.

87. Philadelphia was occupied by the British and Galloway was the leader of the local Loyalist government.

88. Forman was later pardoned on the conditions that he leave New Jersey within two months, the United States within six months and that he never return to either.

89. The King of France

90. John Cozens was exchanged as a prisoner of war over a year and a half later

91. So called by reason of the color of their uniform coats. Many were loyalists recruited locally and sent back to raid their neighbors and kin.

92. Today, Middle Towne Point is called Matawan Borough and the Burrows House still stands on Main Street. One lady, who grew up in the house next door, swears to there having been blood stains on the

inside stairway from this skirmish and that a tunnel ran from its cellar out to nearby Matawan Creek where patriots would board boats to attack British positions. Before the town became a suburb to New York, special respect was shown the house each 4th of July.

93. This report in "Jemmy Rivington's royal, loyal, lying Gazette" was answered by the rebel *New Jersey Gazette* of July 1, asserting that it was the British soldiers who ran away when surprised by the Americans

94. Her real name was Mary Ludwig Hays.

95. Lee was convicted of disobedience of orders in not attacking the enemy as ordered and in making an unnecessary and disorderly retreat by thirteen fellow officers, Major General Lord Stirling acting as President of the Board.

96. The King of France

97. Benjamin Franklin, America's ambassador to France and instrumental in securing France's assistance to the American cause

98. How prophetic this toast was! The American Revolution and its assertion of the rights of man spread to France a decade or so later and then through Europe. Today, it has seized South Africa and toppled Russia and its hope lives in the hearts of those still oppressed in China and elsewhere.

99. Captain Zabriskie died 38 hours later from the bullet wound in the small of his back. He was eulogized by the rebel *Jersey Gazette* as "a terror to the enemies of his country and the aversion of only the people that

deserve to be slaves. We that have experienced and been protected by his valor, weep at his loss." *The New Jersey Gazette,* July 15, 1778

100. England had General William Howe and his brother Admiral Richard Howe, as well as Sir Henry Clinton. The American forces had General George Clinton (also Governor of New York) and, his brother General James Clinton and General Robert Howe of North Carolina. .

101. *The New York Gazette,* June 24, 1776

102. After the Battle of Yorktown, Lafayette returned to France, where he was to play a role in that nation's securing her own liberty. In 1824, he came back to America and was feted throughout the land during a year's tour of the Republic that he and France had helped to birth. Indeed, it was in recognition of America's obligation to men like Lafayette and the nation of France that General Pershing, more than a century and a half later, exclaimed "Lafayette, we have come!" to announce the landing of American troops in France to aid the French to recapture their country from the Germans in World War I.

103. But he was not the Baron he claimed to be, although he was married to a countess

104. which he was to dissipate with high living

105 . He was also the grandfather of America's greatest general, Robert E. Lee.

106. On the other hand, Britain had arguably the finest army in the world and it was familiar with the provinces. Its officers had been seasoned in the decades

of war with France and Spain, much of which fighting took place on the North American continent. The British also had allies. Loyalists, fleeing the rebel sentiment of countryside, formed regiments, such as The New Jersey Volunteers, to join with the regular British army in many major engagements. They also guided commando type raids into their former neighborhoods, gathering provisions for the British troops stationed in New York and kidnapping their former neighbors who had espoused the American cause. Britain also recruited the Indians of the Iroquois confederacy to harass the frontiers. Finally, mercenaries, especially from the German state of Hesse, who were ethnically and politically connected to the House of Hanover, were also employed to put down the rebellion.

107. On rare occasions, some prisoners were able to escape the British prison ships:

"Last Wednesday morning, about one o'clock, made their escape from the Goodhope prison ship, in the North River, nine captains and two privates. Among the number was Captain James Prince, who has been confined for four months, and having no prospect of being exchanged, concerted a plan, in conjunction with the other gentlemen, to make their escape which they effected in the following manner: They confined the mate, disarmed the sentinels and hoisted out the boat which was on deck. They brought off nine stands of arms, one pair of pistols and a sufficient supply of ammunition, being determined not to be taken alive. They had scarce got clear of the ship before the alarm was given, when they were fired on by three different ships, but fortunately no person was hurt. The New Jersey Gazette, October 20, 1779

108. It is fitting and appropriate for one to die on behalf of his fatherland

109. For example, in Trenton, the Tories burned both the Presbyterian and Episcopal churches, as well as the Meeting House of the pacifist, neutral Quakers.

110. Loyalists who had lived in New Jersey before the hostilities

111. The line uttered to Cicero to the Roman Senate regarding Cataline's attempt to usurp the Roman Republic. Bemoaning Rome's more decay, the phrase roughly translates as "Oh Times that we live in, Oh Customs that we hold".

112. This was one of three New Jersey massacres of prisoners by the British during the war, the others occurring at Hancock's Bridge and Osborne Island.

113. The Hessians were more disappointing to the British Command than helpful. They did not get along with the British troops, deserted in large numbers and often failed to fight enthusiastically at several battles including Trenton.

114. Washington was the ultimate spy master for the Americans, personally plotting trails of false clues and disinformation so as to give his out numbered troops a better chance against the British.

115. This is not the Hudson River, which originally had been called the North River, but the Navesink River in Monmouth County, which together with the Shrewsbury River (sometimes called the South River) flanked the Rumson peninsula of today. At the

time of the Revolution, both the Navesink and the Shrewsbury flowed directly into the Atlantic Ocean, although neither does today

116. Today, the location of the bridge connecting Rumson to Sea Bright, the latter at the time being a sandbar just emerging from the Atlantic

117. Lighthorse Henry Lee of Virginia (not to be confused with the unrelated Charles Lee, court-martialed for failing to fight at the Battle of Monmouth). For his action here, Henry Lee was awarded one of the eight medals awarded by the Congress during the entire war.

118. The artillery, which General Knox commanded, was wintering there

119. William Franklin, who, of course, had already been expelled from New Jersey.

120. About 3 or 4 miles above Paterson

121. From Hoppertown, now Hohokus

122. The lighthouse still stands, although now more than a mile from the Hook's tip.

123. Reportedly, Major Byles was shot on the spot because he failed to "present the hilt of his sword in front, while surrendering."

124. A poignant letter, dated January 4, 1782, from an officer of the British army occupying Charleston South Carolina to his friend in London gives some idea of Charleston's period of occupation:

The retrograde progress of our arms in this Country, you have seen in your newspapers, if they dare to tell you the truth. This precious commodity is not to be had in the Government paper printed here, for Rivington hangs over the press and will suffer nothing to pass but what is palpable, that is, in plain terms, what is false. Our victories have been dearly bought, for the rebels seem to grow stronger by every defeat, like Antaeus, of whom it was fabled, being the son of the goddess Teitus, or the earth, every fall he received from Hercules gave him more strength, so that the hero was forced to strangle him in his arms at last. I wish our Ministry would send us a Hercules to conquer these obstinate Americans whose aversion to the cause of Britain grows stronger every day.

If you go into company with any of them occasionally, they are barely civil, and that is, as Jack Falstaff says, "by compulsion". They are in general sullen, silent and thoughtful. The King's Health they dare not refuse but they drink it in such a manner, as if they expected they would choke on it.

The Assemblies which our officers have opened in hopes of giving an air of gaiety and cheerfulness to themselves and the inhabitants are but dull and gloomy meetings. The men play at cards, indeed, to avoid talking. The women are seldom or never persuaded to dance. Even in their dresses, the females seem to bid us defiance; the gay toys that are imported here, they despise. They wear their own home spun manufactures and take care to have on their breast knots, and even on their shoes, something that resembles the flag of thirteen stripes. An officer told Lord Cornwallis not long ago, that he believed that if he had destroyed all the men in North America, we should have enough to do to conquer the women.

I am heartedly tired of this country and wish myself at home.

125. According to *The New Jersey Gazette* of October 4, 1780, Andre was undone by a British deserter who recognized him, despite his disguise, and who alerted Arnold of it. Fortunately, Alexander Hamilton, Washington's aide, was there at West Point at the time, so that Arnold could not suppress the information.

126. "*Poughkeepsie, October 2. Andre was taken by three young men of the militia of Westchester County, Messrs Pawling, Deane, and VanWeert. He offered them for his liberty his gold watch, one thousand guineas and as large a quantity of goods as they could bring from New York, which, with republican virtue, they refused, informing Andre that they were American and were not to be purchased.*" *The New Jersey Gazette*, October 11, 1780.

127. John Cleves Symmes, a resident of Newtown, Sussex County, helped draft New Jersey's Constitution in 1776. After Independence had been achieved, he became one of New Jersey's representatives in the Continental Congress. Illustrative of the American move westward, Symmes then relocated to Ohio where he was appointed Federal Judge in the Northwest Territory, now Ohio. Two his children also received notoriety. His daughter Anne was to become the bride of President William Henry Harrison. His son, John, Jr. proposed and lectured on the proposition that the earth was hollow and its interior inhabited.

128. Cornwallis was the Second Earl of Cornwallis and active politically in the House of Lords

for the last decade and a half. His friend and ally was George Sackville Germain, British Secretary of State for the American colonies who virtually directed the Revolution War from London for the British. Clinton hated Lord Germain too, and he knew the sentiment was reciprocated. The man had been cashiered from the British service for cowardice at the battle of Minden in 1759, where Cornwallis had served under him. Now he was, in effect, the commander in chief of the British forces in America. Another irony.

Cornwallis had another advantage over Clinton, which Clinton knew about --a dormant commission that allowed Cornwallis to take command of the forces in America, should Clinton become incapacitated. Its purpose was to prevent Von Knyphausen, the commander of the Hessians who technically outranked the junior British officer, from taking command in a crisis. But, as a practical matter, Lord Germain easily could classify Clinton as incapacitated with the signing of his name to a proclamation to that effect. Cornwallis would be his successor.

129. George Rex, translating as King George

130. This are had been settled by the Dutch in the 1600's, evident from the "kill" ending of the name Fishkill. In Dutch, kill meant stream.

131. Dr. Scudder, a physician, had been a delegate to the New Jersey Provincial Congress that had declared its Independence from England, the Speaker of the wartime General Assembly and one of New Jersey's representatives in the Continental Congress that sat in Philadelphia during most of the war. He also served in the militia and fought in the Battle of Monmouth in 1778. A description of his burial and the family he left behind

should once more make us more aware of the heroic sacrifices made by the Patriots:

"His remains were removed from the place of action to his own house, with all the decency and solemnity suitable to so mournful and melancholy an occasion. After which his remains, attended by the most numerous and respectable concourse of people ever known on a similar occasion in this county, were interred at the Presbyterian church in Freehold, with the honors of war. Few men have fell in the country that were so useful in life, or so generally mourned for in death. He was a tender husband, an affectionate parent, a sympathetic, generous, real friend, a disinterested, determined patriot, and has since the commencement of the war devoted his time, his talent, and a large part of a comfortable estate to the service of his country, and what will add a luster to the whole, we trust he is the finished Christian.

"Thus has this great and good man fell at the prime of life, and in the midst of his usefulness, having left behind him an inconsolable widow, five amiable children, and a very numerous acquaintance to lament his fall." New Jersey Gazette, October 24, 1781

132. *"The circumstances attending the death of the above mentioned Philip White, were as follows: On Saturday the 30th of March last, he was surprised by a party of our people, and after he had laid down his arms in token of surrendering himself a prisoner, he again took up his musket and killed a son of Col. Hendrickson; he was however taken by our light horse, and, on his way from Colts Neck to Freehold, where they were conducting him, he again attempted to make his escape from the guard, who called on him several times to surrender, but he continued running, although often crossed and re crossed by the light horse, and desired to

stop and finally, when leaping into a bog, impassable by the horse, he received a stroke in the head with a sword, which killed him instantly. The above facts have not only been proved by the affidavits of our friends who were present, but by the voluntary and candid testimony of one Aaron White, who was taken prisoner with the said Philip."

133. It was a difficult relocation for the ex-slaves. But it was better than servitude. Some, calling themselves Black Pioneers, gleefully accepted a special settlement for the "black gentry" and named it Birchtown, in honor of the General who had signed the pass that gave them liberty, free to go wherever and do whatever they wanted. A second settlement was on the other side of Nova Scotia at the Bay of Fundy, at a black township named Brindley Town. Some, led by a Thomas Brownspriggs, went even further north to Chedabucto Bay and Cape Breton Island. It is in Guysborough county in the Cape Breton Islands where one still can find the purer lineage, descendants of the group, led by Thomas Brownspriggs, in 1784.

INDICES

INDEX TO PERSONAL NAMES

A

ADAMS, Samuel -53
ALEXANDER, William (see also Lord Stirling) - 201, 356
ALLAN, Col. - -200
ALLEN, Abraham - 234
ALLEN, Ethan - 74
ALLEN, Lieut. Col. Isaac - 166
ALLEN, Moses -11
ALLENS, Col. William -112
ALLI, Hyder - 322
ANDRE, Maj. John - 289, 290, 291, 370
ANGEL, Col. (first name unknown) - 280
ANNAN, Davis - 349
ANSTRUTHER, Capt. (first name unknown) - 271
ANTOINETTE, Queen Marie - 340
ARBUTHNOT, Adm. Marriot -244, 245, 280
ARMSTRONG, Capt. (first name unknown) - 208

ARNOLD, Benedict - 136, 137, 182, 288, 289, 290, 291, 308, 316, 328, 350, 354, 370
ARNOLD, Mrs. Benedict - 292
ASGILL, Charles - 340
ASGILL, Lady - 340
ATLEE, Col. Samuel - 82, 83
AYRES, (captain of British merchant ship) - 43, 44, 45
AYRES, Col. (first name unknown) - 28
AYRES, William - 11

B

BACHE, Theophilus - 303
BACON, (first name unknown) - 218
BAINBRIDGE, Dr. (first name unknown) - 80
BALDWIN, Nehemiah - 18
BALL, Joseph - 298
BALL, Stephen - 232

BANTA, John - 234
BANTA, Weart - 233
BARBER, Col. Francis - 183
BARNES, (first name unknown) - 131
BARRE, Col. Isaac - 28
BARRET, Lieut. (first name unknown) - 191
BARRY, Commodore John - 142, 143, 302
BARTHOLOMEW, Benjamin - 172
BARTON, John - 159
BARTON, Joseph Jr. - 159
BARTON, Col. Joseph - 158, 159, 232, 236, 238
BARTON, Mrs. Joseph (first name unknown) - 159
BAYLOR, Col. George - 191, 219,
BEACH, Ezekiel - 68, 69, 169
BECKWITH, Maj. George - 312
BEDFORD, Gunning - 353
BEEKMAN, (first name unknown) - 315, 323
BELINDA (Annis Boudinot Stockton pen name) - 108
BELT, Capt. Walter - 296
BELTKIN, Maj. (first name unknown) - 201
BENSON (first name unknown) - 253
BERGEN, (first name unknown) - 317
BICKHAM, Geo. - 95, 120
BIRCH, James - 172
BIRCH, Samuel - 344, 373
BLACK, John - 13, 14, 353
BLAIR, William - 284
BLANCH, Col. (first name unknown) - 274
BLANCHARD, (first name unknown) - 103
BLANCHARD, Cornelius - 292
BLAND, Maj. Theodorick - 157, 205
BLOOMFIELD, Joseph - 207, 299
BLOOMFIELD, Thomas - 232
BOARDMAN, Rev. Benjamin - 86
BOELLISFELT, Widow (first name unknown) - 256
BOGART, Cornelius - 234
BOGART, Matthias - 234
BOGERT, David Ritzema - 261
BONNER, Lieut. Col. (first name unknown) - 183
BOSKIRK, (first name unknown) - 124
BOSKIRK, Col. - 211

BOUDINOT, Annis - 360
BOUDINOT, Elias - 46, 360
BOURKE, Stephen - 252
BOWEN, David - 155
BOWEN, John - 227
BOWNE, Samuel - 332
BOYD, James - 222
BOYD, William - 151
BRACKENRIDGE, Hugh 14, 352
BRADFORD, William, Jr.- 10,
BRADFORD, William Sr. - 351
BRAILEY, Col. (first name unknown) - 247
BRANT, Joseph - 184, 189, 246, 2474
BRANT, Molly - 184, 185
BREEZE, Col. (first name unknown) - 235
BROOK, Capt. (first name unknown) - 22
BROWER, Abraham - 260, 261
BROWN, Maj. Andrew -317
BROWN [E] John - 124, 125
BROWN, John, a Negro man - 299
BROWN, Capt. (first name unknown) - 52
BROWNSPRIGGS, Thomas - 373

BUCHANAN, Capt. (first name unknown) - 301
BUCK, Aaron – 334
BULL, (first name unknown) -61-
BURDGE, Jonathan - 252
BURGOYNE, John - 133, 141, 187,283
BURKE, Edmund - 330
BURKE,[BOURKE] Stephen (*aka* Stephen Emmons) - 252
BURNET, (first name unknown) - 216
BURNEY, William - 89
BURR, Aaron Jr.- 12, 350
BURR, Aaron Sr. - 350
BURROWS, John - 178
BUSKIRK, Lt. Col. Abraham (see also Van Bushkirk) - 166
BUSKIRK, George - 233, 234
BUTE (first name unknown) - 111
BUTLER, John - 184, 185, 246
BUTLER, Walter - 184, 185
BYLES, Maj., (first name unknown) - 272, 273, 368

C

CALDWELL, Mrs. James - 219, 279
CALDWELL, Rev. James -81, 219, 266
CAMBDEN, Lord - 28
CAMPBELL, Donald - 14,
CAMPBELL, George - 234
CAMPBELL, Gen. John - 244
CAMPELL, David - 100, 101
CAMPELL, Donald - 352
CAMPELL, Mr - 271
CANFIELD, Job - 284
CANFIELD, Thomas - 284
CAPE, (first name unknown) - 311
CARLETON, Sir Guy - 331, 334, 338, 340, 341, 342, 343, 344
CASTERLINE, (first name unknown,) - 280
CATALINE - 367
CATTLE, Elisha - 227
CAYFORD, Richard - 168
CHADDOCK, Capt. (first name unknown) - 235
CHAMBERLAIN, John - 256
CHAMBERS, Capt. (first name unknown) - 42, 354
CHAMBERS, Francis - 299
CHAPMAN, Rev. (first name unknown)- 165
CHEESEMAN, Edmund -13,14
CHETWOOD, John- 47
CHEVERS, (first name unknown) - 6
CHEW, Jonathan - 172
CHISWELL, Richard - 359
CHURCHILL, Winston - 226
CHUVER, Dr. Jonathan - 256
CICERO- 367
CLARINDA (see also Susan Livingston) - 116, 117
CLINTON, Gen. George - 365
CLINTON, Gen. Henry - 111, 125, 126, 179, 180, 181, 193, 238, 245, 274, 278, 280, 281, 285, 286, 289, 290, 308, 309, 310, 311, 319, 320, 331, 334, 337, 338, 339, 343, 344, 365, 371
CLINTON, Gen. James - 248, 249, 365
CLOSSON, (first name unknown) - 280
CLOUGH, Maj. (first name unknown) - 219
COCHRAN Dr. John - 81, 212
COLE, Jacob - 233, 234

COLE, William - 257
COLE, (first name unknown) - 254
COLLINS, Isaac - 107, 154, 325
CONNER, Adj. Gen. Morgan - 208
COOK, Maj. (first name unknown - 334
COOK, Col. (first name unknown) - 135
COOK, Paterson - 172
COOPER, Daniel -9
COOPER, Jacob -9
COOPER, William - 9
COREY, Jeremiah - 232
CORLIES, John - 255
CORNWALLIS, Lord Charles - 95, 119, 132, 136, 288, 309, 310, 319, 320, 321, 323, 324, 325, 328, 329, 369, 370, 371
CORTELYOU, Jacques - 304
CORTELYOU, Simon - 304
COTTREL, (first name unknown) - 332
COUSINS, Capt. John (see also John Cozens) - 178
COVENHOUSE, Jacob - 179
COVENHOVEN, John - 171
COVENHOVEN, Justice (first name unknown) - 235

COVENHOVEN, Peter - 332
COWELL, Dr. (first name unknown) - 80
COX, Col. (first name unknown) - 150
COX, Lawrence - 172
COXE, (first name unknown) - 7
COXE, William - 24, 25
COZENS, John - 363
CRAIG, David - 232
CRAIG, Captain (first name not known) - 230
CRANE, Mrs. (first name unknown) - 8
CRANE, Joseph - 312
CRANE, Stephen - 46
CRAUFORD, George - 224
CREIGHTON, Samuel - 299
CRIPS, Whitten -227
CROLIUS, Peter - 147
CUNNINGHAM, Capt. (first name unknown) - 6
CUSHING , - 35
CUSHING, Thomas -52
CUSTIS, John - 203120
CUSTIS, Mrs. John - 200
CUSTIS, Martha - 196

D

D'ESTAING, Count Charles - 106, 300
D'ORVILLERS, Count - 242
DARTMOUTH, Lord William - 28, 39
DAVENPORT, (first name unknown) - 103, 334
DAVIS, Capt. (first name unknown) - 233
DAVIS, Dr. (first name unknown) - 83
DAY, J. - 27
DAY, R. - 27
DAYTON, Elias - 345
DAYTON, (first name unknown) - 103
DAYTON, Capt. - 292
DAYTON, Col. - 198, B280
DE TERNAY, Charles - 277
DE MARELLES, Don Juan - 361
DE GRASSE, Count Francois - 318, 319, 322, 323, 324, 325
DE KALB, Johann - 200, 288
DEANE, (first name unknown) - 370
DEBOW, (first name unknown) - 259
DEHART, Lieut. Jacob Morris - 158
DEHART, John - 46
DEMAREST, Hendrik - 233, 234
DEMAREST, Peter - 234
DEMAREST, Samuel - 233, 234
DENICE, Jacques - 332
DENNIS, John - 148
DENNIS, Capt. Benjamin - 253, 254
DICK, Samuel - 227
DICKERSON, Maj. Gen. - 282
DICKINSON, Gen. Philemon - 124, 205, 206, 313, 322
DICKINSON, Maj. (first name unknown) - 183
DIGBY, Adm. Robert - 331, 339, 342, 343
DILKS, John - 172
DILKS, Joshua - 172
DILL, Joseph - 172
DILLON, William - 190
DONOP, Count Carl - 142, 281
DORSET, Joseph - 284
DOUGLASS, Capt. (first name unknown) - 301
DRAPER, Richard - 38
DRUMMOND, Maj. Robert - 166

E

EARL, (first name unknown) - 124
EDGAR, (first name

unknown) - 273
EDWARDS, Maj. (first name unknown) - 266, 296
EDWARDS, Jonathan - 350
EGBERT, Maj. (first name unknown) - 282
ELLIS, Col. (first name unknown) - 176
ELLIS, Joseph - 52
ELMER, Dr. (first name unknown) - 82
ELMER, Philemon - 147
EMMANS, Stephen - 252
ERSKINE, Sir William - 129, 238
ESTER, Queen - 185
EVANS, Jr., Doctor (first name unknown) - 191, 219
EWING, Thomas - 168

F

FAGAN, Jacob - 252
FARMER, Col. Christopher Billop - 209
FARMER, Jasper - 349
FELL, John - 172
FENNIMORE, Abraham - 172
FENTON, Lewis - 259
FISHER, H. - 54
FITZ RANDOLF, Lieut. Asher - 318
FITZ RANDOLF, Jacob - 170, 171
FITZ RANDOLF, Capt. Nathaniel - 209, 231
FITZ RANDOLF, Ensignr - 311
FLEMING, (first name unknown) - 236
FORD, Col. (first name unknown) - 205, 234, 235
FORD, Jacob, Jr. - 73
FORMAN (first name unknown) - 215
FORMAN, Ezekiel - 173, 364
FRANKLIN, Benjamin - 28, 145, 175, 187, 200, 240, 243, 364
FRANKLIN, John - 172
FRANKLIN, William - 8, 63, 64, 244, 368
FRAUNCES, Samuel - 343
FREDERICK the Great, King - 200
FREEMAN, Justice (first name unknown) - 273
FRELINGHOUSEN, Frederick - 12, 349, 350
FRENEAU, Philip - 13
FUSMAN, Daniel - 172

G

GAGE, General Thomas - 39, 49, 51

GALLOWAY, Joseph - 162, 177, 363
GAMBLE, (first name unknown) - 255
GARDINER, Rufus - 301
GARDNER, Hannah - 152
GARDNER Levy - 152
GARRISON, Gen (first name unknown) - 244
GARTHWAIT, Mrs. 8
GARISTE, Henry - 46
GATES, Lady - 200
GATES, Gen. Horatio - 186, 189, 200, 202, 246, 283, 288
GEORGE III, King - 23, 27, 30, 46, 51, 85, 88, 222, 357, 358
GERMAINE, Lord George - 320; 330, 371
GIBBON, John - 157
GILBERT, Capt. Robert - 296
GILBERTSON, John - 253
GILMORE, David - 309
GLOVER, Col. John - 356, 359
GODWIN, Abraham - 15
GOETSCHIUS, Maj. (first name unknown) - 260
GORDON, Abraham [see also Abraham Godwin] - 15
GORDON, Lieut. Col. Cosmo - 116, 117
GORDON, John - 152, 362
GORDON, Maj. (first name unknown) -
GRAHAM, Charles - 27
GRANDLE, Capt. Thomas - 296
GRANGER, Capt. (first name unknown) - 255
GRAVES, Rear Adm. Thomas - 285, 320
GREEN, Rev. (first name unknown) - 166
GREEN, Col. Christopher - 142
GREEN, Mrs. Nathaniel - 241
GREEN, Gen Nathaniel - 84, 89, 94, 137, 280, 290, 310, 316, 319, 322, 323, 324
GRENVILLE, George - 342
GRIFFIN, Col. (first name unknown) - 93
GRIFFITH, Capt. (first name unknown) - 222
GRIGGS, Matthew - 284
GROOM, Elijah - 252
GROVER, William - 173
GUEST, Henry - 151

H

HALDIMAND Gen.

Frederick - 222, 244
HALL, David - 227, 232
HALL, Edward - 227
HALSEY, Ananias - 67
HAMILTON, Col. Alexander - 116, 290, 350; 370
HAMMEL, (first name unknown) - 124
HAMMET, William - 172
HAMPTON, Jonathan - 102, 103
HANCOCK, (first name not known) - 218
HAND, Col. Elijah - 228, 247
HAND, Jesse - 52
HANKINS, Capt. John - 150, 304
HANKINSON, Kenneth - 150
HARDENBERGH Rev. J.R. [Hardenburgh] - 12, 165, 349
HARRISON, William Henry - 370
HARTLEY, (first name unknown) - 60
HATCH, (first name unknown) - 70
HATCH, Col. (first name unknown) - 70, 83
HAWKINS, Capt. (first name unknown) - 332
HAYDEN, Capt. (first name unknown) - 236
HAYS, Maj. (first name unknown) - 216
HAYS, Mary Ludwig - 216, 364
HAYSE, Maj. Samuel - 284
HEARD, General - 206
HEDDEN, Justice Joseph - 214, 216, 268
HEDDEN, Mrs. Joseph - 268
HENDERSON, Lieut. (first name unknown) - 284
HENDRICKS, Capt. Baker - 313
HENDRICKS, O. - 312
HENDRICKSON, Garret - 332
HENDRICKSON, Hendrick - 332
HENDRICKSON, Col. - 235, 236, 237, 372, 373
HERD, William - 292
HESSE, the Landgrave of - 243
HETFIELD, Cornelius - 232, 268, 292
HETFIELD, Job - 268,
HETFIELD, Smith - 232, 268, 292, 312
HETFIELD, (first name unknown) - 281
HEULINGS, Isaac - 149
HOAR (first name unknown) - 14
HODGE, Hugh - 13
HOLLAND, John - 299

HOLMES, Benjamin - 227
HOLMES, Col. Asher - 332
HOLMES, Justice (first name unknown) - 235
HOLT, John - 104
HOOD, Admiral - 317
HOPPER, Capt. Jonathan - 257
HORNBLOWER, Josiah - 311
HORTENTIUS [see also William Livingston] - 198, 199
HOUSTON, William - 161
HOWARD, Lieut. Col. (first name unknown) - 270, 271
HOWARD, General Frederick - 28
HOWE, Adm. Richard - 192, 358, 365
HOWE, Maj. Gen..Robert - 286, 365
HOWE, Gen. William - 62, 74, 77, 78, 80, 88, 91, 96, 103, 108, 109, 120, 127, 132, 133, 134, 136, 179, 180 138, 139, 140, 141, 210, 221, 297, 309, 310, 344, 358, 362, 365
HOWELL, Ebenezer - 227
HUDDY, Capt. Joshua - 334, 335, 336, 337,338, 340
HUFTY, Jacob - 227
HUMPHREYS, William - 25
HUNTER, Rev. Andrew - 197
HUNTINGTON, Samuel - 121
HUTCHINSON, (first name unknown) - 280
HUYLER, Cornelius - 234
HUYLER, J. - 233
HYLER, Adam - 299, 304, 305, 306, 333

I

ILIFF (first name unknown) - 124, 125
INNESS, William - 149
INSLEE, (first name unknown) - 280
IRVINE, Gen. William -265

J

JACKSON, Charles - 231, 299
JACKSON, Harry - 299
JAY, Sir James - 324
JAY John - 351
JEFFRIES (first name unknown) - 53
JOHNSON, Dr. (first name unknown - 16

JOHNSON, James- 284
JOHNSON, John - 184
JOHNSTON, Guy - 184,
JOHNSTON, G. - 207
JOHNSON, Col. Philip - 213
JOHNSON, Sir William 184 -
JONES, Aquilla - 259
JONES, Capt. John Paul - 300, 301
JONES, Maj. Gen. Valentine - 162
JULIUS, Maj. (Count of Mont Fort) - 201

K

KEARNEY, Maj. (first name unknown) - 197
KEEN, Nicholas - 227
KEESBY, Edmund - 227
KENNEDY, Capt. (first name unknown) - 10
KEPPLE, Adm. Augustus - 242
KEYS, (first name unknown) - 49
KIMBLE, (first name unknown) - 250
KING, Frederick - 149
KIRKPATRICK, (first name unknown) - 324
KNOWLTON, Lieut. Col. (first name unknown) - 87

KNOX, Mrs. Henry - 241
KNOX, Gen. Henry - 74, 240, 368
KNYPHAUSEN, Gen. Wilhelm - 244, 278, 279, 281, 282
KOSCIUSZKO, Tadeusz - 200
KOWATCH, Col. (first name unknown) - 201

L

LAFAYETTE, Marquis de - 181, 200, 278, 284, 286, 365
LAING, Capt. John - 296
LAMB, Col. John - 280
LANE, Sukey - 152, 362
LEE, Gen. Charles - 181, 182, 183, 184, 364, 368
LEE, Henry - 12, 13, 201, 202, 239, 240, 259, 269, 284, 351; 358, 368
LEE, Robert E. - 351
LESEGH, (first name unknown)- 280
LESHIER, John; see also Lozler, Le Sheair - 260
LEWIS, Warner - 200
LIGHT [Leydt], Matthew - 349

LINCOLN, Benjamin - 202, 210, 283
LINN, William - 12, 13,
LIPPINCOTT, Capt. Richard - 305, 338, 440
LITTLE, Capt. Christopher - 178
LITTLE, John - 235
LIVINGSTON, Col. Henry - 182
LIVINGSTON, Henry Brocholst - 12, 351
LIVINGSTON, Susan - 116
LIVINGSTON, William - 46, 71, 72, 91, 116, 117, 163, 165, 173, 176, 182, 198, 225, 226, 251, 325, 326, 327, 339, 351;
LLOYD, David - 118, 123, 124, 125, 126, 172
LONGWORTH, Isaac - 215
LONGWORTH, Thomas - 215
LORD, Isaac - 172
LOT, Capt. Jeromus - - 304
LOUIS XVI, King - 240, 243, 322, 323, 324, 340, 363
LOW, John - 10
LOWTHER, Sir James - 329
LOZLER, [le Sheair, Leshier] John - 260, 261
LUCE, Capt. (first name unknown) - 232
LUCERNE, Monsieur - 121
LUDLOW, (first name unknown) - 264
LYON, Zophar - 284

M

MCCALLISTER, Lieut. (first name unknown) - 240
MCCUTCHEN, Capt. (first name unknown) - 6
MCDOUGALL, Brig. Gen. Alexander - 120
MCKNIGHT, Rev. Charles - 348
MCKNIGHT, Dr. Charles Jr. - 13, 14, 28, 366, 379
MCKNIGHT, Capt. Richard - 235, 236, 237
MCLEAN Gen. Francis - 244
MCMULLEN, Robert - 190
MCNAIR, Lieut. (first name unknown) - 157, 212
MACPHERSON, Lieut. Col. (first name unknown) - 270, 271
MADISON, James - 14, 353

MAGAW, Col. Robert - 79, 88, 208
MANN, Elias - 312
MARCH, Christopher - 232
MARCH, Lewis - 232
MARION, Francis - 310
MARRINER, William - 303, 304
MARSH, Ephraim - 312
MARTIN, Lieut. (first name unknown) - 135
MARTIN, Col. Ephraim - 69, 169
MARTIN, Gov Josiah - 244
MATTHEWS, Mayor David - 123, 244, 303
MAWHOOD, Col. Charles - 227
MAXWELL, Gen. William - 128, 130, 135, 198, 232, 247, 279
MAXWELL, George - 27
MEE, John - 124, 125
MEEKER, Capt. Samuel - 232
MELCOMBE, Capt. (first name unknown) - 320
MERCER, Hugh Gen. - 86, 89, 96, 122, 123, 242, 355, 359
MEYERS, Ensign (first name unknown) - 119

MIDDLETON, Mary - 148
MIFFLIN, Gen. Thomas - 136
MIFFLIN, Maj. (first name unknown) - 128
MILES, Col. Samuel - 82, 83
MILLER, Nathan - 253
MILLRIDGE, Maj. Thomas - 166
MINUIT, Peter - 357
MONCKTON, Col. - 183
MONROE, James - 359
MONTCRIEFFE, Maj. James - 303
MONTGOMERY, Gen. Richard - 242, 322, 354
MONTGOMERY, (first name unknown) - 6
MOODY, Ensign John - 236
MOORE, (first name unknown) - 224
MOORE, Jotham - 232
MORGAN, Col. Daniel - 137
MORRIS, Col. John - 128
MORRIS, Lewis - 19
MORROW, Lieut. (first name unknown) - 191
MORTON, Joseph - 151
MOTT, James - 284
MURRAY, John - 67,

68, 167, 355
MURRAY, Robert - 67, 68, 167, 355
MYER, Peter - 233

N

NASH, Gen. Francis - 242
NICHOLS, Nathaniel - 298
NEILL, .Robert Jr. - 268
NIEL, Robert - 292
NIGHTINGALE, Thomas - 172
NIXON, (first name unknown) - 230
NORRIS, Richard - 148
NORTH, Frederick Lord - 51, 60, 107, 111, 329, 330, 331, 332
NUTMAN, James - 109

O

OATMAN, Frank - 299
OGDEN, Maj. Aaron – 232
OGDEN, Isaac - 47
OGDEN, (first name unknown) - 308
OGDEN, Col. Matthias - 292
OKERSON, Lieut. (first name unknown) - 236
ORSOE, Abraham - 120
OTIS, James - 35

P

PACE, William - 170
PAINE, Thomas - 13, 92, 94, 96
PALFRY (first name unknown) - 230
PARKER, James - 172
PARKES, Maj. (first name unknown) - 292
PATERSON, William - 65, 66
PATTEN, Capt. (first name unknown) - 269
PATTERSON, [Pattison] Adj. Gen. James - 162
PAWLING, (first name not known) - 370
PEAK, Capt. David - 233
PEARCE (first name unknown) - 179
PEARSE, Jonathan - 284
PENTON, Abner - 227
PERSHING, Gen. John - 366
PETERS, Rev. Samuel - 70
PETERS, Mrs. Samuel - 70
PETERS, Peter - 299
PETIT, C. - 81
PETTIT, Charles - 226
PETTIT, Nathaniel -

PHARIS, Capt. (first name unknown) - 6
PHILLIPS, Jacob - 151
PHILLIPS, Col. - 281
PHILLIPS, Gen. - 210
PIKE, Capt. (first name unknown) - 121
PIPER, Col. (first name unknown) - 83
PITCHER, Molly - 183
PITT, Lord William - 28, 30, 46
PLOUGHMAN, (first name unknown) - 27
POLHEMUS, John - 173
POLHEMUS, (first name unknown) - 250
POWERS, (first name unknown) - 329, 330
PRAT, Joseph - 172
PRESCOT, Gen. -(first name unknown) - 244
PREVOST, Gen. Augustine - 244
PRICE (first name unknown) - 8
PRICE, Richard - 150
PRINCE, James Capt. - 366
PULASKI, Count Casmir - 176, 200, 201
PUTNAM, Col. Israel - 49, 137, 202, 350, 354

Q

QUIGLEY, Capt. Robert - 296
QUIXOTE, Don – 130

R

RALL, Col. - 94
RANDOLF, Thomas - 68
RANDOPH, Justice Daniel - 334
RANDOPH, Lieut. (first name unknown) - 191
REDMAN, Doctor (first name unknown) - 7
REED, Joseph - 115
REVERE, Paul - 51
REVES, Capt. (first name unknown) - 277
REYNOLDS, Col. (first name unknown) - 208
RICE, Capt. John - 296
RICHARDS, John - 260, 261, 299
RIDER, Stephen - 258
RIGGS, Joseph - 46
RIVINGTON, Charles - 359
RIVINGTON, James - 99, 100, 101, 102, 103, 104, 114, 115, 116, 117, 121, 122, 132, 178, 209, 214, 232, 236, 270, 279, 325, 346, 359, 360, 364
RIVINGTON, James Jr. - 359
RIVINGTON, John -

100, 359
ROBERTSON, James - 123, 124, 257
ROBERTSON, Gov - 278
ROBINSON, Col. Beverley - 289, 292
ROBINSON, John - 332
ROCHAMBEAU, Count Donatien - 319, 322, 323, 324
ROSALINDA - 117
ROSS, Joseph - 14
ROSSELL, Zachariah - 298
RUDOLF, [Rudolph] Capt. Michael - 269
RUECASTLE, Lieut. John - 232
RUTGERS, Anthony - 10
RUTHERFORD, Walter - 172
RYERSON, (first name unknown) - 333
RYKER, Dr. (first name unknown) - 250

S

SANDWICH, John, Earl of - 48
SAWBRIDGE, Alderman (first name unknown) - 61
SCAMMELL, Adjt. Gen Alex - 226
SCHAAK, Capt. (first name unknown) - 305
SCHANK, Garrit - 298
SCHANK, Lt. (first name unknown) - 303
SCHENK, Capt. John - 232, 233
SCHURMAN, James - 349
SCOTT, Col. Charles - 130
SCUDDER, John - 151
SCUDDER, Joseph - 151
SCUDDER, Dr. Nathaniel -151, 318, 348, 371
SEARS, Isaac - 103, 116
SHADWICK, Capt. (first name unknown) - 237
SHARP, Anthony - 227
SHEA, Col. (first name unknown) - 79
SHELDON, Col. (first name unknown) - 291
SHIPPEN, Dr. William Jr. - 80, 212
SHOTWILL, James - 152
SHREVE, Col. Israel- 176
SHUTE, William - 227
SIMCOE, John - 249, 250
SINNICKSON, Andrew - 227
SINNICKSON, Thomas - 227
SKINNER, Cortland -

32, 134, 179, 193, 313, 353
SKINNER, Capt. (first name unknown) - 232, 236
SLOANE, William - 147
SMALLWOOD, Col. William - 83
SMITH, Belcher Peartree - 12, 151
SMITH, Claudius - 253, 254
SMITH, James - 253
SMITH, Joshua - 289
SMITH, Tom - 289, 290, 292
SMITH, William - 289
SMITH, William P. - 46
SMOCK, Barnes Capt. - 255
SMOCK, Lieut. John - 178
SPENCER, Rev. Elihu - 322
SPENCER, , Col. (first name unknown) -247
SPRING, Samuel - 14, 352
STEPHENS, [Stevens] Gen. Adam - 136
STEPHENS, Joseph - 232
STEUART, Col. (first name unknown) - 284
STEVENS, Capt. David - 299
STEVENS, Richard - 324
STEPHENS (STEVENS) Gen. (first name unknown) - 134, 135
STEPHENS, Col. (first name unknown) - 241
STEVENSON, John – 3
STEVENSON, Lieut. (first name unknown) - 332, 362, 364
STEWARD, Capt. (first name unknown) - 267
STEWART, Col. Walter - 182
STIRLING, Countess of - 197
STIRLING, Lord [Sterling]; see also William Alexander - 83, 89, 140, 194, 201, 202, 226, 231, 239, 240, 265, 267, 279, 281, 304 356,
STIRLING, Lieut. Colonel (first name unknown) - 231
STITH, Capt. (first name unknown) - 191
STOCKTON, Annis Boudinot - 360
STOCKTON, Richard - 171, 358, 360
STOCKTON, Samuel Witham - 2
STOREY, Capt. (first name unknown) - 318
STRAW, Thomas [alias Thomas Welcher]- 254, 257
STRING, Charles - 172
STUDSON, (first name

unknown) - 334
STUYVESANT, Peter - 359
STUYVESANT, (first name unknown) - 85
SULLIVAN, Gen. John - 94, 136, 248, 249
SULLIVAN, Samuel H. - 156, 204, 213
SUMTER, Thomas - 310
SUTHERLAND, Maj. (first name unknown) - 261
SWAN, Capt. (first name unknown) - 191
SYMMES, Anne - 371
SYMMES, John - 303, 370
SYMMES, John, Jr. - 370

T

TALBOT, Maj. Silas - 300
TALLMADGE, Maj. Benjamin - 287, 345, 346,
TALLMAN, Cornelius - 233
TALLMAN, Dow - 233
TARLETON, Col. Banastre - 310
TAYLOR, James - 13, 14
TAYLOR, Capt Yelverton - 296
TENNENT, William - 11, 348
THARP, John - 232
THATCHER, Elizabeth - 8
THAYER, Maj. (first name unknown) - 144
THOMPSON, Mark - 69, 169
THOMPSON, Capt. Thomas - 280
THOMPSON, Brig. Gen. William - 208
THOMSON, Charles - 217
THOMSON, Thomas - 227
THOMSON, William - 332
THROCKMORTON, Lieut. (first name unknown) - 236
TILGMAN, Tench - 25
TILTON, John - 336, 337
TITUS - 236, 255
TOWNSEND, Robert - 104, 287, 346
TRAPP, Capt. (first name unknown) - 254
TRECOTHIC AND HANBURY - 28
TRECOTHIC, Barlow - 29
TRENCHARD, George - 227
TRUMBULL, Col. (first name unknown) - 260
TUCKER, Samuel - 64, 73, 76
TUTTLE, John - 309

TY, Col. - 236, 255, 335
TYRON, Gov. - 243, 244

U

URINE, Gideon - 172

V

VAN ALLEN, Capt. (first name unknown, Loyalist officer) - 233, 261
VAN BREENCK, Sheriff (first name unknown) - 235
VAN BROCKLE (first name unknown) -179
VAN BRUNT, Maj. (first name unknown) -235, 237
VAN BUSKIRK, Col. Abraham - 267
VAN CAMP, Thomas - 170, 171
VAN DIKE, John - 349
VAN EMBURG, Maj. (first name unknown) - 273
VAN HEISTER, (first name not unknown) - 221
VAN KIRK, John - 253
VANMARTER, Gilbert - 255
VAN METER, Cyrenus - 171
VAN METER, (first name unknown) - 259
VANNOTE, Jacob - 252
VANNOTE, William - 252
VAN VORST, Cornelius - 260
VAN WEERT, (first name unknown) (370
VAN ZANDT, Wynant - 172
VEESTERVELT, Jeremiah - 233
VESTERVELT, John - 234
VICKERS Samuel - 349
VON KNYPHAUSEN, Gen. [see also KNYPHAUSEN] 371
VON STEUBEN, Baron Frederick - 175, 200, 205, 206
VOORHEES, Capt. Peter - 250

W

WADE, Deacon (first name unknown, from Connecticut Farms, NJ) - 211
WALL, James - 284
WALL, Capt. Joseph - 179
WALLING, James- 284

WALLING, Philip - 284
WALLING, Thomas - 284
WALLING, Capt. (first name unknown) - 284
WARD, Uzal - 215
WARD, Lieut. Ebenezer - 284
WARD., Capt (first name unknown) - 292
WARDILL, William - 235
WARING, (first name unknown) - 6
WARREN, Joseph - 242, 323
WARREN, General - 322
WASHINGTON, George - 62, 72, 74, 79, 82, 83, 84, 86, 88, 89, 90, 93, 94, 95, 96, 110, 111, 112, 114, 122, 124, 125, 12, 128, 133, 135, 136, 137, 138, 139, 141, 144, 154, 163, 164, 165, 175, 178, 181, 182, 183, 186, 187, 189, 190, 194, 195, 196, 197, 198, 199, 200, 201, 202, 203, 206, 209, 225, 229, 237, 238, 239, 240, 241, 243, 250, 263, 265, 274, 277, 278, 282, 284, 285, 286, 287, 288, 289, 290, 291, 293, 307, 309, 310, 311, 316, 317, 321, 322, 323, 324, 325, 334, 337, 338, 340, 342, 344, 345, 346, 350, 356, 357, 359, 361, 367
WASHINGTON, Martha Custis - 196, 200, 241
WASHINGTON, Capt. William - 94
WATSON, Capt. (first name unknown) - 102
WAYNE, Gen. Anthony - 137, 175, 176, 202, 239, 307, 308,
WELCHER, Thomas - 257
WELLS, Harrison - 172
WEST, Stephen - 252
WESTCOTT, Richard - 299
WHITE, Aaron - 377, 372, 373
WHITE, John - 299
WHITE, Philip - 336, 337, 372, 373
WHITE, Robert - 299
WHITE, (first name unknown) 26, 70
WHITEHEAD, (first name unknown) -

14
WHITEHEAD, Jesse - 232
WIGSTAFF, Capt. (first name unknown) - 178
WILLET, Lieut. (first name unknown) - 266
WILLIAMS, Ezekiel - 250, 253
WILLIAMS, Plato - 299
WILLIAMSON, Jacob - 13, 14
WILLIS, Benjamin - 232
WILLIS, Elizabeth, - 180
WILLIS, William - 153
WILSON, (first name unknown) - 177
WINANS, Doctor (first name unknown) - 312
WINANS, Mrs. (first name unknown) - 312
WINANTS, Lieut. Daniel - 209
WIND, Gen. (first name unknown) - 206
WITHERSPOON, David - 12, 353, 351
WITHERSPOON, John Sr. -151, 160, 161, 351
WITHERSPOON, John, Jr - 12, 351
WOODHULL, Samuel - 287
WOOSTER, David. - 242
WORLY, Henry - 7
WORMB, Col. (first name unknown) - 117
WRIGHT, Samuel - 252
WYCOFF, Col. (first name unknown) - 235
WYLIE, Capt.(first name unknown) - 156, 204

Z

ZABRISKIE, Joost - 211, 234
ZABRISKIE, Capt. George - 191, 364

PLACE NAMES AND
GEOGRAPHIC LOCATIONS

A
Absequean River - 156
Acquaconack NJ -89
Albany - 133, 185
Allegheny Mountains - 24
AllenTown - 53, 181
Alloways Creek - 218
Amboy [See also Perth Amboy and South Amboy] NJ - 2, 3, 49, 81,82, 96, 120, 129, 130, 131, 134, 137, 138, 139, 140, 155, 181, 210, 231, 249, 286, 311, 354, 356
Amwell - 256
Annapolis - 47
Antigua - 4, 296
Appalachia - 5
Arch Street, Phila. - 161
Arthur Kill – 265, 277
Ash Swamp, NJ - 218
Augusta, Ga. - 229, 309
Azores - 4

B
Bahanna Island - 84
Baltimore – 27, 47, 140
Barbados - 4
Barbados Neck -
Baskenridge, NJ- 194, 263, 264
Bath, Eng. – 15
Battery – 79, 356
Bavaria - 200
Bay of Fundy - 373
Bay of Honduras -4
Bedlow's Island - 78
Belfast – 6
Benedict on Patuxent - 27
Bergen County – 56, 86, 172, 206, 233, 234, 257, 258, 260, 273, 347, 358, 359
Bergen Neck NJ - 90, 285
Bergen Point, NJ – 275
Bergen Town, NJ – 83, 85, 88, 115, 121, 127, 171, 214, 261, 268, 284
Bermuda – 4, 296, 299
Billingsfort - 178, 245
Billop's Point - 245
Birchtown - 373
Black Horse, NJ - 93
Black Point, NJ – 85, 236, 318, 348
Blackwell's Island –84
Bonham Town, NJ – 134, 139, 231
Boon Town, NJ - 239
Bordentown, NJ - 93, 298, 358
Boston - 3, 22, 30, 40, 45, 47, 49, 50, 51, 52, 53, 58, 62, 63, 75, 79, 100,157, 254, 317
Bound Brook, NJ – 133, 166, 249
Bound Creek - 311
Bowery, the – 85
Bowery Lane - 346
Bowling Green - 356, 357
Branford, Ct. - 52
Breed's Hill - 62, 354
Brest - 300
Bridgetown NJ - 82
Brindley Town - 373

Brinker's Mills - 248
Bristol - 3, 297
Broad Street, NYC - 344
Broadway, NYC – 87, 356, 357
Bronx, the - 87
Brooklyn - 356
Brotherton, NJ - 5
Brunswick [See also New Brunswick] NJ – 66, 67, 120,129, 130, 131, 132, 133, 134, 135, 136, 137, 138, 139, 212, 216, 249, 250, 304, 362
Brunswick Hills - 134
Bucks County, Pa. - 177
Bull's Ferry - 158
Bunker Hill – 62
Burlington Path - 236
Burlington, NJ – 3, 28, 56, 63, 93, 149, 151, 184, 206, 269, 297, 298, 299, 347, 358
Burnt Island - 179
Burrows House - 363

C
Cambridge, Mass - 354
Cambridge NJ - 200
Camden, NJ - 9, 175 273
Camden, SC – 288
Camp Tappan – 291
Canada - 1, 63, 74, 133, 184, 222, 244, 249, 340, 344, 354
Cape Breton Island -373
Cape Charles - 320
Cape Cod - 300
Cape Francois - 300
Cape Henlopen – 300
Cape May County- 2, 52, 57, 192, 206, 363
Caribbean - 2, 4, 155, 295
Carlisle, Pa. – 156, 185, 204

Carpenter Hall, Phila. - 47
Castle William, Boston - 50
Charles River - 62
Charleston [Charlestown] SC – 3, 202, 274, 275, 279, 283, 319, 368
Charlestown, Mass. - 241
Charlotburg Iron Works - 256
Chatham Square - 85
Chatham, NJ- 117, 308
Chedabucto Bay - 373
Cheesequake Creek, NJ - 298
Chemung - 248
Cherry Valley – 185, 246
Chesapeake Bay - 141, 274, 318
Chester, Pa. – 47, 297
Chestnut St., Phila. - 9
Christeen, Del. - 178
Christiana Creek - 302
Cinque Ports - 332
Closter [Kloster] NJ-118, 119, 270, 273
Colt's Neck, NJ – 236, 252, 318, 333, 372, 373
Columbus, County – 359
Conascung - 284
Concord – 51
Connecticut – 4, 47, 49, 52, 69, 103
Connecticut Farms, NJ – 166, 219, 220, 279, 292
Coopers Ferry, NJ - 9, 143, 175, 180
Corell's Ferry [Coryell's Ferry] NJ - 178
Cork – 6, 190
Crane's Ferry - 231
Cross-Roads, Monmouth County - 181
Crosswicks NJ- 95, 148, 181

Cuhichtun - 246
Cumberland County 2- 57, 69, 155, 168, 176, 206
Curacao - 4

D
De Hart's Point, NJ – 268
Decker's House - 266, 275
Decker's Ferry - 275
Delaware – 4, 302, 353
Delaware River – 3, 9, 93, 94, 95, 96, 108, 109, 110, 138, 139, 140, 141, 142, 144, 153, 155, 175, 176, 177, 178, 180, 181, 195, 246, 263, 300, 302, 307, 310, 358
Dismal Swamp, NJ - 135
Dobb's Ferry – 88, 200, 286
Dover Castle - 332
Dublin - 3, 35
Dutchess County - 194

E
East Indies - 322
East River –84, 87, 139, 186, 285, 356
Easton, Pa. - 201, 247, 248
Egg Harbor [Egg Harbour] NJ; see also Little Egg Harbor and Great Egg Harbor - 3, 155, 190, 300, 301
Elizabeth Town - 7, 25, 49, 58, 77, 78, 81, 83, 96, 101, 102, 106, 112, 113, 114, 128, 129, 147, 155,165, 192, 193, 200, 209, 210, 216, 220, 231, 246, 248, 265, 268, 277,280, 281, 282, 292, 312, 313, 354, 355
Elizabeth Town Point, NJ – 53, 77, 179, 206, 277,279, 280,281, 282, 312
English Neighbourhood, NJ- 271
Eustatia- 316
Eutaw Springs - 323
Essex County – 45, 46, 54, 55, 56, 57, 77, 88, 104, 206, 311
Exuma - 4

F
Fairfield, Ct. – 52
Falls at Tinton Manor - 236
Falmouth - 241
Farmingham, Mass. - 49
Fire of 1776 - 356
First Avenue, NYC -
Fishkill, NY - 255, 289, 317, 371
Flatbush, Brooklyn – 83, 303
Flemming Town, [Flemington] NJ - 136
Florida – 290, 244, 344
Forks of Little Egg Harbour – 156, 297, 299
Fort Clinton - 238
Fort Constitution - 90
Fort George – 87, 331, 357
Fort Hill, Boston - 50
Fort Hoorn's Hook - 84
Fort Independence - 193
Fort Lafayette - 208
Fort Lee – 86, 89, 90, 270, 271, 284
Fort Mercer - 142
Fort Mifflin – 142, 143, 144
Fort Niagara – 247, 249
Fort Paulus Hook –358
Fort Richmond - 318
Fort Ticonderoga - 74

Fort Washington - 86, 89, 91, 112, 193
Forty Fort, Pa. - 185
France - 1, 100, 106, 141, 145, 175, 190, 200, 202, 205, 240, 334, 343, 364, 365, 366
Freehold - 36, 53, 181, 298, 318, 348, 372, 373

G

Garret's Hill, NJ - 314
Genesee, NY - 249
Georgia - 3, 47, 189, 229, 244
Glasgow - 3
Glouster County –9, 52 , 57, 69, 176, 206
Glouster Point, NJ – 43, 45, 162, 181, 296, 325
Glouster Town, NJ – 55,142
Goshen - 253
Governor's Island - 113
Grand Street, Jersey City - 358
Great Egg Harbor, NJ – 296, 304
Great Swamp, Amwell, NJ - 256
Groton, Ct. – 300
Guilford, Ct. 52, 303
Guilford Courthouse - 319

H

Hackensack River – 192, 261, 275
Hackensack Town, NJ - 5, 88, 89, 93, 254, 258, 270, 271, 349
Haddonfield - 226
Halifax – 74, 77, 79, 244

Halstead's Point, NJ - 312
Hamburg, Germany -
Hamburg, Del. - 302
Hancock's Bridge – 218, 228, 367
Hanover, N J – 110
Hanover Square, NY – 99, 100
Harlem, NY - 84
Hartford, Ct. - 194, 288, 289
Haverstraw, NY – 79, 238, 289
Hebron, Ct. – 69
Heights- Town - 147
Hell Gate , NY -84
Hesse-Cassel, state of - 77, 366
Highlands, NJ - 82, 235, 335, 340
Hoboken, NJ [Hoebuck, Hoobuck] - 86, 190, 193, 233
Hohokus - 368
Holland - 255
Hoorn's Hook - 84
Hopper's Town, NJ - 270, 368
Hospital Wharf, Phila - 144
Hudson River [see also North River] - 3, 74, 78, 88, 89, 91, 127, 133, 138, 141, 145, 184, 185, 190, 202, 237, 238, 263, 269, 270,278, 281, 286, 287, 288, 317, 358, 367
Hudson Valley - 5
Hunterdon County – 26, 53, 56, 206
Huntington Bay, NY - 286

I

India - 1
Ireland - 4, 5, 102, 149

J
Jamaica - 4, 102
JamesTown - 6
Japan - 1
Jersey City, NJ – 86, 239
Jockey Hollow, NJ - 250, 263, 264
Jumping Point Inlet, NJ - 237

K
Kakiate - 238
Kansas - 2
Kent on Delaware - 47
Kingsbridge, NY – 87, 111, 186, 189, 190, 193, 270
King's Ferry – 237, 239, 285, 286
King's Highway, Newark - 15
Kingson, NJ - 216, 241
Kingson, RI - 241
Kingwood NJ - 8
Kloster [see also Closter] NJ - 273

L
Lancaster - 206
Learn - 6
Lexington - 51
Liberty Island - 355
Lisbon - 3,
Little Egg Harbor, NJ – 156, 192, 276, 296, 297, 299
Little Ferry, NJ - 233
Liverpool -3
London - 3, 27, 39, 41, 60, 99, 111, 148, 179, 297, 320, 321, 326, 354, 368
Londonderry - 6
Long Beach, NJ - 154
Long Branch - 298

Long Island - 5, 79, 83, 84, 86, 112, 210, 221, 231, 245, 253, 284, 285, 287, 297, 300, 303, 304, 317
Long Island Sound - 287
Long Pond - 256
Longstreet's Mill, Mon. County - 259
Lower Freehold, NJ - 11
Lower Marlborough - 27
Lyme, Ct. - 52

M
M'Conkey's Ferry - 94
Madeira -4
Manhattan - 79, 83, 84, 85 87, 202, 344, 356, 357
Mantua Creek - 177
Marblehead, Mass. – 358, 359
Market Street, Phila - 9
Marlborough - 27
Martinico - 4
Maryland - 4, 27, 35, 47, 60, 79, 163, 164
Massachusetts - 4, 30, 31, 36, 39, 40, 47, 51, 68, 74, 103, 169, 202, 203, 358
Matawan, NJ – 178, 276, 303, 363
Matawan Creek, NJ - 364
Matuchin [Metuchen], NJ - 135
Mendham, NJ – 68, 169
Middle Haddam, Ct. - 86
Middlebrook NJ- 133, 134, 154, 229
Middlebush NJ - 136
Middlesex.County - 27, 56, 68, 168, 206, 256

Middletown NJ - 2, 183, 209, 234, 235, 237, 298, 333, 348
Middletowne Point, NJ – 178, 276, 303, 363
Mill Creek - 178
Millstone, NJ - 136
Minisinks - 246
Mississippi River – 350
Monmouth Court House - 128, 181, 182, 252
Monmouth County -2, 36, 52, 56 , 155, 171, 173, 181, 183, 190, 206, 234, 236,,251, 252, 253, 255, 259, 298, 313, 318, 332,333, 334, 337, 348, 353
Montreal - 354
Montrefour Island - 84
Moorestown, NJ - 93, 176
Morris County - 56, 68, 131, 149, 169, 194, 205, 250
Morristown, NJ – 73, 96, 97, 110, 114, 121, 122, 127, 128, 133, 154, 157, 205, 207, 229, 238, 250, 254, 255, 258, 263, 264, 267, 274, 279, 361
Morrissania - 84
Mount Holly, NJ - 93, 150, 158, 176, 358
Mount Pleasant, NJ - 333
Mud Island - 142
Mushankunk - 247

N
Narragansett Bay - 36
Narrows - 305, 333
Navesink River - 367
Nebraska - 2
Nevis - 4
New Barbadoes, Bergen County - 223
New Barbados Neck - 260
New Bridge - 271
New Brunswick, NJ [See also Brunswick] – 25, 81, 89, 90, 91, 93, 95, 97, 127, 132, 137, 140, 148, 151, 155, 229, 303, 304, 305, 324, 349
New Brunswick, Can. -343
New Castle, Del. - 302
New Dock - 233
New Hampshire – 3, 4, 47, 54
New Haven Ct.- 52
New Kittanning - 248
New London, Ct. - 52
New Market, -Eng - 99
New Market, NJ - 361
New Utrecht, NY – 83, 304
New Windsor, NJ – 254, 293
Newark, NJ – 9, 10, 15, 18, 19, 36, 45, 57, 77, 80, 90, 91, 96,106, 165, 200, 214, 215, 216, 242, 249, 267, 268, 284, 286, 292
Newark Bay - 85
Newark Mountain - 165
New Bridge - 271
Newcastle - 47
Newfoundland - 50
Newmarket , London -
Newport – 3, 37, 38, 277, 287
Newry, Ireland - 3, 6
Newtown, Pa. - 177
Newtown Township, Sussex County N.J. - 69, 100, 370
Newtown, Glouster County, NJ - 258
Norfolk - 241
North Castle, NY - 189
North Carolina – 4, 47, 76, 115, 243, 244, 365

North River [see also Hudson River] - 79, 85, 86, 87, 139, 186, 192, 194, 200, 237, 238, 239, 258, 268, 281, 286, 293, 300
North River [see also Navesink River] - 235, 367
Norwich, Ct. - 52
Notch below Passaic Falls - 250
Nova Caseseria - 348
Nova Scotia - 343, 344, 347, 373

O

Ohio - 370
Ohio River - 188
Oklahoma - 5
Old Tappan - 219
Ontario River - 191
Osborne Island. -367
Ossining, NY - 361

P

Pacquanock, NJ -114
Painter's Point - 235
Palisades NJ – 86
Paramus NJ - 191, 270, 271, 272
Paris - 341, 342, 343, 345
Passaic Falls, NJ - 250
Passaic River – 5, 10, 192
Paternoster Row - 99
Paterson - 368
Pauling's Purchase, NY - 194
Paulus Hook, NJ [see also Powles Hook] – 86, 193, 202, 239, 240, 260, 261, 284, 358
Pearl Street, NY - 344

Peekskill, NY - 120, 361
Penn's Neck, NJ - 178
Pennytown N.J. - 119
Perth Amboy, NJ [See also Amboy and South Amboy] - 3, 77, 86, 127, 133, 137, 347, 355
Pine Barrens - 251
Piscataqua Township, NJ [See also Piscataway, NJ] – 168
Piscataway, NH - 3,
Piscataway, NJ [See also Piscataqua Township] – 68, 127, 135, 137
Pitts-Town - 112
Pleasant Valley NJ – 313, 332
Pluckemin, NJ - 128
Point Judith, RI - 300
Point-no-point - 296
Poland - 200
Pomfret, CT - 49
Pompton, NJ – 114, 257
Portsmouth, Eng. - 331
Poughkeepsie - 370
Powles Hook, NJ [See also Paulus Hook] – 10, 79, 85, 88, 268
Powles Hook Ferry - 10
Prackness - 286
Princeton, Town, NJ - 8, 14, 80, 93, 95, 96, 96, 115, 122, 140, 151, 165, 166, 187, 216, 217, 293, 303, 307, 308, 315, 323
Prior's Mill - 260
Providence Plantations, RI - 47
Province Island – 142
Pumpton - 121

Q
Quebec – 49, 50, 288, 343, 354
Quibble Town, NJ - 68, 110, 127, 168
Quintin's Bridge, NJ - 7, 227

R
Raccoon Creek - 178
Rahway, NJ - 89, 105, 127, 155, 170, 232, 268, 354
Raritan River – 5, 7, 93, 128, 129, 133, 138, 159, 229, 273, 305, 324
Raritan Town, NJ -
Red Bank, Monmouth County, NJ - 235
Red Bank on Delaware, - 142, 143
Reedy Island - 44
Refugee Town – 335
Rhode Island – 4, 36, 37, 38, 39, 47, 142, 192, 245, 246, 276, 277, 285, 287, 300
Ridgbury, NJ, village of - 58
Ridgefield, NJ - 58
Ringwood - 238
Rock-Pond - 253
Rome - 367
Rumson, NJ – 236, 348, 367, 368

S

Salem, Mass. - 52
Salem County – 53, 57, 176, 206, 227
Salem town, NJ - 3, 176
Sandy Hook, NJ - 42, 77, 78, 82, 106, 132, 133, 155, 178, 183, 186, 190, 192, 193, 230, 235, 236, 255, 269, 270, 274, 275, 276, 304, 306, 317, 318, 320, 321, 332, 335, 336, 349, 368
Sandy Hook Bay - 2, 3, 185, 351
Sandy Hook Lighthouse - 269
Sandy Point - 249
Santo Domingo - 4, 6
Savannah, GA. - 201, 319
Saybrook, Ct. - 52
Scarborough, Eng. - 15
Schoolie's Mountain - 152, 170
Schuykill River - 143
Scotch Plains, NJ - 166, 280
Scotland - 5, 347
Seabright - 368
Setauket - 287
Shamokin NY - 185
Shark River - 178
Short Hills, NJ - 194, 362
Shrewsbury River - 305, 367
Shrewsbury NJ - 105, 106, 132, 215, 235, 251, 252, 255, 274, 318
Shutter's Island - 85
Sing Sing - 120
Slab Town, NJ - 93
Smith's Clove - 238, 253, 254, 255
Smith's Farm - 131
Somerset County - 7, 56, 152, 159, 170, 206, 347, 362
Somerset Courthouse - 120, 136, 137, 138, 139, 249
South Amboy [See also Amboy and Perth Amboy] NJ- 80, 181, 249, 250

South Carolina - 4, 6, 54, 60, 246, 288, 296, 310, 319, 321, 353
South Hanover, NJ. -166
South River - 367
Spain - 1, 205, 351, 366
Spanktown, NJ - 127, 129, 170
Springfield, NJ - 166, 192, 277, 280, 281
Squabble Town, NJ - 127
Squam [Manasquan], NJ - 178
St. Christopher - 4
St. Eustatia -4
St. Kitts - 4
St. Lucia - 244
St. Martin's - 4
St. Ubes - 296
Staten Island - 58, 76, 77, 78, 82, 102, 118, 124, 125, 127, 132, 133, 134, 139, 140, 155, 170, 179, 192, 193, 209, 216, 231, 232, 234, 238, 245, 265, 266, 267, 275, 277, 288, 280, 281, 285, 292, 311, 312, 313, 317, 318, 354, 355, 356, 362
Staten Island Sound - 80, 139
Statue of Liberty - 356
Stoney Point -(on Hudson River) - 202, 378, 239, 240, 246
Stoney Point -(on Raritan River) - 273
Surinam - 4
Susquehanna River - 247
Sussex County - 56, 69, 102, 158, 169, 205, 247, 370
Sussex, Del - 47

T

Tappan, NJ – 114, 237
Tarrytown, NY - 79, 238, 278
Teller's Point - 279
Tennessee - 310
Tinton Falls, NJ - 236
Tioga – 248
Tom's River Inlet - 190
Tom's River, NJ - 191, 253, 297, 334, 335
Trembley's Point, NJ - 267
Trenton, NJ – 7, 53, 56, 64, 73, 80, 81, 93, 94, 95, 96, 111, 112, 124, 127, 140, 147, 154, 167, 176, 177, 195, 201, 206, 208, 212, 216, 217, 221, 229, 238, 282, 308, 310, 367
Tunbridge, Eng. - 15
Turk's Island – `297
Turky, NJ - 166

U
Ulster – 5
Ushant – 242

V
Valley Forge- 127, 144, 174, 175, 177, 200, 209, 212, 229, 263, 350
Van Vegher's Bridge - 249, 250
Verplank's Point - 246, 290
Versailles - 187
Vienna - 316
Virginia – 3, 4, 28, 35, 47, 60, 76, 112, 115, 163, 164, 183, 196, 202, 222, 247, 306, 310, 319, 320, 351, 368
Virginia Capes - 5,

W

Wachung Mountains, NJ - 133
Wales - 5
Wall Street, NY - 100, 357
Washington Street, Jersey City - 358
Water Street, Phila. - 161
Watering Place, the – 3, 78
Weathersfield, [Whethersfield] Ct. - 159
Weehawkin, NJ - 270, 350
West Indies - 6, 79, 100, 193, 246, 297, 343, 344
West Point - 198, 237, 238, 240, 250, 27, 281, 287, 288, 289, 290, 291, 292, 370
Westchester, NY – 79, 86, 120, , 185, 189, 194, 216, 238, 370
Westfield, NJ – 140, 147, 218
WhiteHall, London - 38
White Hall, NY - 238
Whitehall Slip, NY - 356

White Plains - 88, 91, 157, 189, 213, 238, 286
Windsor township, NJ – 8, 256, 348
Wioming Valley – 184, 185, 247
Woodbridge, NJ – 24, 26, 105, 107, 120, 127, 129, 139, 192, 209, 216, 231, 232, 318
Woodbridge Neck, NJ - 130
Woodbury - 129, 130, 155, 273
Woodruff's Farms - 231

Y

York Island - 85
York, Pa -206
York River - 325
Yorktown – 28, 306, 319, 320, 321, 325

GENERAL SUBJECT MATTER INDEX

Articles of Confederation - 360
Baptists - 5
Battle of Augusta - 309
Battle of Bennington - 141
Battle of Brandywine – 141, 200, 202
Battle of Bunker Hill – 203
Battle of Camden (SC) - 200, 202, 309
Battle of Charleston (SC) - 202, 283, 354
Battle of Charlestown (Mass) - 309
Battle of Concord – 17, 74
Battle of Cowpens - 310
Battle of Eutaw Springs -323
Battle of Fort Lee - 97
Battle of Germantown – 202
Battle of Green Spring - 141, 202
Battle of King's Mountain – 310
Battle of Kingsbridge - 97
Battle of Lexington – 17, 74, 81
Battle of Long Island - 97, 127, 202, 203, 213
Battle of Manhattan – 246, 350
Battle of Minden - 371

Battle of Monmouth – 155, 182, 183, 185, 187, 194, 200, 350, 368, 371
Battle of Paulus Hook – 239
Battle of Princeton –97, 122, 127, 155, 197, 217, 310, 351
Battle of Saratoga – 141, 145, 175, 200, 240, 242, 283
Battle of Savannah -309
Battle of Stoney Point – 202
Battle of Trenton - 97, 127, 155, 350, 359
Battle of White Plains – 97
Battle of Yorktown – 200, 202, 321, 323, 340, 365
Beekman's Tavern - 315, 323
Black Pioneers - 373
Blazing Star – 170, 179
Blue Ball - 85
Board Of Loyalist Refugees - 342
Book Of Negroes – 344
Boston Massacre - 30, 36
Boston News Letter - 38
Boston Port Bill - 47
Boston Tea Party – 40
British Coffee House – 104, 287, 346
Brussels Gazette of America - 361
Bull Head Tavern - 346
Butlers Rangers -184, 246
Carolina Brigade - 233
Cayugas - 184
Cherry Valley Massacre - 185, 221
Civil War - *351*
Cockpit of the Revolution - 74
Columbia University School of Medicine - 353
Committee of Correspondence - 348
Committee of Inspection- 105
Committee of merchants, London - 28
Committee of North American Merchants - 29, 30
Committee of Observation - 55, 56, 58, 82, 355
Committee of Provincial Saltpetre - 355
Committee of Safety – 52, 120, 354
Common Sense - 92
Confederate Nations - 184
Connecticut, New Jersey, Hudson's River and Quebec Weekly Advertiser, The - 100
Conoys - 184
Continental Congress – 47, 48, 51, 54, 55, 58, 60, 62, 64, 65, 67, 68, 69, 71, 72, 75, 76, 102, 104, 105, 114, 116, 121, 122,138, 142, 167, 169, 170, 182, 183, 196, 201, 203, 211, 239, 240, 241, 243, 246, 264, 265,282, 295, 308, 315, 322, 323, 324, 338, 339, 348, 350, 351, 353, 360, 368, 370
Courts of Admiralty –
Crisis - 92, 94, 96
Culper Network – 287, 346
Declaration of Independence – 19, 81, 82, 91, 103, 186, 189, 282, 315, 357, 360
Delaware Indians [See also Lenni Lenape] - 5
Dutch Reformed Church -12
East India Company - 43, 45
Evacuation Day - 344
Father of the American Navy

– 362
Father of the Constitution - 353
Fighting Cocks Tavern - 358
Fighting Parson - 358
Flying Camp – 86, 91, 355, 359
Fraunces Tavern - 344
Gaspee Affair, the -36, 37, 39
Good Hope prison ship - 366
Hanover, House of - 367
Hessians, the – 88, 93, 94, 107, 111, 112, 113, 117, 129, 134, 135, 142, 183, 195, 220, 221, 225, 243, 244, 245, 279, 328, 367, 371
Hibernia Iron Works - 256
Highland Watch - 131
Highlanders – 128, 134, 135, 245
History of England by Smollet - 99
House of Commons - 331, 332, 342
House of Lords - 370
Huguenots – 5
Intolerable Acts – 40
Iroquois – 155, 184
King's College [See also Princeton University and Old Nassau] – 12
Lee's Legion - 202
Lenni Lenape [see also Delaware Indians] - 5, 184
Longstreet' Mill - 259
Magna Carta - 32
Marriner's tavern - 324
Mattisonia Grammar School - 11
Maxwell's Brigade - 198

Mohawk Indians – 40, 184, 185, 246
Mount Holly Iron Works - 150
Nanticokes - 184
Nassau Hall [See also Princeton University and Kings College] 11, 81, 160
New Jersey Journal - 99

New Jersey Gazette[er] - 99, 319, 364, 370
New Jersey Provincial Congress – 350, 371
New York Evening Post - 22
Old Nassau – 12
Oneidas - 184
Onondaga -184
Pennsylvania Chronicle, the - 38
Pennsylvania Evening Post, the - 360
Pennsylvania Journal, the - 38, 351
Pennsylvania Ledger, the - 359
Pennsylvania Post, the - 86, 359
Philipsburg Proclamation of 1779 - 343
Pine Robbers – 252
Poet of the American Revolution – 352
Presbyterian church - 279, 321, 348, 353, 367, 372
Prior's Mill - 260
Princeton Grammar School – 12, 151, 152, 161, 350, 353
Princeton College [See also College of New Jersey] - 12, 13, 14, 151, 152, 159,

160, 282, 283, 317, 323, 348, 349, 350, 351, 352
Proclamation Act of 1763, the - 24
Pulaski Legion - 200, 201
Quakers – 24, 61, 66, 218, 367
Quartering Act of 1765, the - 24
Queens College [See also Rutgers University] – 11, 349
Queens Head Tavern – 42, 343
Rising Glory of America - 352
Rivington's New York Gazetteer -99, 103, 214, 359
Rivington's New York Loyal Royal Gazette - 99, 103, 178, 236, 270, 325, 333, 360, 361, 364
Rouba tavern - 341
Royal American Gazette -
Royal Gazette, The - 99, 346
Royal, Loyal Gazette - 99
Rutgers University – 11, 14, 159, 349, 350

Senecas - 184, 222
Skinner's Greens - 353
Society of Friends - 61
Sons of the American Revolution - 341
Sons of Liberty – 24, 26, 27, 30, 70, 103, 357
Stamp Act - 24, 25, 26, 27, 28, 29, 30, 60, 357
Statue of Liberty - 355
Sugar Act - 24
Tea Act - 39
Three Pigeons – 260
Townshend Acts - 30
Treaty of Paris - 1, 23
Trenton Ordinance, the - 82
Trinity Church - 357
Tuscaroras - 184
Waldeckers – 128,
White Hall Inn - 358
Whitehead's Long Room - 14
Wioming Valley Massacre - 185, 221
Zabriskie's Mills -271

Other Heritage Books by Richard B. Marrin:

Abstracts from the New London Gazette*:*
Covering Southeastern Connecticut, 1763-1769

Abstracts from the New London Gazette*:*
Covering Southeastern Connecticut, 1770-1773

Abstracts from The Connecticut Gazette
(Formerly The New London Gazette*):*
Covering Southeastern Connecticut, 1774-1776

A Glance Back in Time: Life in Colonial New Jersey (1704-1770)
as Depicted in News Accounts of the Day

Going to Court in Texas: Riding the Circuit, 1842-1861

New Jersey During the Revolution, as Related in the News Items of the Day

The Paradise of Texas, Volume 1: Clarksville and Red River County, 1846-1860

Passage Point: An Amateur's Dig into New Jersey's Colonial Past

Runaways of Colonial New Jersey: Indentured Servants,
Slaves, Deserters, and Prisoners, 1720-1781

Other Heritage Books by Richard B. Marrin and Lorna Geer Sheppard:

Abstracts from The Northern Standard *and the Red River District [Texas]:*
Volume 1: August 20, 1842-August 19, 1848

Abstracts from The Northern Standard *and the Red River District [Texas]*
Volume 2: August 26, 1848-December 20, 1851

Abstracts from The Clarksville Standard
(Formerly The Northern Standard*)*
Volume 4: 1854-1855

Abstracts from The Clarksville Standard
(Formerly The Northern Standard*)*
Volume 5: 1856-1857

Other Fireside Fiction by Richard B. Marrin:

The Retaking of America

www.ingramcontent.com/pod-product-compliance
Lightning Source LLC
Chambersburg PA
CBHW050832230426
43667CB00012B/1968